File:06

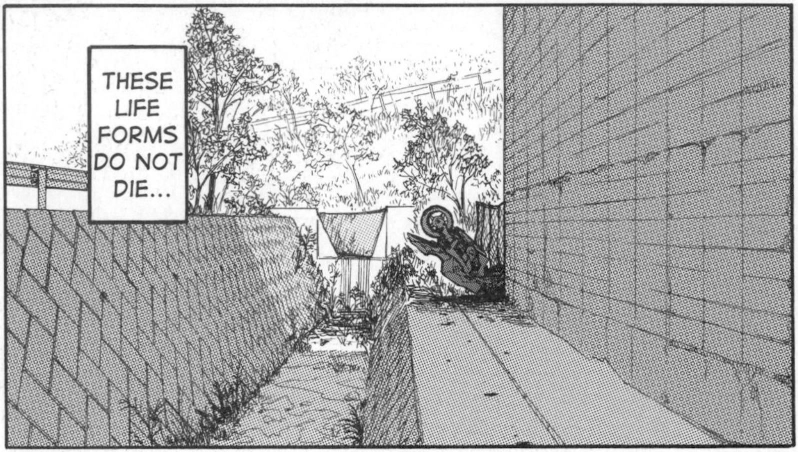
THESE LIFE FORMS DO NOT DIE...

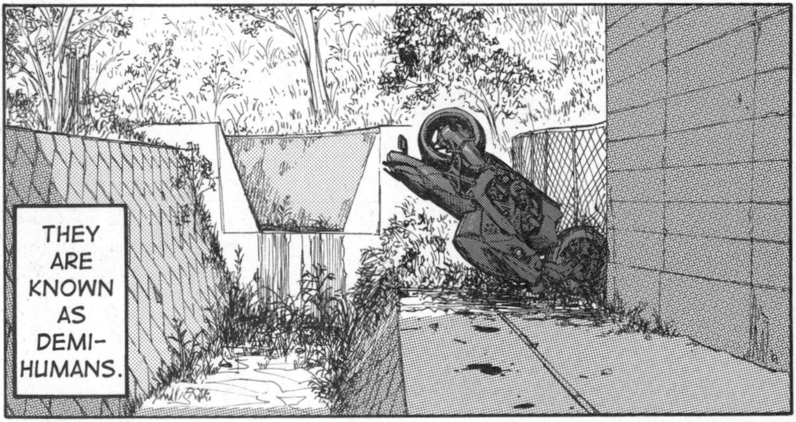
THEY ARE KNOWN AS DEMI-HUMANS.

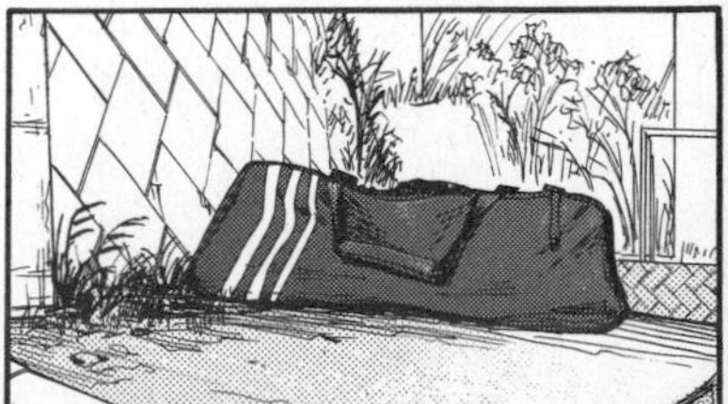

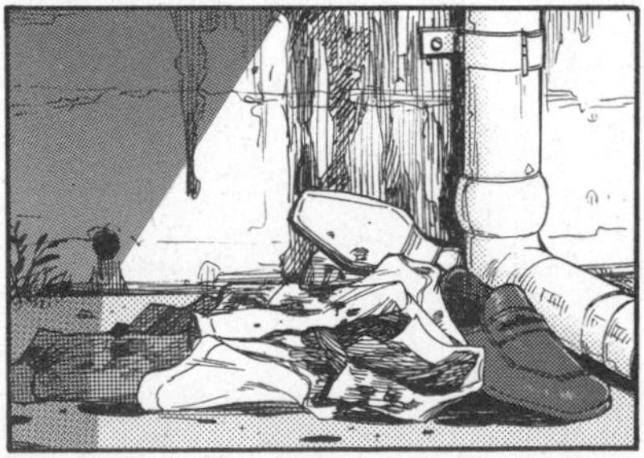

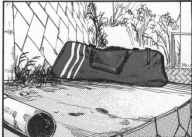

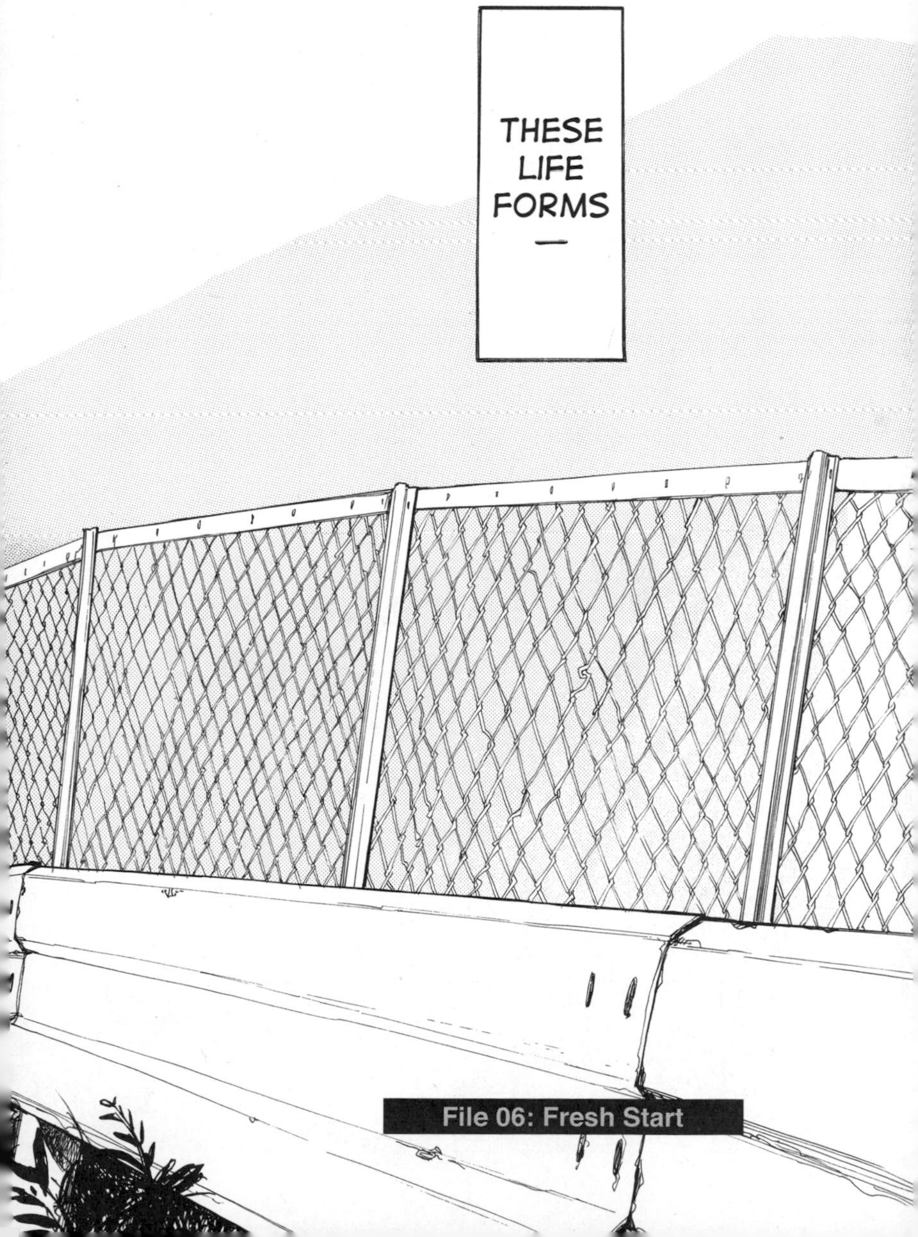
THESE LIFE FORMS —
File 06: Fresh Start

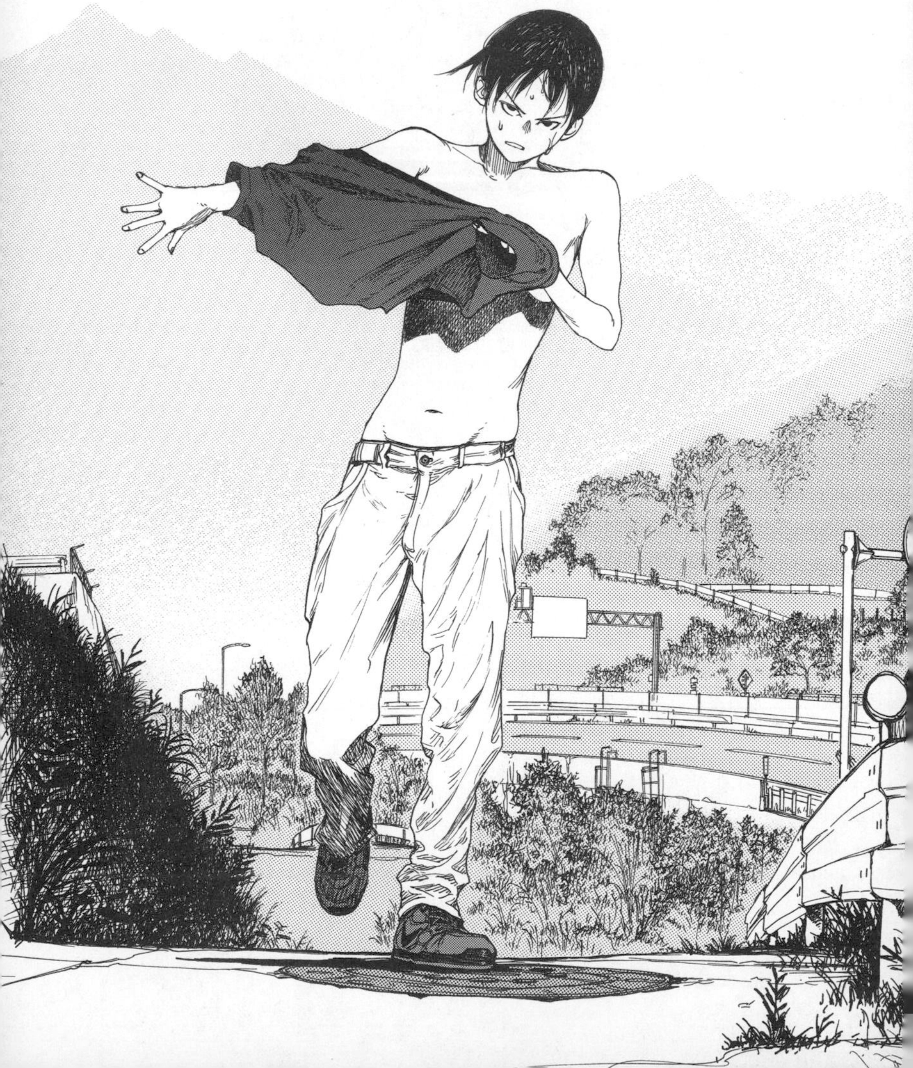

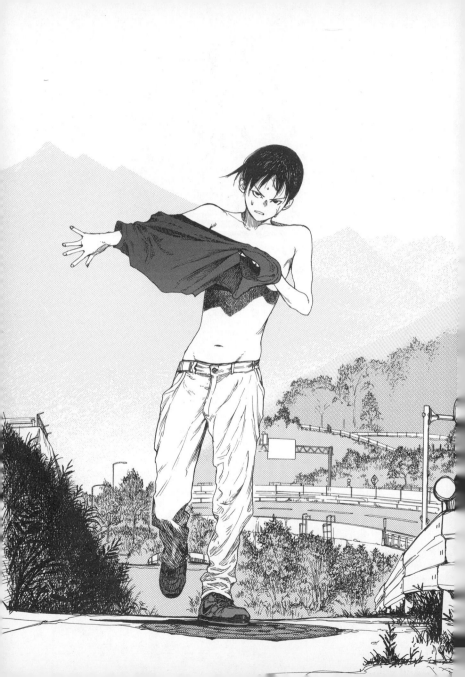

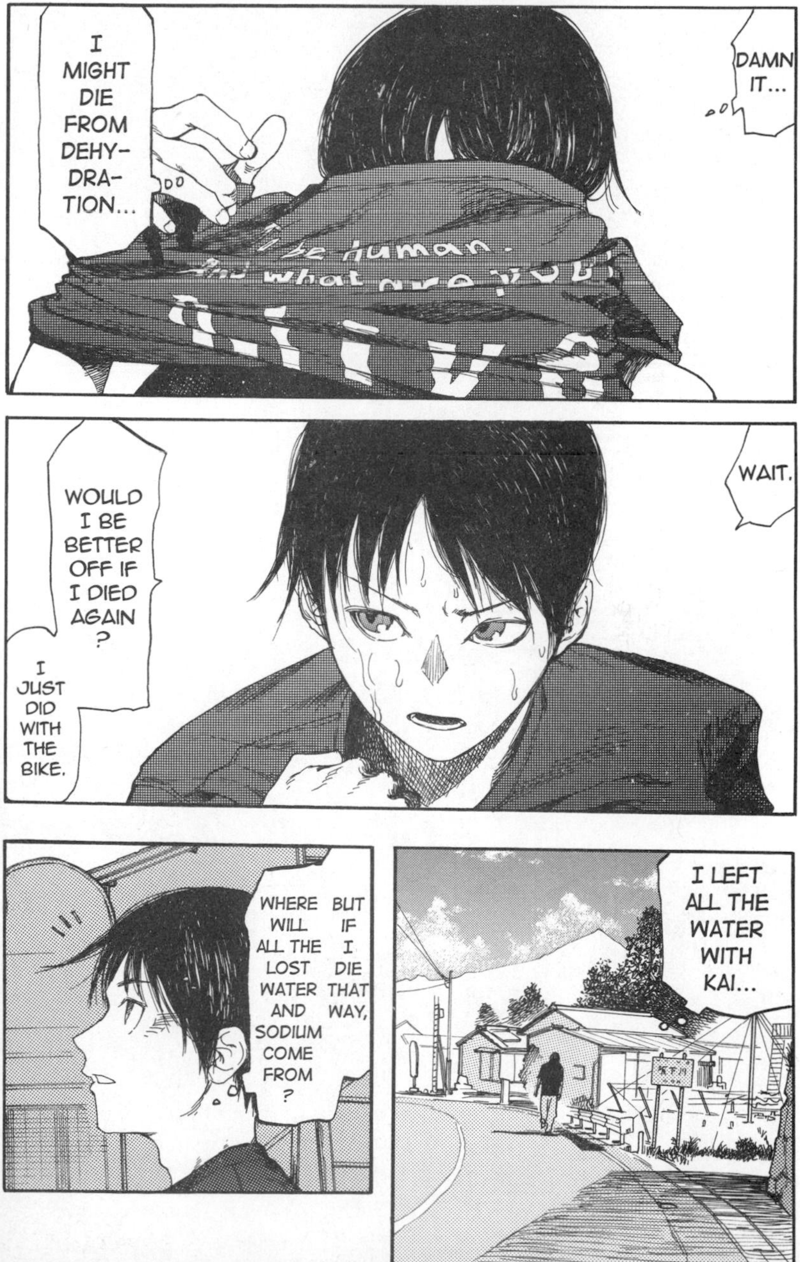
DAMN IT...
I MIGHT DIE FROM DEHYDRATION...
WAIT.
WOULD I BE BETTER OFF IF I DIED AGAIN?
I JUST DID WITH THE BIKE.
I LEFT ALL THE WATER WITH KAI...
BUT IF I DIE THAT WAY,
WHERE WILL ALL THE LOST WATER AND SODIUM COME FROM?

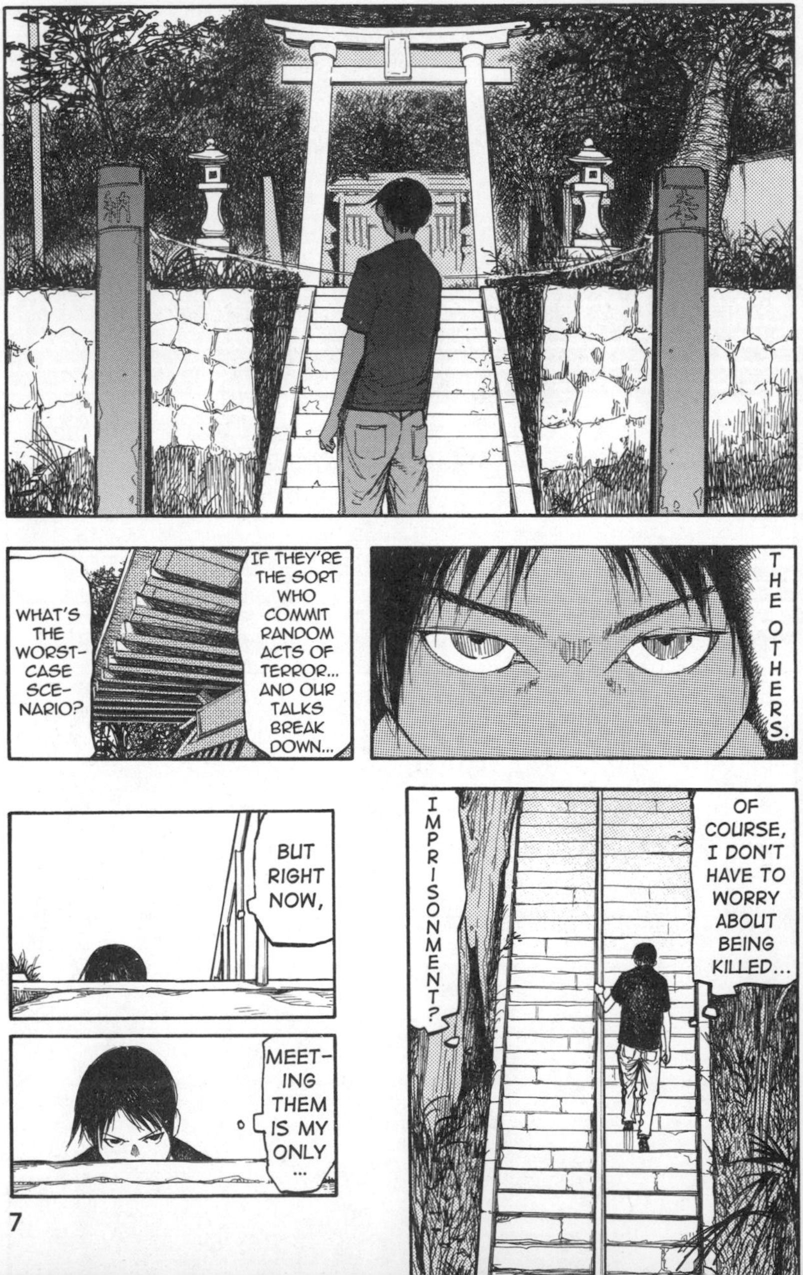
THE OTHERS.
IF THEY'RE THE SORT WHO COMMIT RANDOM ACTS OF TERROR... AND OUR TALKS BREAK DOWN...
WHAT'S THE WORST-CASE SCE-NARIO?
OF COURSE, I DON'T HAVE TO WORRY ABOUT BEING KILLED...
IMPRISONMENT?
BUT RIGHT NOW,
MEET-ING THEM IS MY ONLY ...

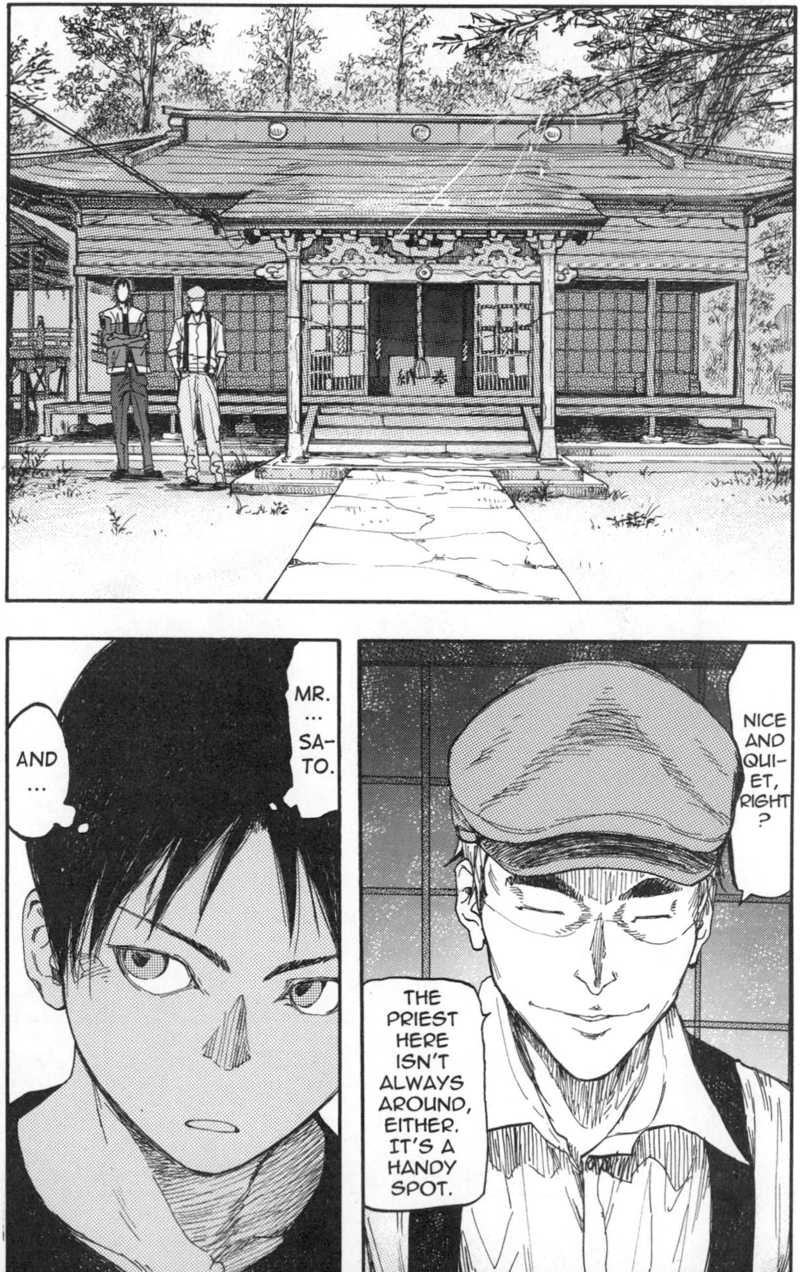
NICE AND QUIET, RIGHT?
THE PRIEST HERE ISN'T ALWAYS AROUND, EITHER. IT'S A HANDY SPOT.
MR. ... SATO.
AND ...

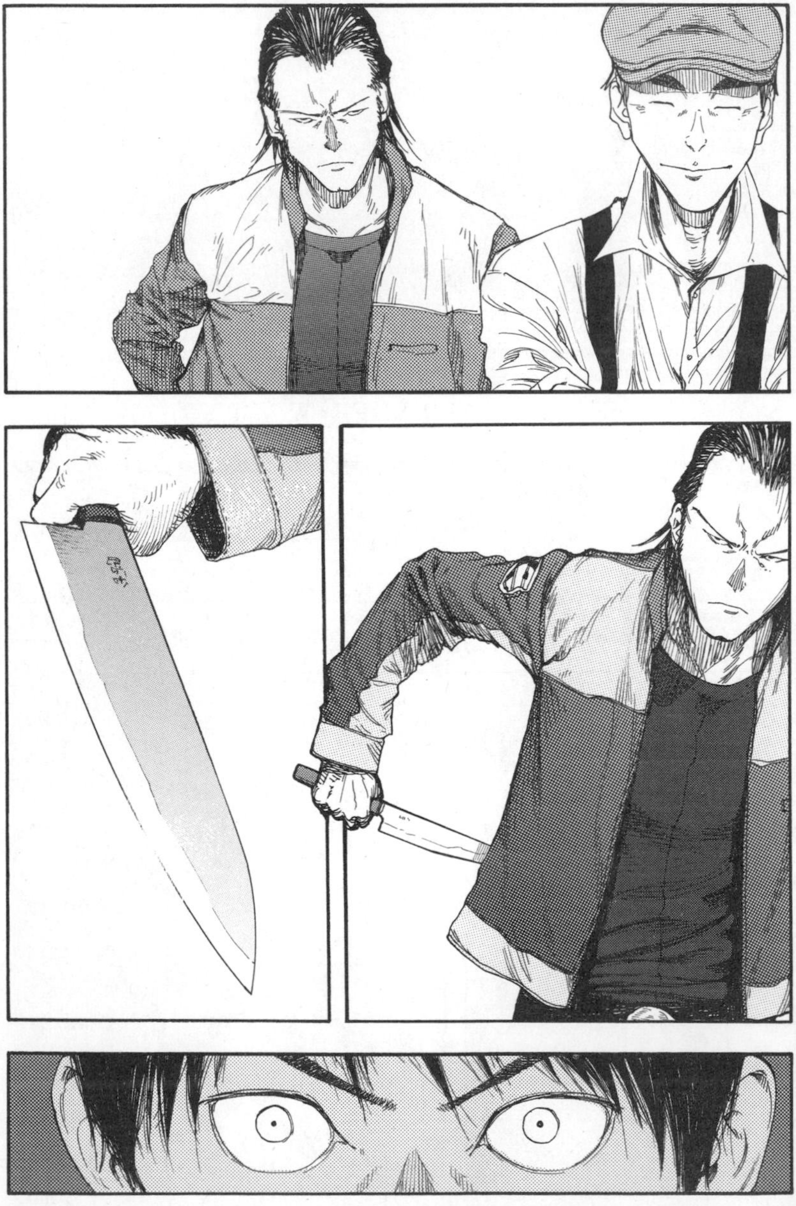

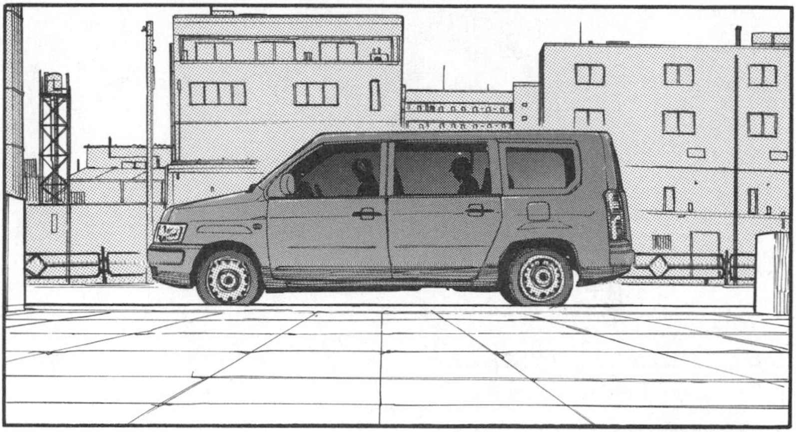

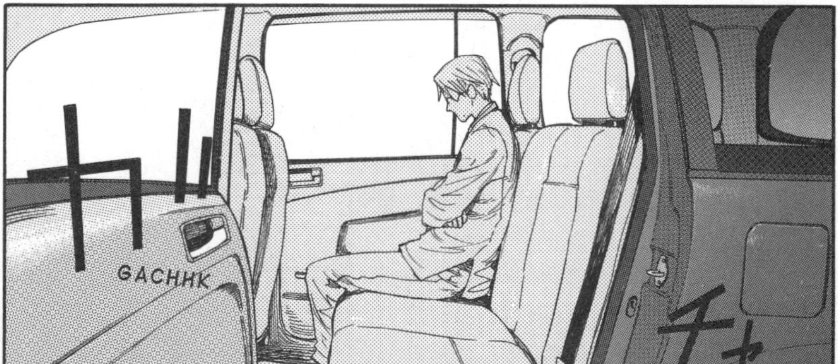
GACHHK

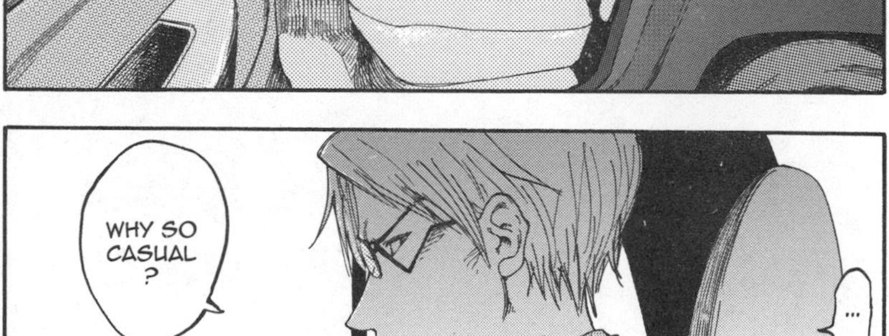
WHY SO CASUAL ?
...

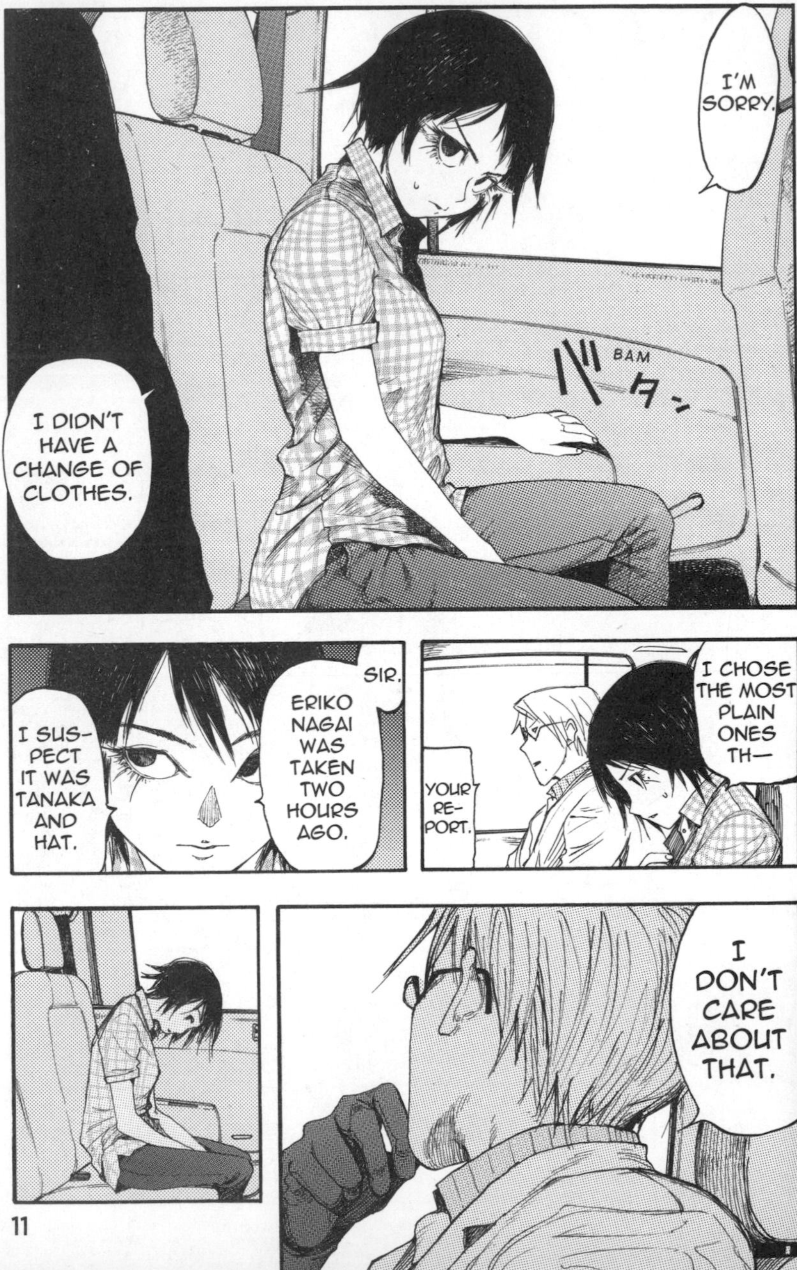
I'M SORRY.
BAM
バタン
I DIDN'T HAVE A CHANGE OF CLOTHES.
I CHOSE THE MOST PLAIN ONES TH—
YOUR RE-PORT.
SIR.
ERIKO NAGAI WAS TAKEN TWO HOURS AGO.
I SUS-PECT IT WAS TANAKA AND HAT.
I DON'T CARE ABOUT THAT.

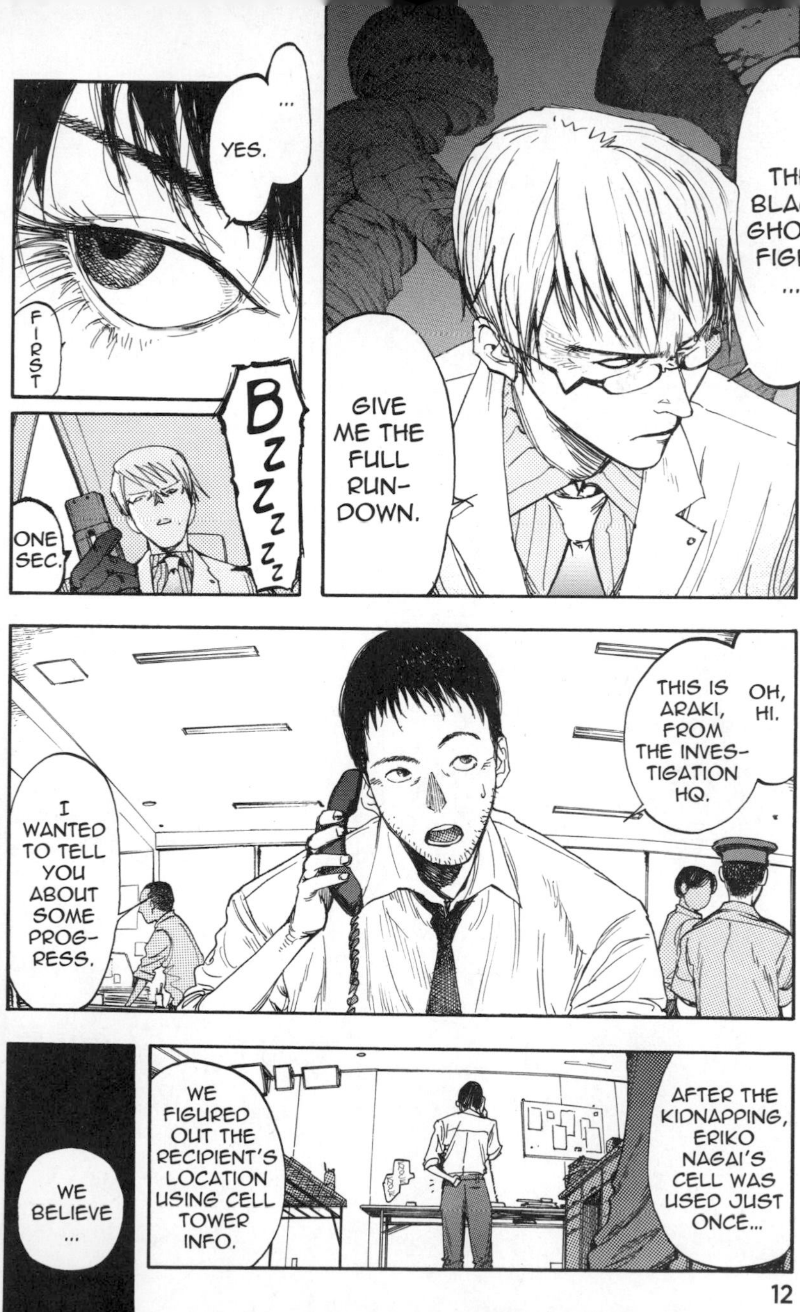
THE BLACK GHOST FIGHT ...
GIVE ME THE FULL RUN-DOWN.
... YES.
FIRST
BZZZZZ
ONE SEC.
OH, HI.
THIS IS ARAKI, FROM THE INVESTIGATION HQ.
I WANTED TO TELL YOU ABOUT SOME PROGRESS.
AFTER THE KIDNAPPING, ERIKO NAGAI'S CELL WAS USED JUST ONCE...
WE FIGURED OUT THE RECIPIENT'S LOCATION USING CELL TOWER INFO.
WE BELIEVE ...

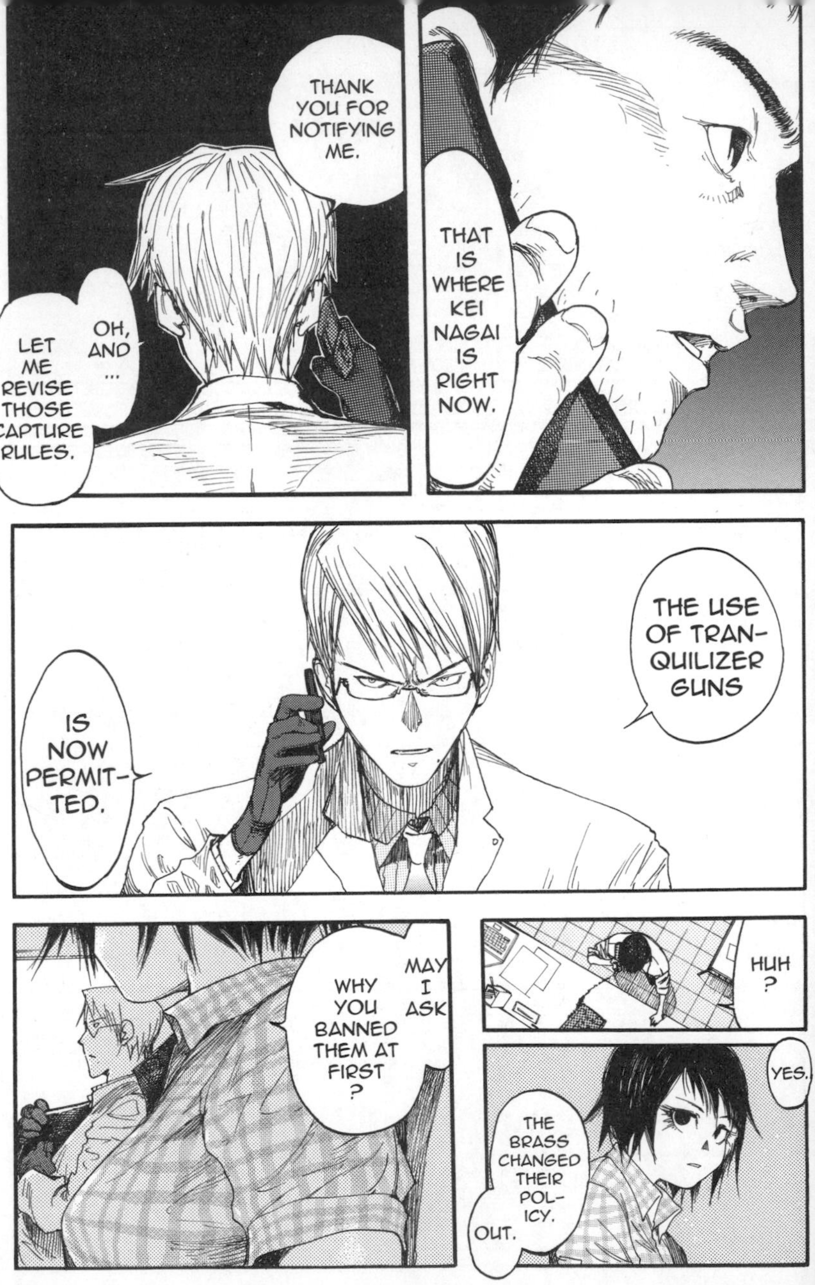
THAT IS WHERE KEI NAGAI IS RIGHT NOW.
THANK YOU FOR NOTIFYING ME.
OH, AND ...
LET ME REVISE THOSE CAPTURE RULES.
THE USE OF TRANQUILIZER GUNS
IS NOW PERMITTED.
HUH?
YES.
THE BRASS CHANGED THEIR POLICY.
OUT.
MAY I ASK
WHY YOU BANNED THEM AT FIRST?

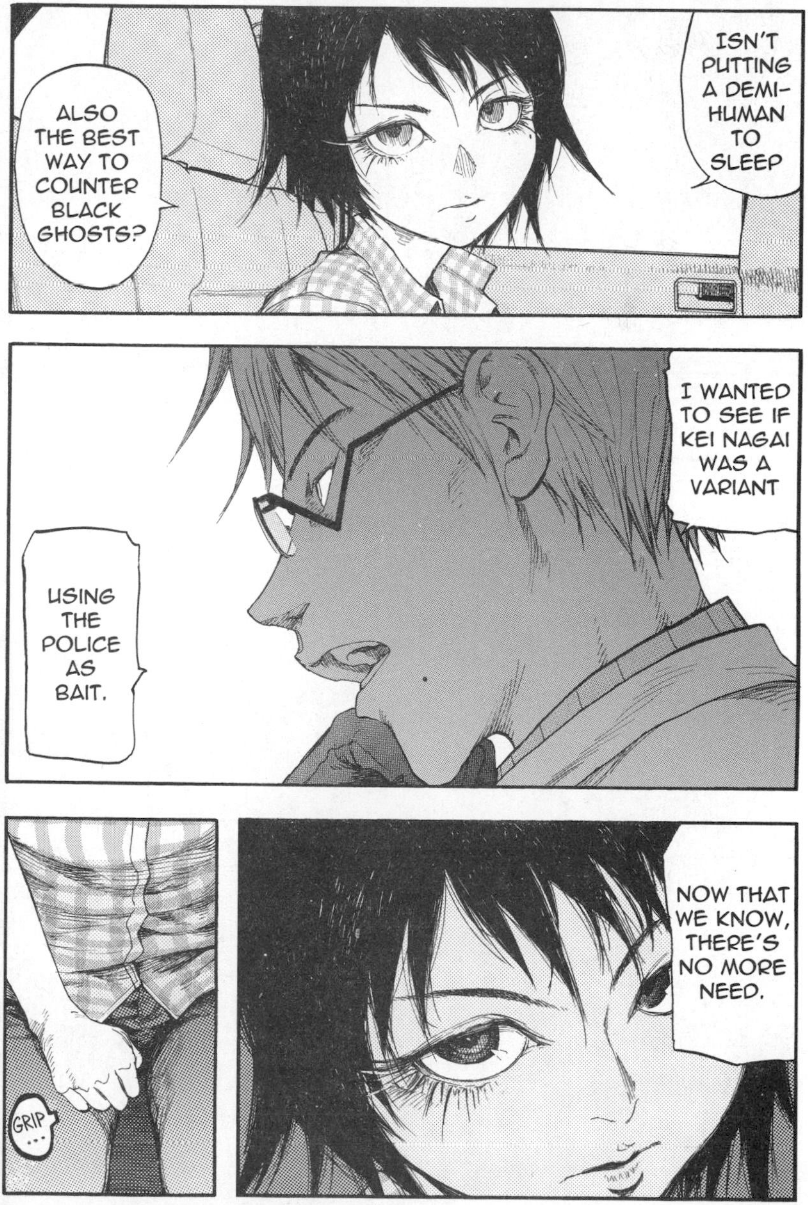
ISN'T PUTTING A DEMI-HUMAN TO SLEEP
ALSO THE BEST WAY TO COUNTER BLACK GHOSTS?
I WANTED TO SEE IF KEI NAGAI WAS A VARIANT
USING THE POLICE AS BAIT.
NOW THAT WE KNOW, THERE'S NO MORE NEED.
GRIP...

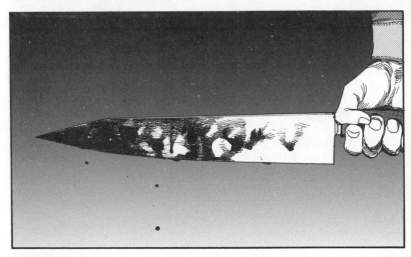

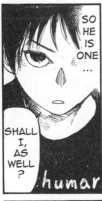

SO HE IS ONE ...

SHALL I, AS WELL?

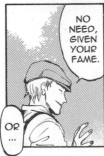

NO NEED, GIVEN YOUR FAME.

OR ...

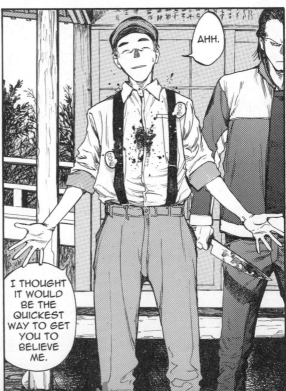

AHH.

I THOUGHT IT WOULD BE THE QUICKEST WAY TO GET YOU TO BELIEVE ME.

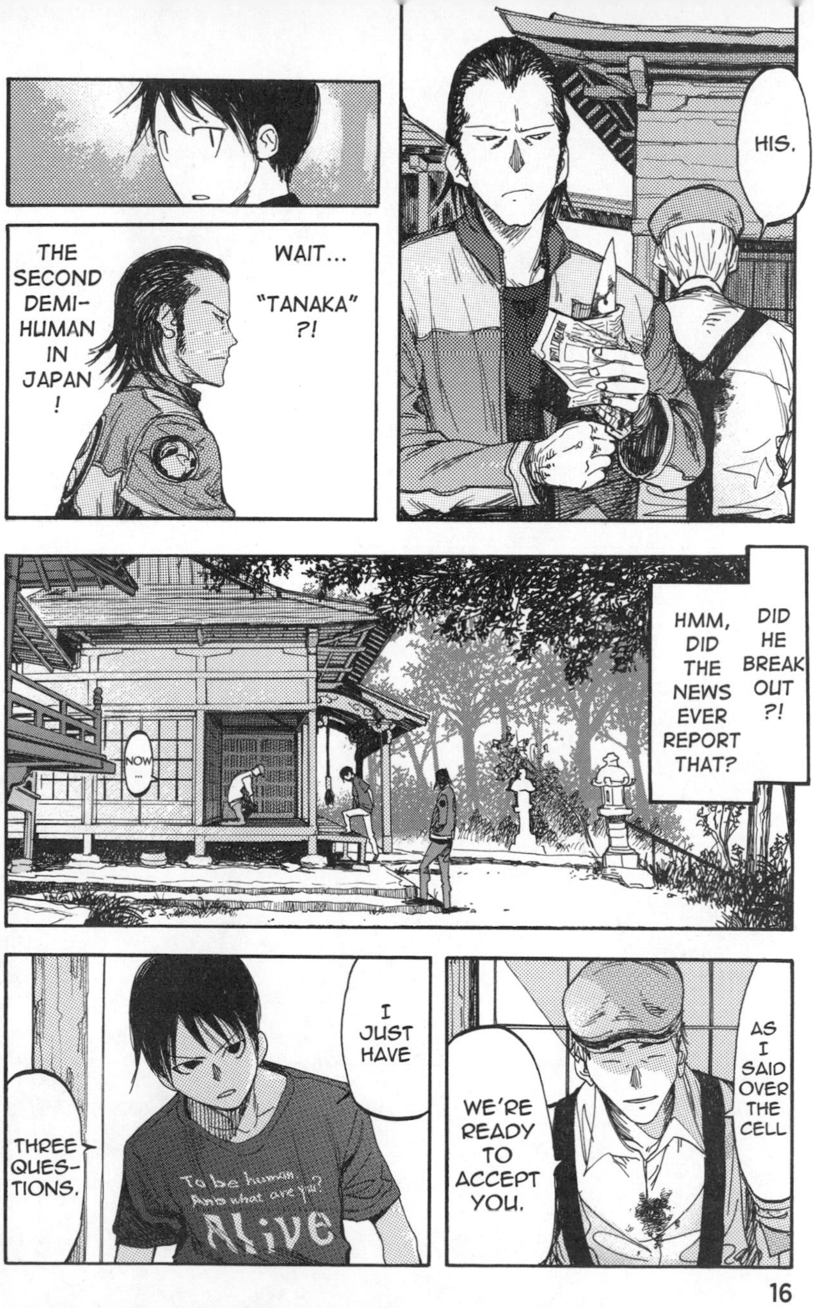
HIS.
WAIT... "TANAKA" ?!
THE SECOND DEMI-HUMAN IN JAPAN !
DID HE BREAK OUT ?!
HMM, DID THE NEWS EVER REPORT THAT?
NOW...
AS I SAID OVER THE CELL
WE'RE READY TO ACCEPT YOU.
I JUST HAVE
THREE QUES-TIONS.
To be human And what are you? Alive

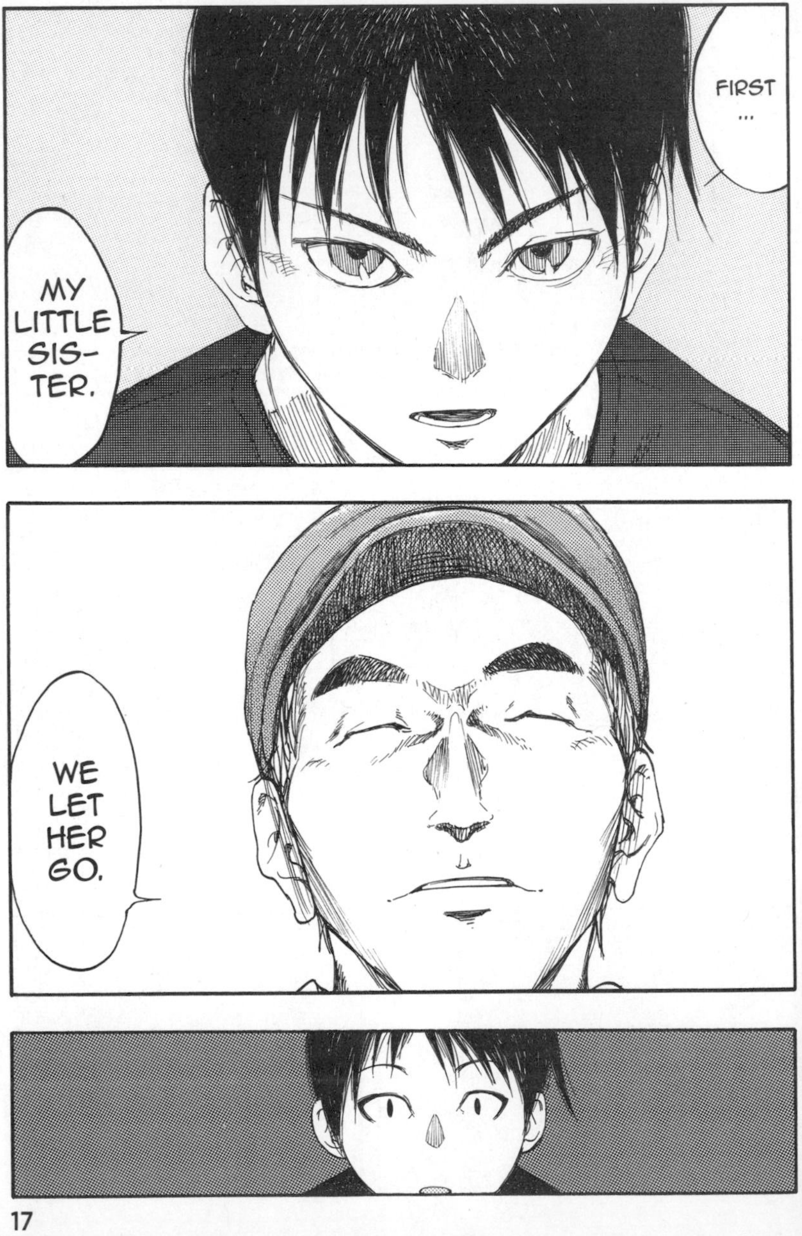
FIRST ...
MY LITTLE SIS-TER.
WE LET HER GO.

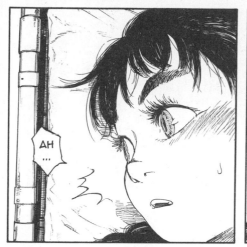

AH
...

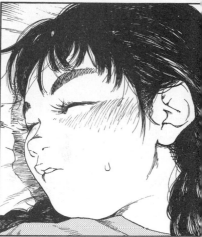

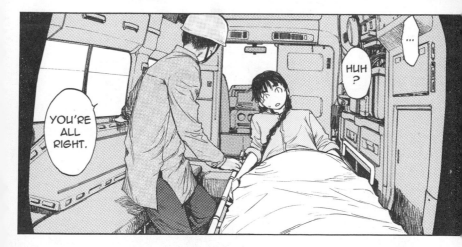

...

HUH
?

YOU'RE
ALL
RIGHT.

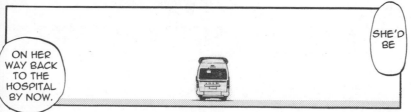

SHE'D
BE

ON HER
WAY BACK
TO THE
HOSPITAL
BY NOW.

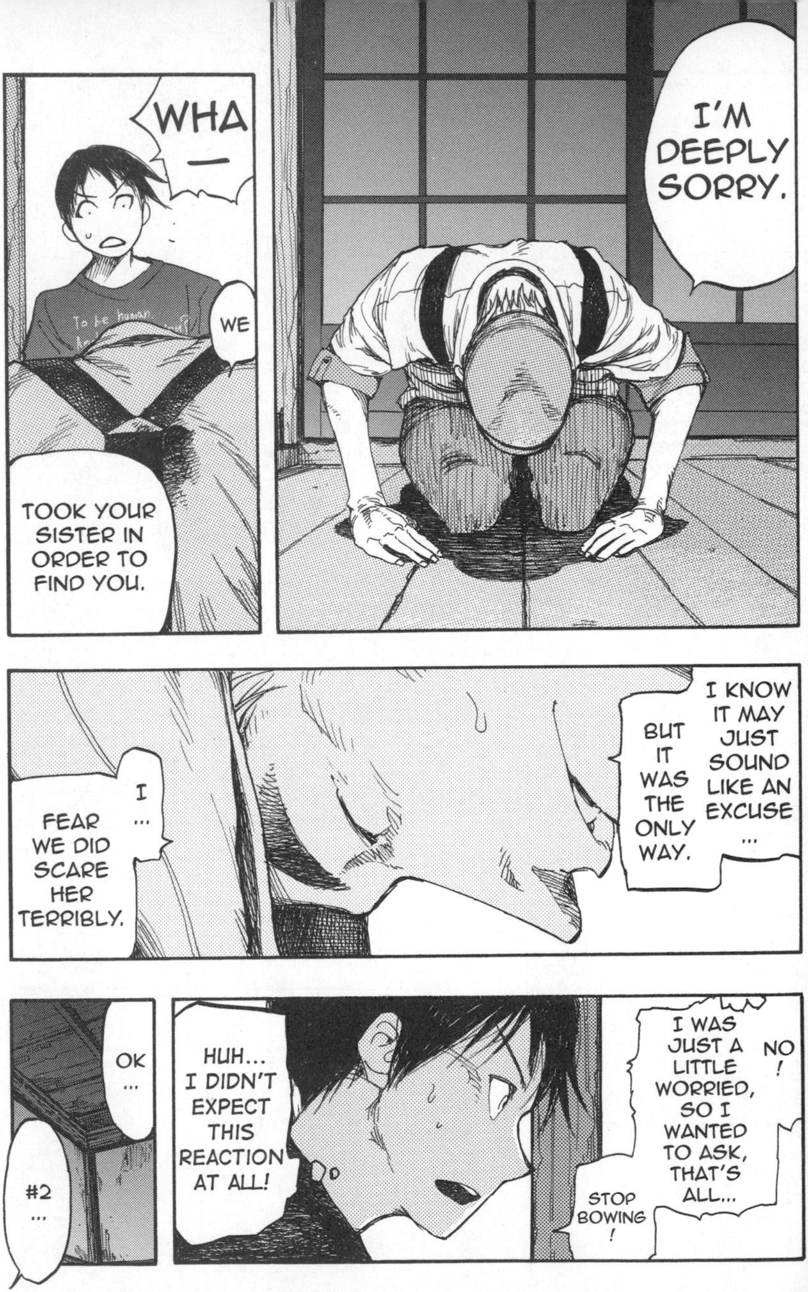
I'M DEEPLY SORRY.
WHA —
WE
TOOK YOUR SISTER IN ORDER TO FIND YOU.
I KNOW IT MAY JUST SOUND LIKE AN EXCUSE ...
BUT IT WAS THE ONLY WAY.
I ... FEAR WE DID SCARE HER TERRIBLY.
NO!
I WAS JUST A LITTLE WORRIED, SO I WANTED TO ASK, THAT'S ALL...
STOP BOWING!
HUH... I DIDN'T EXPECT THIS REACTION AT ALL!
OK ...
#2 ...

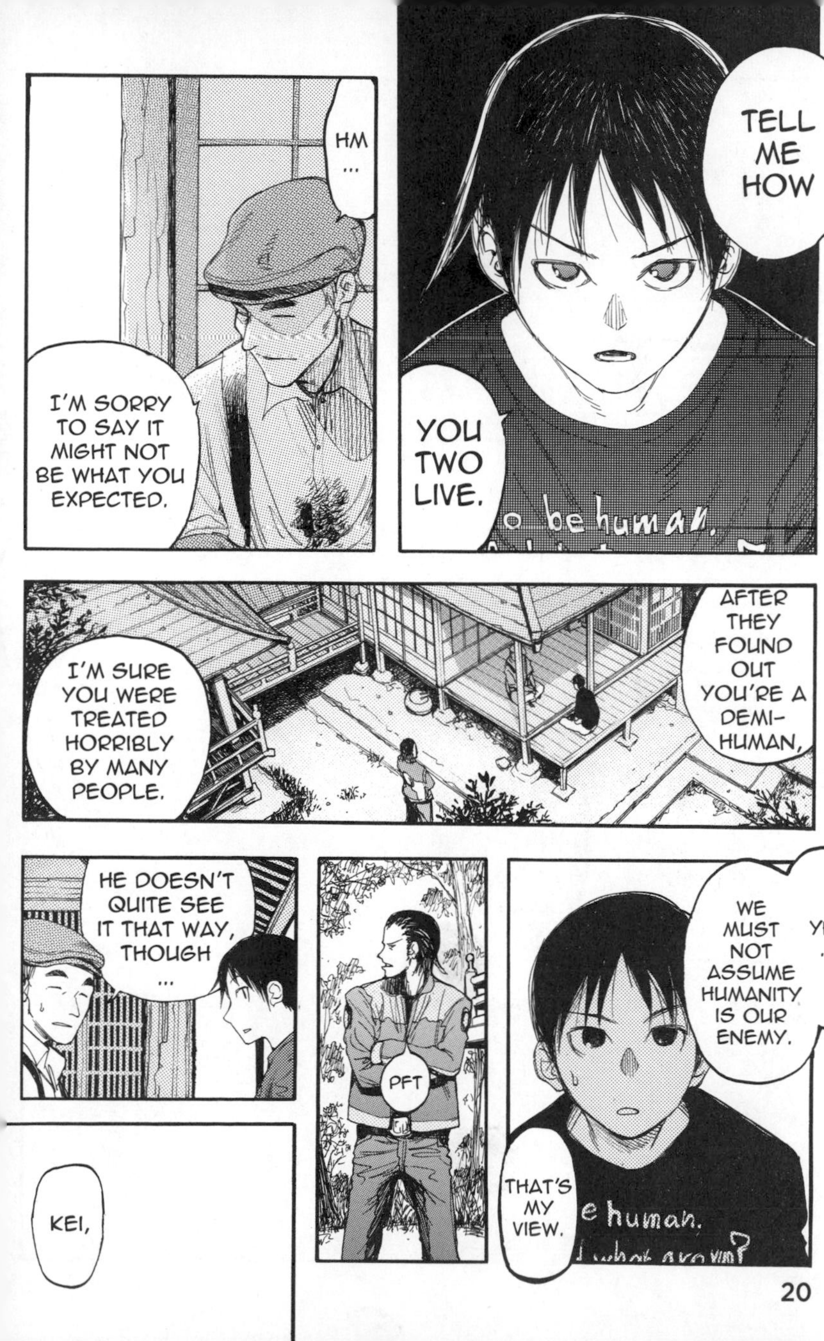
TELL ME HOW
YOU TWO LIVE.
HM ...
I'M SORRY TO SAY IT MIGHT NOT BE WHAT YOU EXPECTED.
AFTER THEY FOUND OUT YOU'RE A DEMI-HUMAN,
I'M SURE YOU WERE TREATED HORRIBLY BY MANY PEOPLE.
YET ...
WE MUST NOT ASSUME HUMANITY IS OUR ENEMY.
THAT'S MY VIEW.
e human.
PFT
HE DOESN'T QUITE SEE IT THAT WAY, THOUGH ...
KEI,

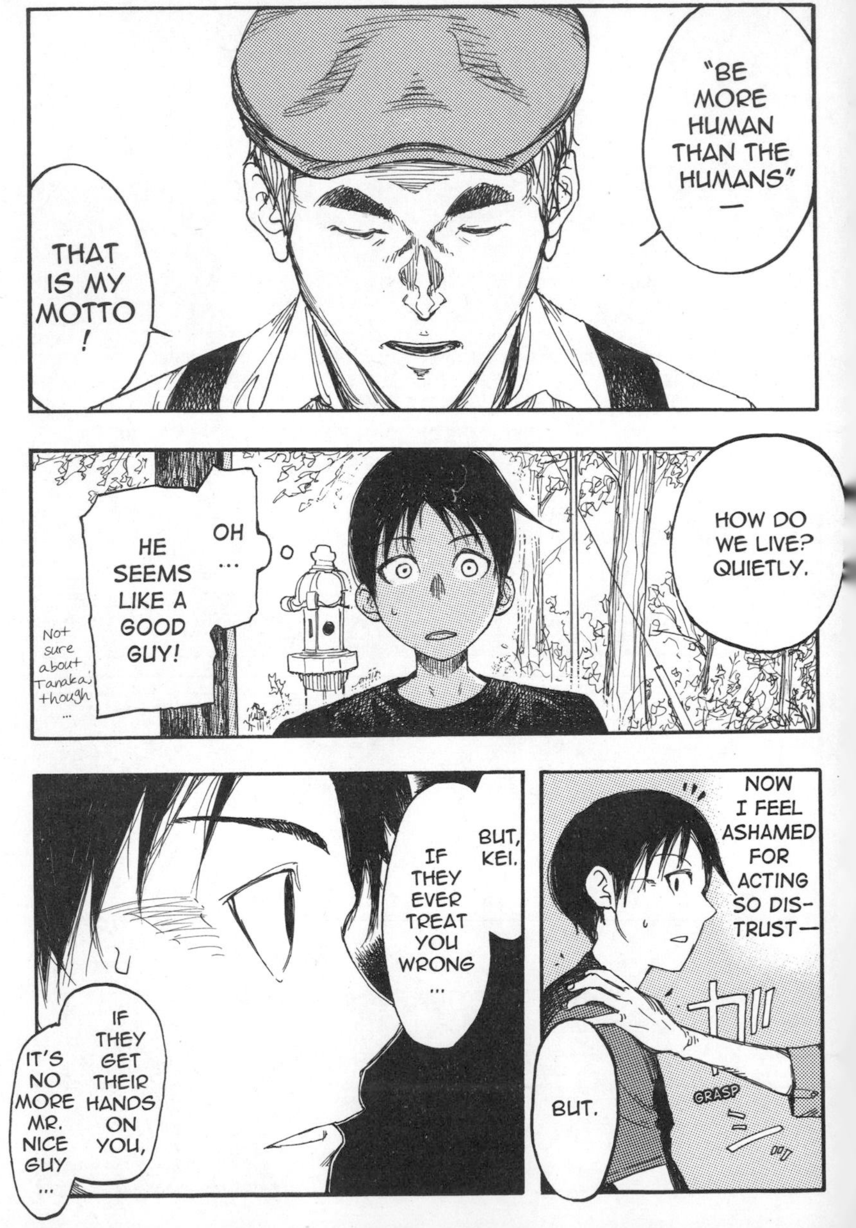
"BE MORE HUMAN THAN THE HUMANS" —
THAT IS MY MOTTO!
HOW DO WE LIVE? QUIETLY.
OH ...
HE SEEMS LIKE A GOOD GUY!
Not sure about Tanaka, though ...
NOW I FEEL ASHAMED FOR ACTING SO DIS-TRUST—
GRASP
BUT.
BUT, KEI.
IF THEY EVER TREAT YOU WRONG ...
IF THEY GET THEIR HANDS ON YOU,
IT'S NO MORE MR. NICE GUY ...

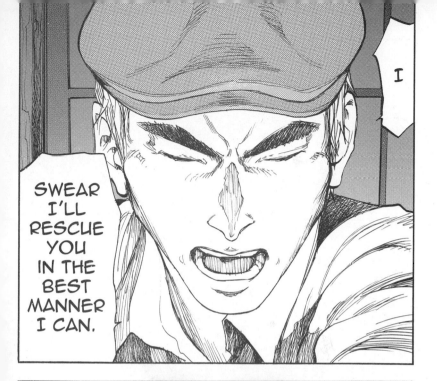

I
SWEAR I'LL RESCUE YOU IN THE BEST MANNER I CAN.

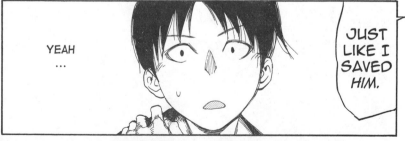

JUST LIKE I SAVED *HIM.*
YEAH ...

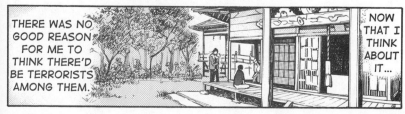

NOW THAT I THINK ABOUT IT...
THERE WAS NO GOOD REASON FOR ME TO THINK THERE'D BE TERRORISTS AMONG THEM.

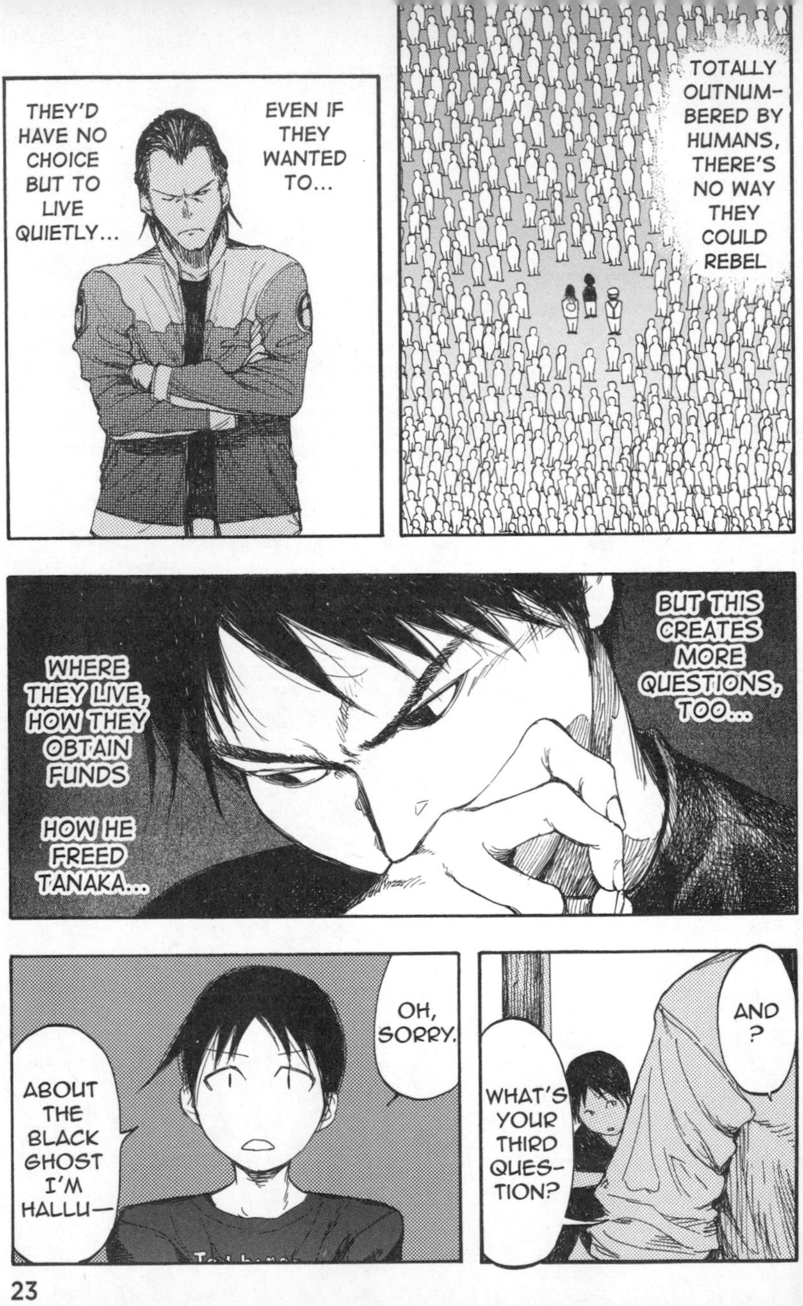
TOTALLY OUTNUMBERED BY HUMANS, THERE'S NO WAY THEY COULD REBEL
EVEN IF THEY WANTED TO...
THEY'D HAVE NO CHOICE BUT TO LIVE QUIETLY...
BUT THIS CREATES MORE QUESTIONS, TOO...
WHERE THEY LIVE, HOW THEY OBTAIN FUNDS
HOW HE FREED TANAKA...
AND?
WHAT'S YOUR THIRD QUESTION?
OH, SORRY.
ABOUT THE BLACK GHOST I'M HALLU—

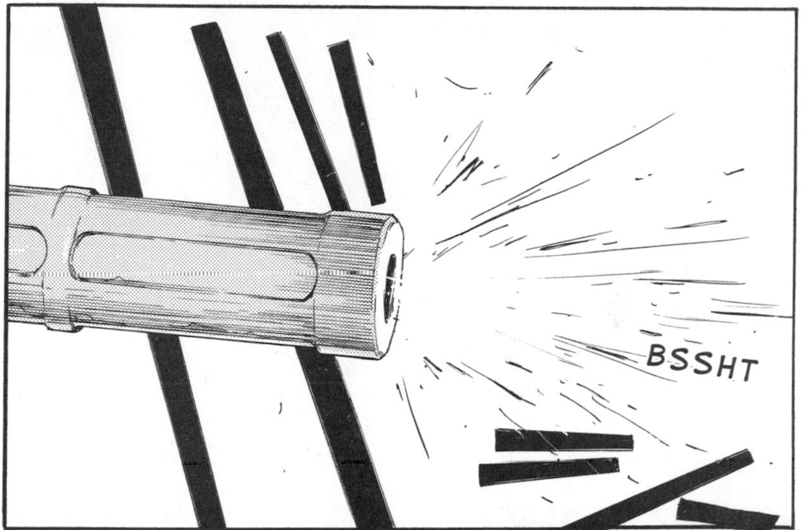
BSSHT

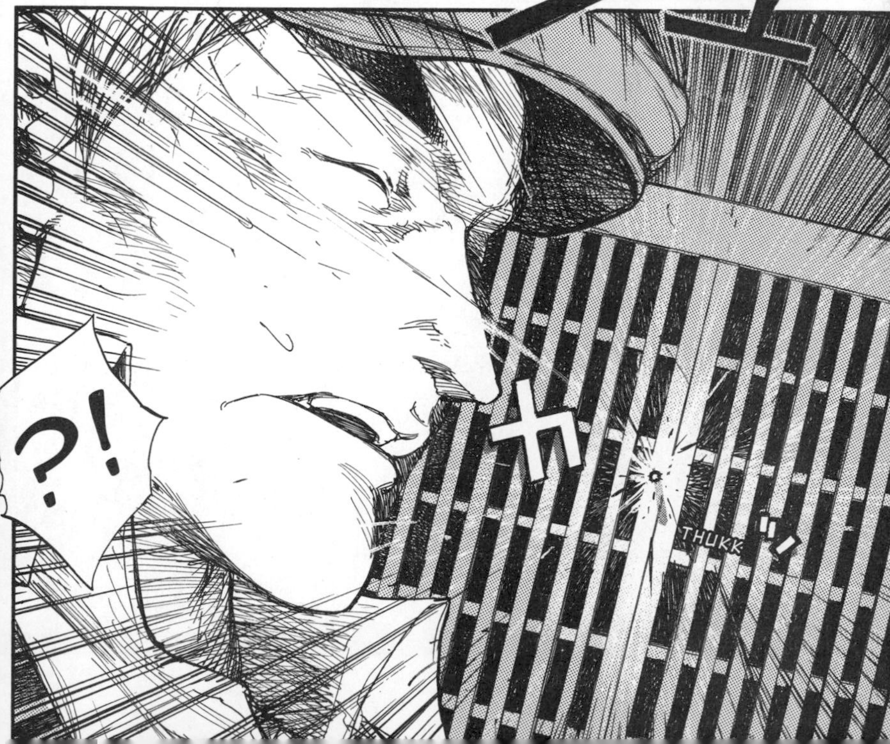
?!
THUKK

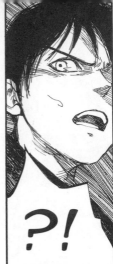

?!

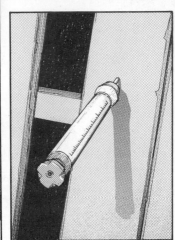

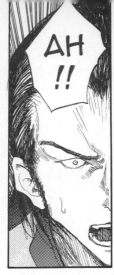

AH!!

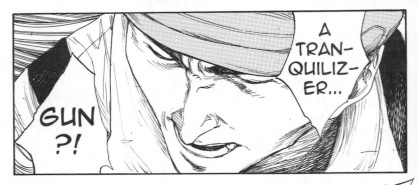

GUN?!

A TRAN-QUILIZ-ER...

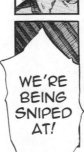

WE'RE BEING SNIPED AT!

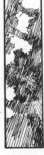

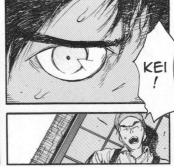

KEI!

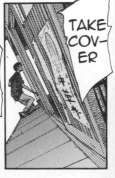

TAKE COVER

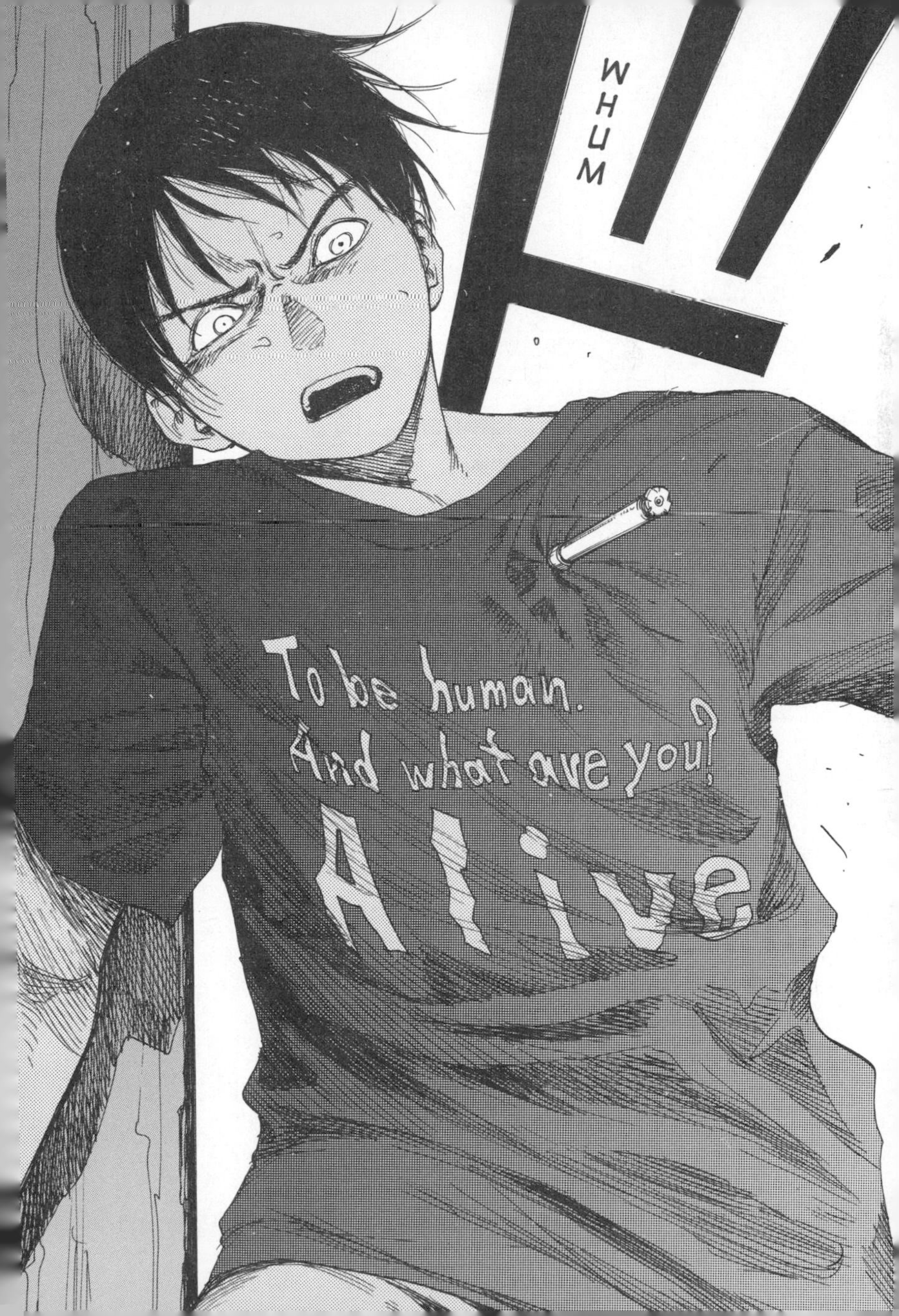
WHUM
To be human.
And what are you?
Alive

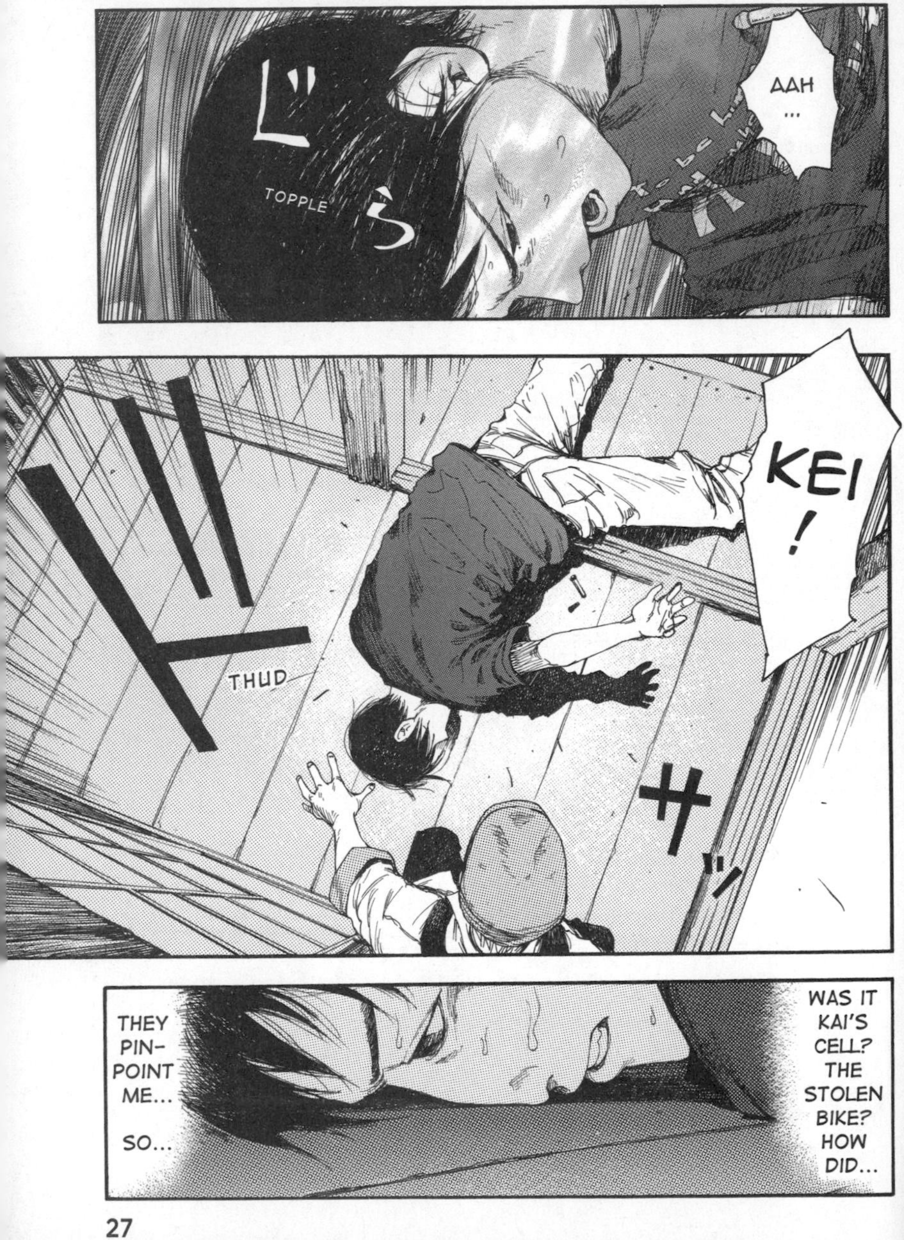
AAH ...
ビ
TOPPLE
ら
KEI!
ド
サ
THUD
WAS IT KAI'S CELL? THE STOLEN BIKE? HOW DID...
THEY PIN-POINT ME... SO...

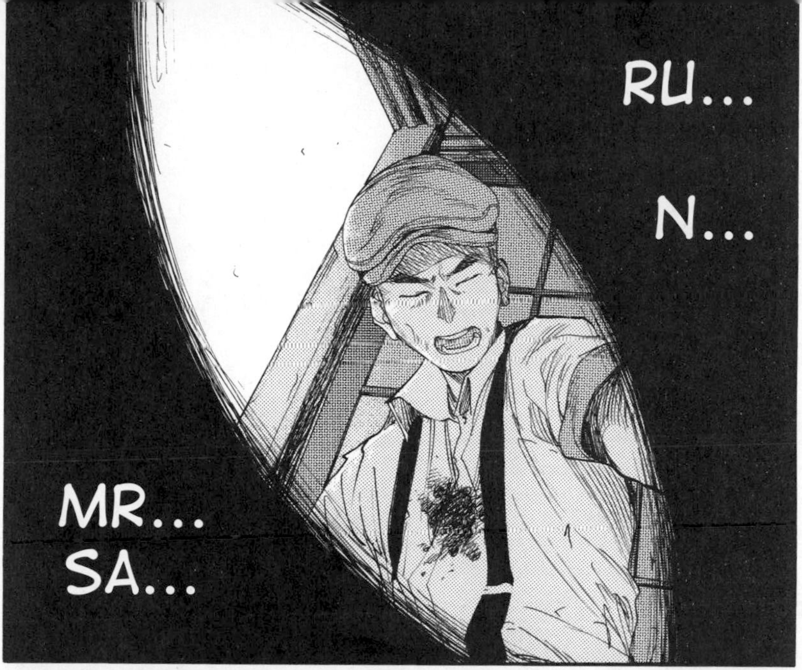
RU...
N...
MR...
SA...

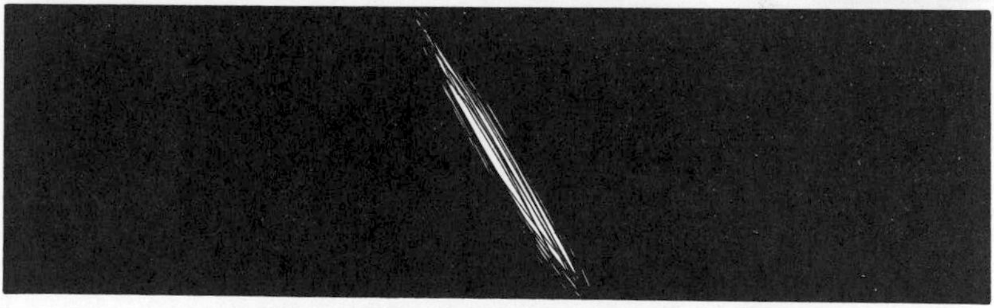

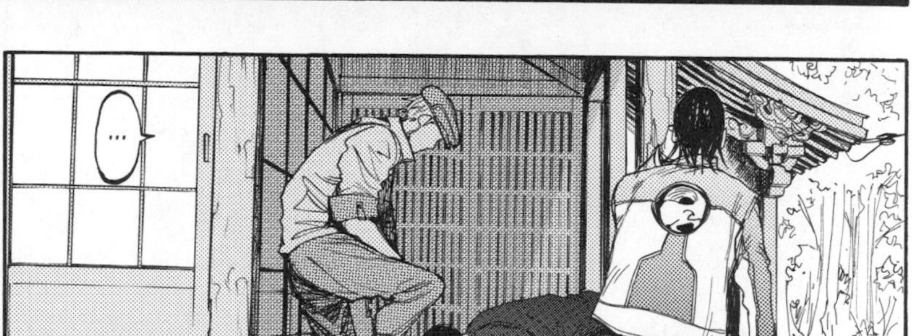
...

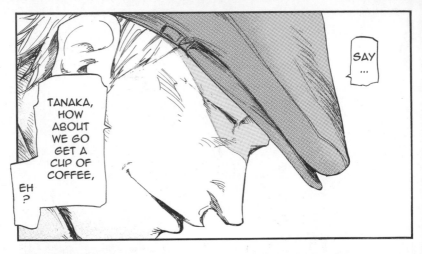

SAY ...
TANAKA, HOW ABOUT WE GO GET A CUP OF COFFEE,
EH?
SO HE FAILS.
YES, FROM THE MOMENT HE ASKED ABOUT HIS SISTER.
HE HASN'T KISSED GOOD-BYE TO HUMAN SOCIETY.
BUT
I DID LIKE HOW THE FIRST SHOT CAME HURTLING MY WAY.
IT ADDED REALISM.
HUH, SORRY ...

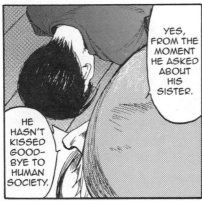

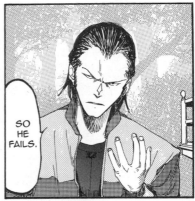

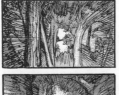

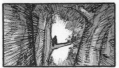

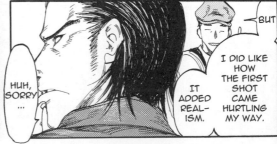

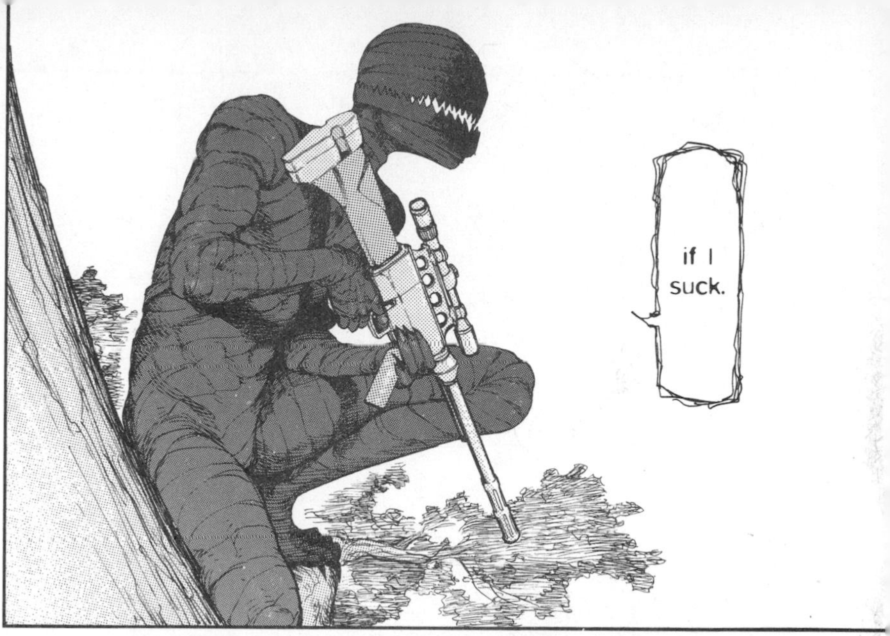
if I suck.

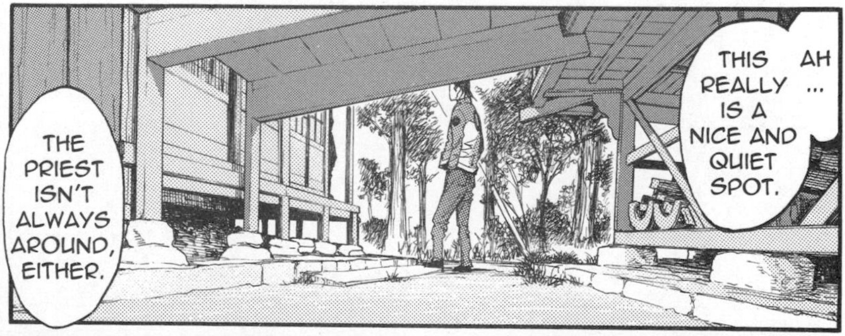
AH ...
THIS REALLY IS A NICE AND QUIET SPOT.
THE PRIEST ISN'T ALWAYS AROUND, EITHER.

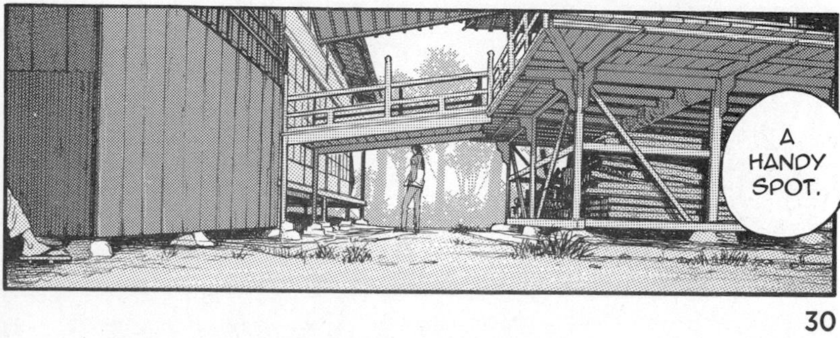
A HANDY SPOT.

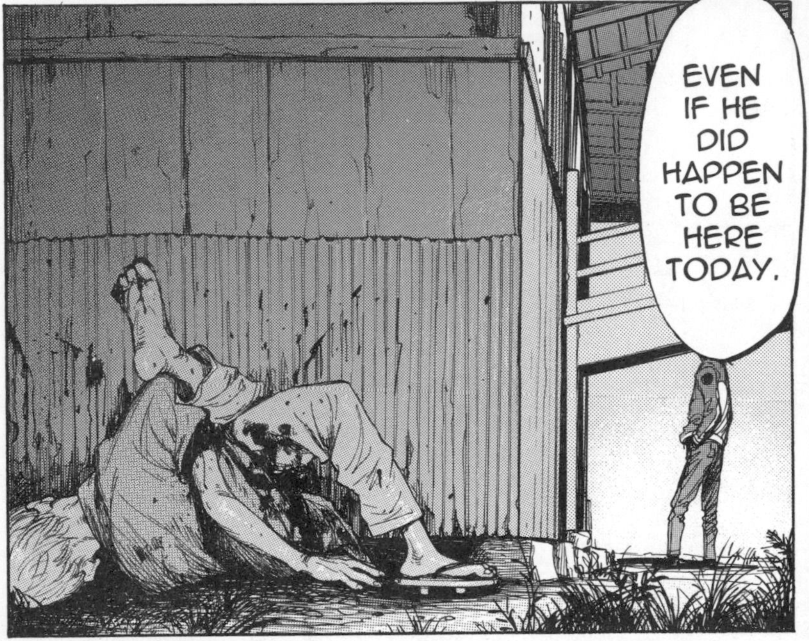
EVEN IF HE DID HAPPEN TO BE HERE TODAY.

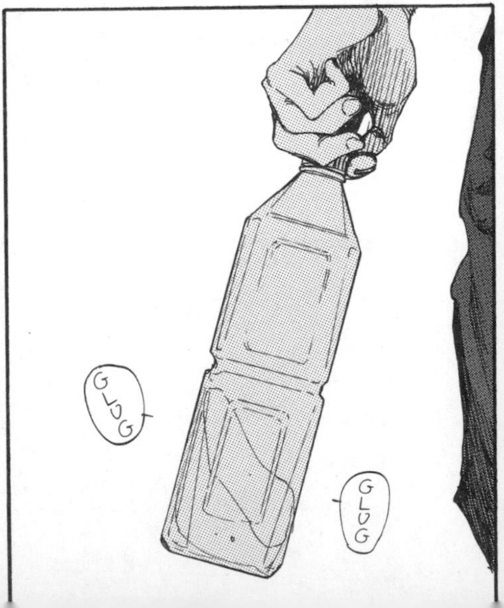
GLUG
GLUG

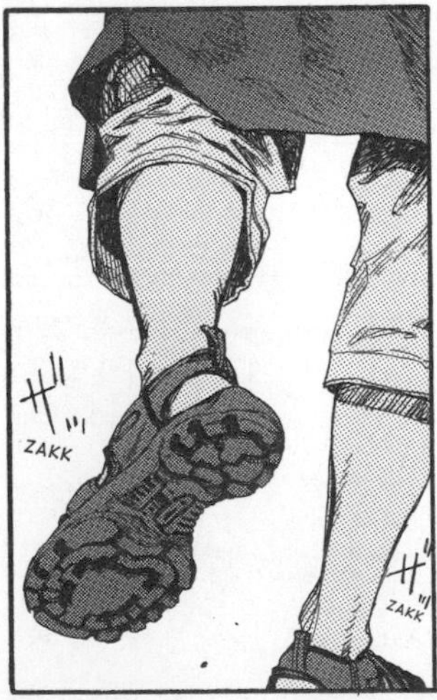
ZAKK
ZAKK

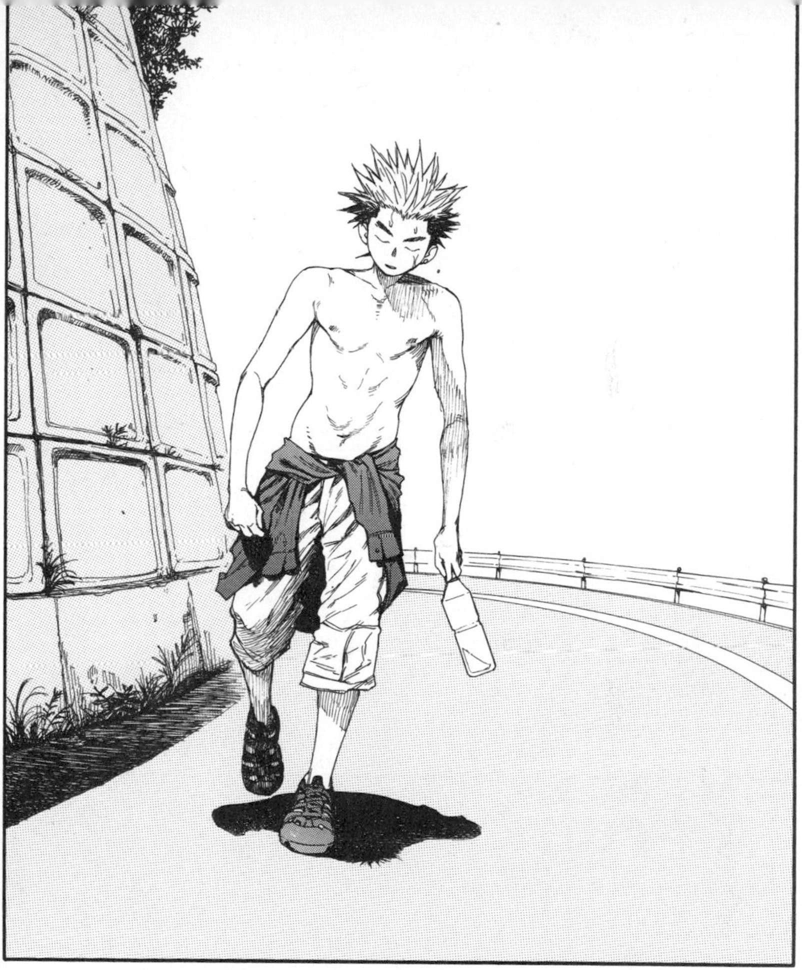

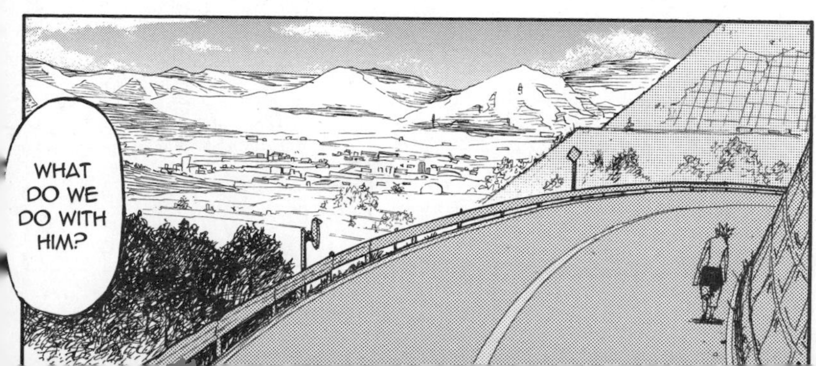
WHAT DO WE DO WITH HIM?

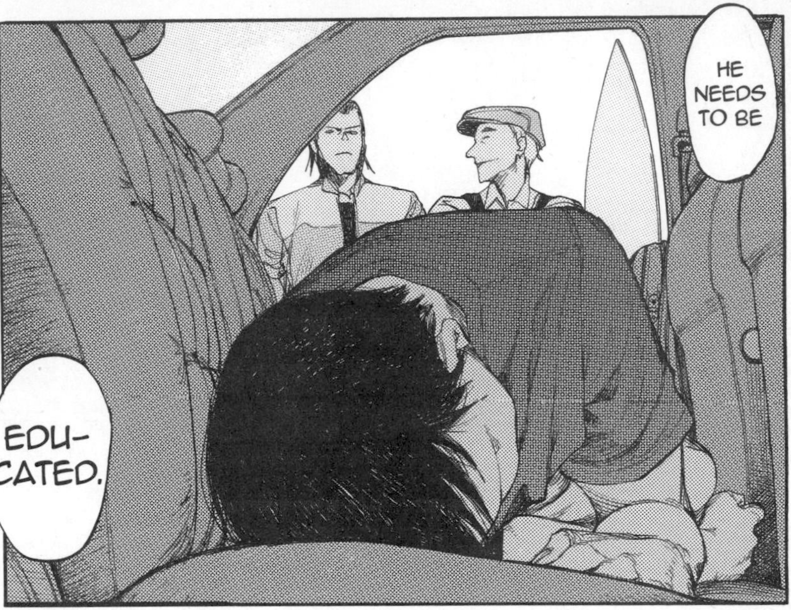
HE NEEDS TO BE
EDU-CATED.

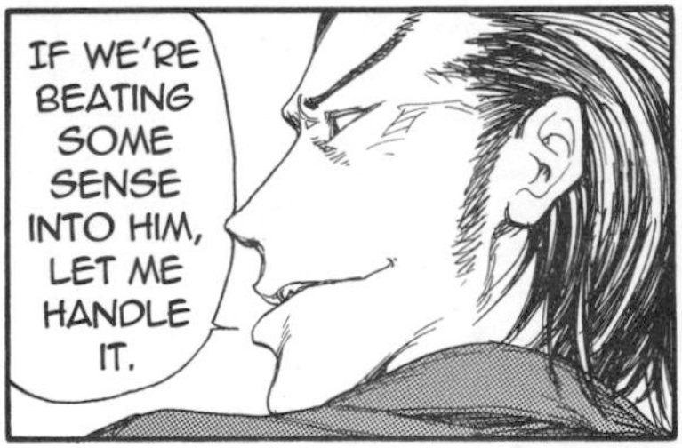
IF WE'RE BEATING SOME SENSE INTO HIM, LET ME HANDLE IT.

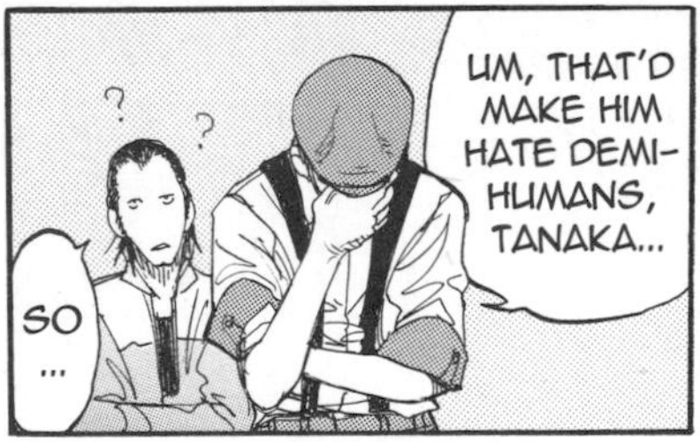
UM, THAT'D MAKE HIM HATE DEMI-HUMANS, TANAKA...
SO ...

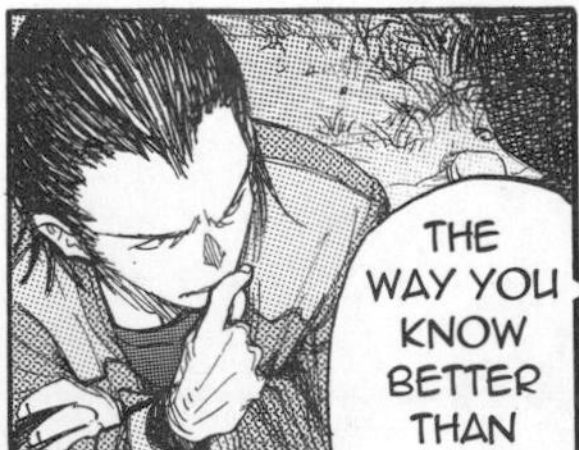
THE WAY YOU KNOW BETTER THAN ANYONE ELSE.

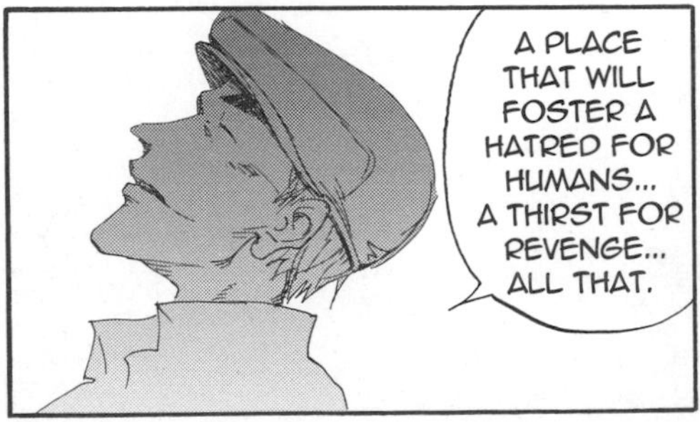
A PLACE THAT WILL FOSTER A HATRED FOR HUMANS... A THIRST FOR REVENGE... ALL THAT.

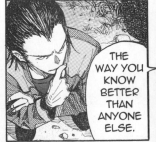

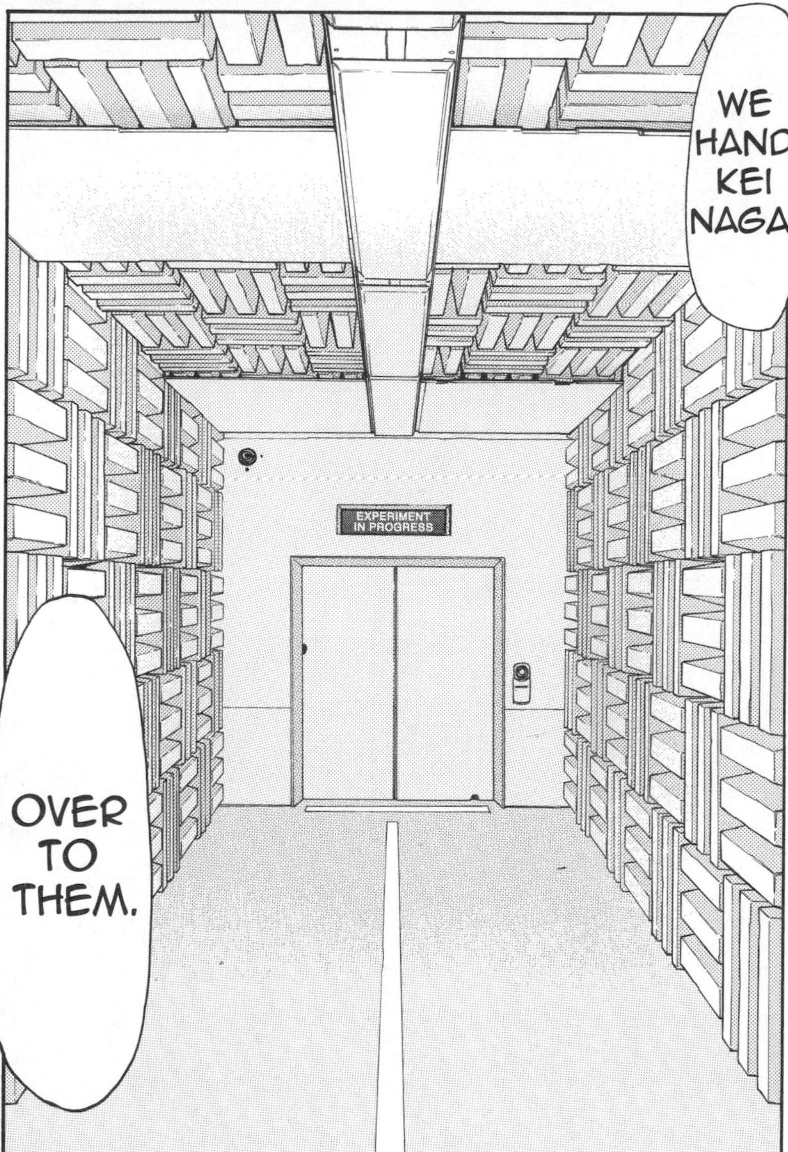
WE HAND KEI NAGAI
EXPERIMENT IN PROGRESS
OVER TO THEM.

File:06 End

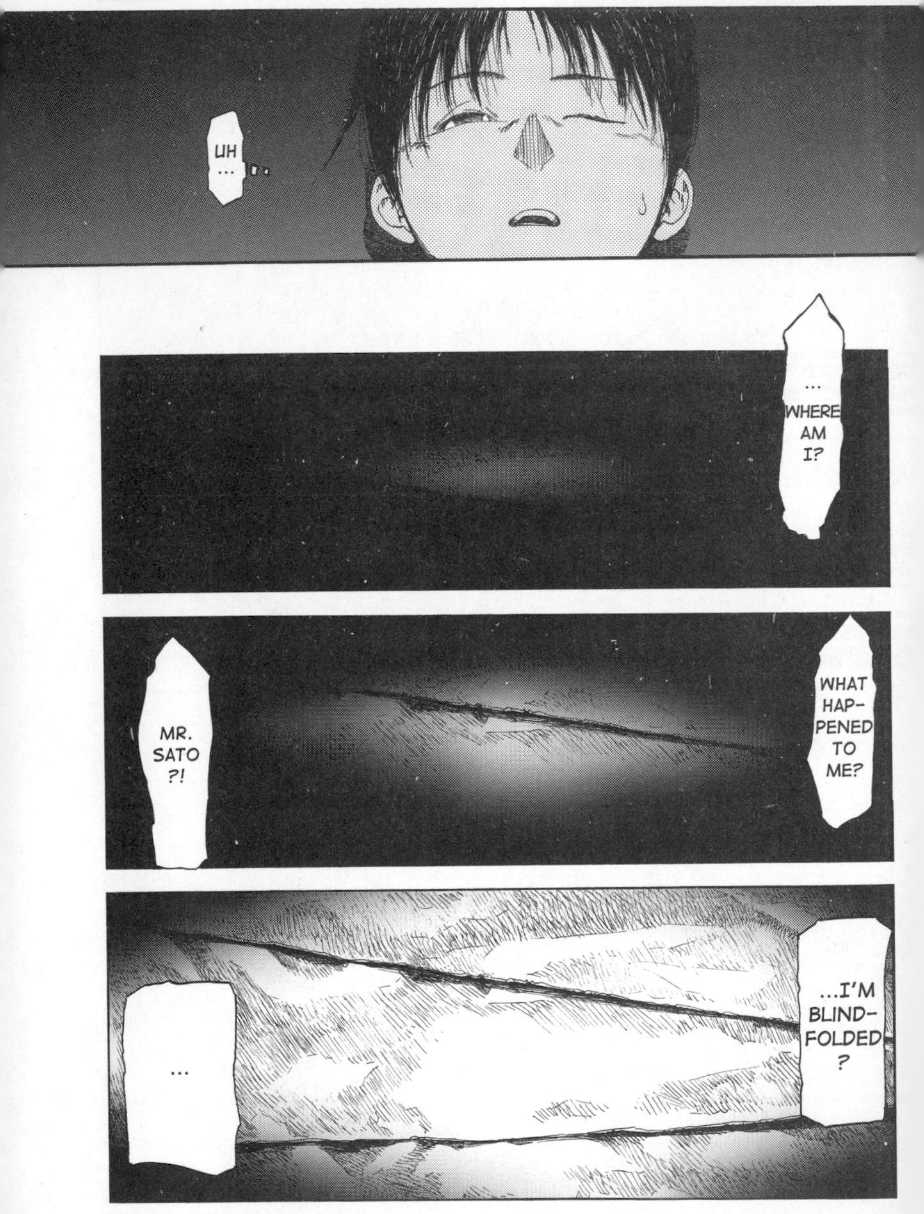
UH ...
... WHERE AM I?
WHAT HAP-PENED TO ME?
MR. SATO ?!
...I'M BLIND-FOLDED ?
...

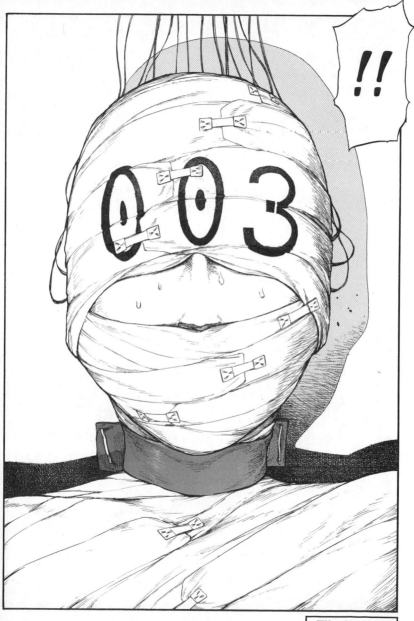

File 07: 003

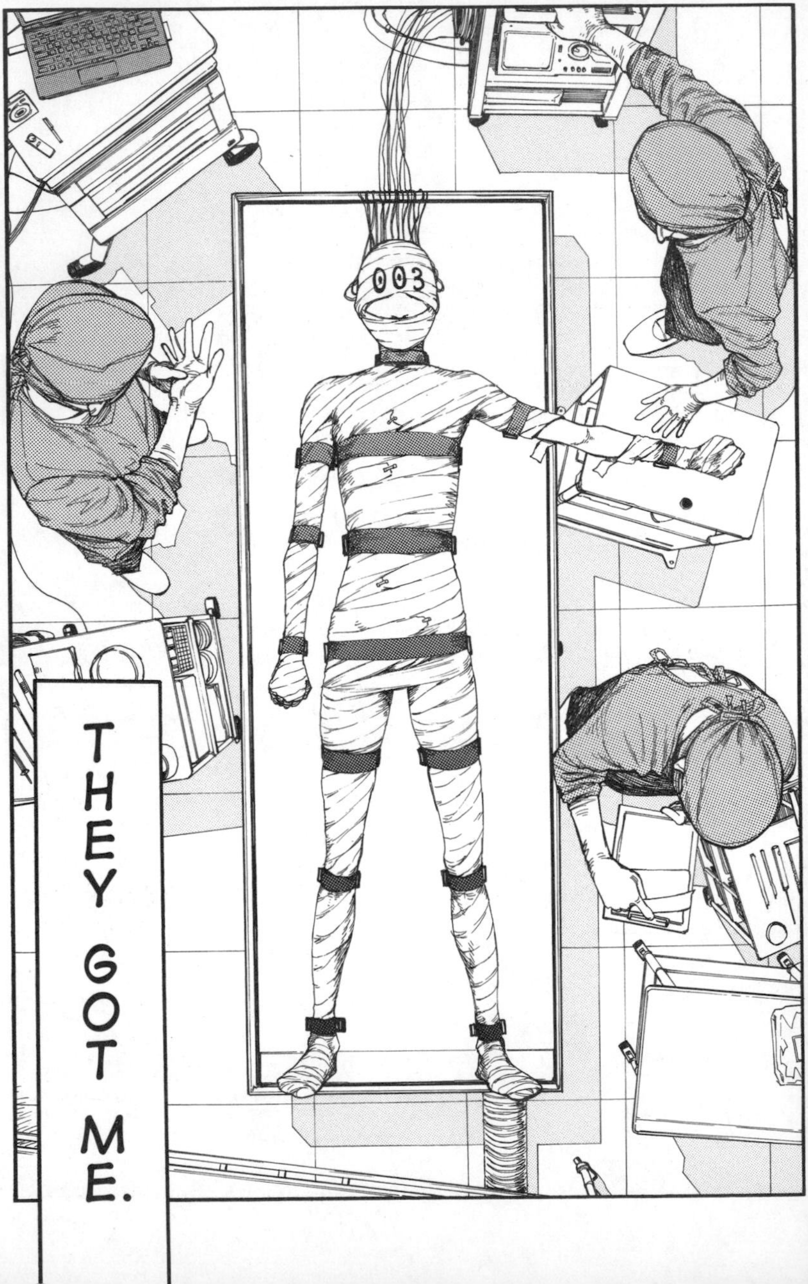
003
THEY GOT ME.

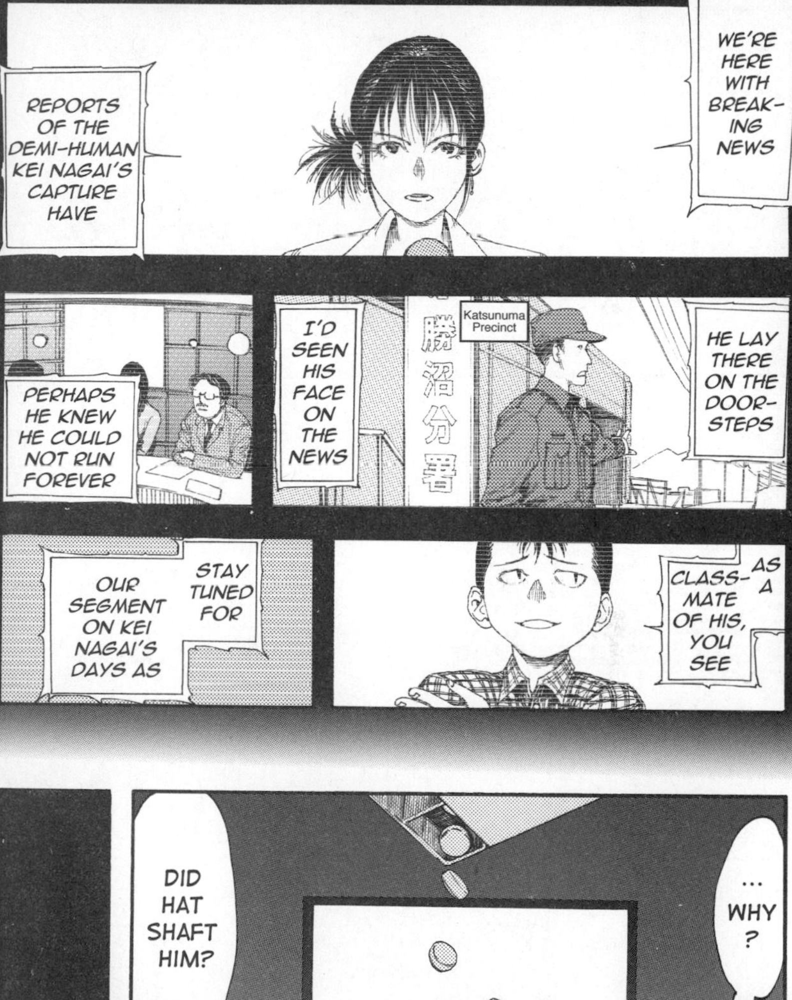
WE'RE HERE WITH BREAKING NEWS
REPORTS OF THE DEMI-HUMAN KEI NAGAI'S CAPTURE HAVE
HE LAY THERE ON THE DOORSTEPS
Katsunuma Precinct
勝沼分署
I'D SEEN HIS FACE ON THE NEWS
PERHAPS HE KNEW HE COULD NOT RUN FOREVER
AS A CLASSMATE OF HIS, YOU SEE
STAY TUNED FOR OUR SEGMENT ON KEI NAGAI'S DAYS AS
... WHY?
DID HAT SHAFT HIM?
BE THAT AS IT MAY ...

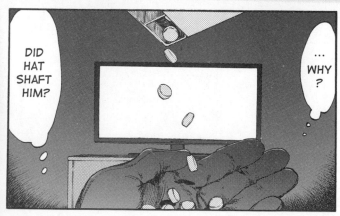

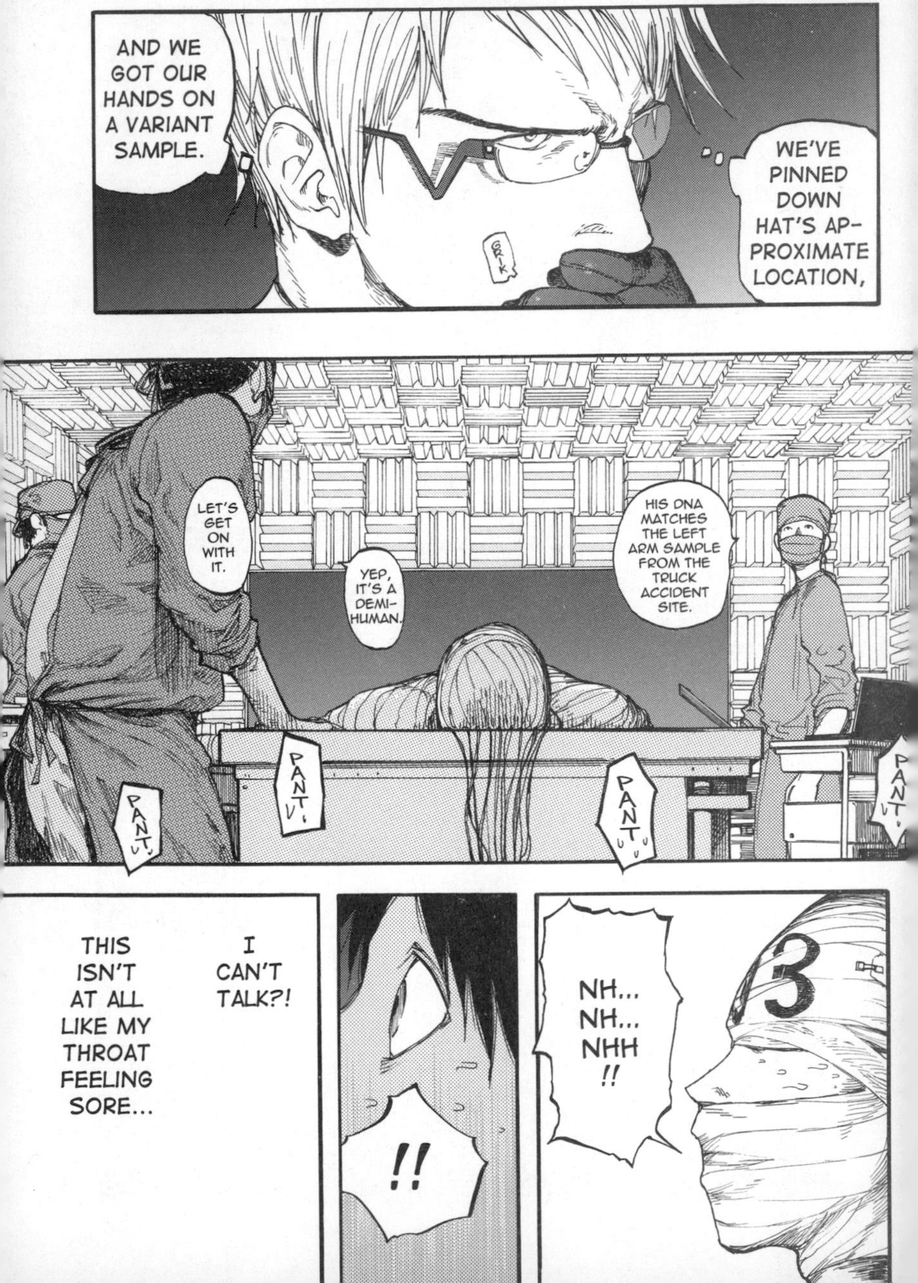
WE'VE PINNED DOWN HAT'S AP-PROXIMATE LOCATION,
GRIK
AND WE GOT OUR HANDS ON A VARIANT SAMPLE.
HIS DNA MATCHES THE LEFT ARM SAMPLE FROM THE TRUCK ACCIDENT SITE.
YEP, IT'S A DEMI-HUMAN.
LET'S GET ON WITH IT.
PANT
PANT
PANT
PANT
NH... NH... NHH !!
!!
I CAN'T TALK?!
THIS ISN'T AT ALL LIKE MY THROAT FEELING SORE...

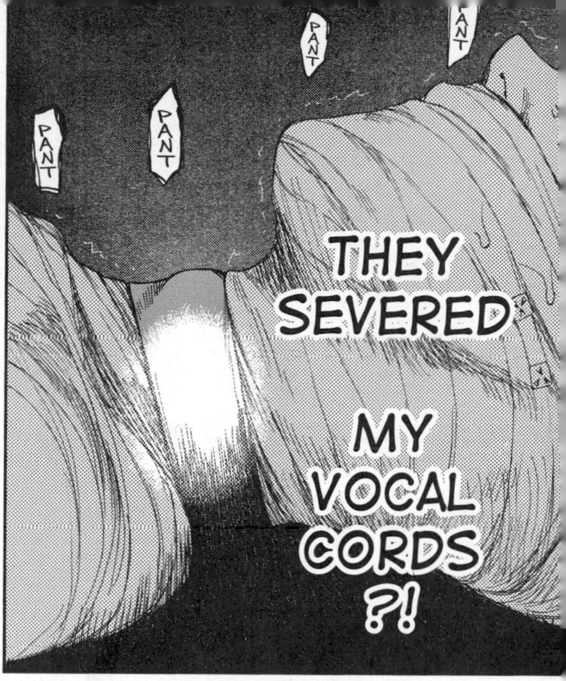
PANT
PANT
PANT
THEY SEVERED MY VOCAL CORDS ?!

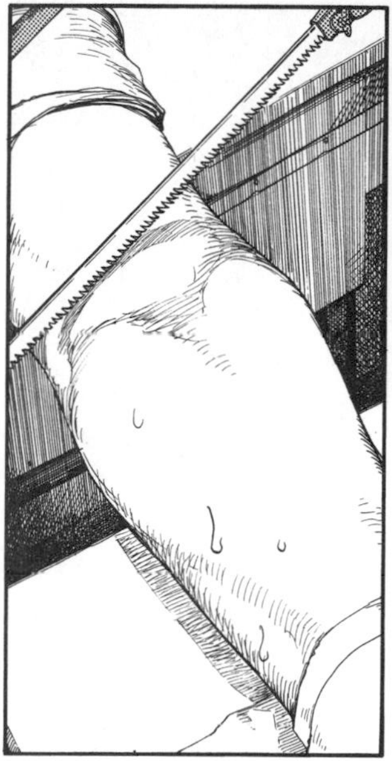

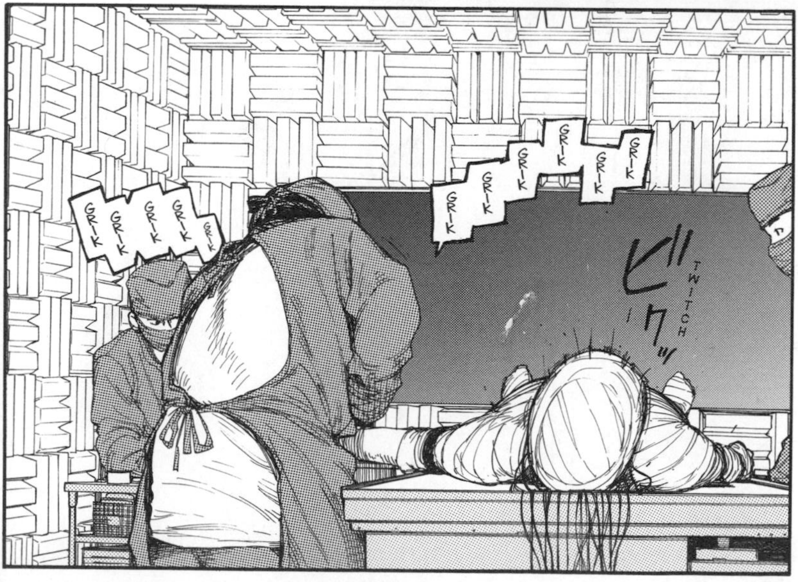
GRIK GRIK GRIK GRIK GRIK GRIK
TWITCH
GRIK GRIK GRIK GRIK GRIK

...NH NH NH!!
ガタ RATTLE
ガタ RATTLE
ガタ RATTLE
NHH NKK!!
ガタ RATTLE
ガタ RATTLE
ガタ RATTLE
GRIK GRIK GRIK GRIK GRIK GRIK GRIK
GRRK GRRK GRRK GRRK
ガタ RATTLE
...NHH!!!
...NNN HHHHH!!!
カタ... KLAK
カタ... KLAK
GRRT GRRT GRRT GRRT GRRT GRRT GRRT

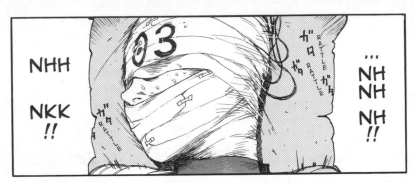

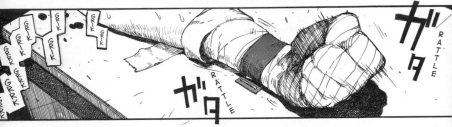

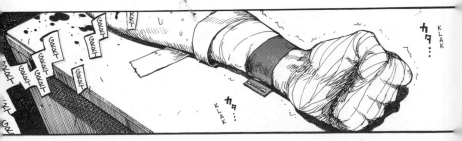

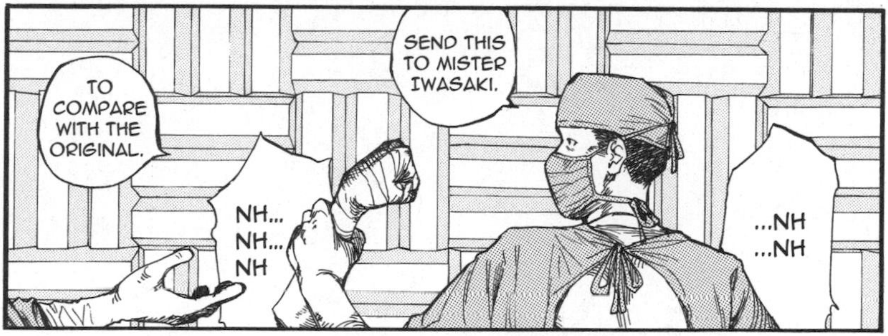
SEND THIS TO MISTER IWASAKI.
...NH ...NH
TO COMPARE WITH THE ORIGINAL.
NH... NH... NH

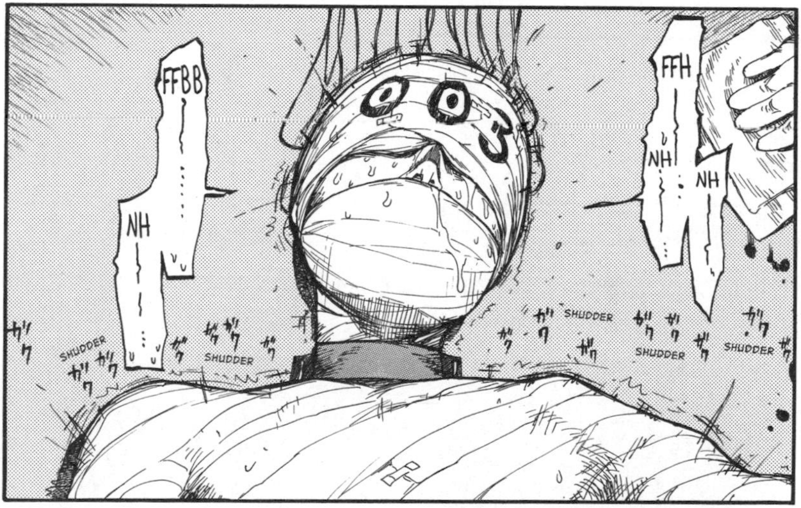
FFH NH NH
FFBB NH
SHUDDER
SHUDDER
SHUDDER
SHUDDER
SHUDDER

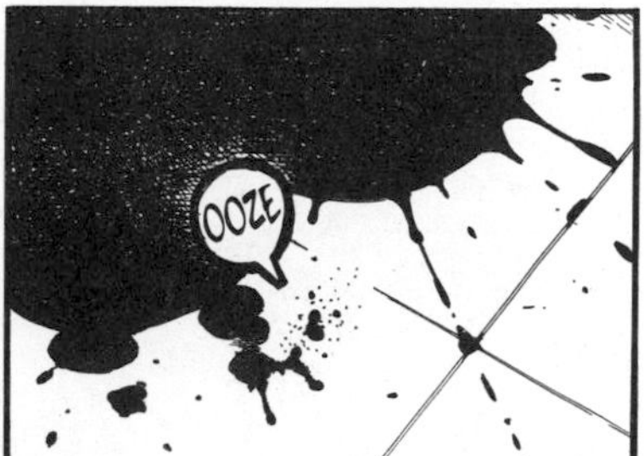
OOZE

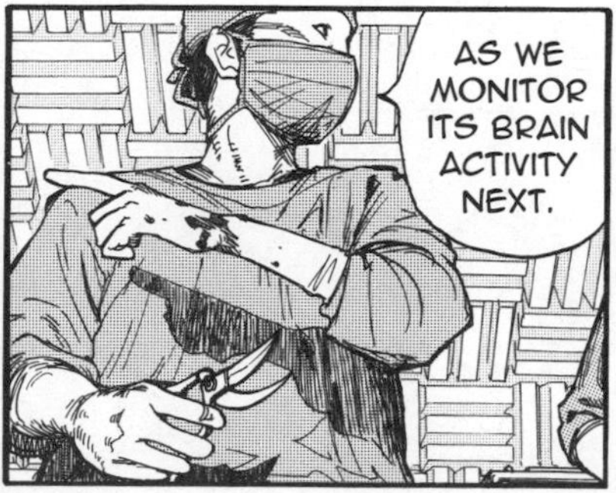
AS WE MONITOR ITS BRAIN ACTIVITY NEXT.

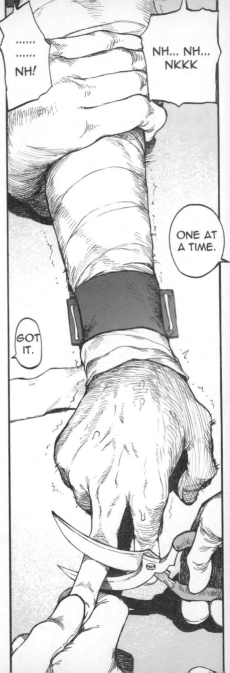

.... NH!

NH... NH... NKKK

ONE AT A TIME.

GOT IT.

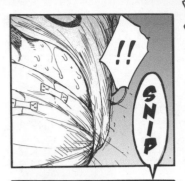

!!

SNIP

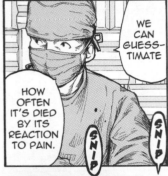

WE CAN GUESS-TIMATE

HOW OFTEN IT'S DIED BY ITS REACTION TO PAIN.

SNIP

SNIP

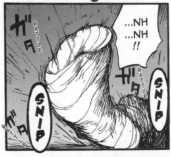

...NH ...NH !!

SNIP

SNIP

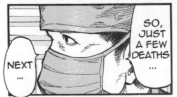

SO, JUST A FEW DEATHS ...

NEXT ...

43

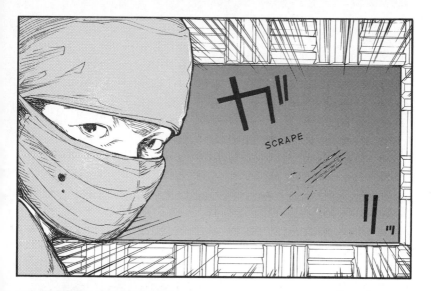

SCRAPE

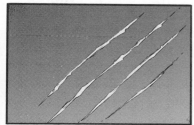

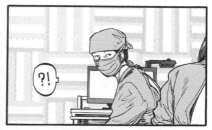

?!

UM
...

DID THAT GLASS ...

ALWAYS HAVE THOSE SCRATCH- ES?

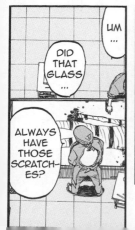

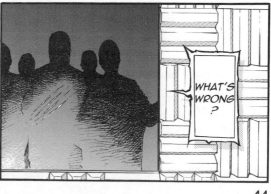

WHAT'S WRONG ?

44

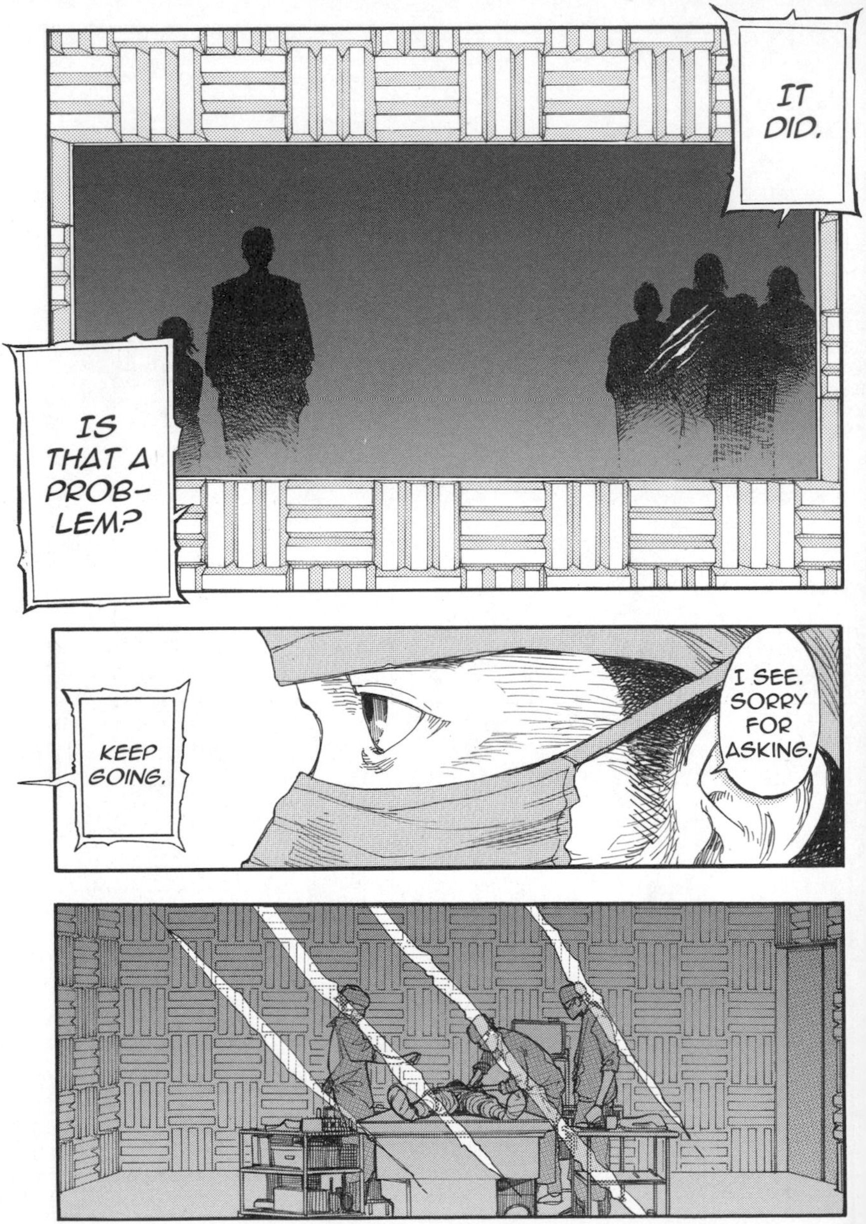
IT DID.
IS THAT A PROB-LEM?
I SEE. SORRY FOR ASKING.
KEEP GOING.

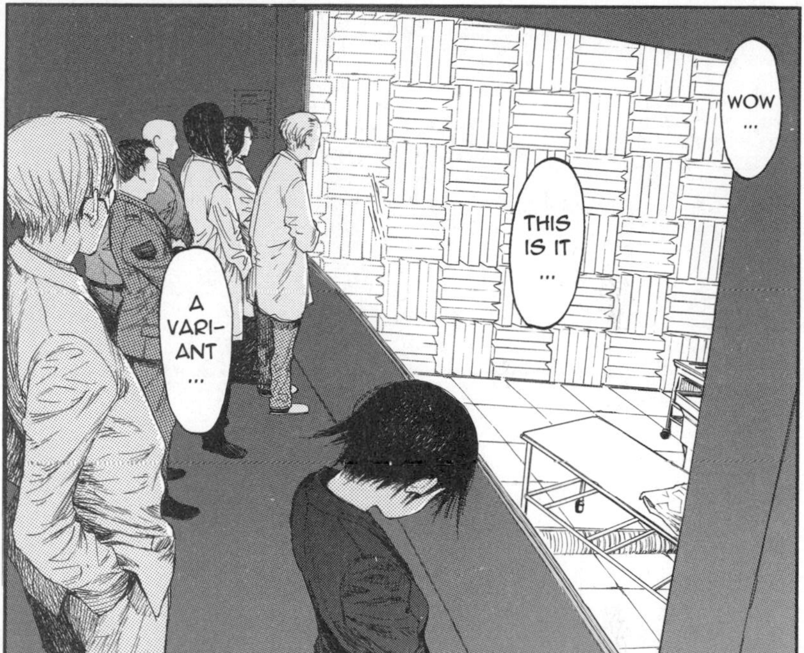
WOW ...
THIS IS IT ...
A VARIANT ...
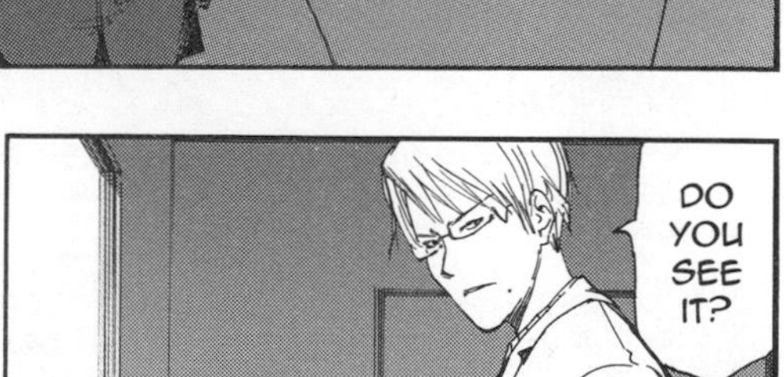
DO YOU SEE IT?
...
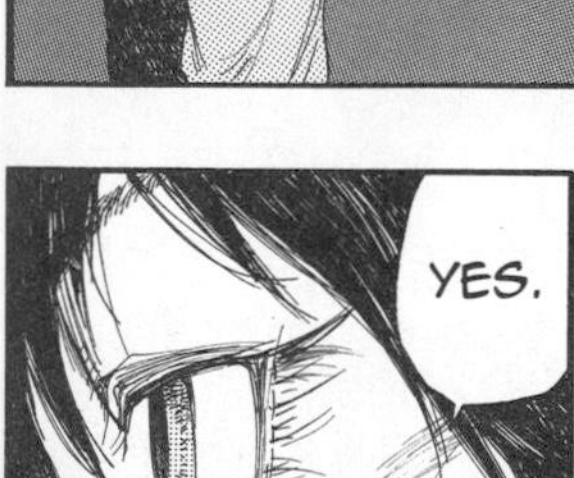
YES.

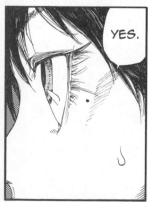

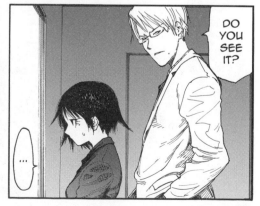

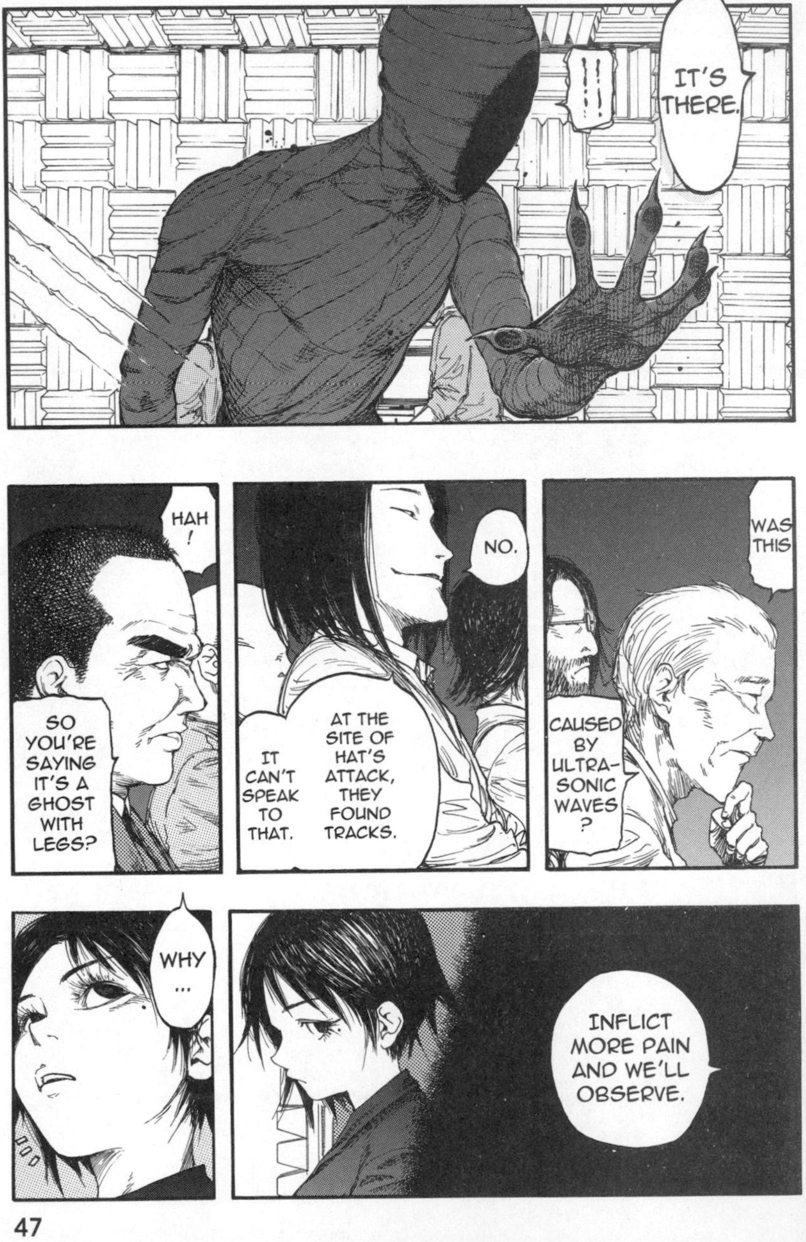
IT'S THERE.
!!
WAS THIS
CAUSED BY ULTRA-SONIC WAVES?
NO.
AT THE SITE OF HAT'S ATTACK, THEY FOUND TRACKS.
IT CAN'T SPEAK TO THAT.
HAH!
SO YOU'RE SAYING IT'S A GHOST WITH LEGS?
INFLICT MORE PAIN AND WE'LL OBSERVE.
WHY ...

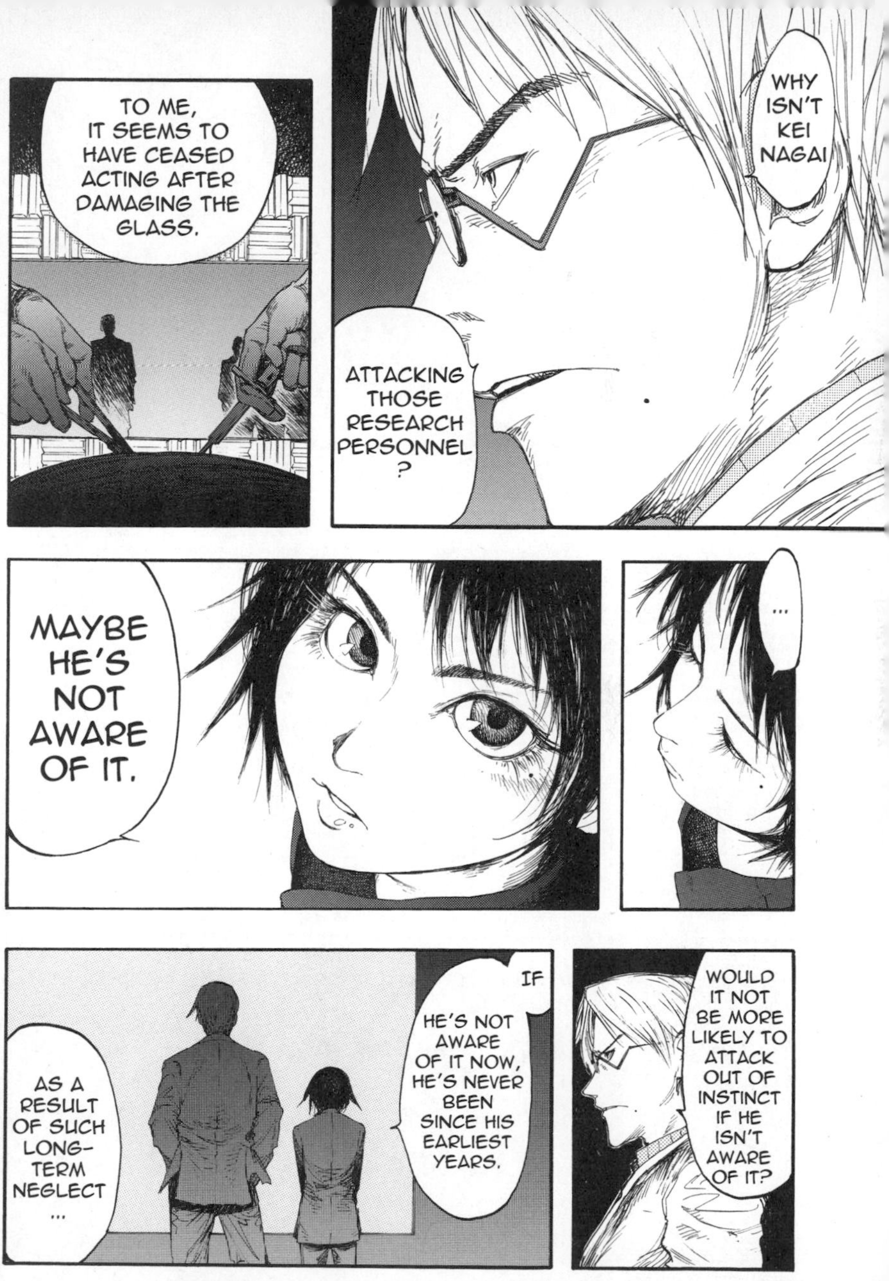
WHY ISN'T KEI NAGAI
ATTACKING THOSE RESEARCH PERSONNEL ?
TO ME, IT SEEMS TO HAVE CEASED ACTING AFTER DAMAGING THE GLASS.
...
MAYBE HE'S NOT AWARE OF IT.
WOULD IT NOT BE MORE LIKELY TO ATTACK OUT OF INSTINCT IF HE ISN'T AWARE OF IT?
IF
HE'S NOT AWARE OF IT NOW, HE'S NEVER BEEN SINCE HIS EARLIEST YEARS.
AS A RESULT OF SUCH LONG-TERM NEGLECT ...

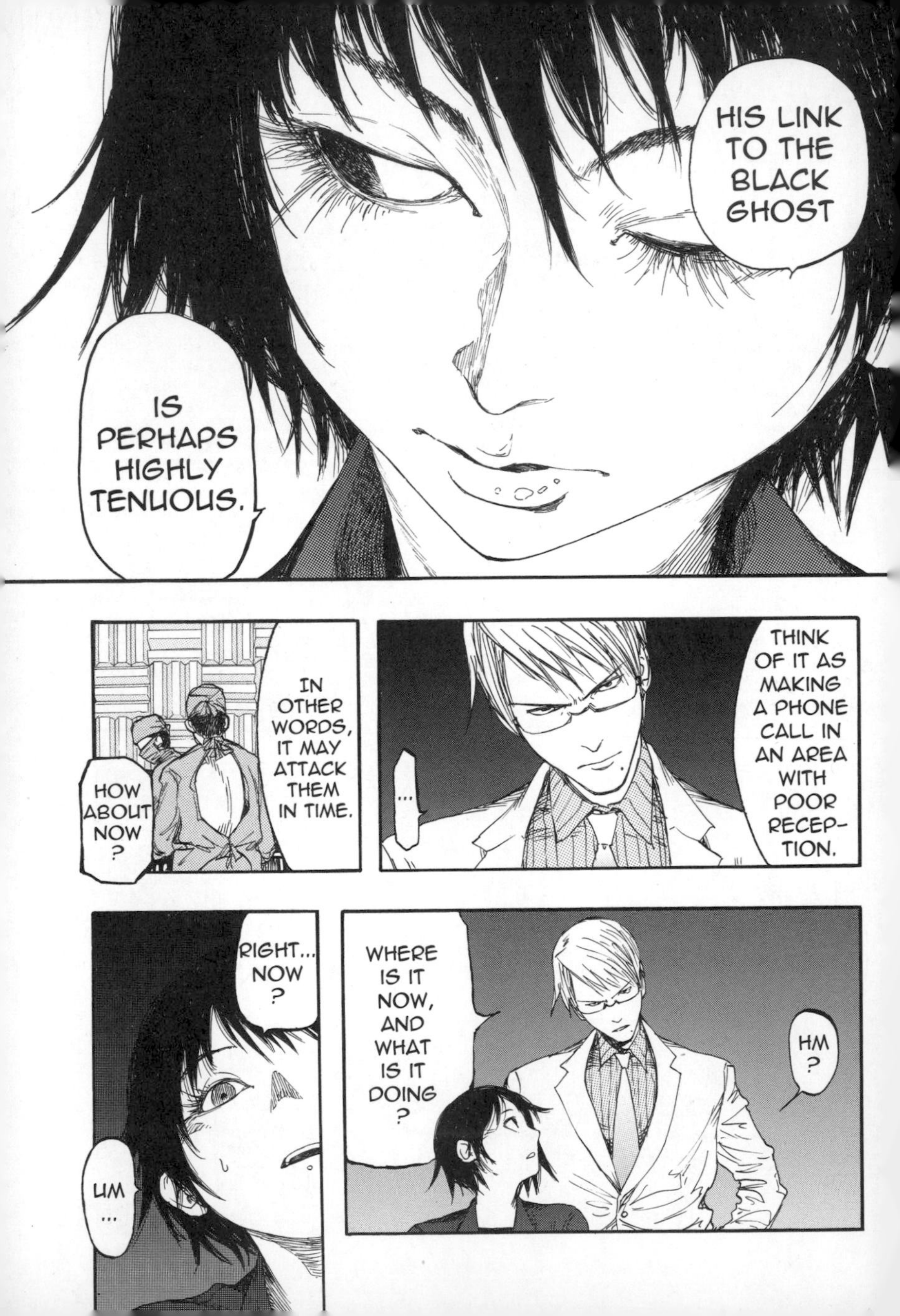
HIS LINK TO THE BLACK GHOST
IS PERHAPS HIGHLY TENUOUS.
THINK OF IT AS MAKING A PHONE CALL IN AN AREA WITH POOR RECEPTION.
...
IN OTHER WORDS, IT MAY ATTACK THEM IN TIME.
HOW ABOUT NOW?
HM?
WHERE IS IT NOW, AND WHAT IS IT DOING?
RIGHT... NOW?
UM...

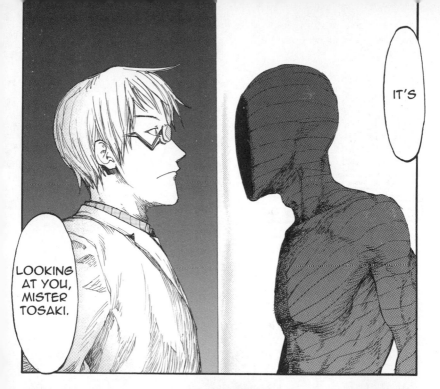

IT'S

LOOKING AT YOU, MISTER TOSAKI.

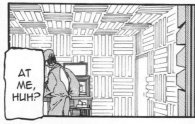

AT ME, HUH?

...

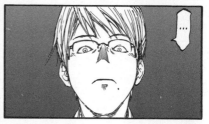

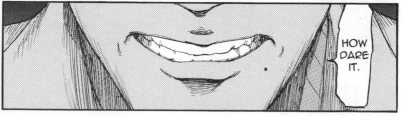

HOW DARE IT.

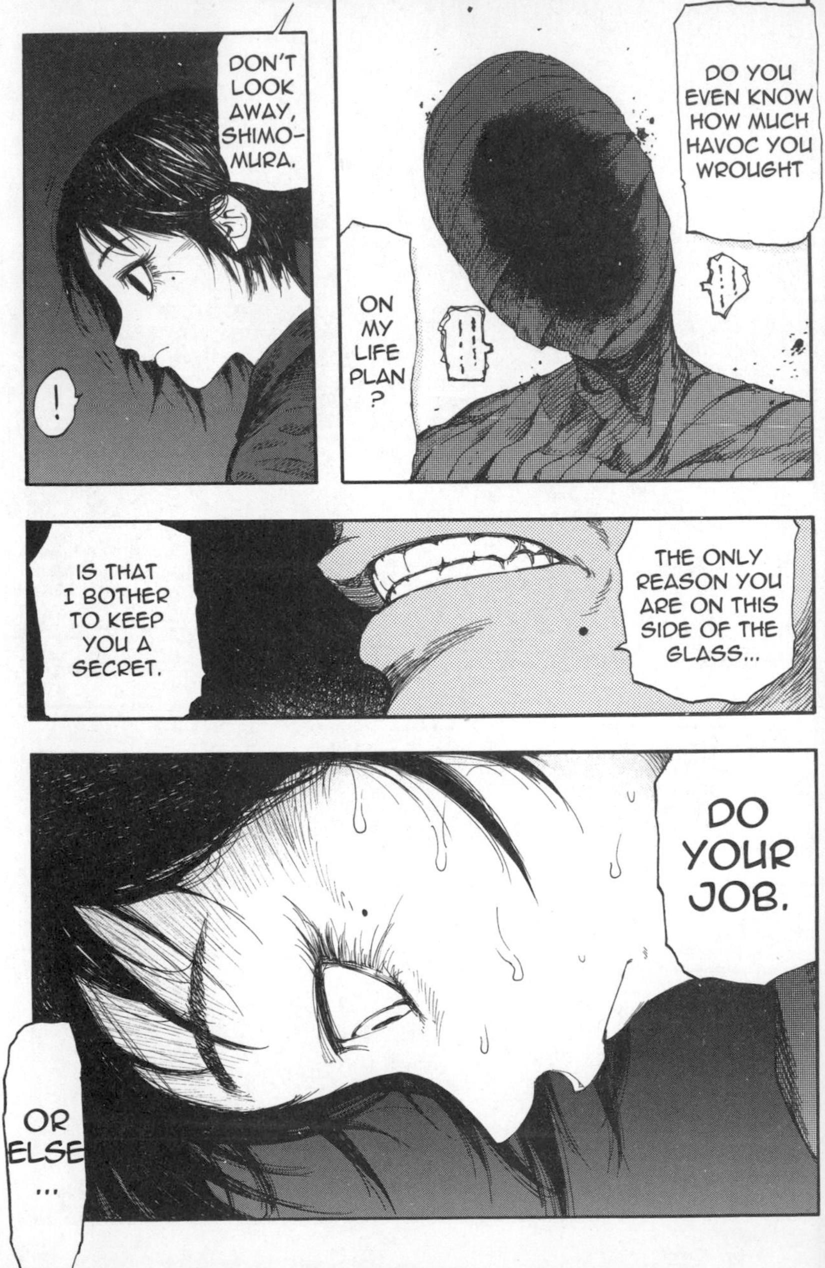
DO YOU EVEN KNOW HOW MUCH HAVOC YOU WROUGHT
ON MY LIFE PLAN?
DON'T LOOK AWAY, SHIMO-MURA.
!
THE ONLY REASON YOU ARE ON THIS SIDE OF THE GLASS...
IS THAT I BOTHER TO KEEP YOU A SECRET.
DO YOUR JOB.
OR ELSE...

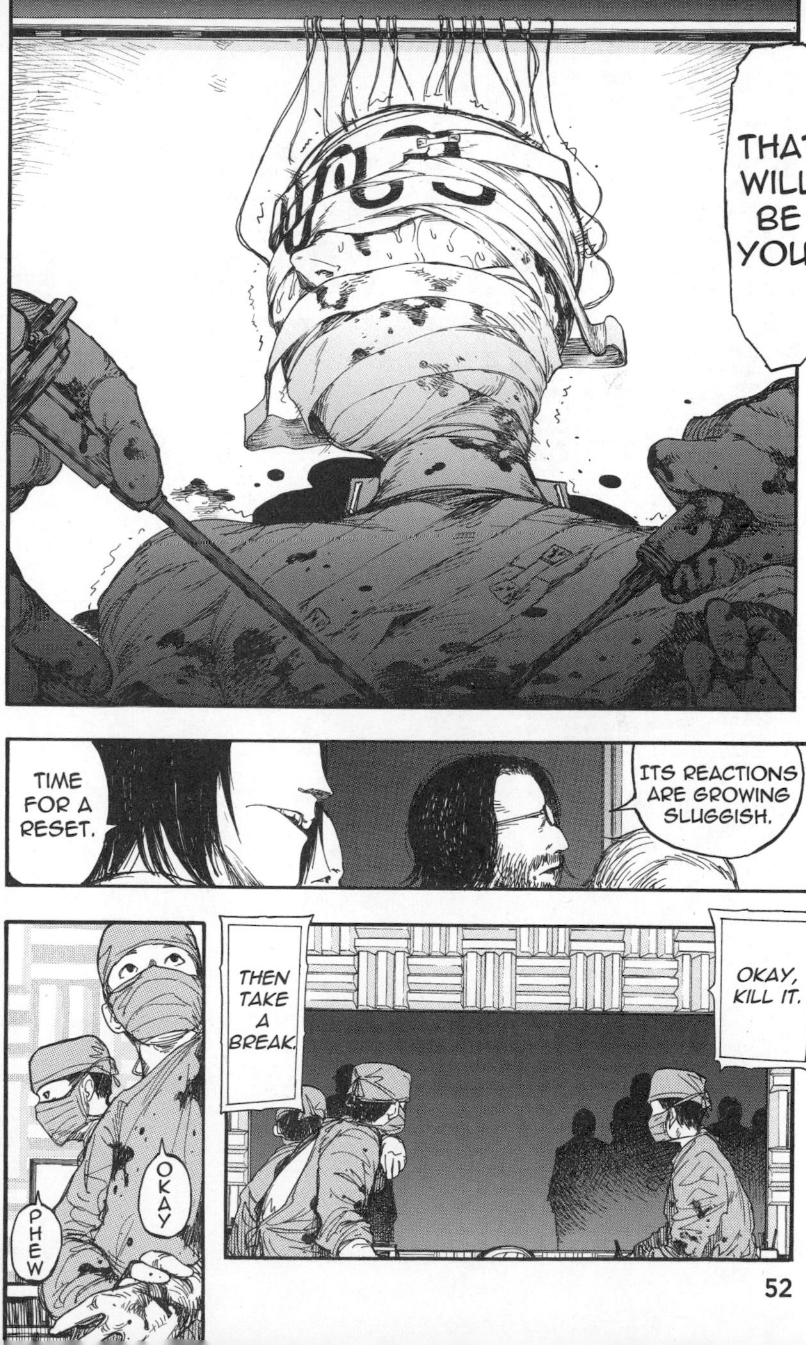
THAT WILL BE YOU.
ITS REACTIONS ARE GROWING SLUGGISH.
TIME FOR A RESET.
OKAY, KILL IT.
THEN TAKE A BREAK.
OKAY
PHEW

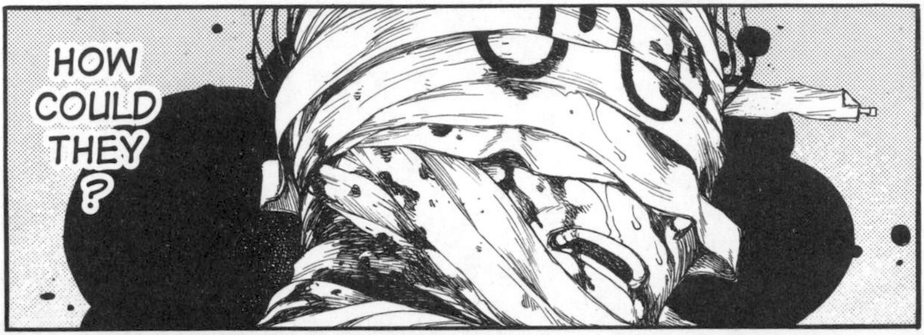
HOW COULD THEY ?

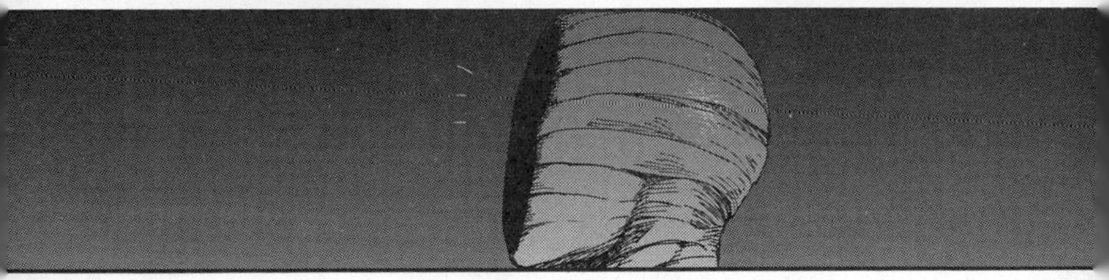

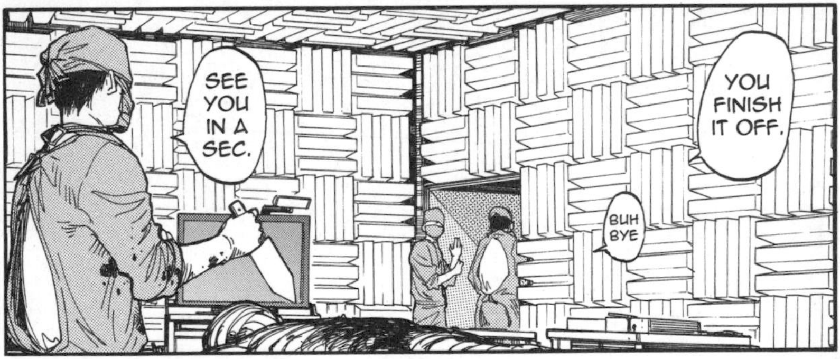
YOU FINISH IT OFF.
BUH BYE
SEE YOU IN A SEC.

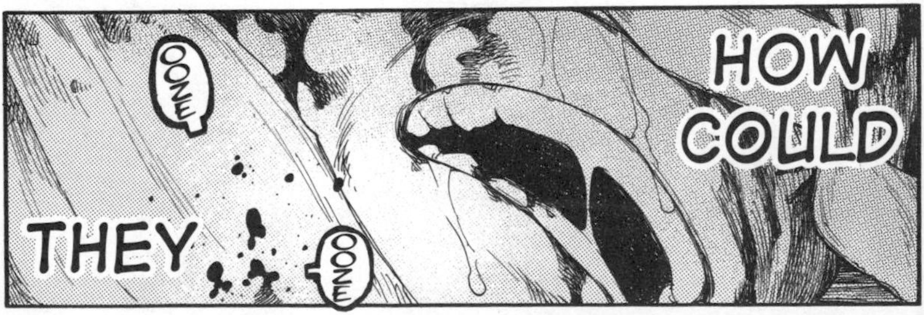
HOW COULD
OOZE
THEY
OOZE

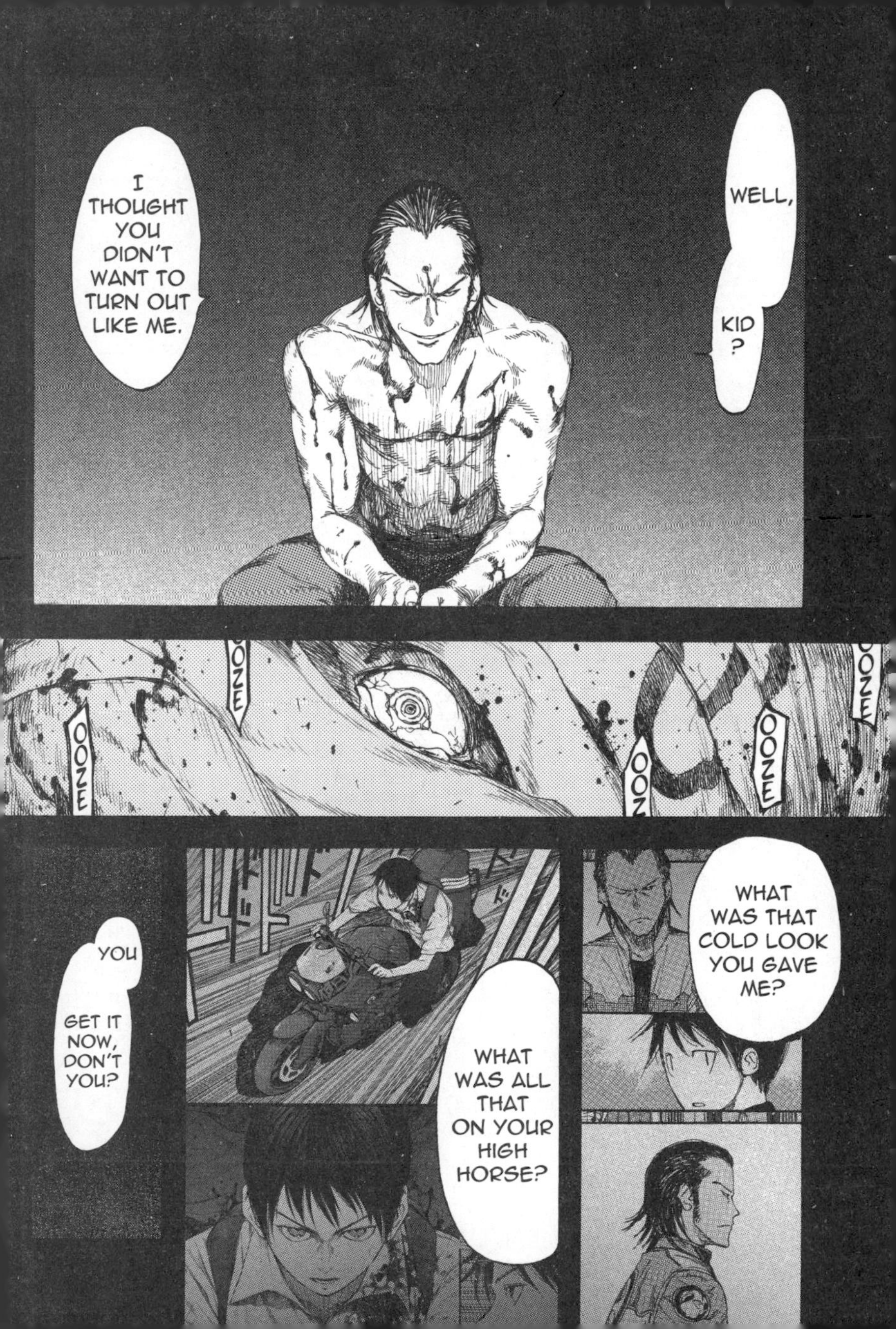
WELL,
KID?
I THOUGHT YOU DIDN'T WANT TO TURN OUT LIKE ME.
OOZE
OOZE
OOZE
OOZE
OOZE
WHAT WAS THAT COLD LOOK YOU GAVE ME?
WHAT WAS ALL THAT ON YOUR HIGH HORSE?
YOU
GET IT NOW, DON'T YOU?

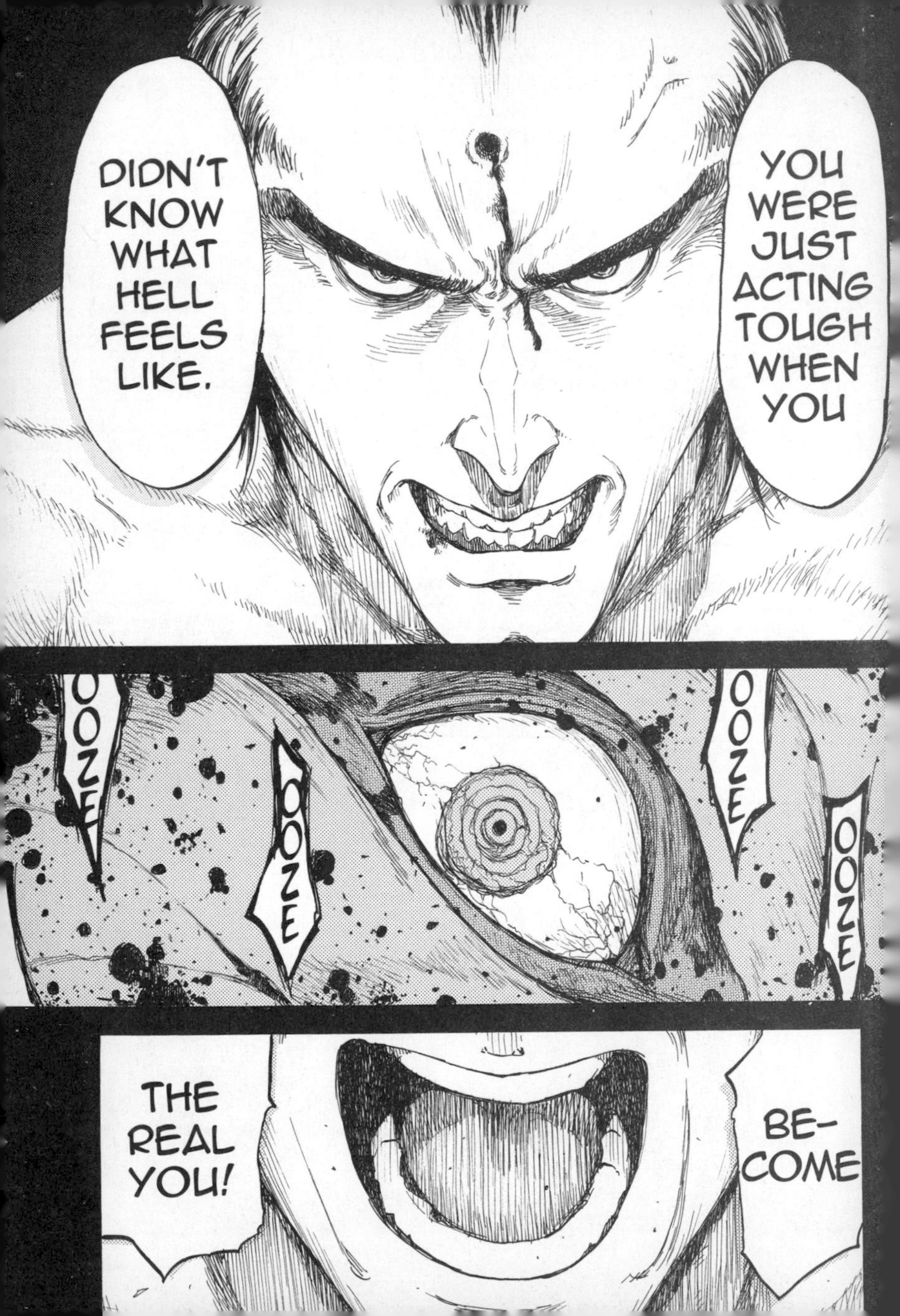
YOU WERE JUST ACTING TOUGH WHEN YOU
DIDN'T KNOW WHAT HELL FEELS LIKE.
OOZE
OOZE
OOZE
OOZE
BE-COME
THE REAL YOU!

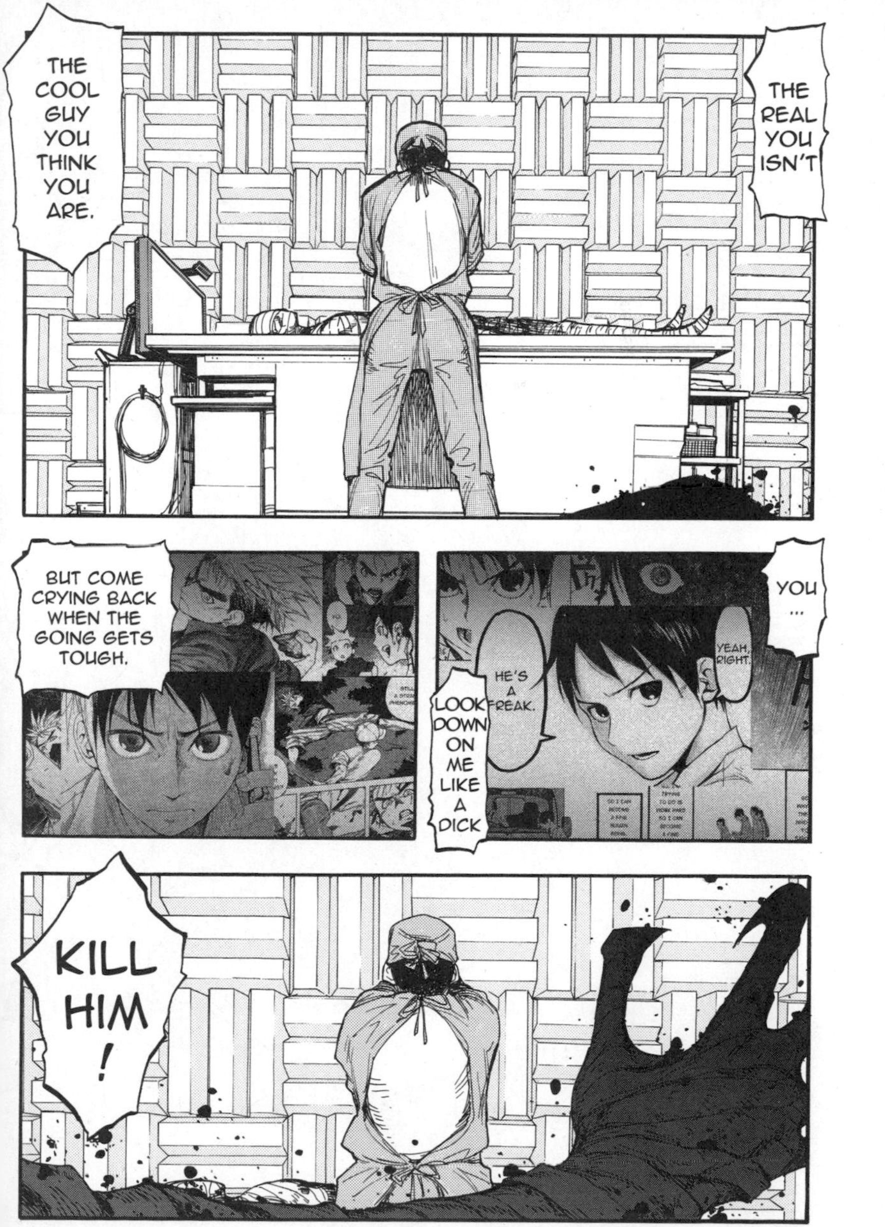
THE REAL YOU ISN'T
THE COOL GUY YOU THINK YOU ARE.
YOU ...
YEAH, RIGHT.
HE'S A FREAK.
LOOK DOWN ON ME LIKE A DICK
BUT COME CRYING BACK WHEN THE GOING GETS TOUGH.
KILL HIM!

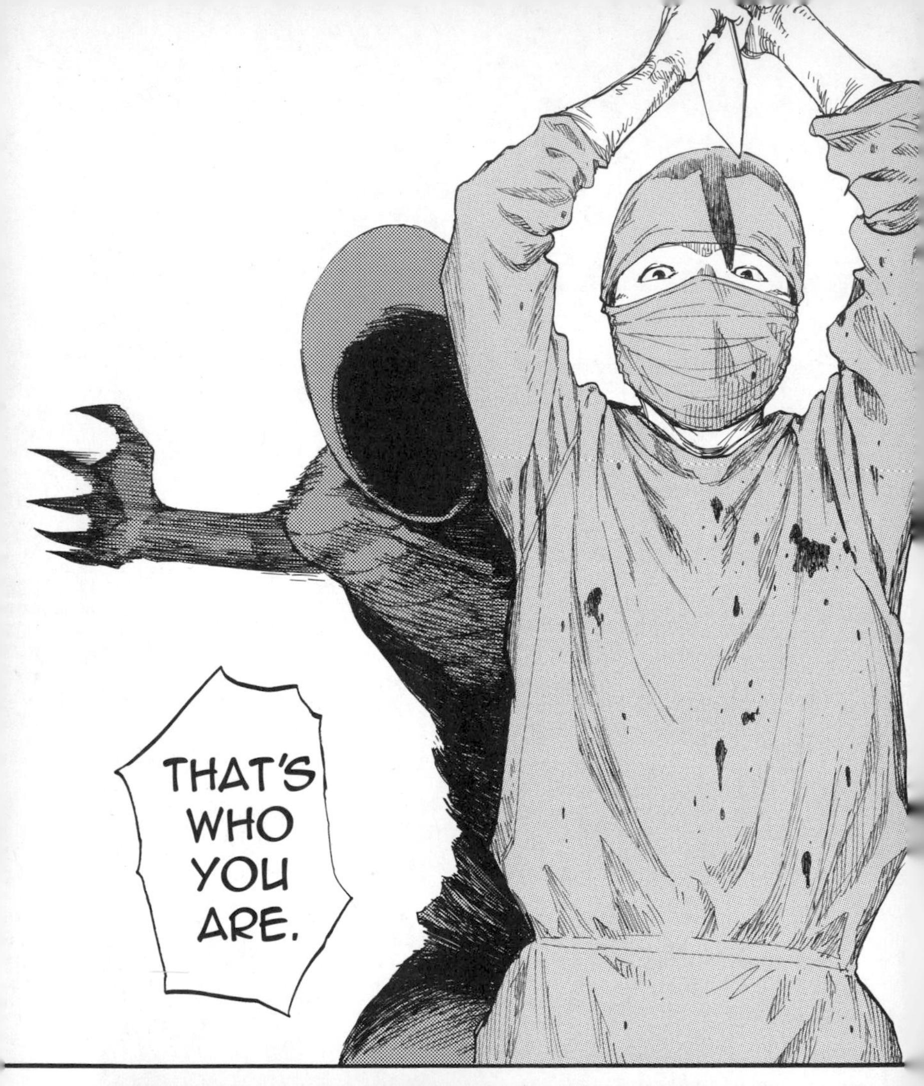
THAT'S WHO YOU ARE.
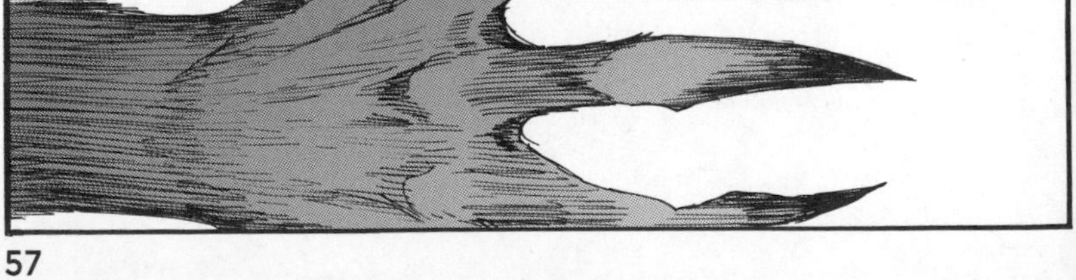

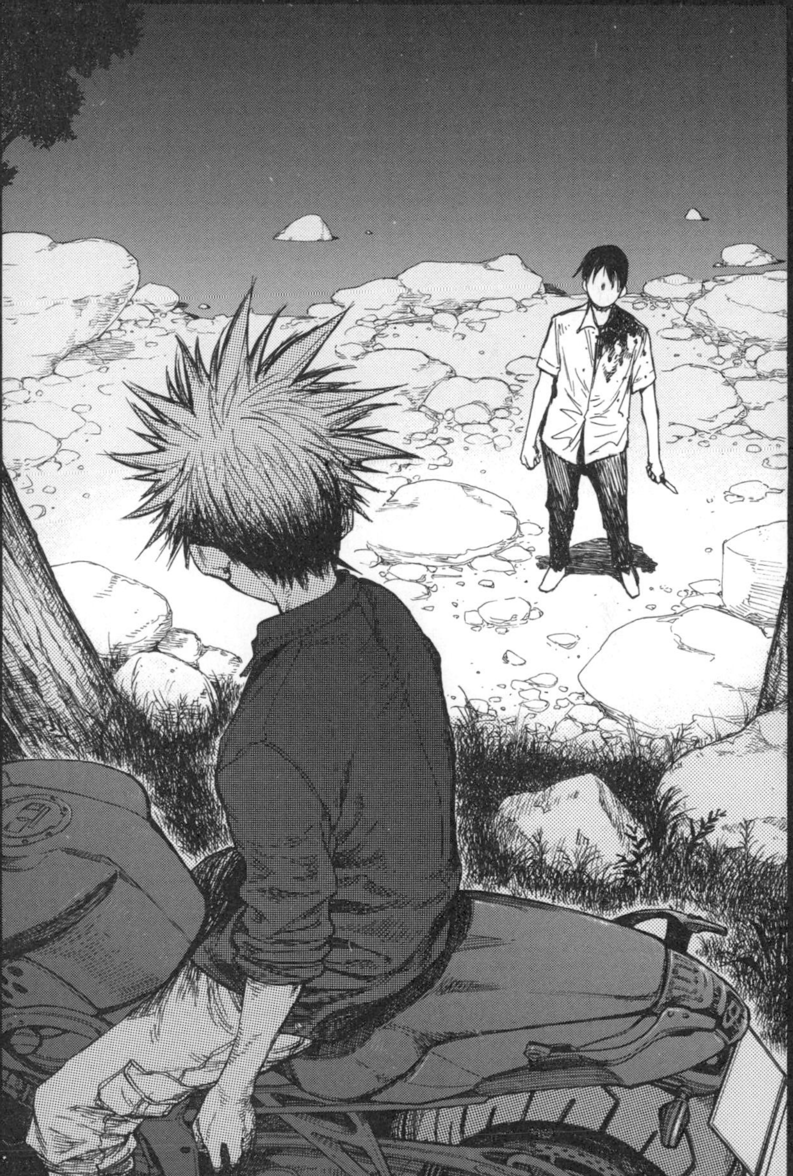

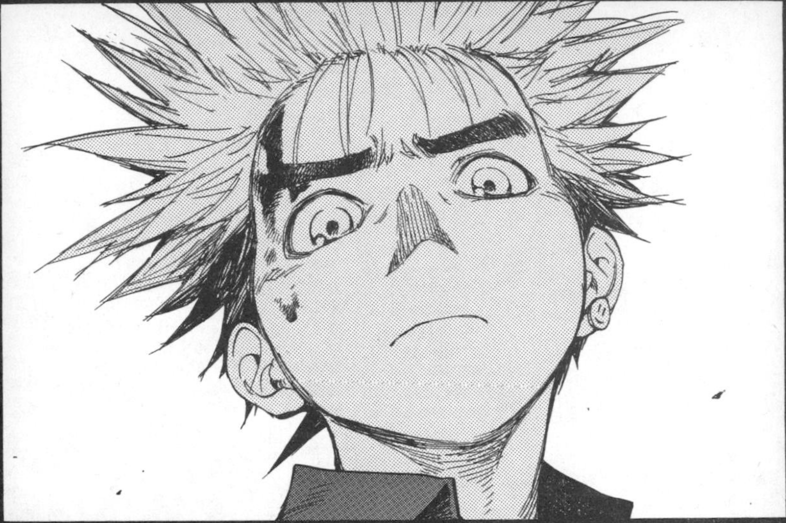
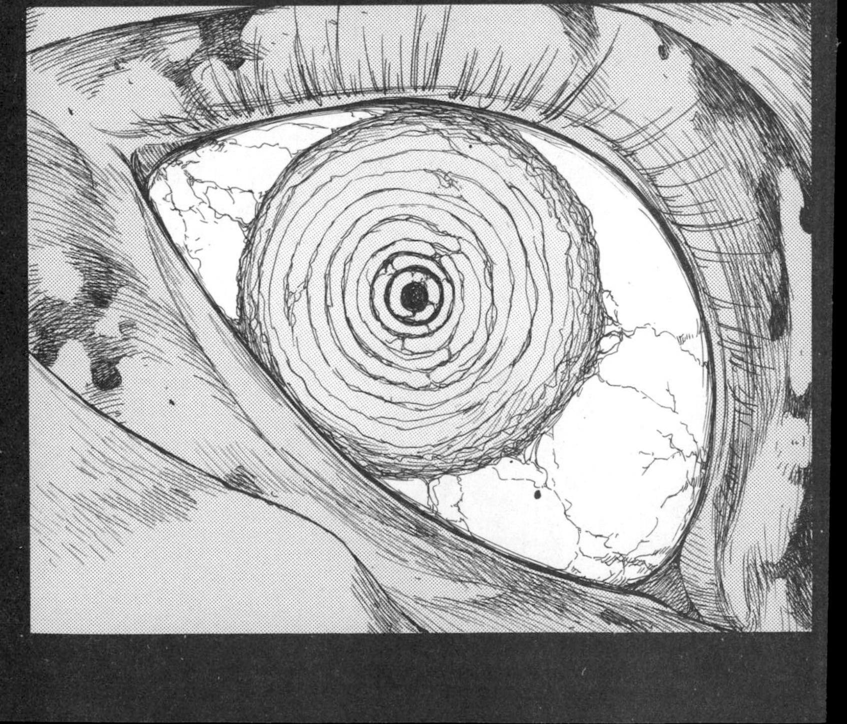

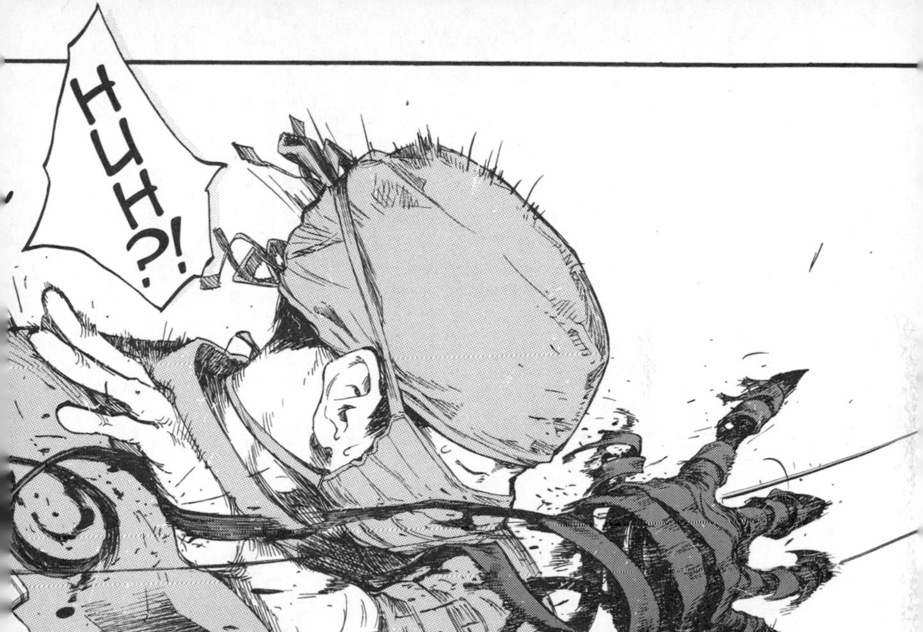
HUH?!
BWOOOSH
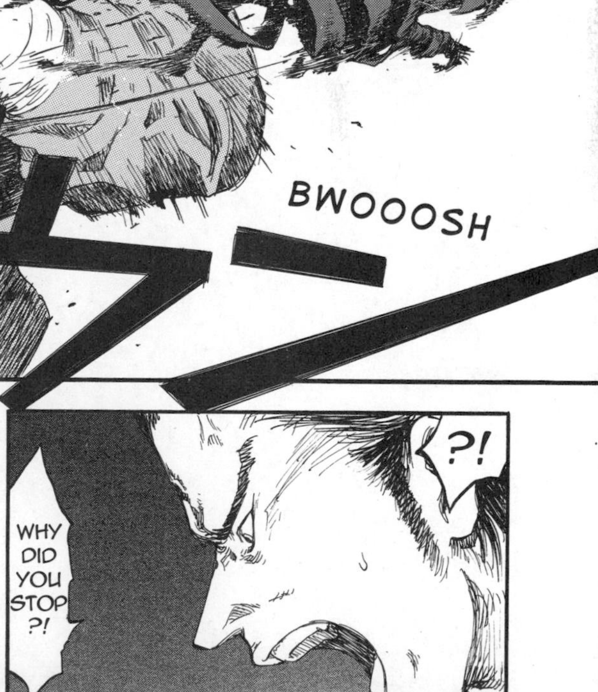
?!
WHY DID YOU STOP?!
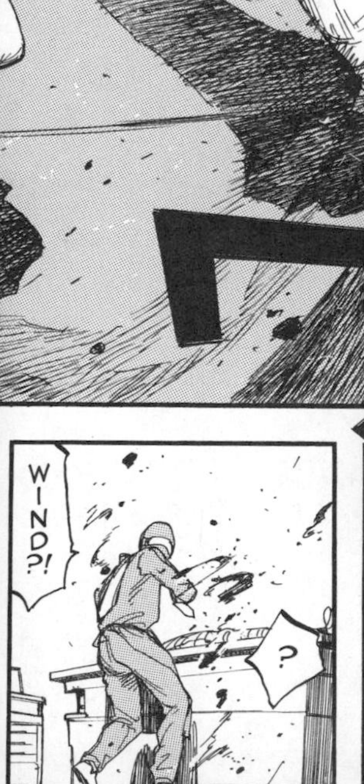
WIND?!
?

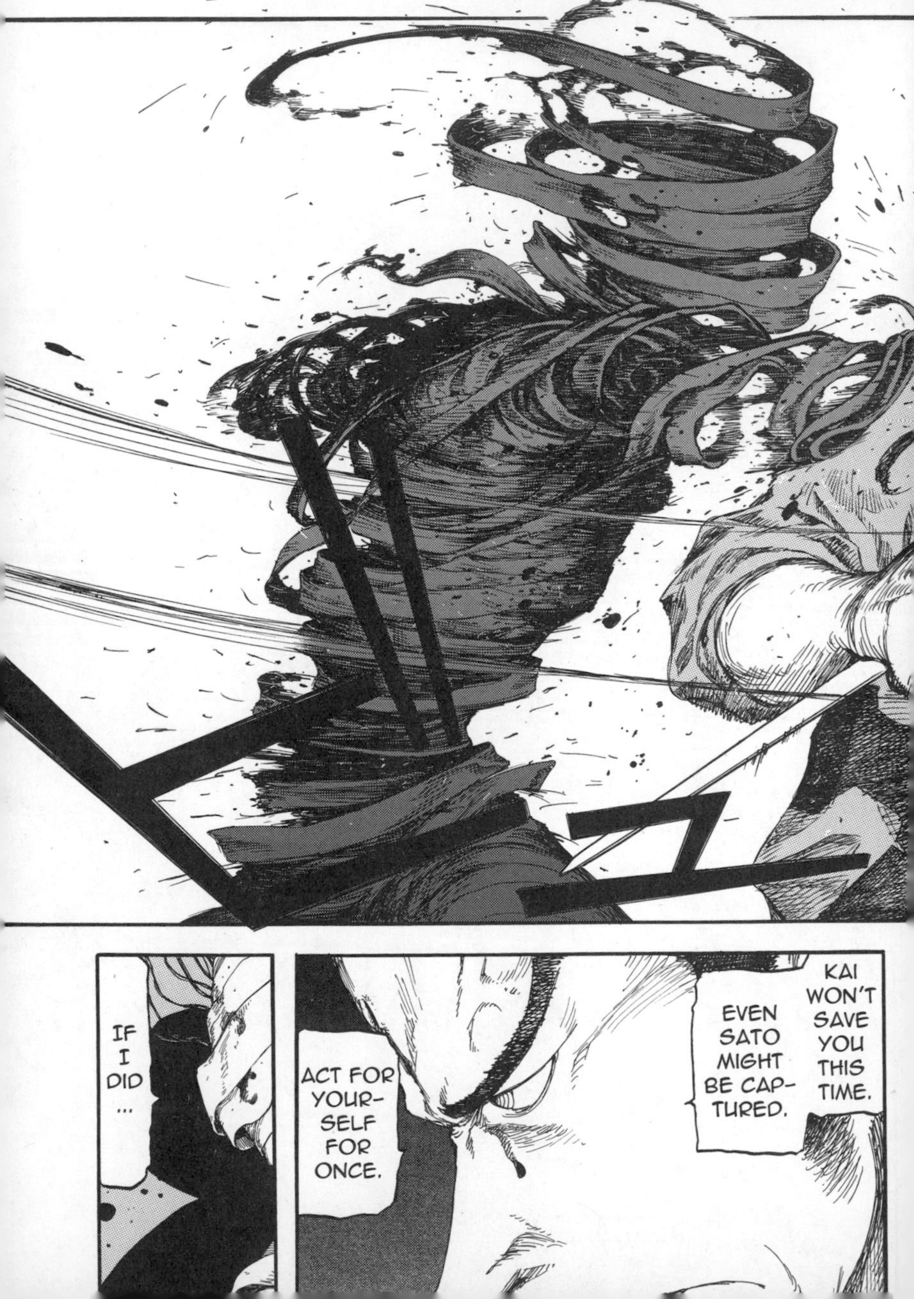
KAI WON'T SAVE YOU THIS TIME.
EVEN SATO MIGHT BE CAPTURED.
ACT FOR YOURSELF FOR ONCE.
IF I DID ...

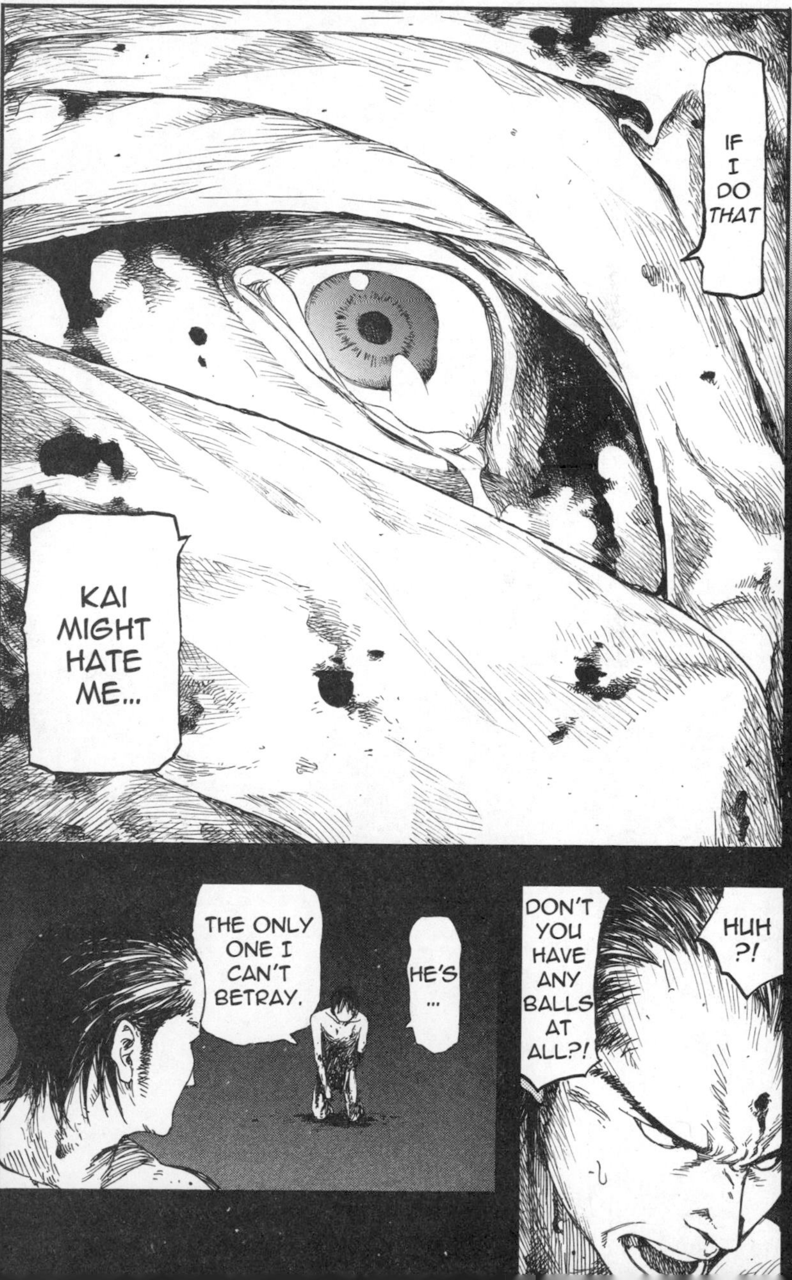
IF I DO THAT
KAI MIGHT HATE ME...
HUH?!
DON'T YOU HAVE ANY BALLS AT ALL?!
HE'S...
THE ONLY ONE I CAN'T BETRAY.

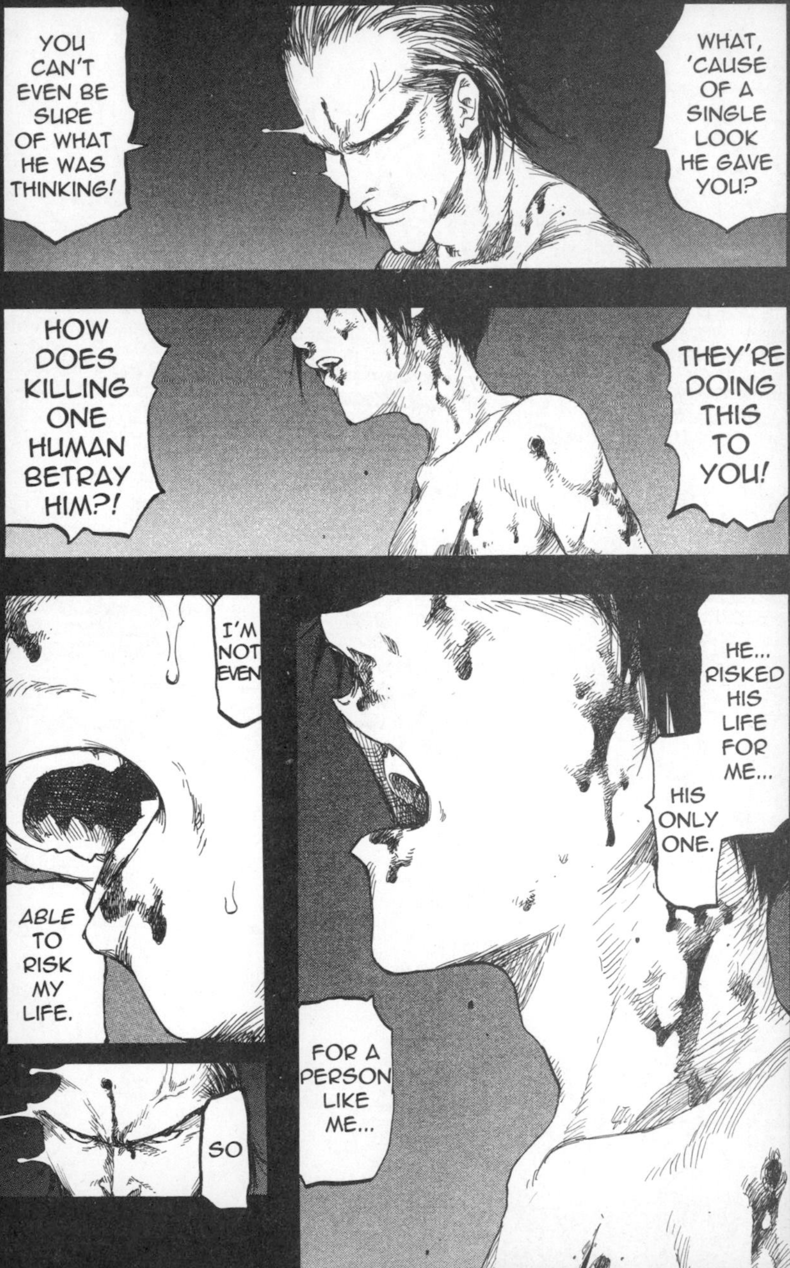
WHAT, 'CAUSE OF A SINGLE LOOK HE GAVE YOU?
YOU CAN'T EVEN BE SURE OF WHAT HE WAS THINKING!
THEY'RE DOING THIS TO YOU!
HOW DOES KILLING ONE HUMAN BETRAY HIM?!
HE... RISKED HIS LIFE FOR ME...
HIS ONLY ONE.
FOR A PERSON LIKE ME...
I'M NOT EVEN
ABLE TO RISK MY LIFE.
SO

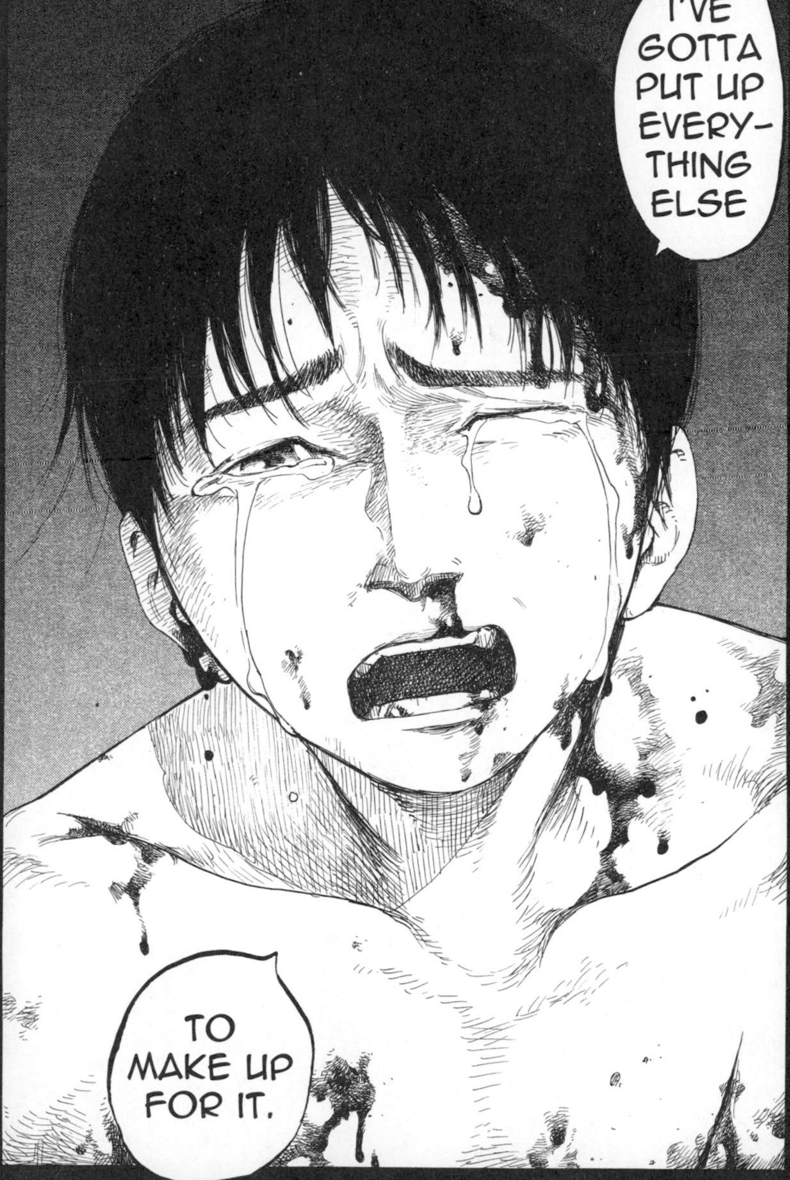
I'VE GOTTA PUT UP EVERY-THING ELSE
TO MAKE UP FOR IT.

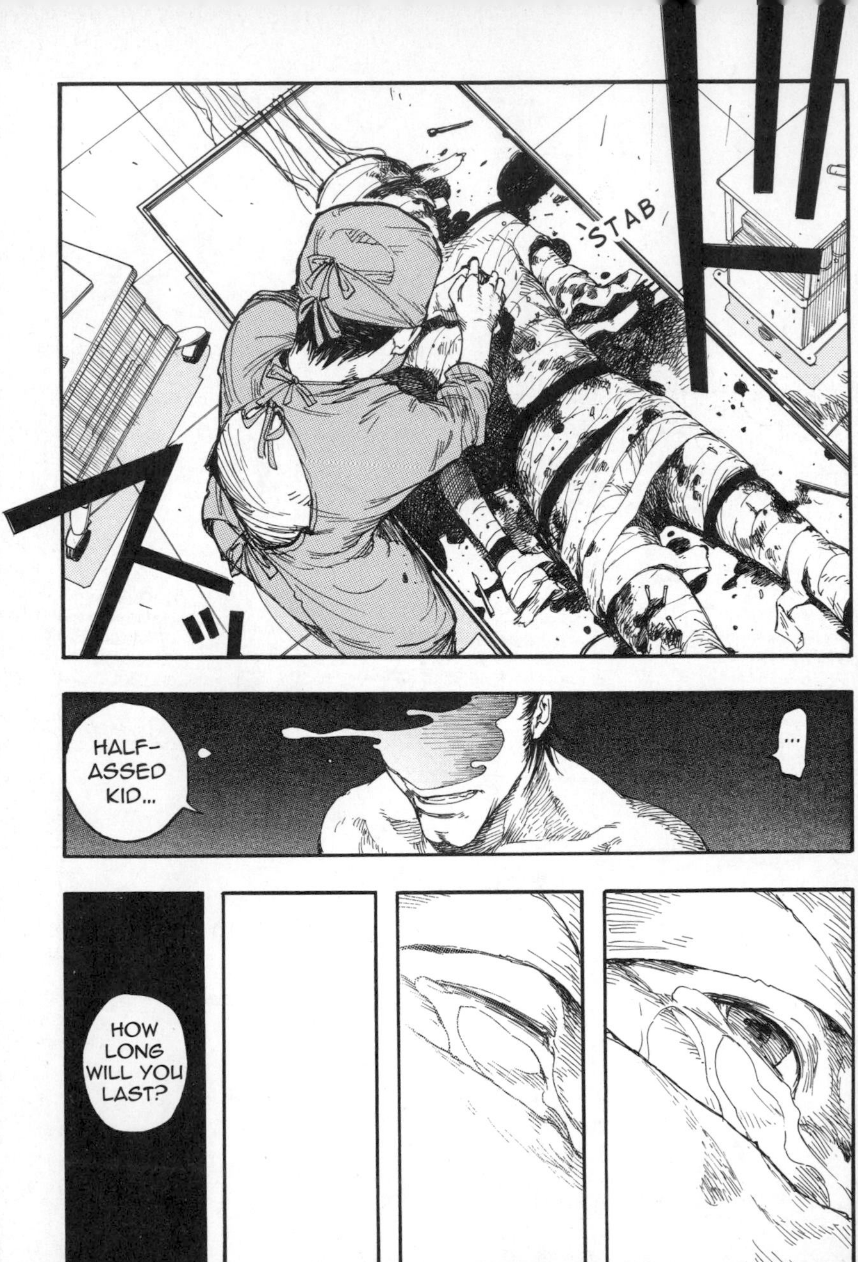
STAB
...
HALF-ASSED KID...
HOW LONG WILL YOU LAST?

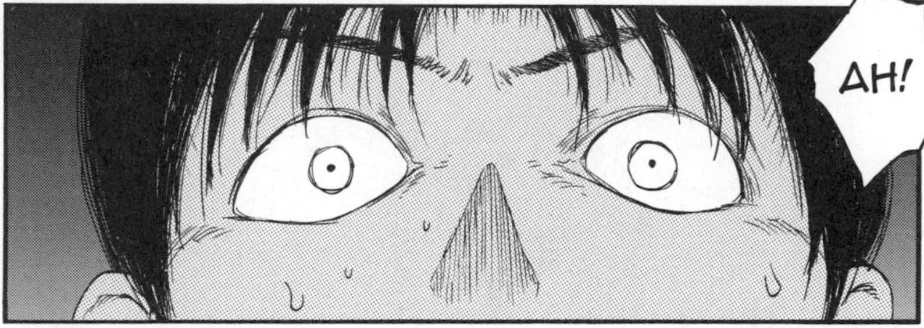
AH!

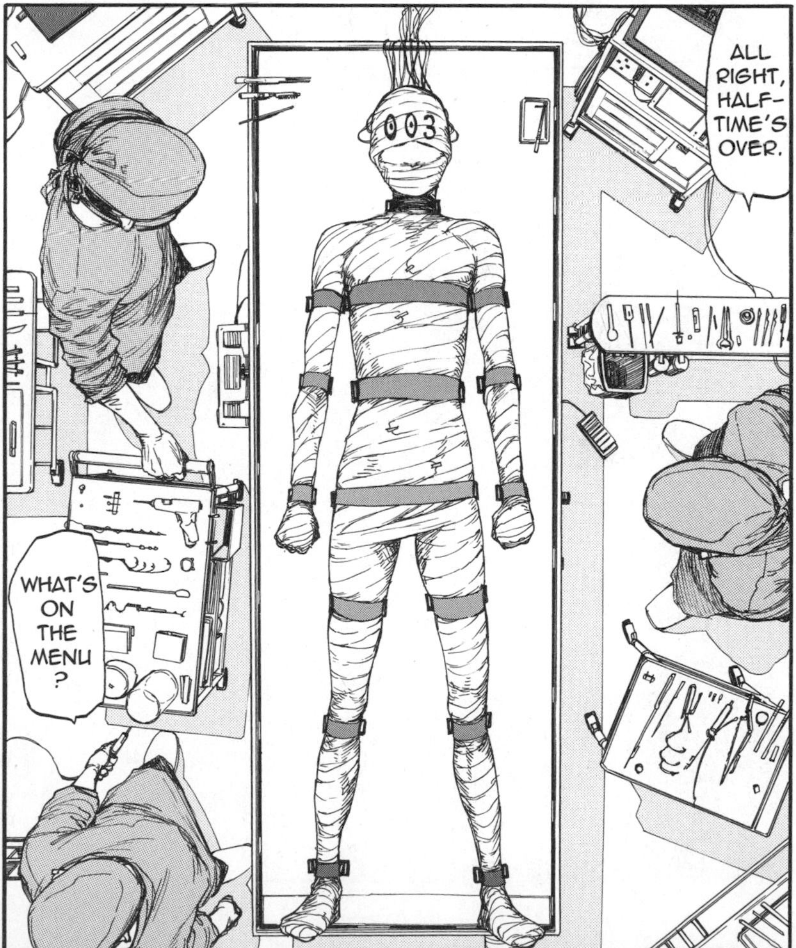
ALL RIGHT, HALF-TIME'S OVER.
WHAT'S ON THE MENU ?
003

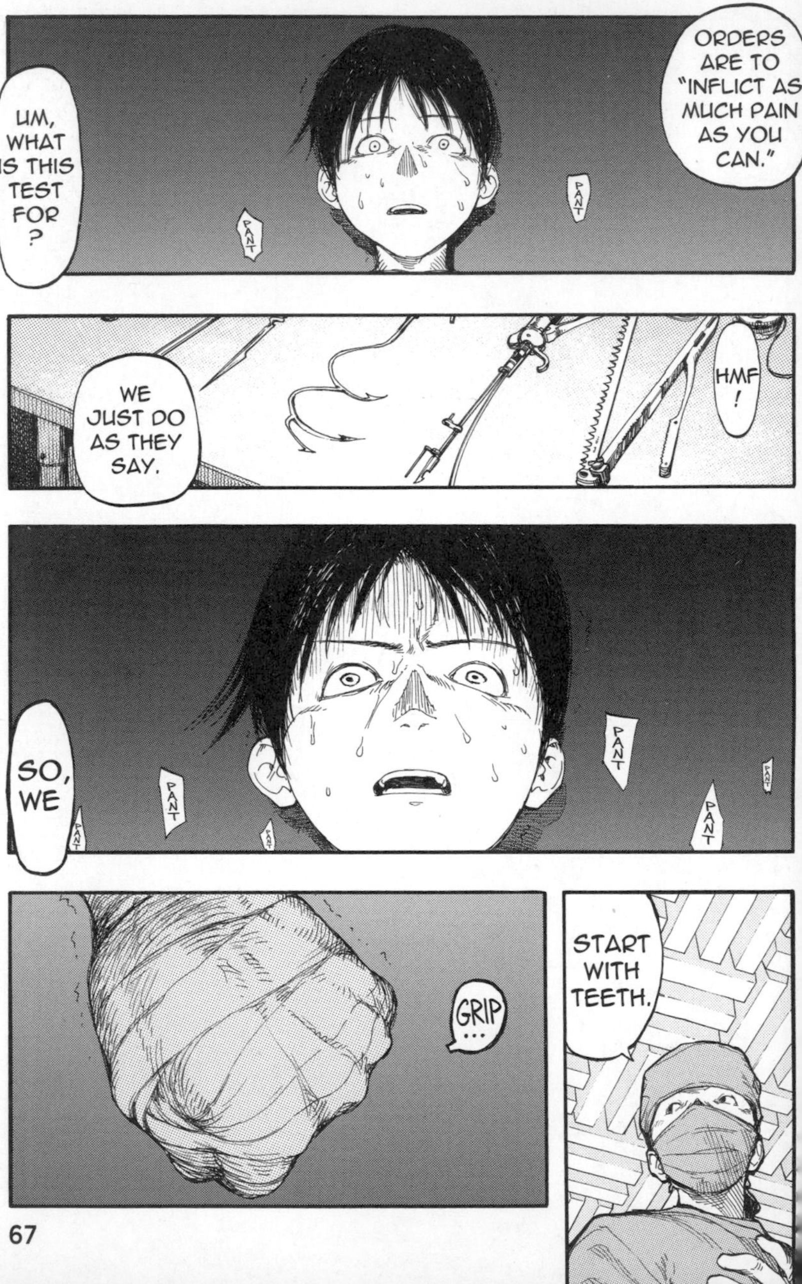
ORDERS ARE TO "INFLICT AS MUCH PAIN AS YOU CAN."
PANT
PANT
UM, WHAT IS THIS TEST FOR?
HMF!
WE JUST DO AS THEY SAY.
PANT
PANT
PANT
PANT
PANT
PANT
SO, WE
START WITH TEETH.
GRIP...

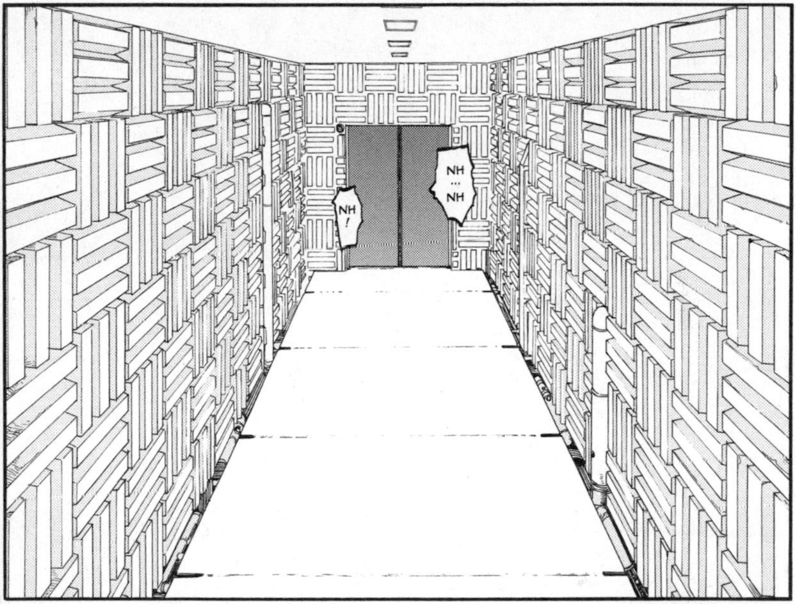
NH
...
NH
NH!
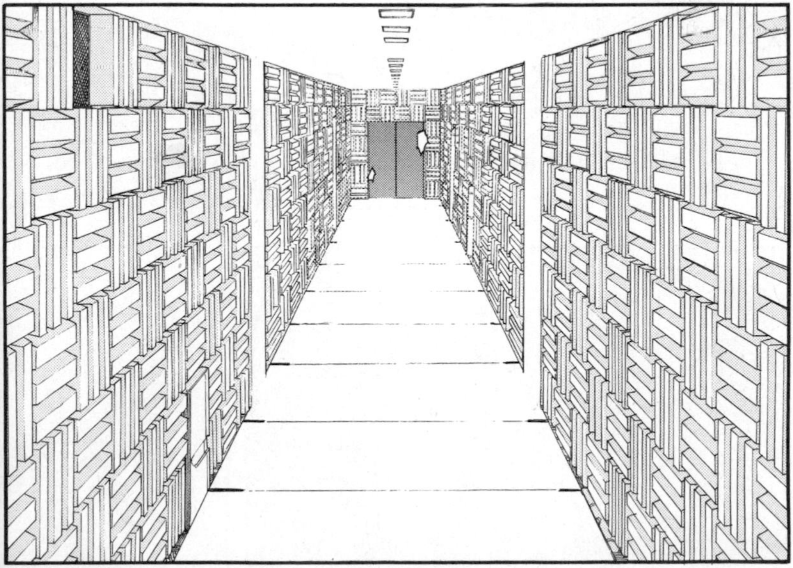
File:07 End

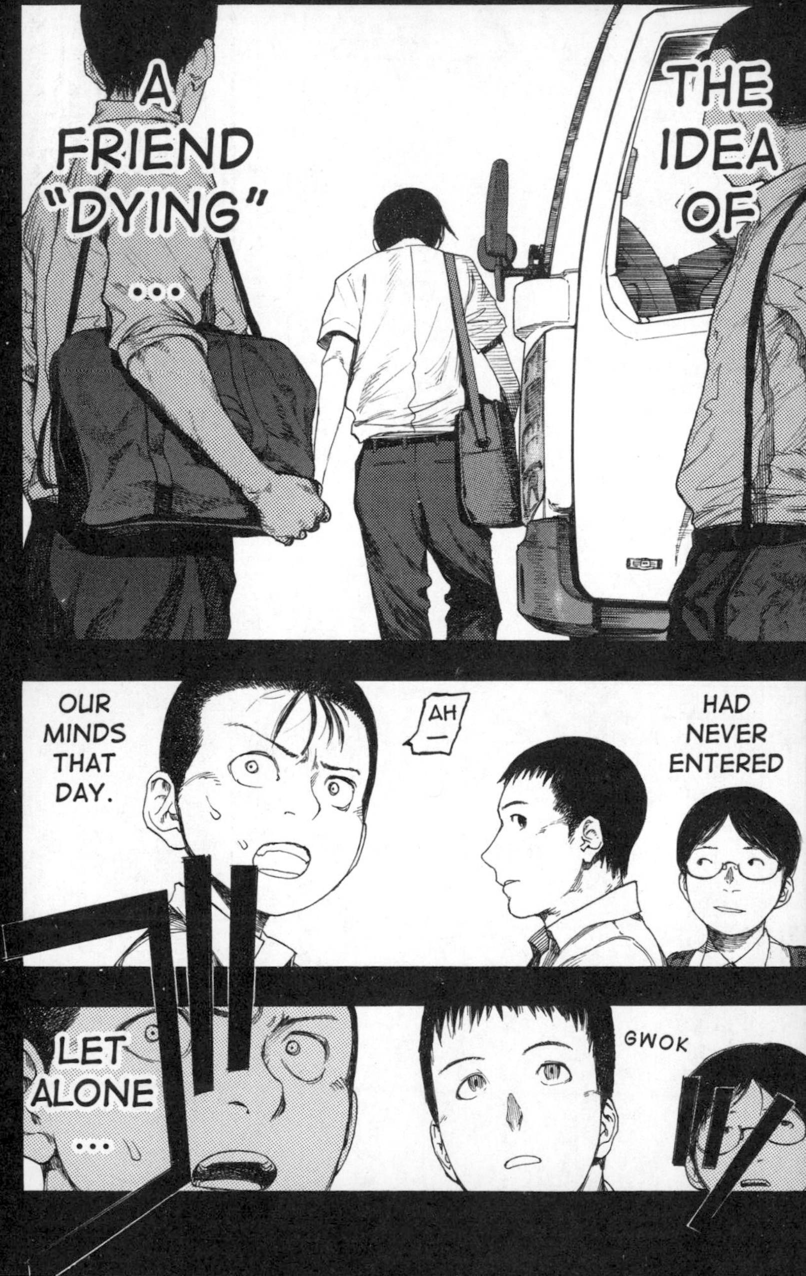
THE IDEA OF
A FRIEND "DYING"
...
HAD NEVER ENTERED
AH—
OUR MINDS THAT DAY.
GWOK
LET ALONE
...

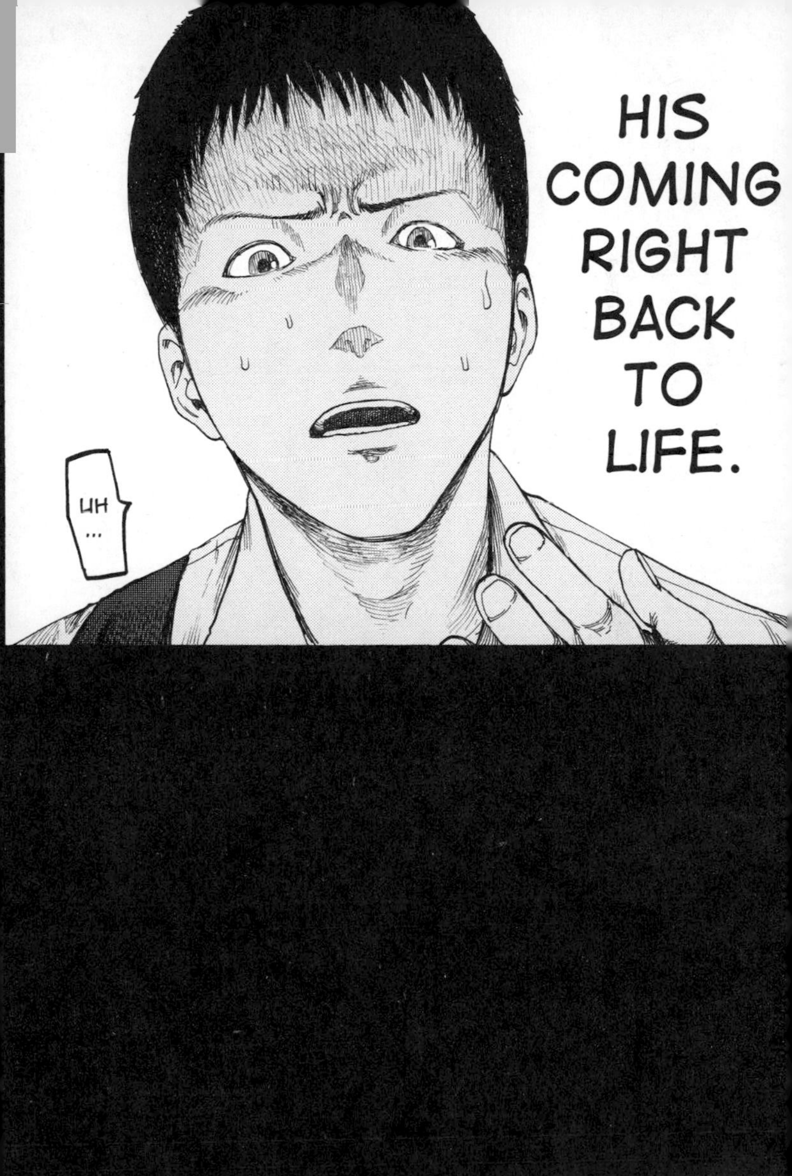
HIS COMING RIGHT BACK TO LIFE.
UH ...

File 08: Blindness

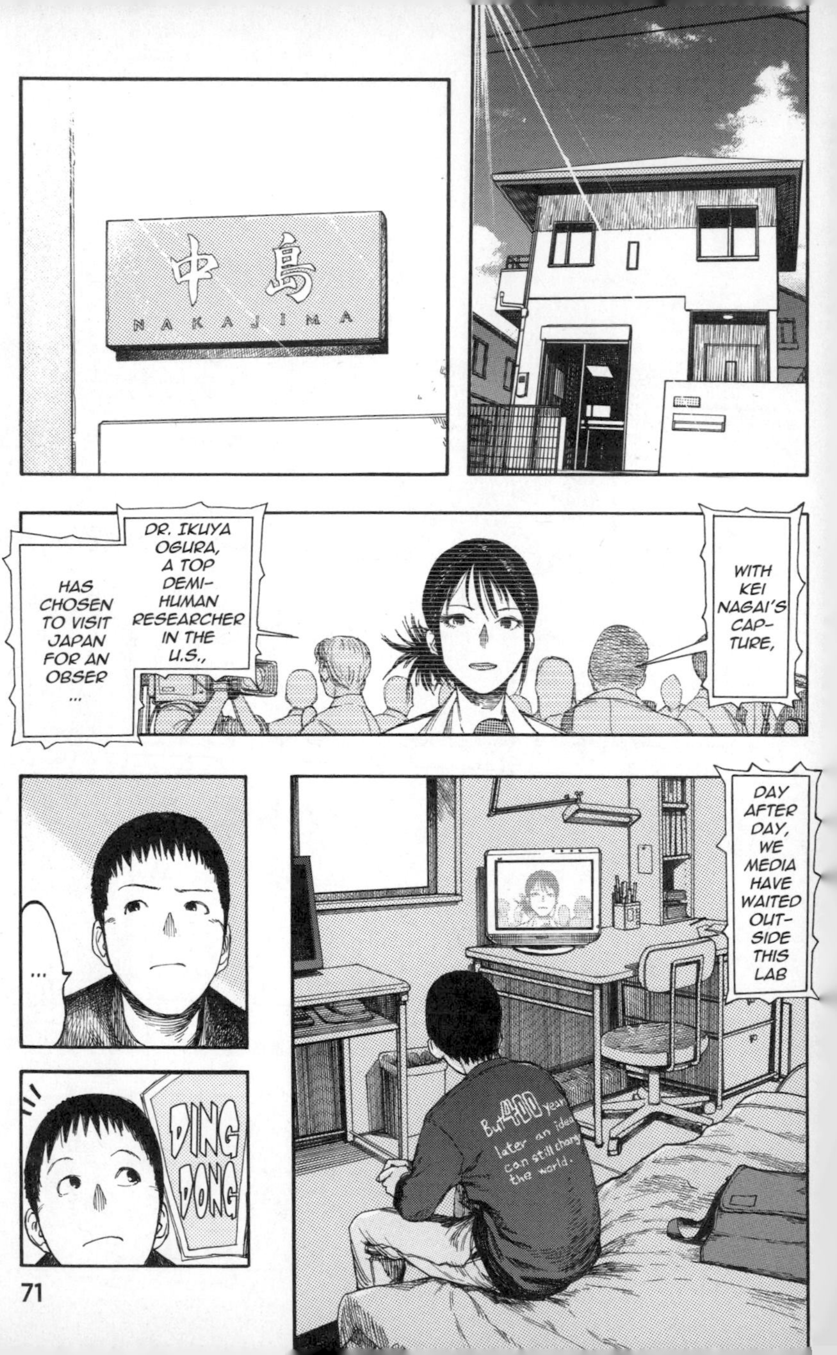
中島
NAKAJIMA
WITH KEI NAGAI'S CAPTURE,
DR. IKUYA OGURA, A TOP DEMI-HUMAN RESEARCHER IN THE U.S.,
HAS CHOSEN TO VISIT JAPAN FOR AN OBSER ...
DAY AFTER DAY, WE MEDIA HAVE WAITED OUTSIDE THIS LAB
But 400 years later an idea can still change the world.
...
DING DONG

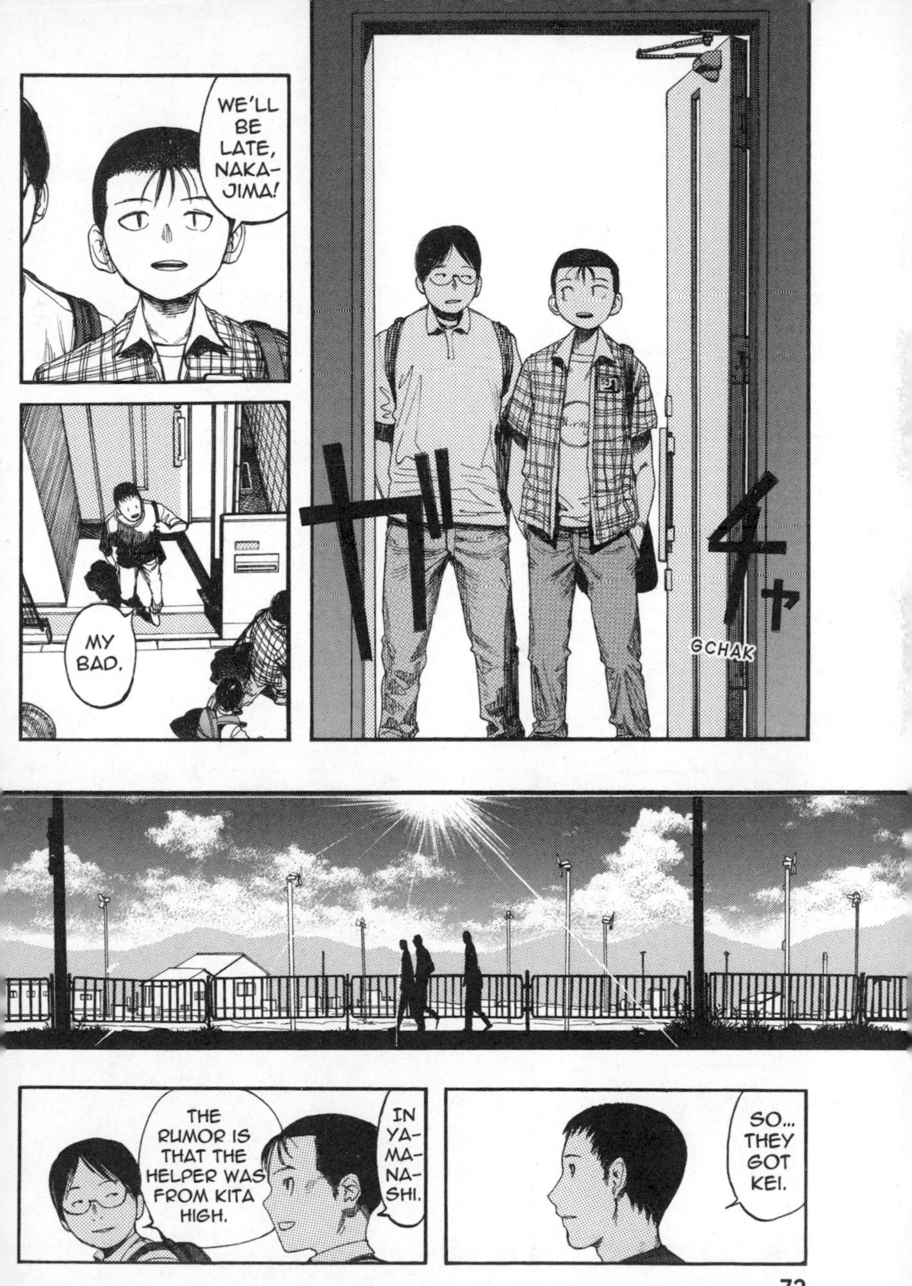
GCHAK
WE'LL BE LATE, NAKA-JIMA!
MY BAD.
SO... THEY GOT KEI.
IN YA-MA-NA-SHI.
THE RUMOR IS THAT THE HELPER WAS FROM KITA HIGH.

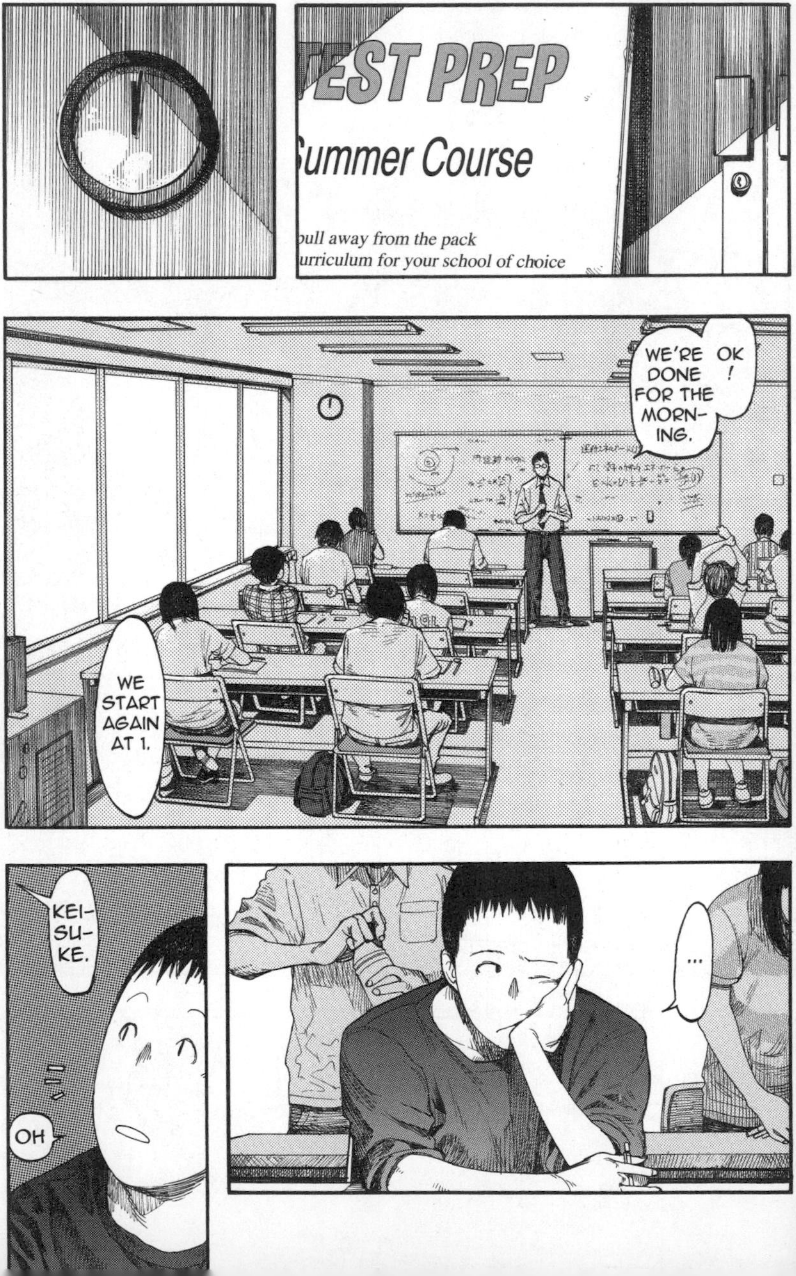
TEST PREP
Summer Course
pull away from the pack
curriculum for your school of choice
OK!
WE'RE DONE FOR THE MORNING.
WE START AGAIN AT 1.
...
KEI-SUKE.
OH

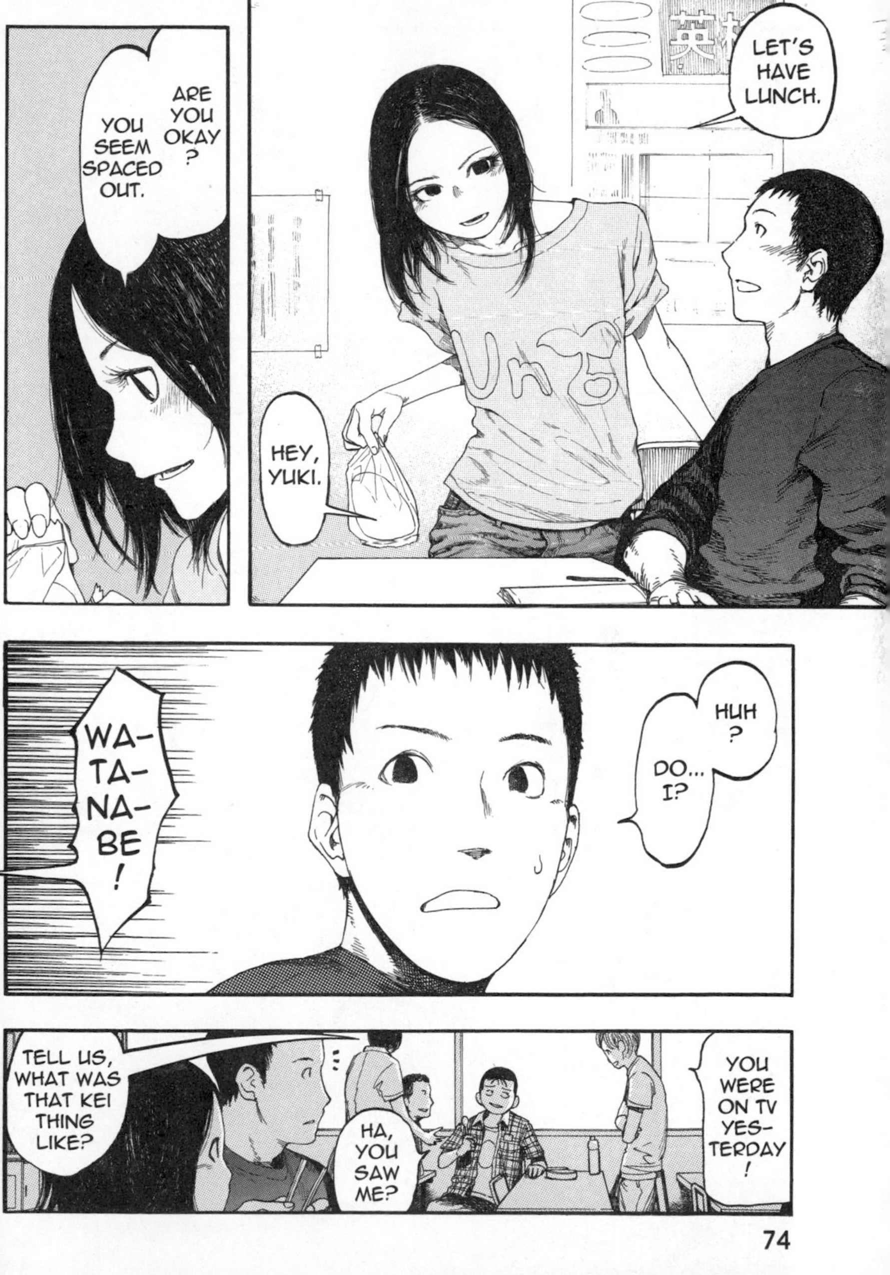
LET'S HAVE LUNCH.
HEY, YUKI.
ARE YOU OKAY? YOU SEEM SPACED OUT.
HUH? DO... I?
WA-TA-NA-BE!
YOU WERE ON TV YES-TERDAY!
HA, YOU SAW ME?
TELL US, WHAT WAS THAT KEI THING LIKE?

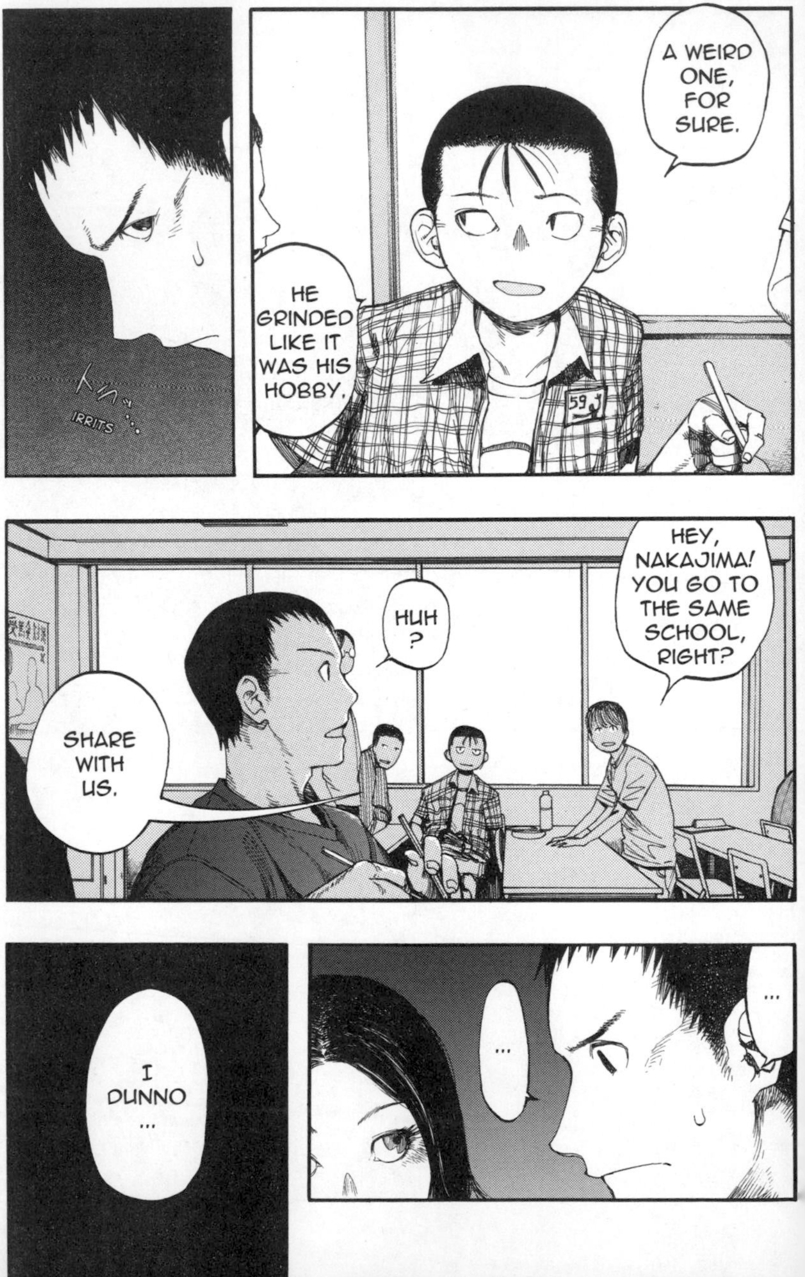
A WEIRD ONE, FOR SURE.
HE GRINDED LIKE IT WAS HIS HOBBY.
IRRITS
HEY, NAKAJIMA! YOU GO TO THE SAME SCHOOL, RIGHT?
HUH?
SHARE WITH US.
...
...
I DUNNO ...

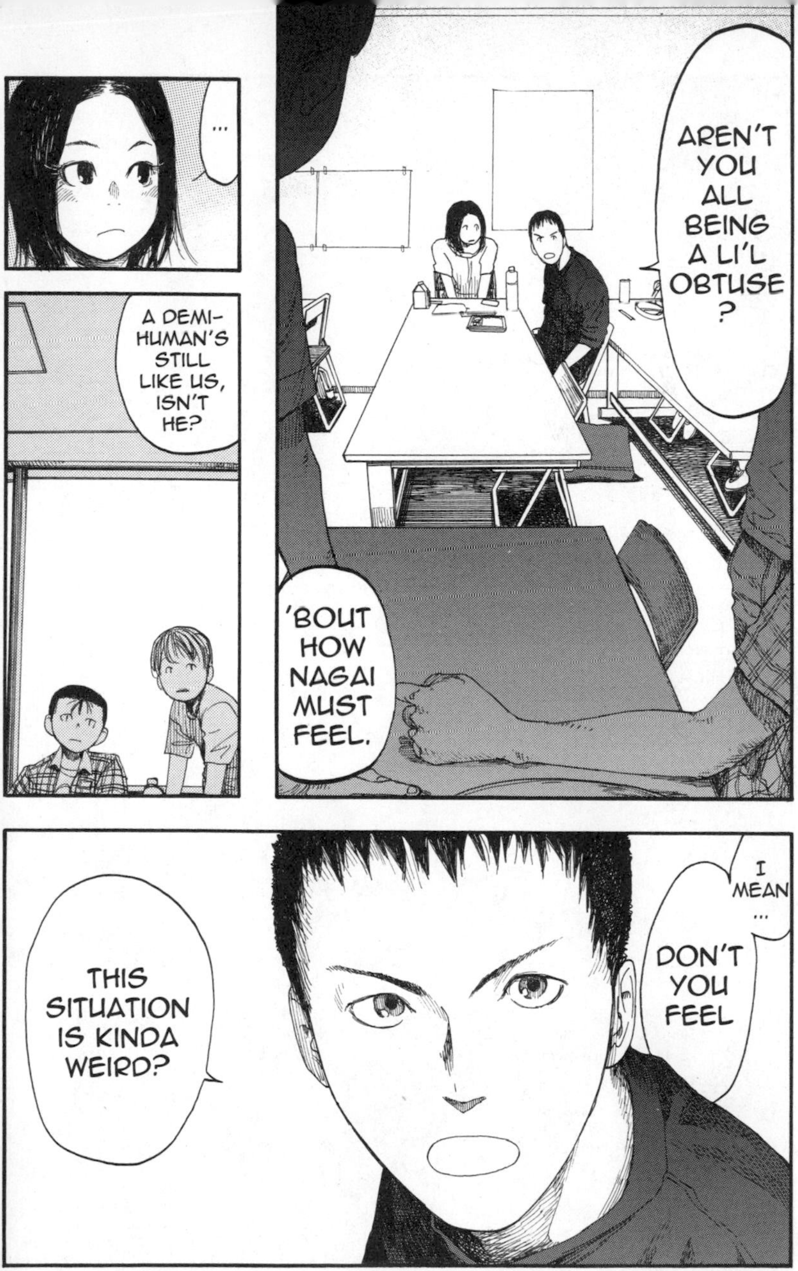
AREN'T YOU ALL BEING A LI'L OBTUSE?
'BOUT HOW NAGAI MUST FEEL.
...
A DEMI-HUMAN'S STILL LIKE US, ISN'T HE?
I MEAN ...
DON'T YOU FEEL
THIS SITUATION IS KINDA WEIRD?

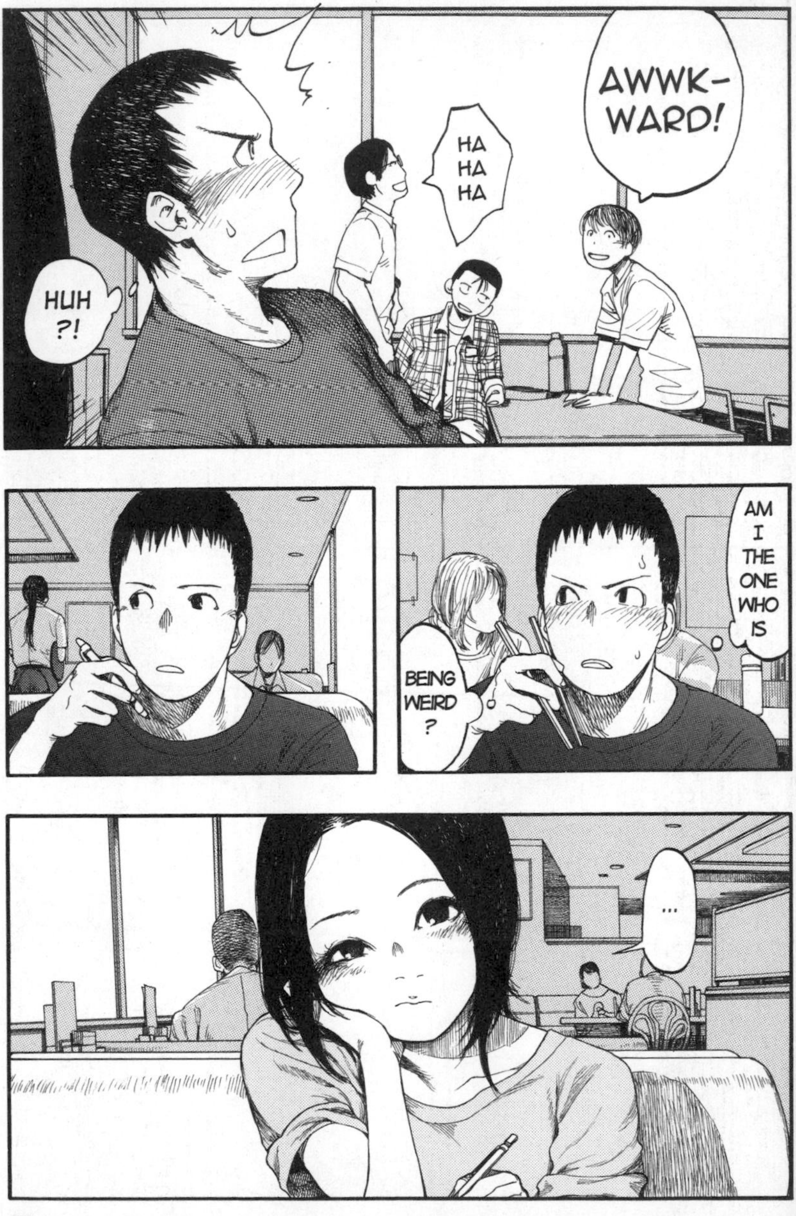
AWWK-WARD!
HA HA HA
HUH ?!
AM I THE ONE WHO IS
BEING WEIRD ?
...

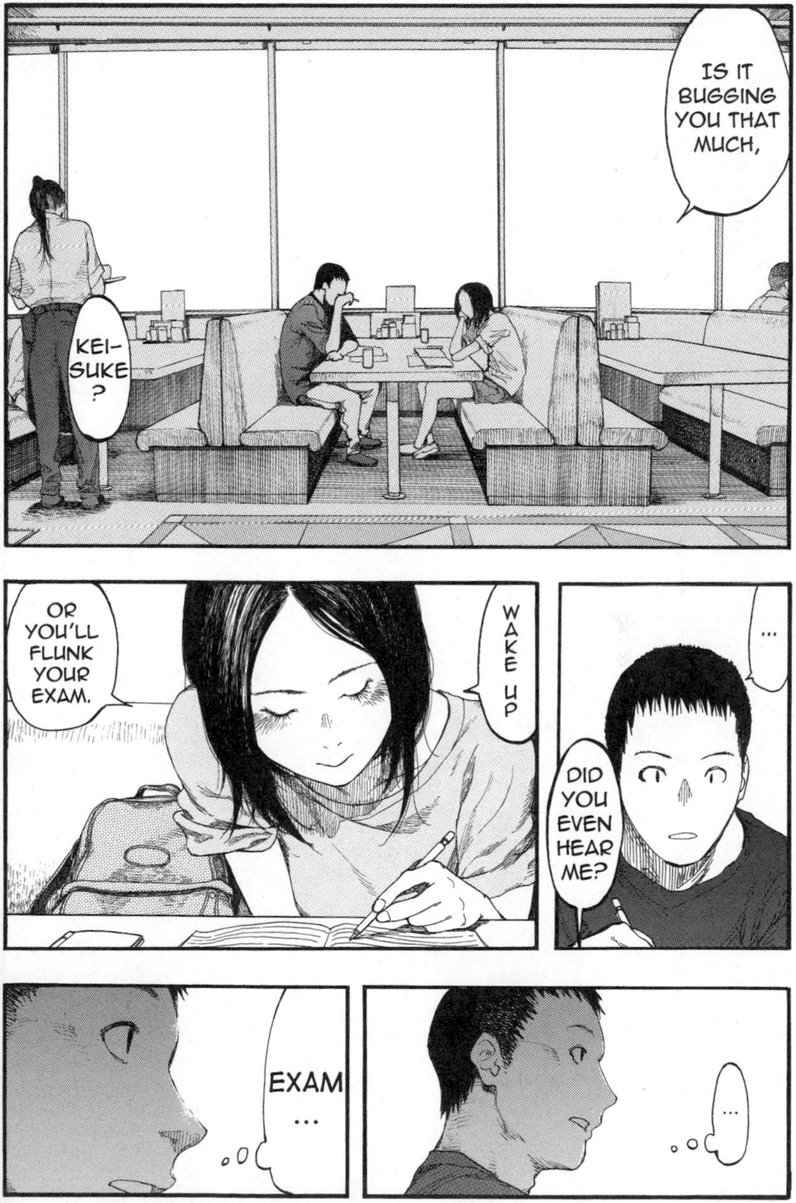
IS IT BUGGING YOU THAT MUCH,
KEI-SUKE?
...
DID YOU EVEN HEAR ME?
WAKE UP
OR YOU'LL FLUNK YOUR EXAM.
...
EXAM ...

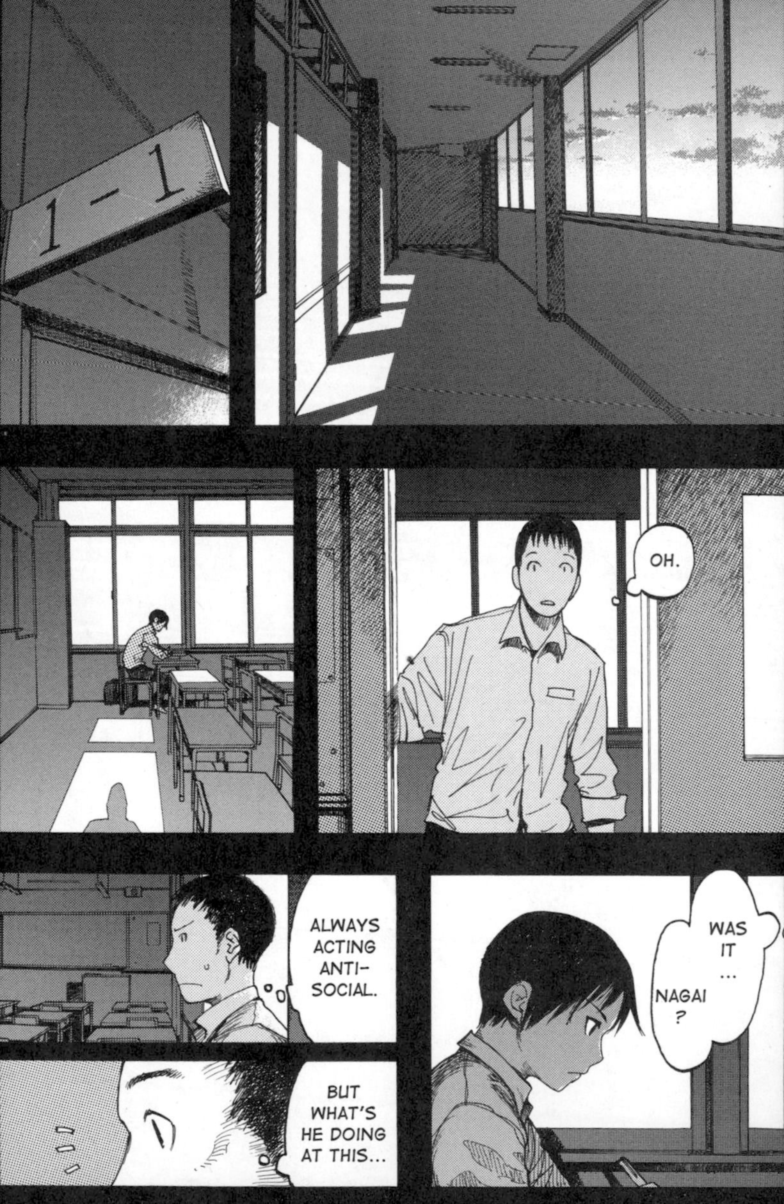

OH.
WAS IT ... NAGAI ?
ALWAYS ACTING ANTI-SOCIAL.
BUT WHAT'S HE DOING AT THIS...

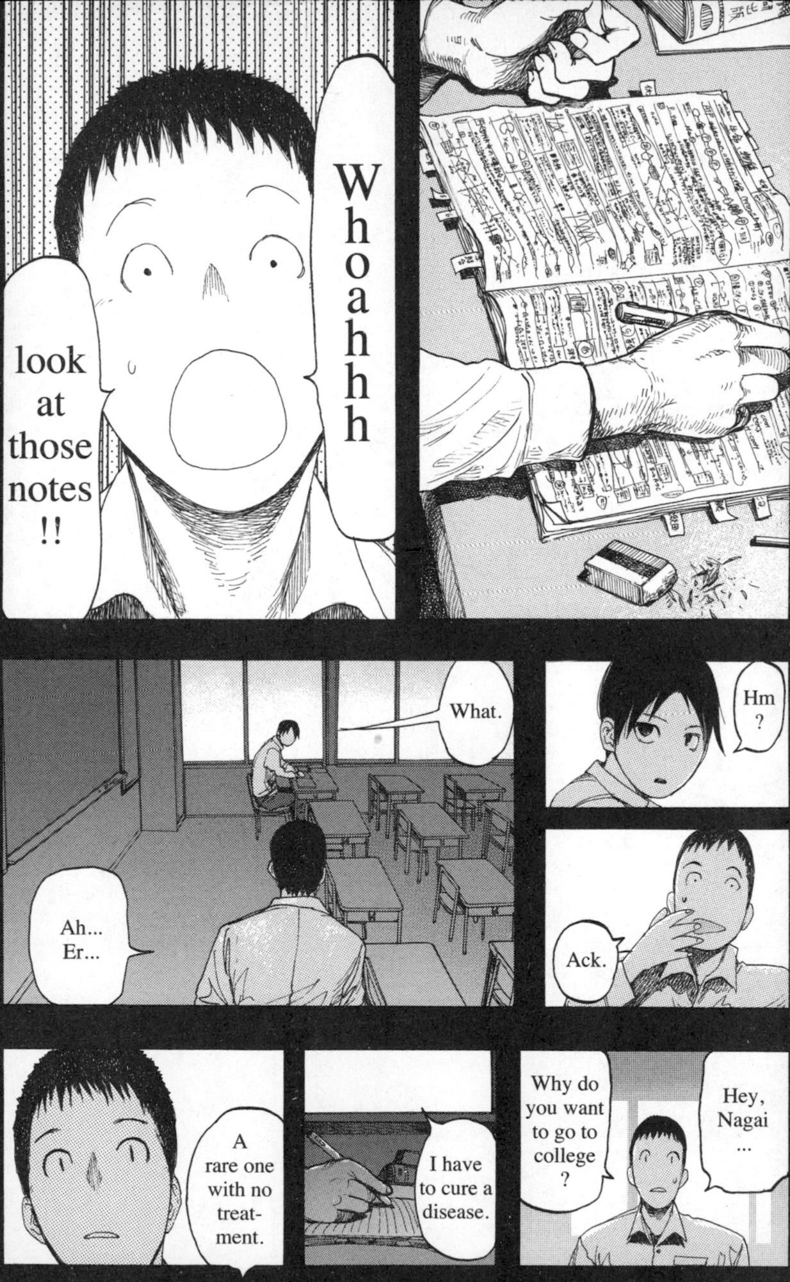
Whoahhh
look at those notes!!
Hm?
Ack.
What.
Ah... Er...
Hey, Nagai...
Why do you want to go to college?
I have to cure a disease.
A rare one with no treatment.

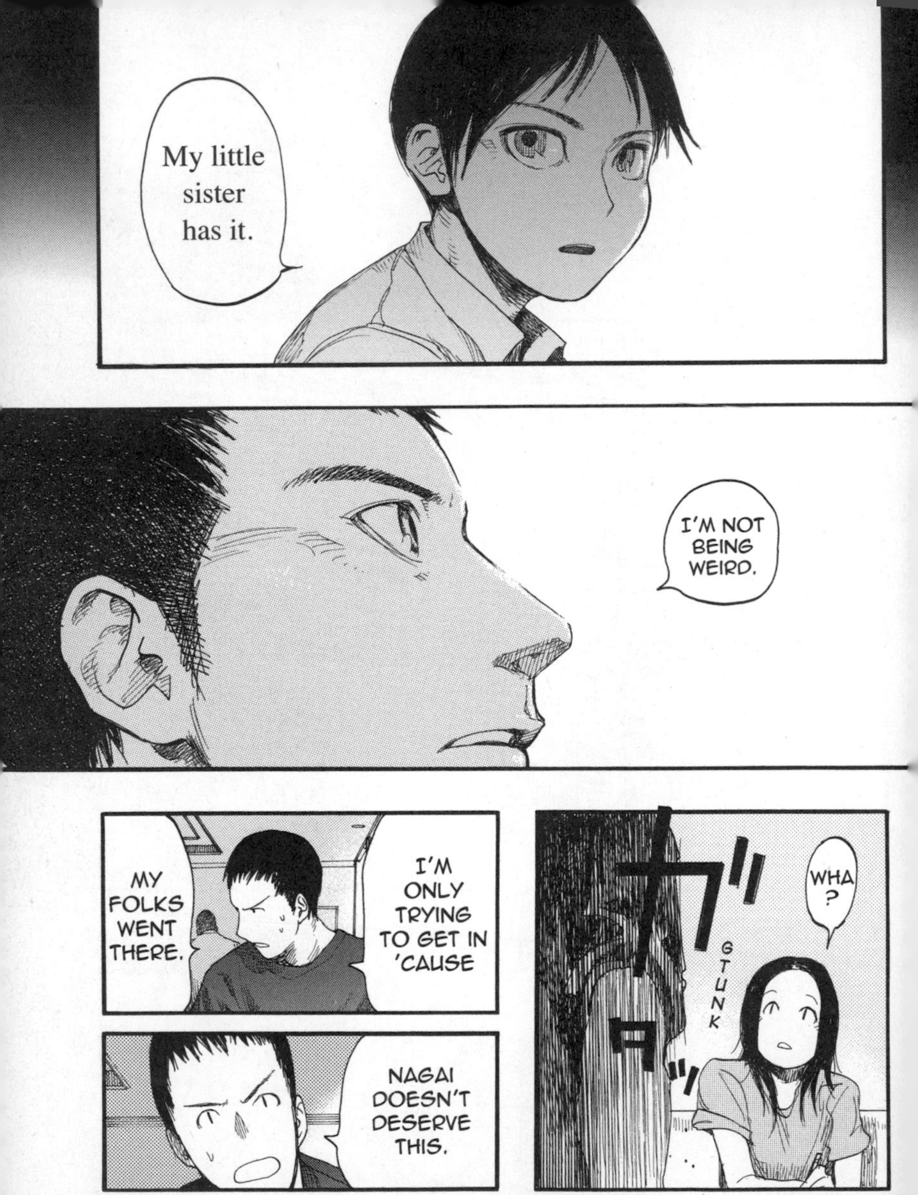
My little sister has it.
I'M NOT BEING WEIRD.
WHA?
GTUNK
I'M ONLY TRYING TO GET IN 'CAUSE
MY FOLKS WENT THERE.
NAGAI DOESN'T DESERVE THIS.

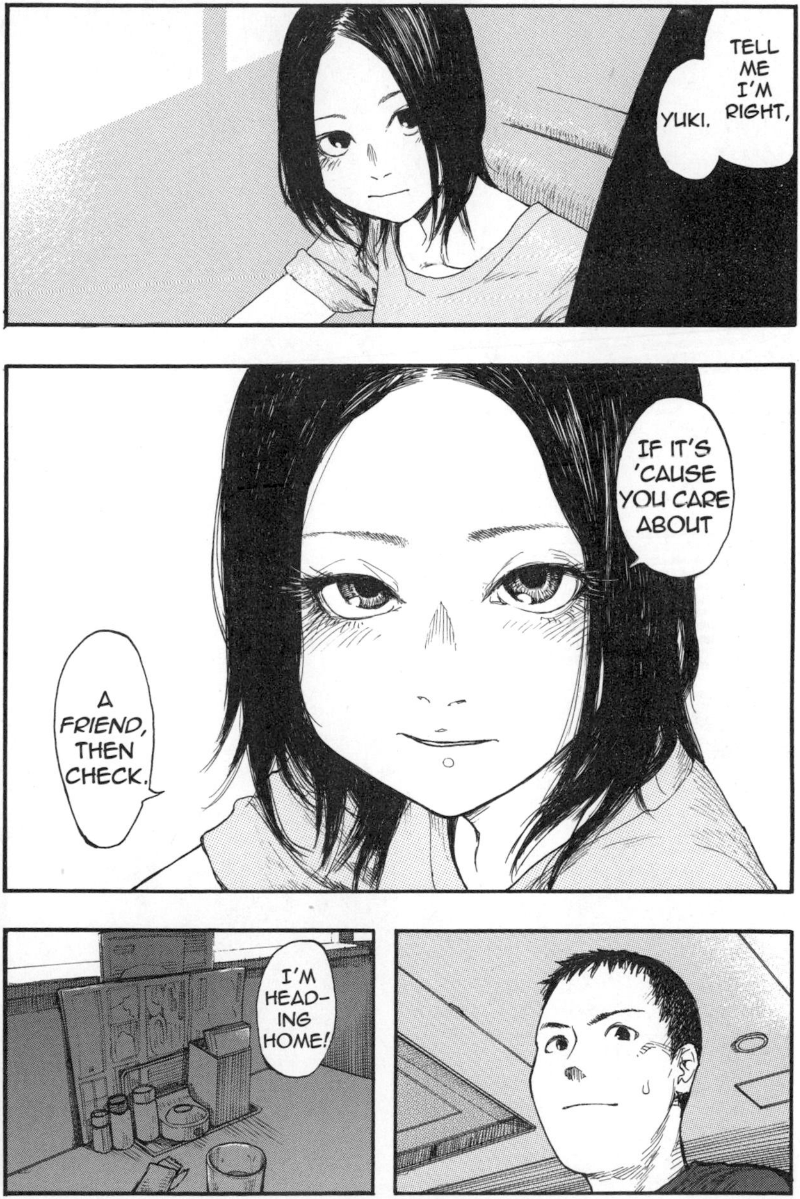
TELL ME I'M RIGHT, YUKI.
IF IT'S 'CAUSE YOU CARE ABOUT
A FRIEND, THEN CHECK.
I'M HEAD-ING HOME!

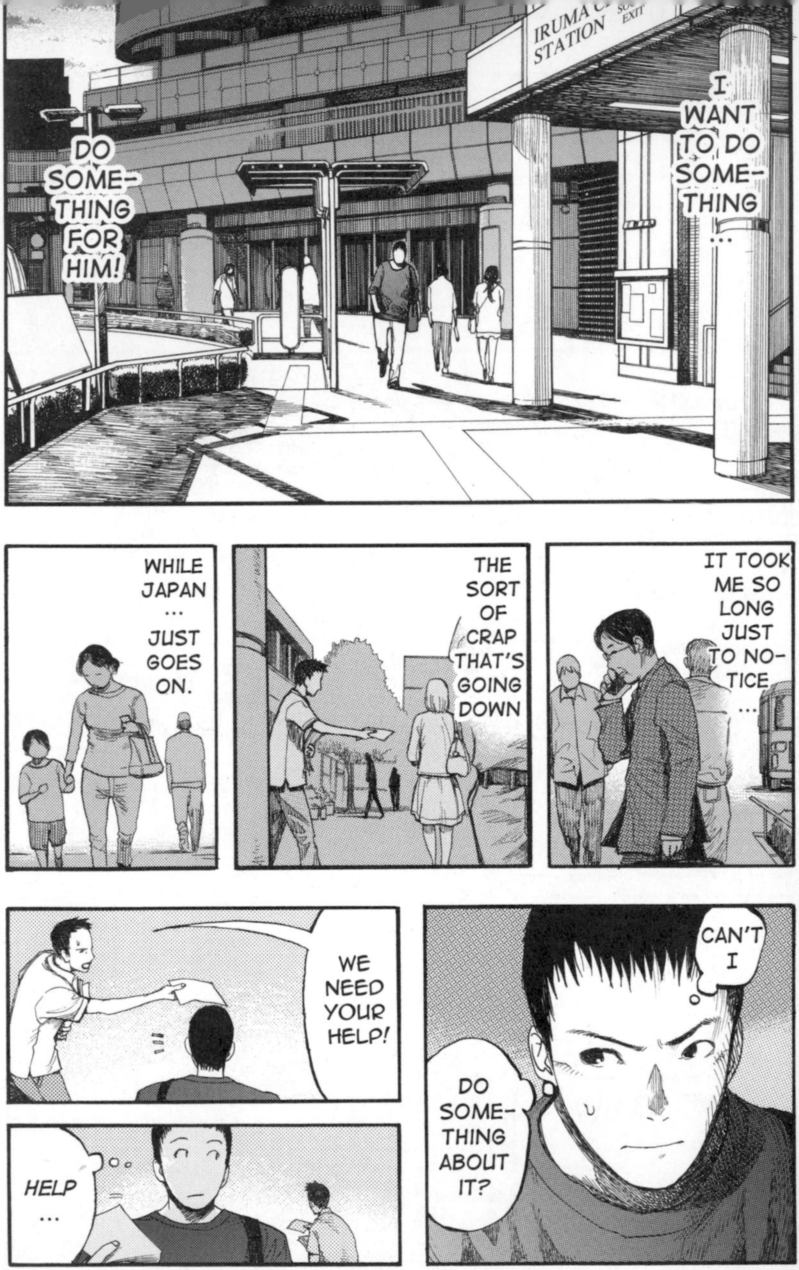
STATION
EXIT
I WANT TO DO SOME-THING ...
DO SOME-THING FOR HIM!
IT TOOK ME SO LONG JUST TO NO-TICE ...
THE SORT OF CRAP THAT'S GOING DOWN
WHILE JAPAN ... JUST GOES ON.
CAN'T I
DO SOME-THING ABOUT IT?
WE NEED YOUR HELP!
HELP ...

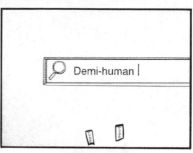

Demi-human |
TYPE
TYPE
Demi-human save|
TYPE
TYPE
TYPE
I DON'T USE THE INTERNET MUCH...
MAYBE ...
CLICK
C
C
Association for the Abolition of Discrimination against Demi-Humans
DH
ABOUT
NEWS
ACTIVITIES
Q&A
JOIN
CLICK
I KNEW IT.
JACKPOT!
DH
JOIN
CLICK

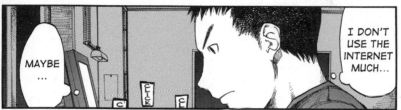

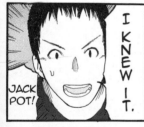

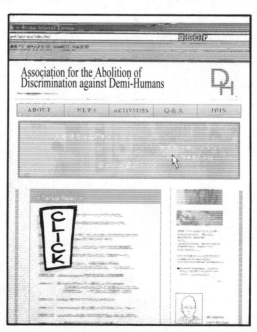

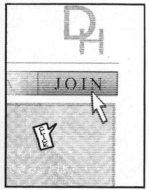

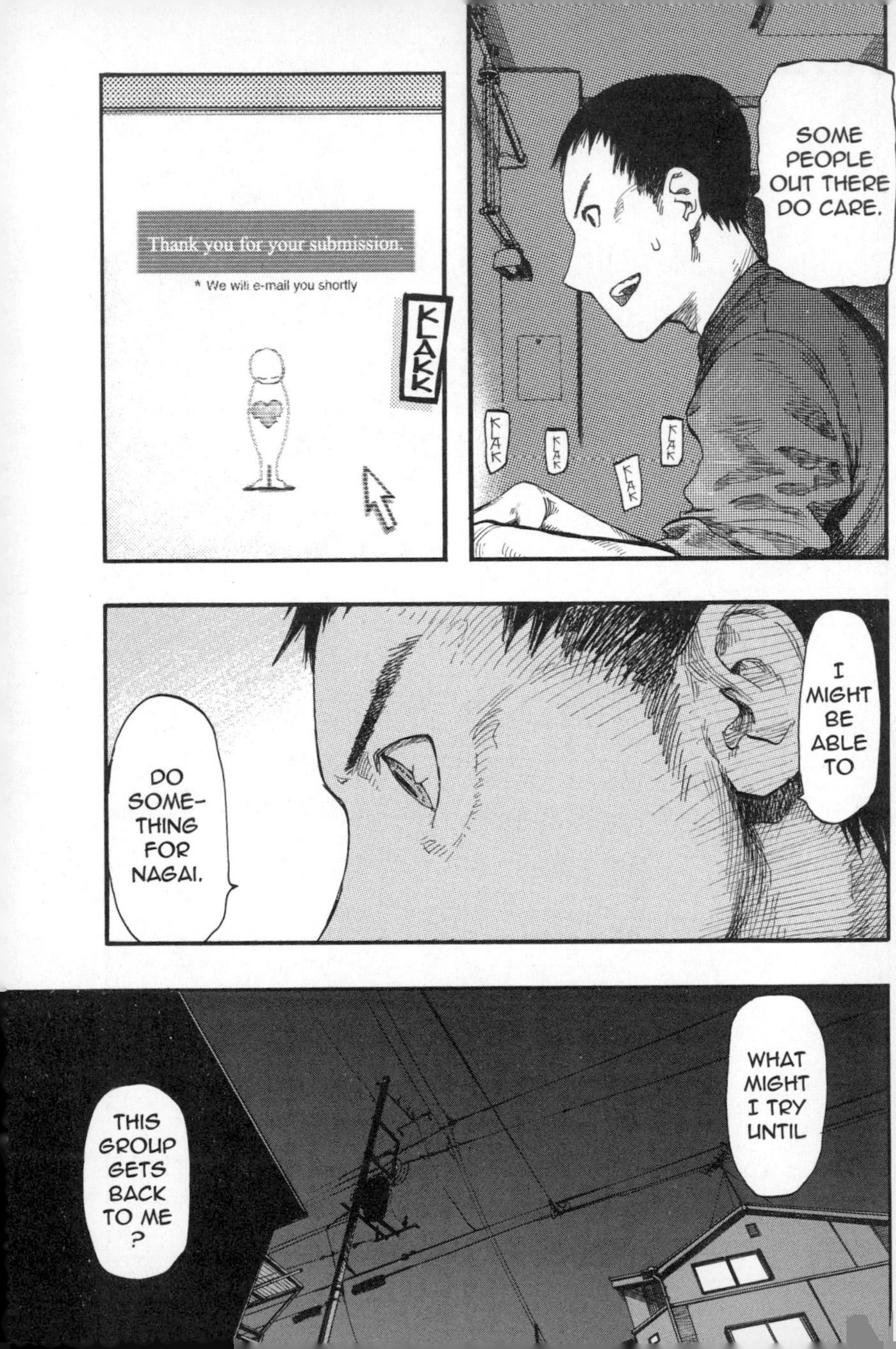
SOME PEOPLE OUT THERE DO CARE.
KLAK KLAK KLAK KLAK
Thank you for your submission.
* We will e-mail you shortly
KLAKK
I MIGHT BE ABLE TO
DO SOME-THING FOR NAGAI.
WHAT MIGHT I TRY UNTIL
THIS GROUP GETS BACK TO ME ?

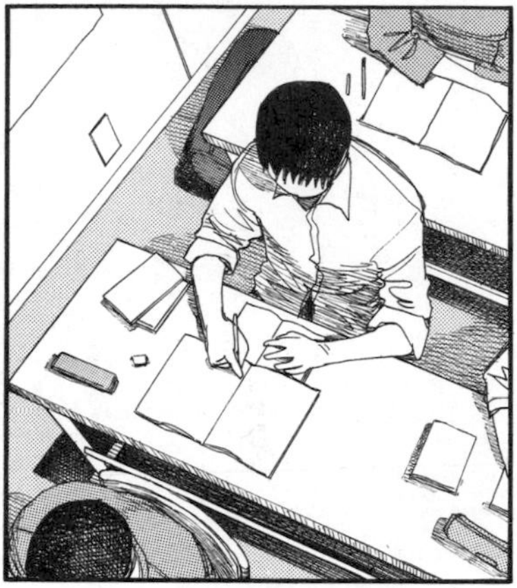
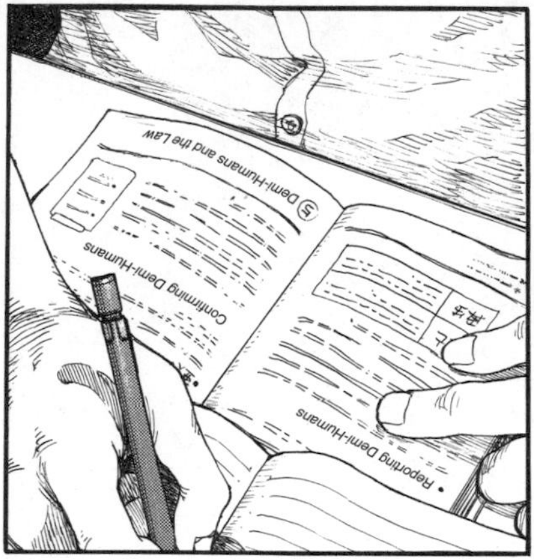
5 Demi-Humans and the Law
Confirming Demi-Humans
Reporting Demi-Humans
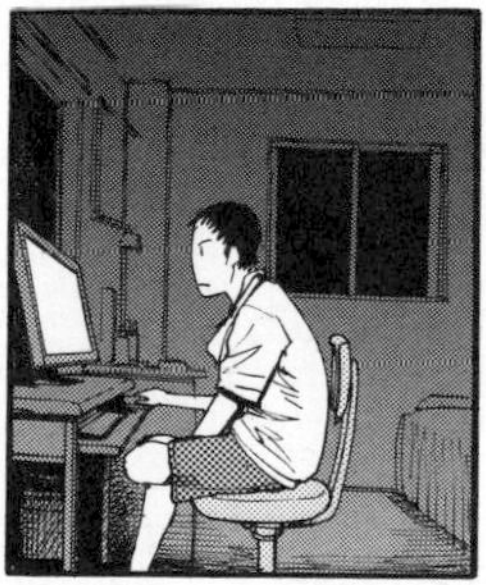
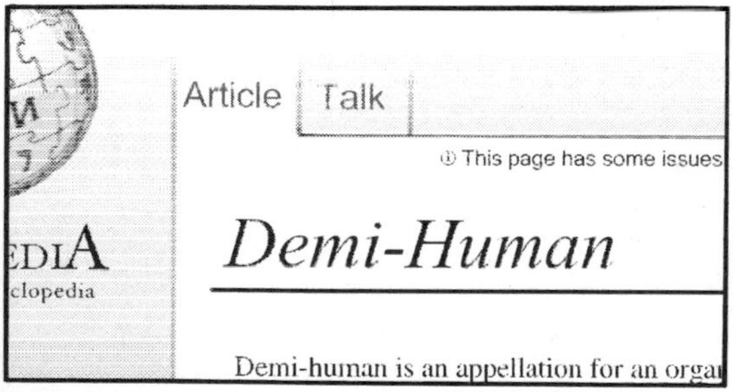
Article
Talk
ⓘ This page has some issues
EDIA
clopedia
Demi-Human
Demi-human is an appellation for an orga
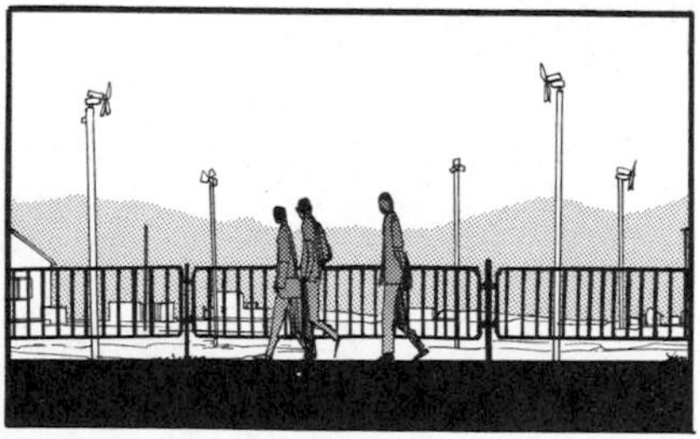
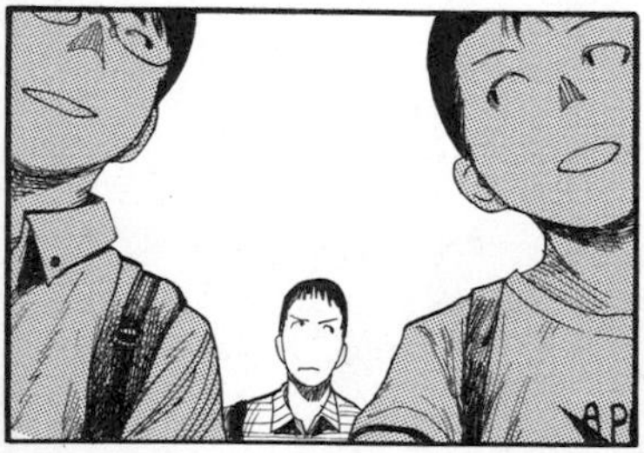

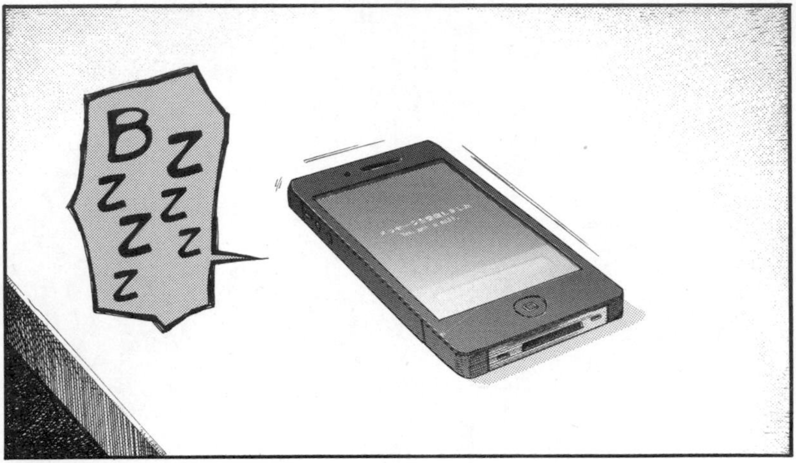
BZZZZZZ
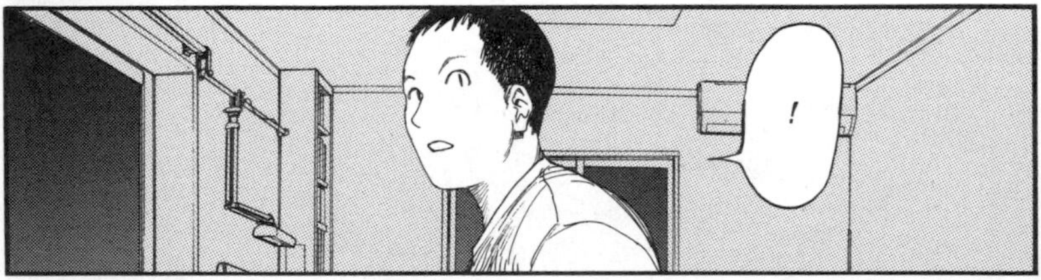
!
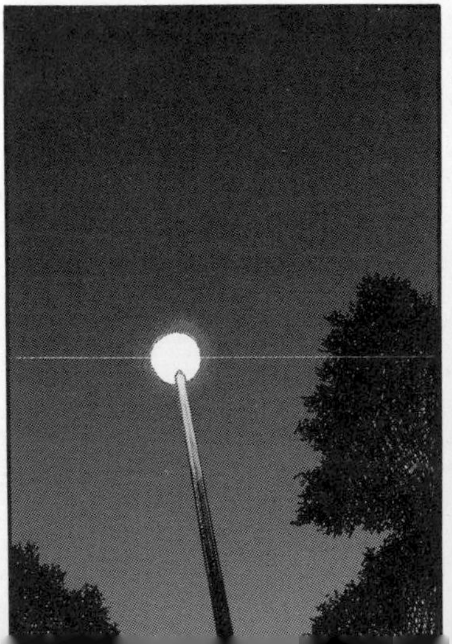
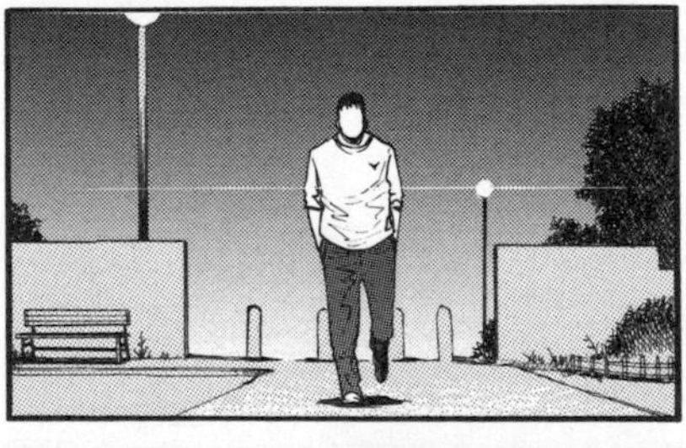
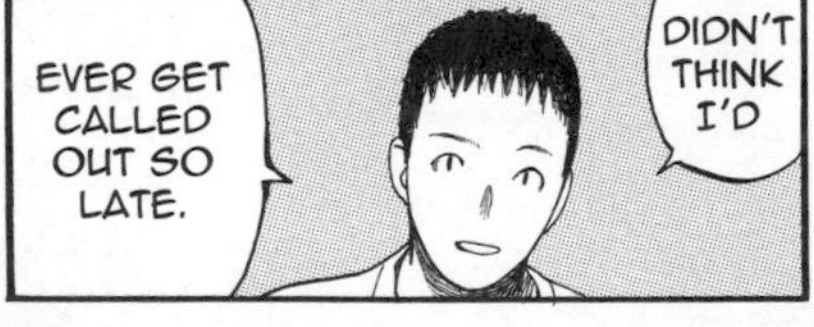
DIDN'T THINK I'D
EVER GET CALLED OUT SO LATE.

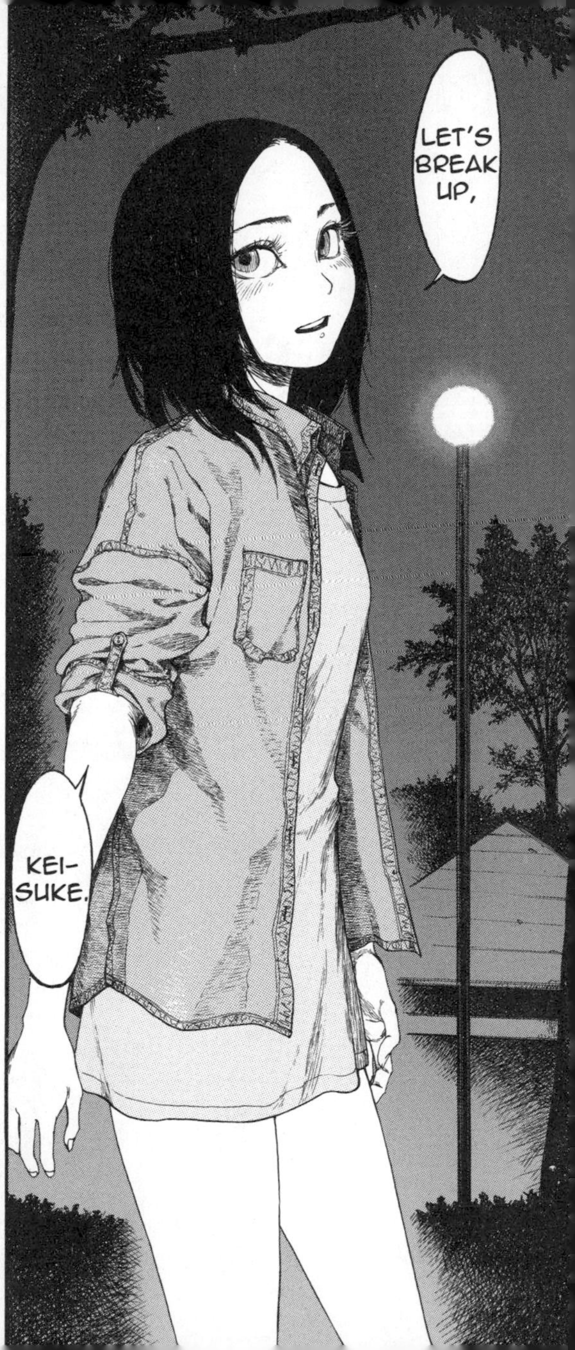
LET'S BREAK UP,
KEI-SUKE.
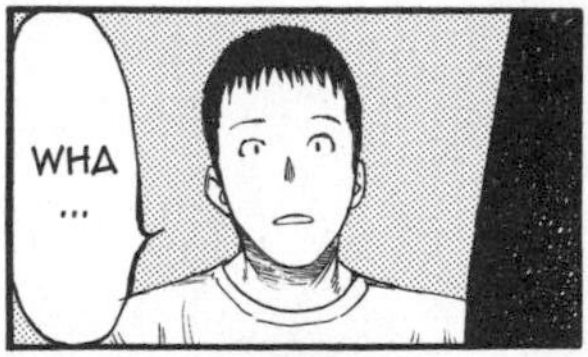
WHA ...
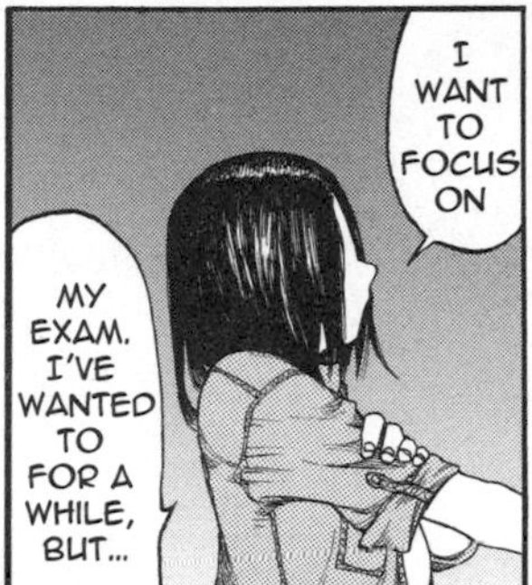
I WANT TO FOCUS ON
MY EXAM. I'VE WANTED TO FOR A WHILE, BUT...
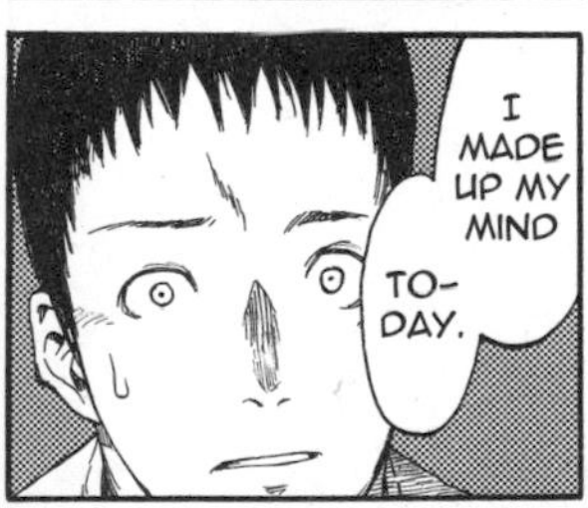
I MADE UP MY MIND
TO-DAY.
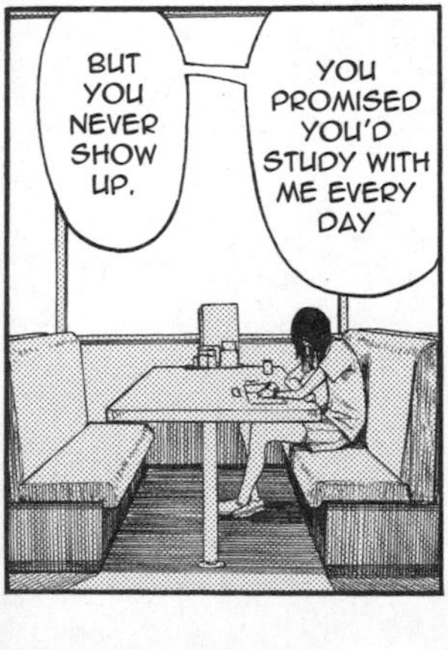
YOU PROMISED YOU'D STUDY WITH ME EVERY DAY
BUT YOU NEVER SHOW UP.

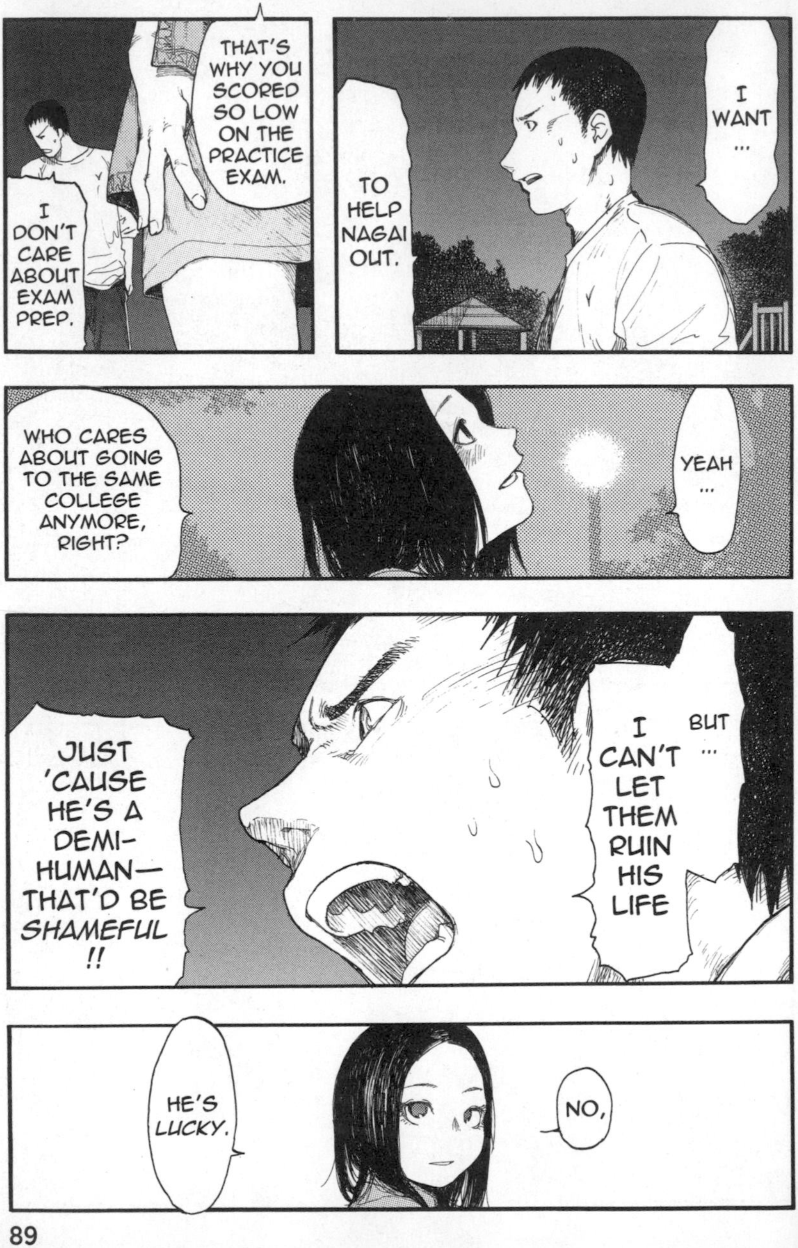
I WANT ...
TO HELP NAGAI OUT.
THAT'S WHY YOU SCORED SO LOW ON THE PRACTICE EXAM.
I DON'T CARE ABOUT EXAM PREP.
YEAH ...
WHO CARES ABOUT GOING TO THE SAME COLLEGE ANYMORE, RIGHT?
BUT ...
I CAN'T LET THEM RUIN HIS LIFE
JUST 'CAUSE HE'S A DEMI-HUMAN—THAT'D BE *SHAMEFUL* !!
NO,
HE'S *LUCKY*.

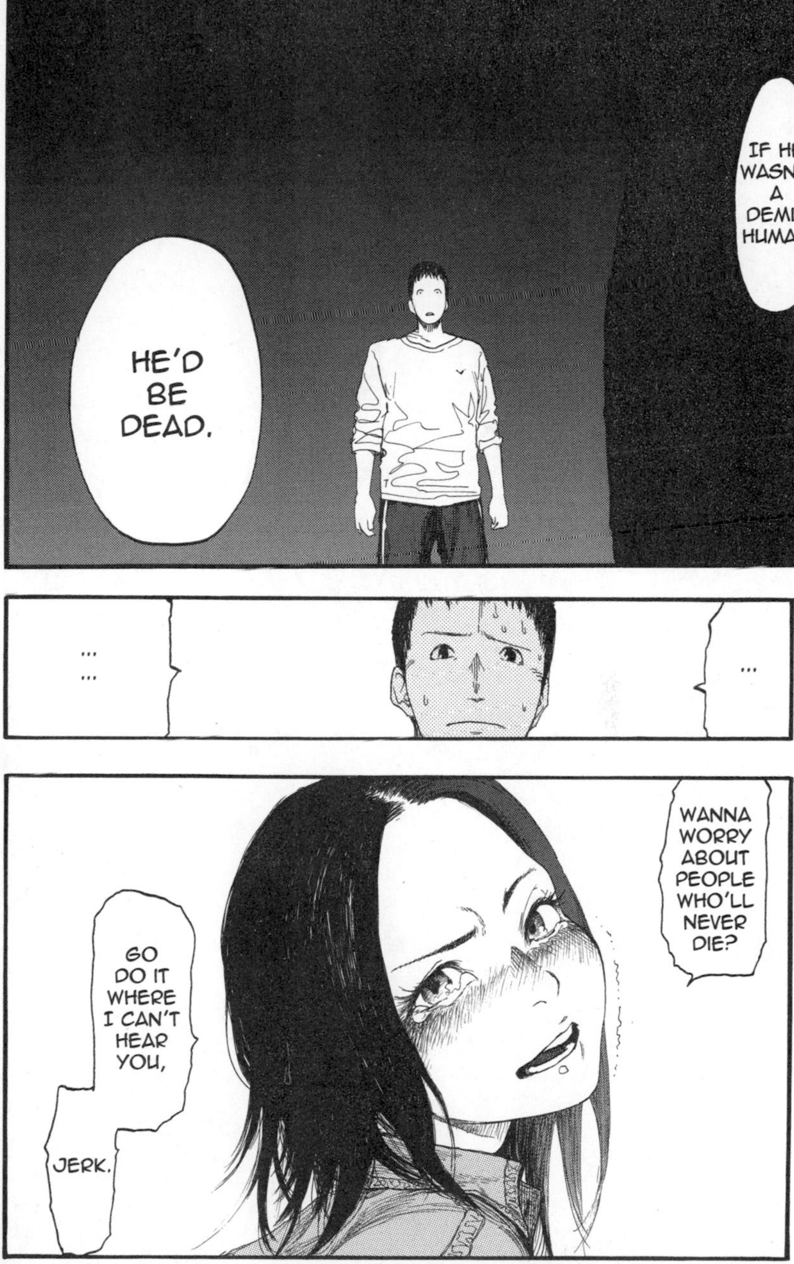
IF HE WASN'T A DEMI-HUMAN
HE'D BE DEAD.
...
...
...
WANNA WORRY ABOUT PEOPLE WHO'LL NEVER DIE?
GO DO IT WHERE I CAN'T HEAR YOU,
JERK.

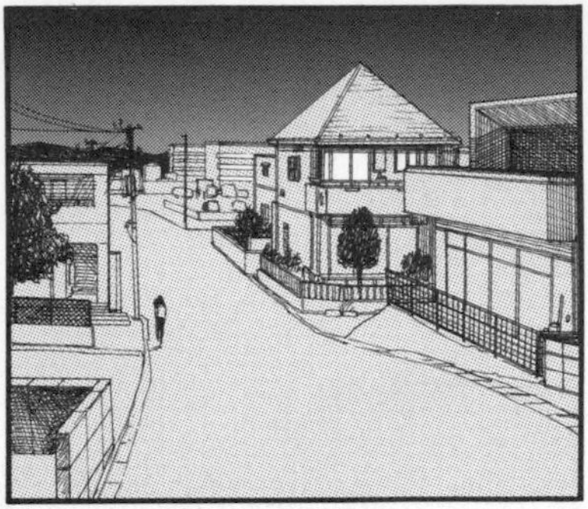
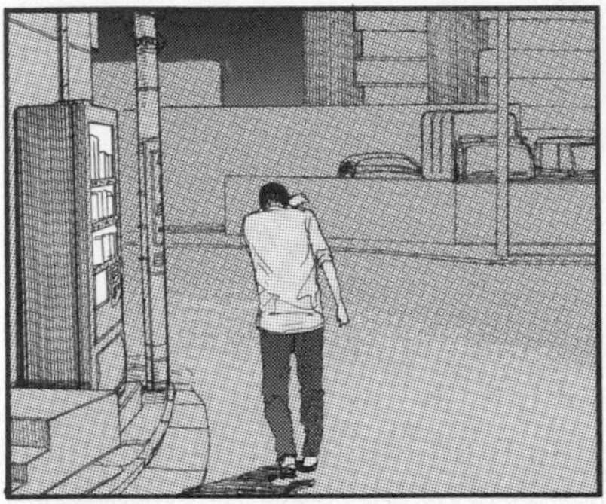
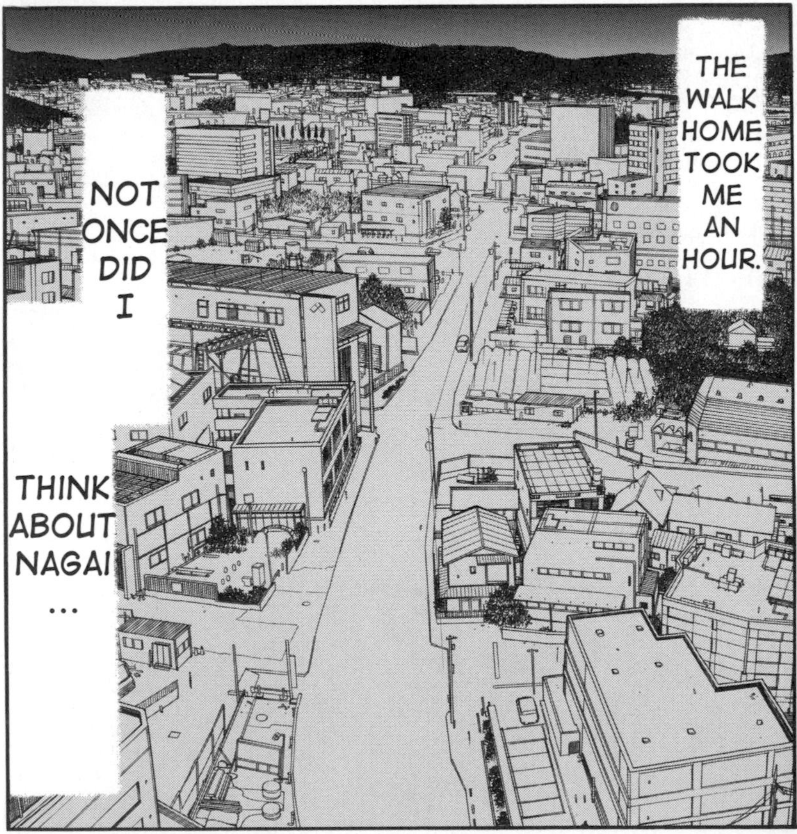
THE WALK HOME TOOK ME AN HOUR.
NOT ONCE DID I
THINK ABOUT NAGAI ...

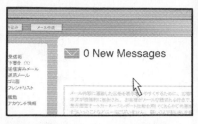

0 New Messages

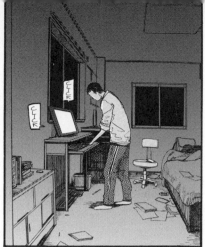

AH

...

Association Discrimination

Site last updated: 2000.4.21

ABOUT

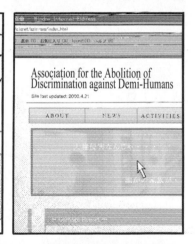

Association for the Abolition of Discrimination against Demi-Humans

Site last updated: 2000.4.21

| ABOUT | NEWS | ACTIVITIES |

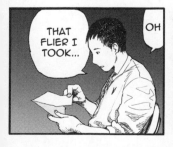

THAT FLIER I TOOK...

OH

?

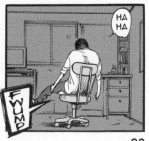

HA HA

FWUMP

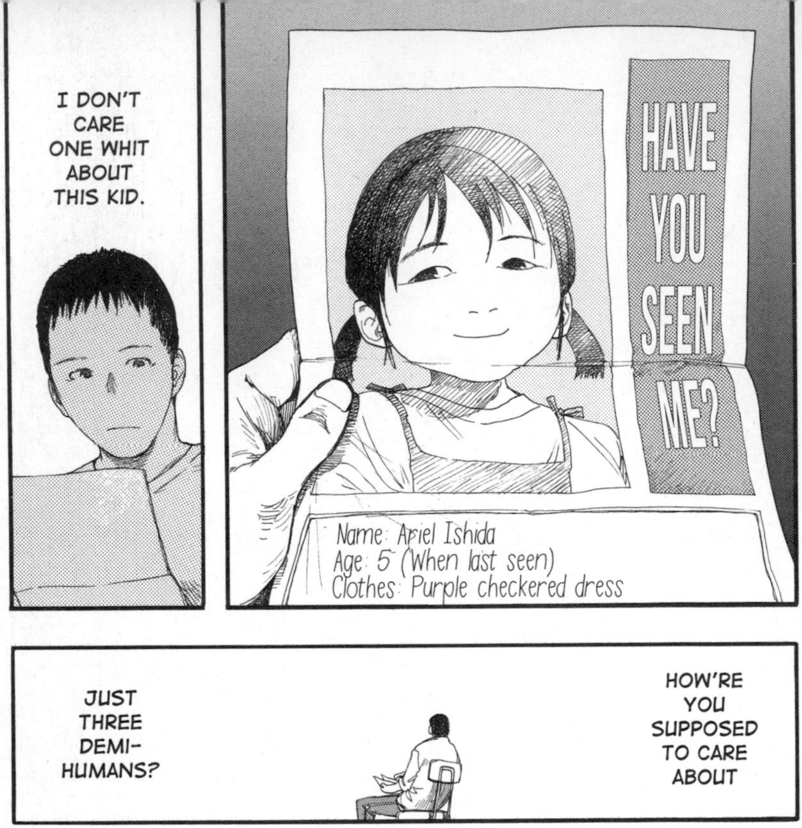
HAVE YOU SEEN ME?
Name: Ariel Ishida
Age: 5 (When last seen)
Clothes: Purple checkered dress
I DON'T CARE ONE WHIT ABOUT THIS KID.
HOW'RE YOU SUPPOSED TO CARE ABOUT
JUST THREE DEMI-HUMANS?

I WAS THE WEIRD ONE.

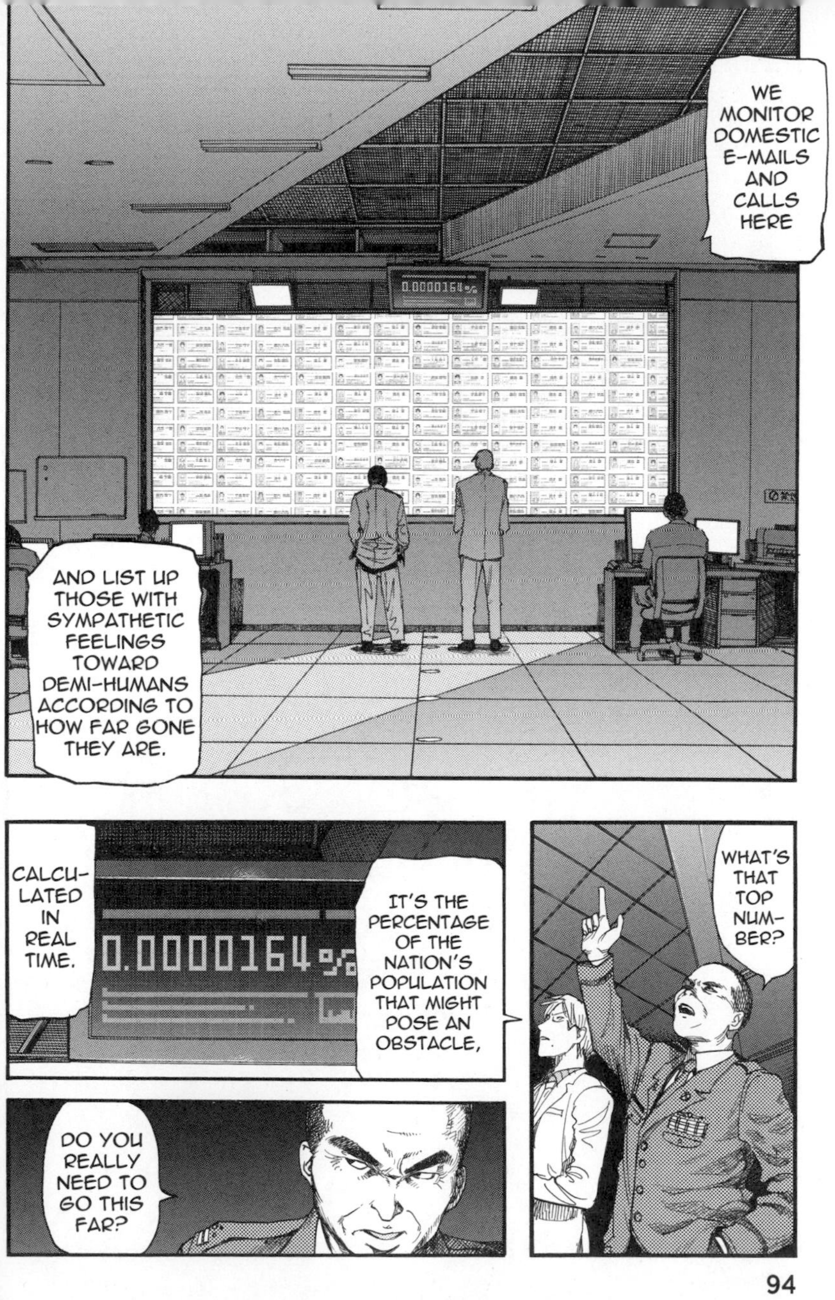
WE MONITOR DOMESTIC E-MAILS AND CALLS HERE
0.0000164%
AND LIST UP THOSE WITH SYMPATHETIC FEELINGS TOWARD DEMI-HUMANS ACCORDING TO HOW FAR GONE THEY ARE.
WHAT'S THAT TOP NUM-BER?
IT'S THE PERCENTAGE OF THE NATION'S POPULATION THAT MIGHT POSE AN OBSTACLE,
CALCU-LATED IN REAL TIME.
0.0000164%
DO YOU REALLY NEED TO GO THIS FAR?

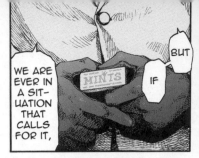
WE ARE EVER IN A SITUATION THAT CALLS FOR IT,

BUT

IF

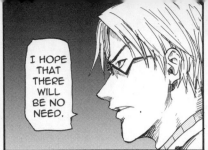
I HOPE THAT THERE WILL BE NO NEED.

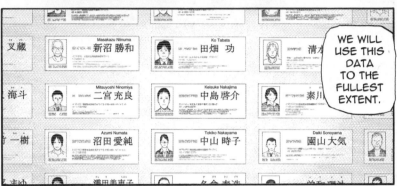

WE WILL USE THIS DATA TO THE FULLEST EXTENT.

Masakazu Niinuma
新沼勝和

Ko Tabata
田畑 功

清水

Mitsuyoshi Ninomiya
二宮充良

Keisuke Nakajima
中島啓介

素川

Azumi Numata
沼田愛純

Tokiko Nakayama
中山時子

Daiki Sonoyama
園山大気

叉蔵

海斗

一樹

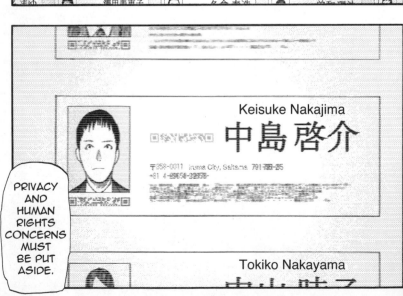

Keisuke Nakajima
中島 啓介

〒358-0011　Iruma City, Saitama　791-785-85
+81 4-2856-2878

PRIVACY AND HUMAN RIGHTS CONCERNS MUST BE PUT ASIDE.

Tokiko Nakayama

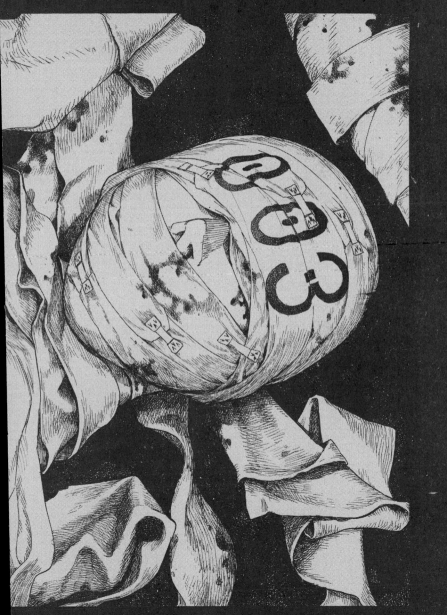

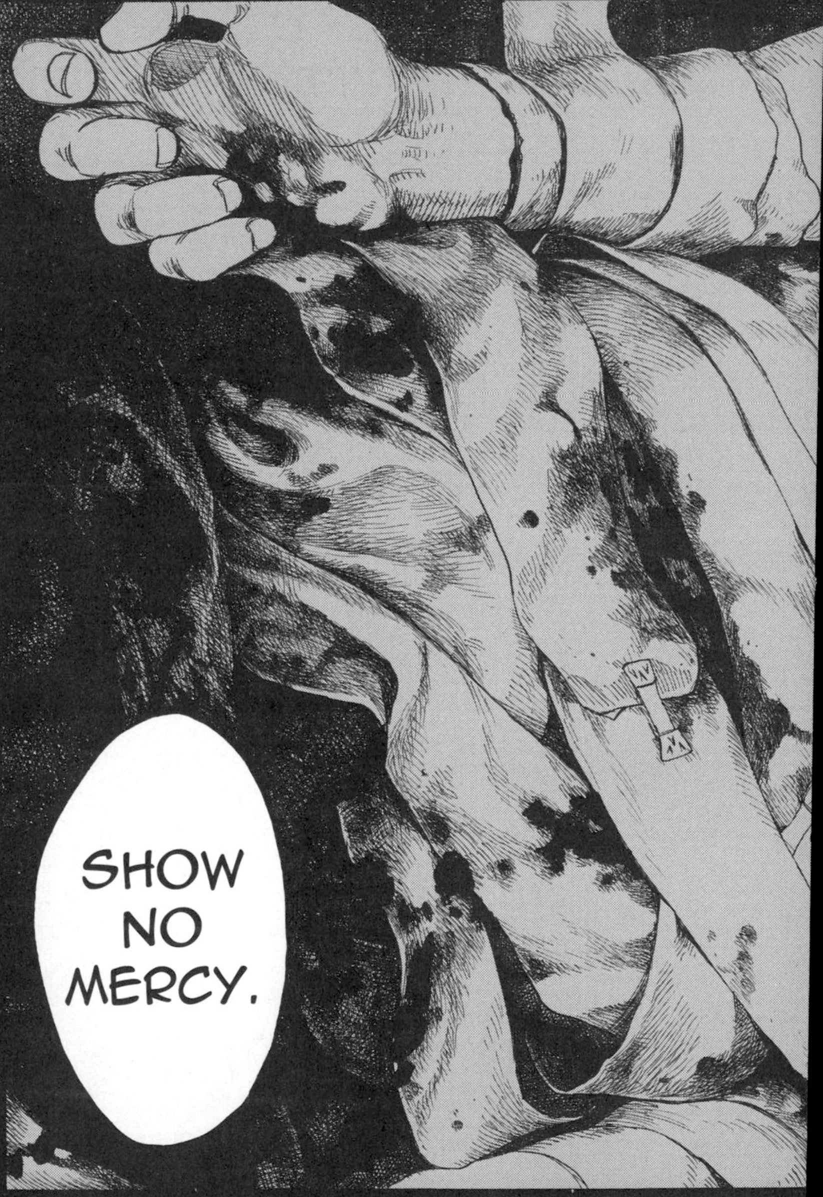
SHOW NO MERCY.

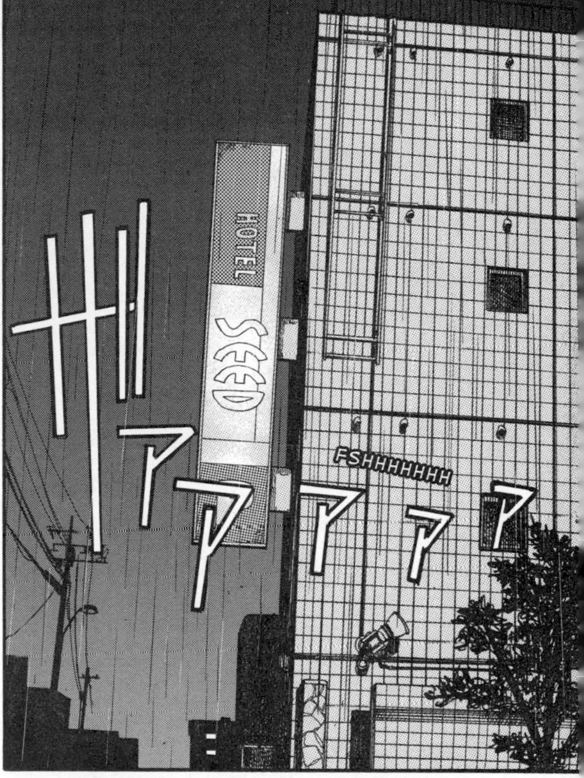
HOTEL
SEED
FSHHHHHHH

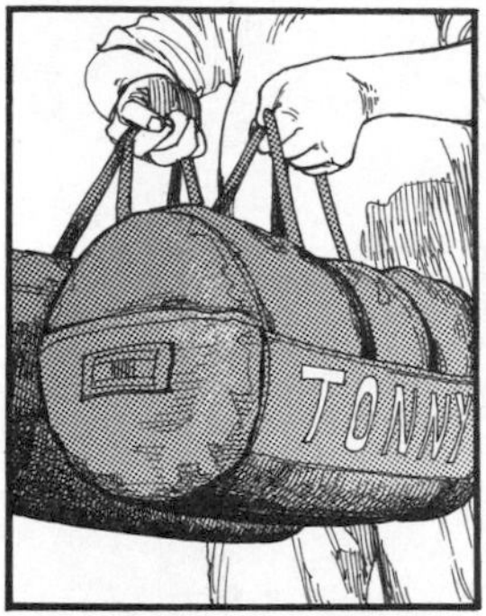
TONNY

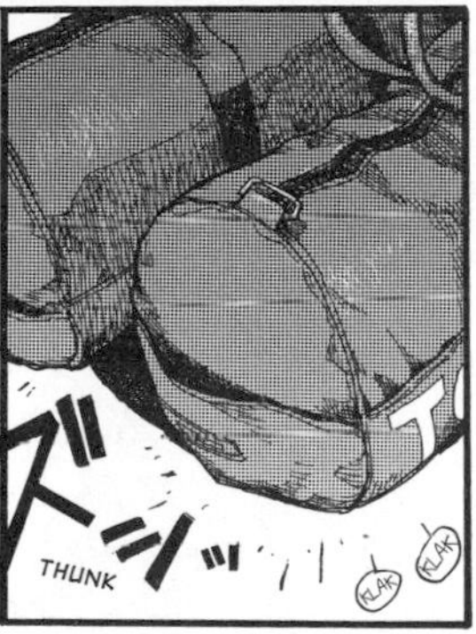
ズシッ
THUNK
KLAK
KLAK

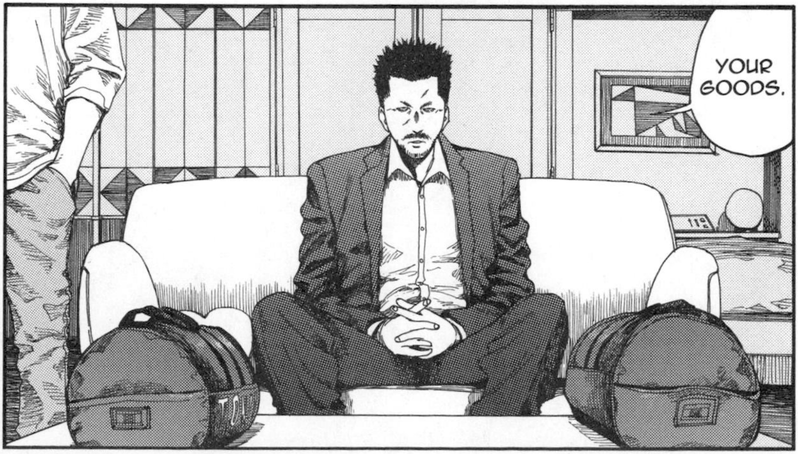
YOUR GOODS.

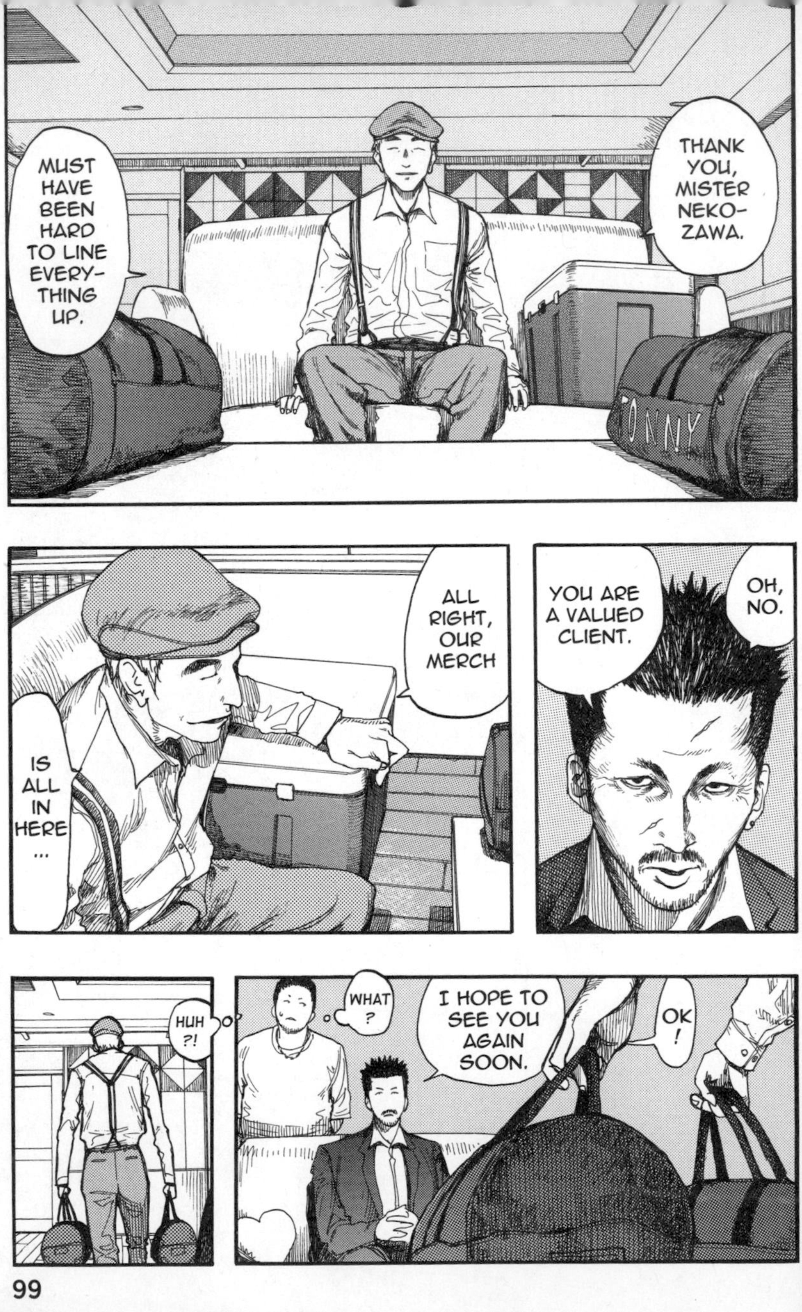
THANK YOU, MISTER NEKO-ZAWA.
MUST HAVE BEEN HARD TO LINE EVERY-THING UP.
TONNY
OH, NO.
YOU ARE A VALUED CLIENT.
ALL RIGHT, OUR MERCH
IS ALL IN HERE ...
OK!
I HOPE TO SEE YOU AGAIN SOON.
WHAT?
HUH?!

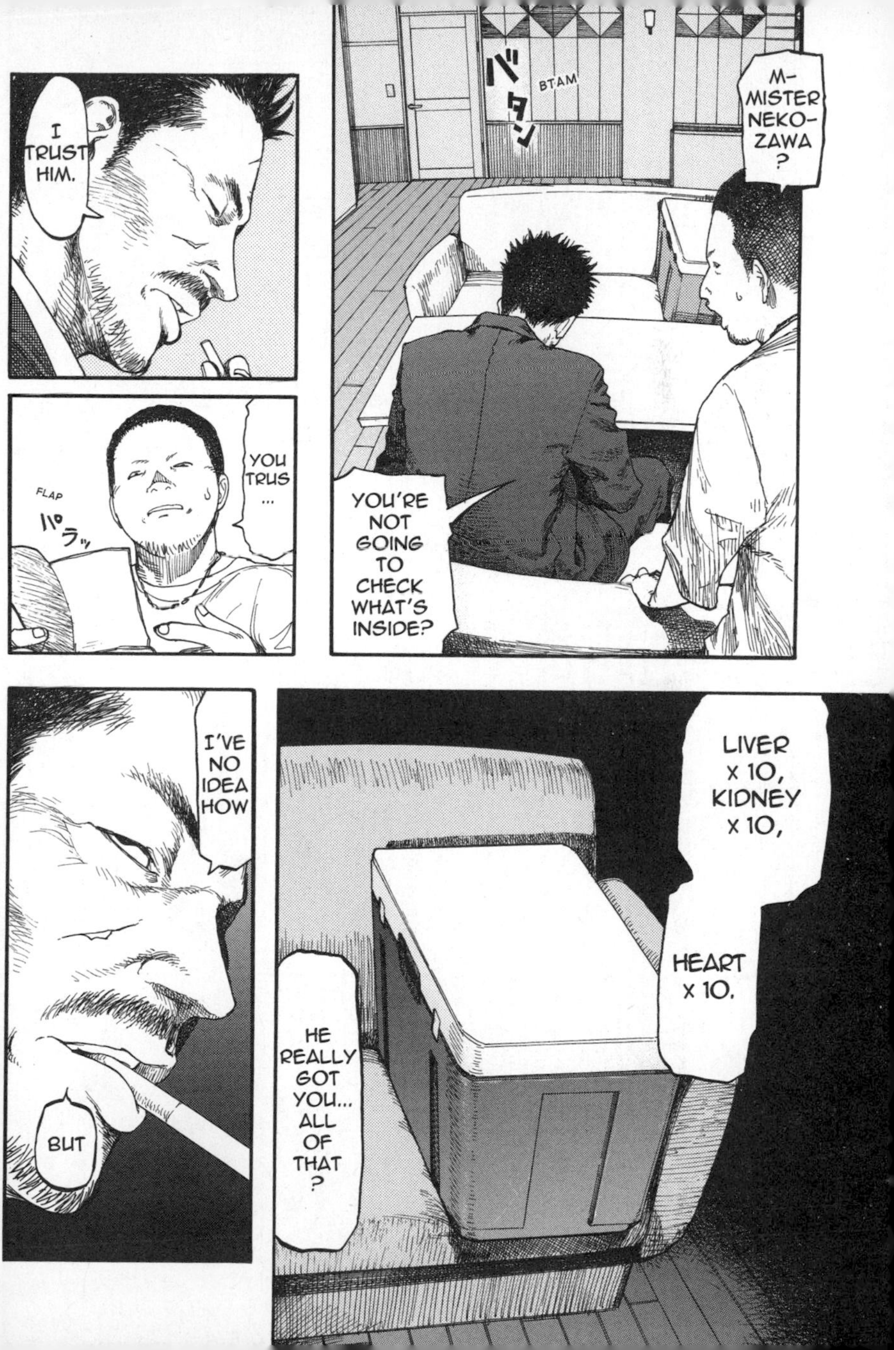
バタン
BTAM
M-MISTER NEKO-ZAWA?
YOU'RE NOT GOING TO CHECK WHAT'S INSIDE?
I TRUST HIM.
YOU TRUS...
FLAP
パラッ
LIVER x 10, KIDNEY x 10,
HEART x 10.
HE REALLY GOT YOU... ALL OF THAT?
I'VE NO IDEA HOW
BUT

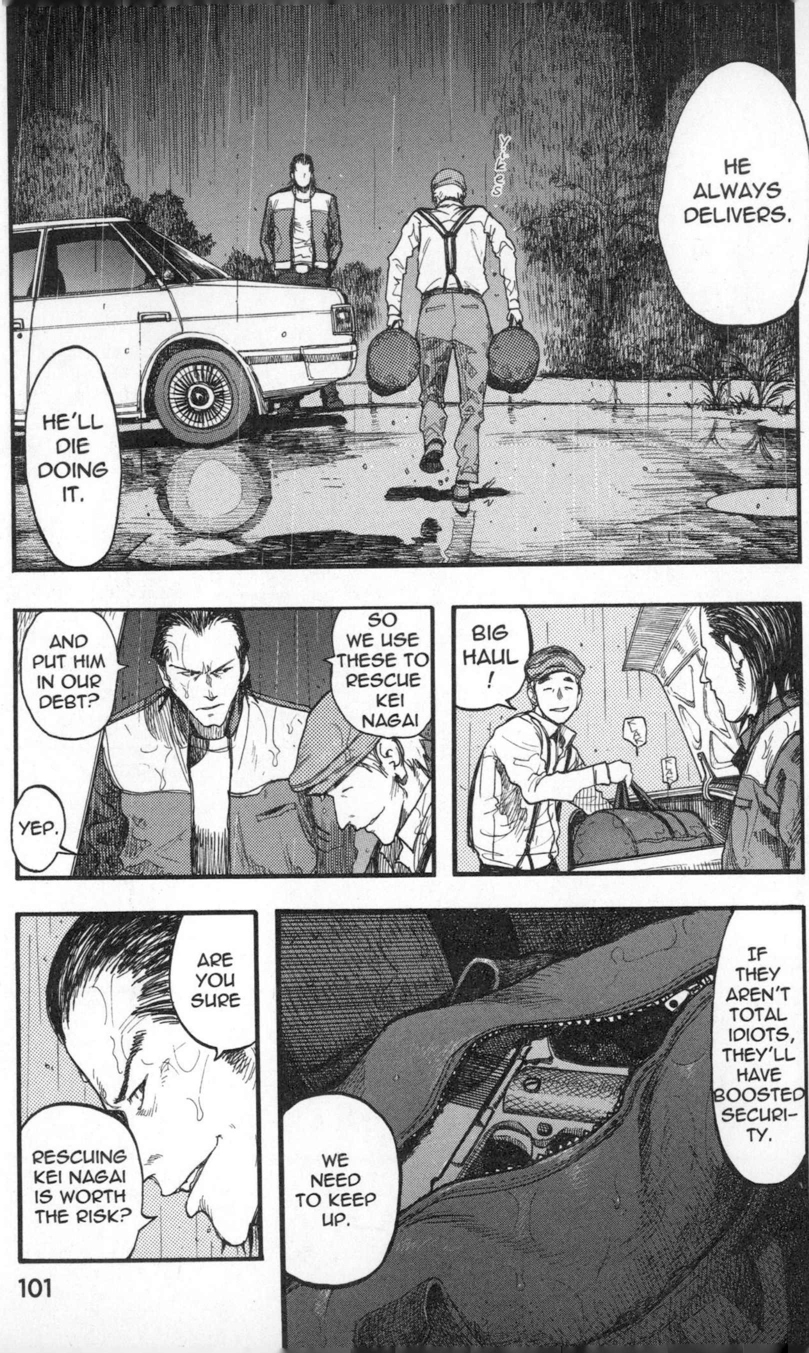
HE ALWAYS DELIVERS.
HE'LL DIE DOING IT.
BIG HAUL!
SO WE USE THESE TO RESCUE KEI NAGAI
AND PUT HIM IN OUR DEBT?
YEP.
IF THEY AREN'T TOTAL IDIOTS, THEY'LL HAVE BOOSTED SECURITY.
WE NEED TO KEEP UP.
ARE YOU SURE
RESCUING KEI NAGAI IS WORTH THE RISK?

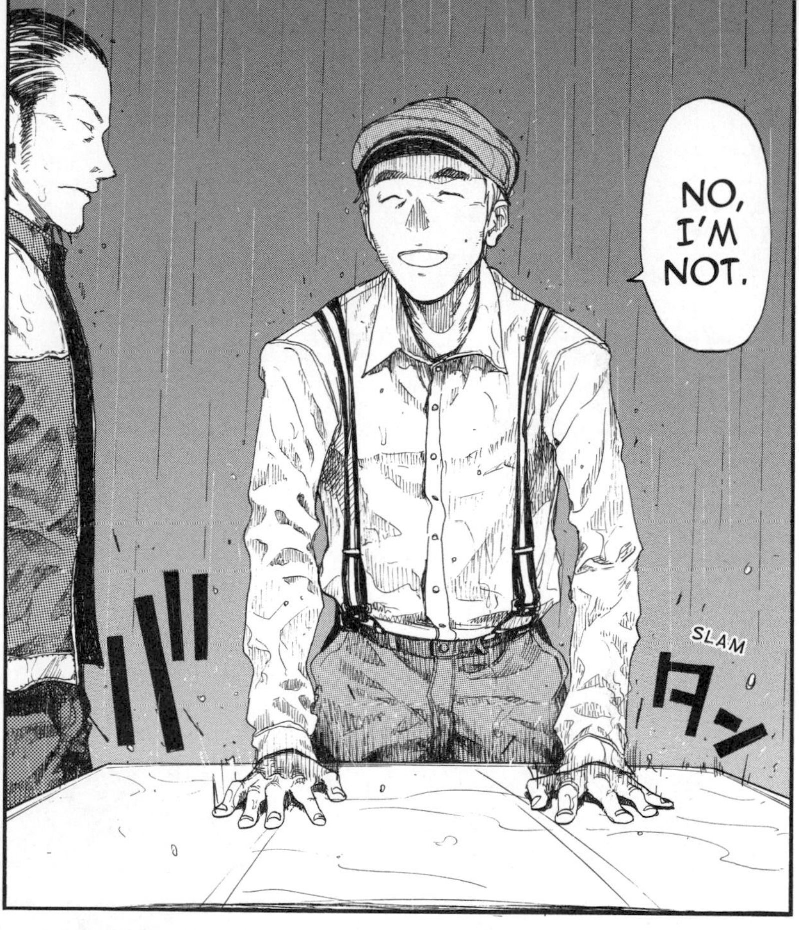
NO, I'M NOT.
SLAM
タン

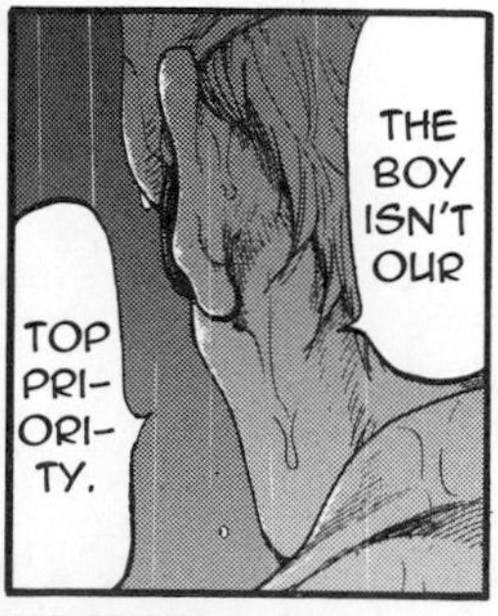
THE BOY ISN'T OUR
TOP PRI-ORI-TY.

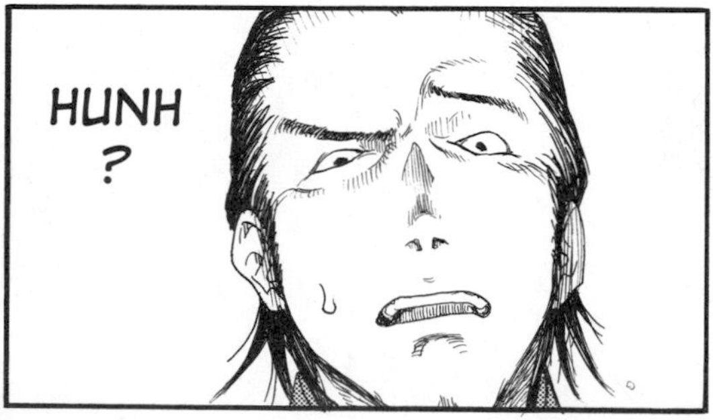
HUNH ?

File:08 End

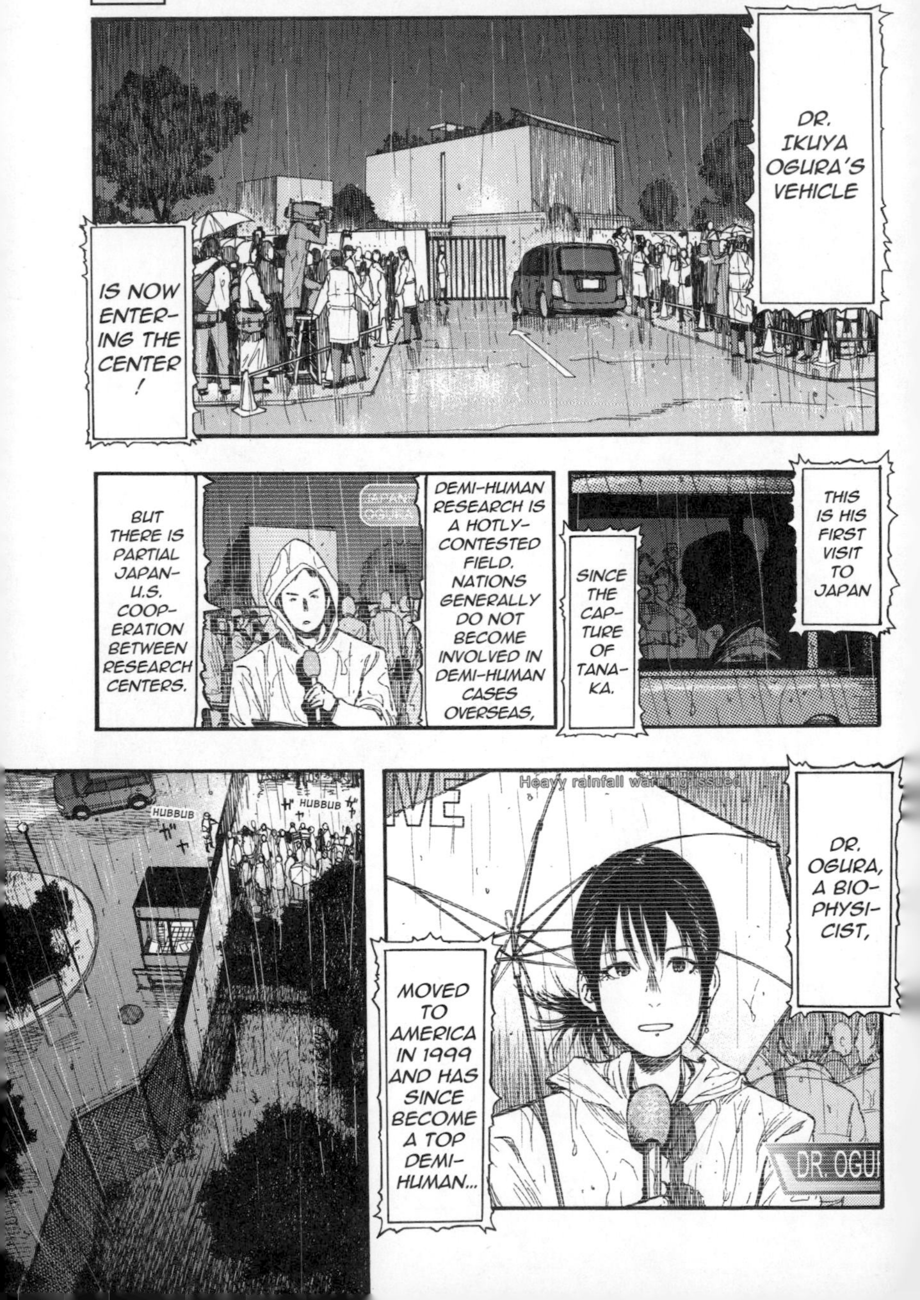
DR. IKUYA OGURA'S VEHICLE
IS NOW ENTERING THE CENTER!
THIS IS HIS FIRST VISIT TO JAPAN
SINCE THE CAPTURE OF TANAKA.
DEMI-HUMAN RESEARCH IS A HOTLY-CONTESTED FIELD. NATIONS GENERALLY DO NOT BECOME INVOLVED IN DEMI-HUMAN CASES OVERSEAS,
BUT THERE IS PARTIAL JAPAN-U.S. COOPERATION BETWEEN RESEARCH CENTERS.
Heavy rainfall warning issued
DR. OGURA, A BIOPHYSICIST,
MOVED TO AMERICA IN 1999 AND HAS SINCE BECOME A TOP DEMI-HUMAN...
HUBBUB
HUBBUB

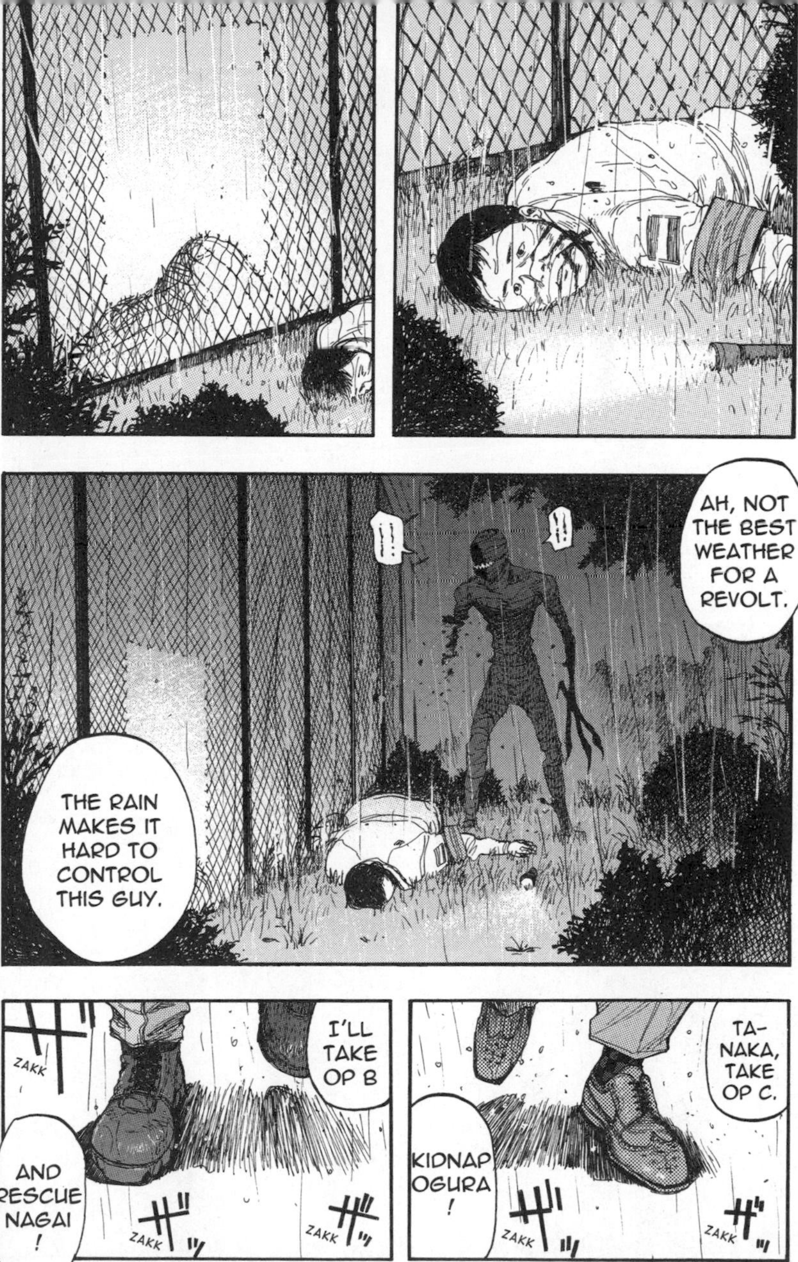
AH, NOT THE BEST WEATHER FOR A REVOLT.
!!
!!
THE RAIN MAKES IT HARD TO CONTROL THIS GUY.
TA-NAKA, TAKE OP C.
KIDNAP OGURA!
ZAKK
ZAKK
I'LL TAKE OP B
AND RESCUE NAGAI!
ZAKK
ZAKK

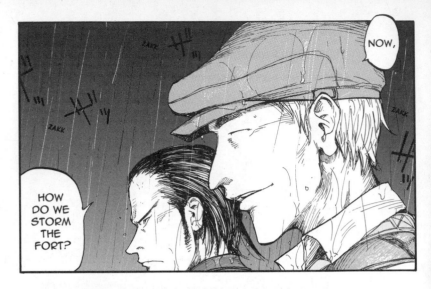

NOW,
ZAKK
ZAKK
ZAKK
HOW DO WE STORM THE FORT?
EASY!
AMASS MORE FIRE-POWER THAN THE ENEMY EXPECTS.
ZAKK
WITH THE MAXIMUM FIRE-POWER WE CAN MUSTER...
ZAKK
ZAKK
WE ROLL OVER THEM.

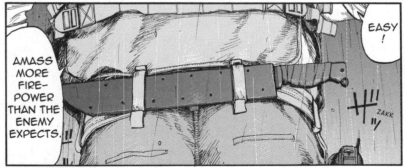

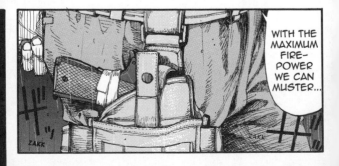

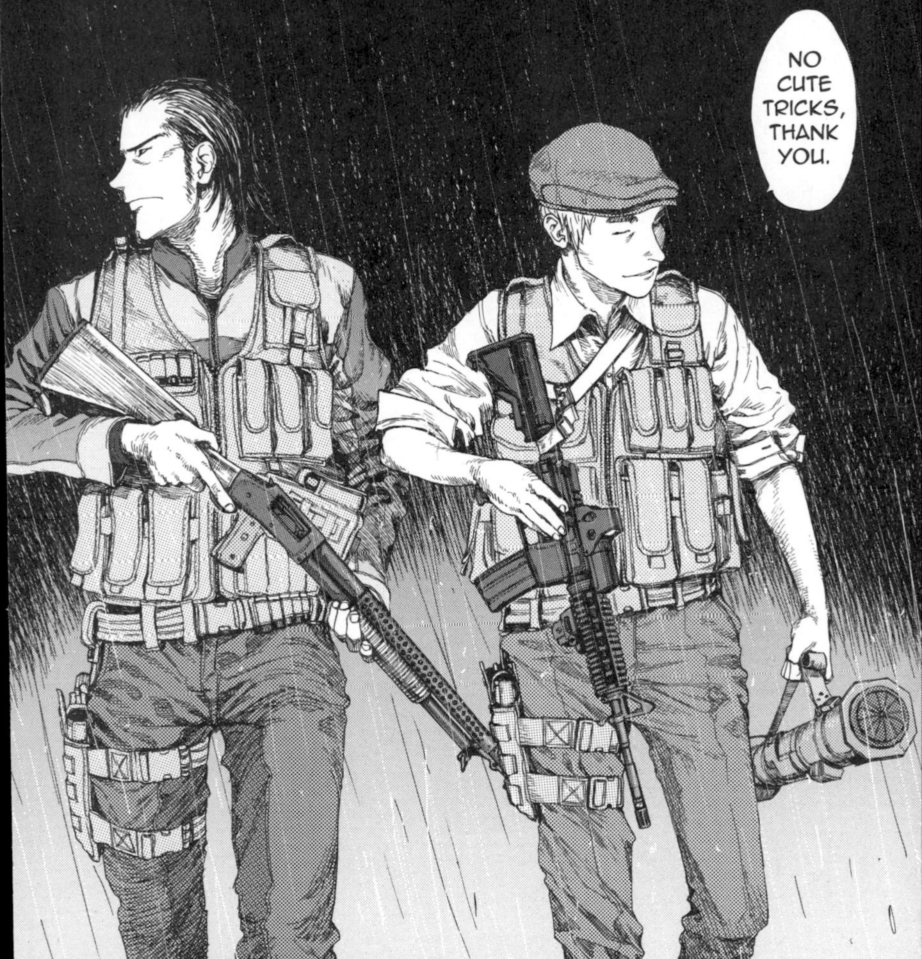
NO CUTE TRICKS, THANK YOU.

File 09: Killtacular

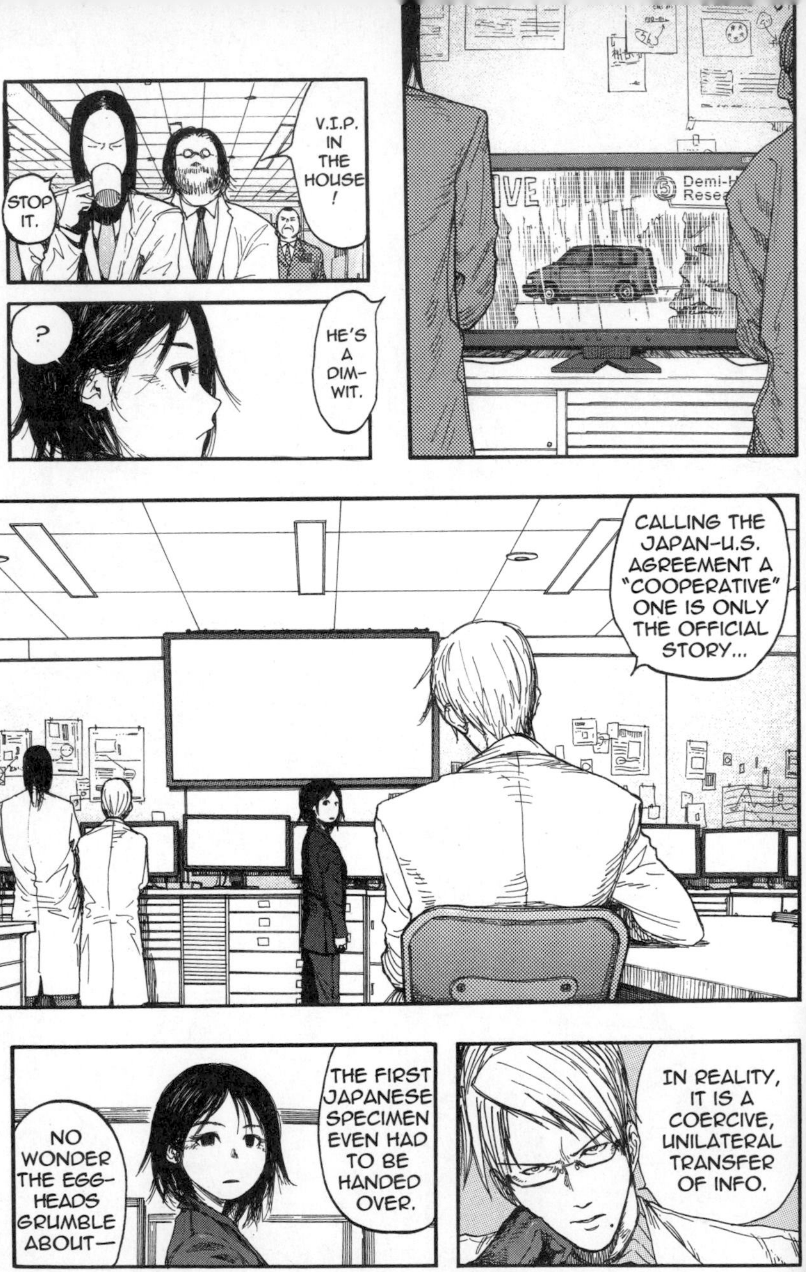
V.I.P. IN THE HOUSE!
STOP IT.
HE'S A DIM-WIT.
?
CALLING THE JAPAN-U.S. AGREEMENT A "COOPERATIVE" ONE IS ONLY THE OFFICIAL STORY...
IN REALITY, IT IS A COERCIVE, UNILATERAL TRANSFER OF INFO.
THE FIRST JAPANESE SPECIMEN EVEN HAD TO BE HANDED OVER.
NO WONDER THE EGG-HEADS GRUMBLE ABOUT—

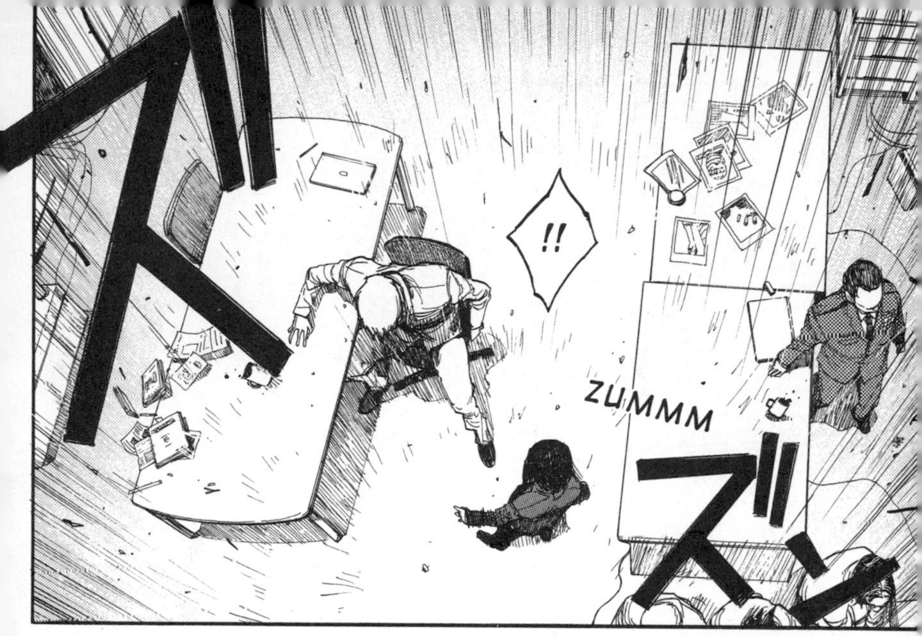
!!
ZUMMM

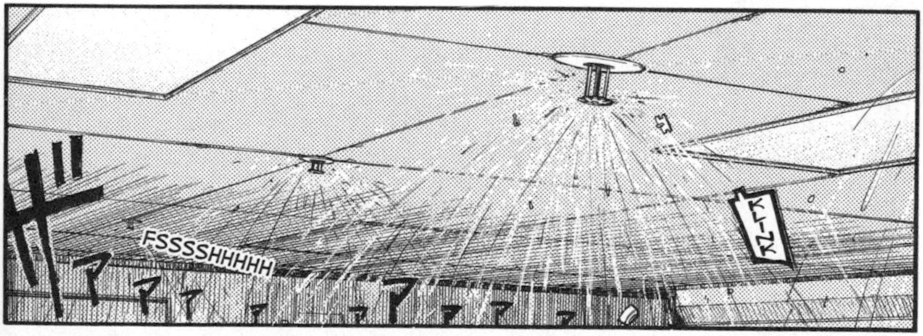
FSSSSHHHHH
KLINK

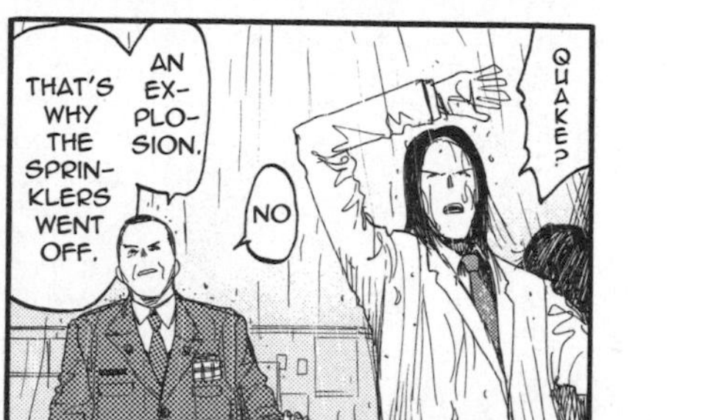
QUAKE?
NO
AN EX-PLO-SION.
THAT'S WHY THE SPRIN-KLERS WENT OFF.

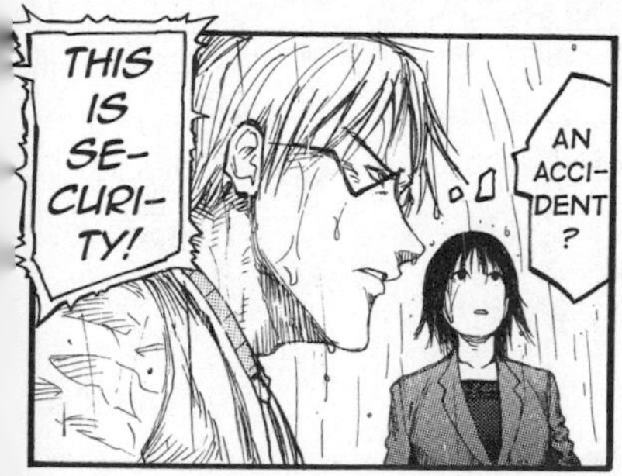
AN ACCI-DENT?
THIS IS SE-CURI-TY!

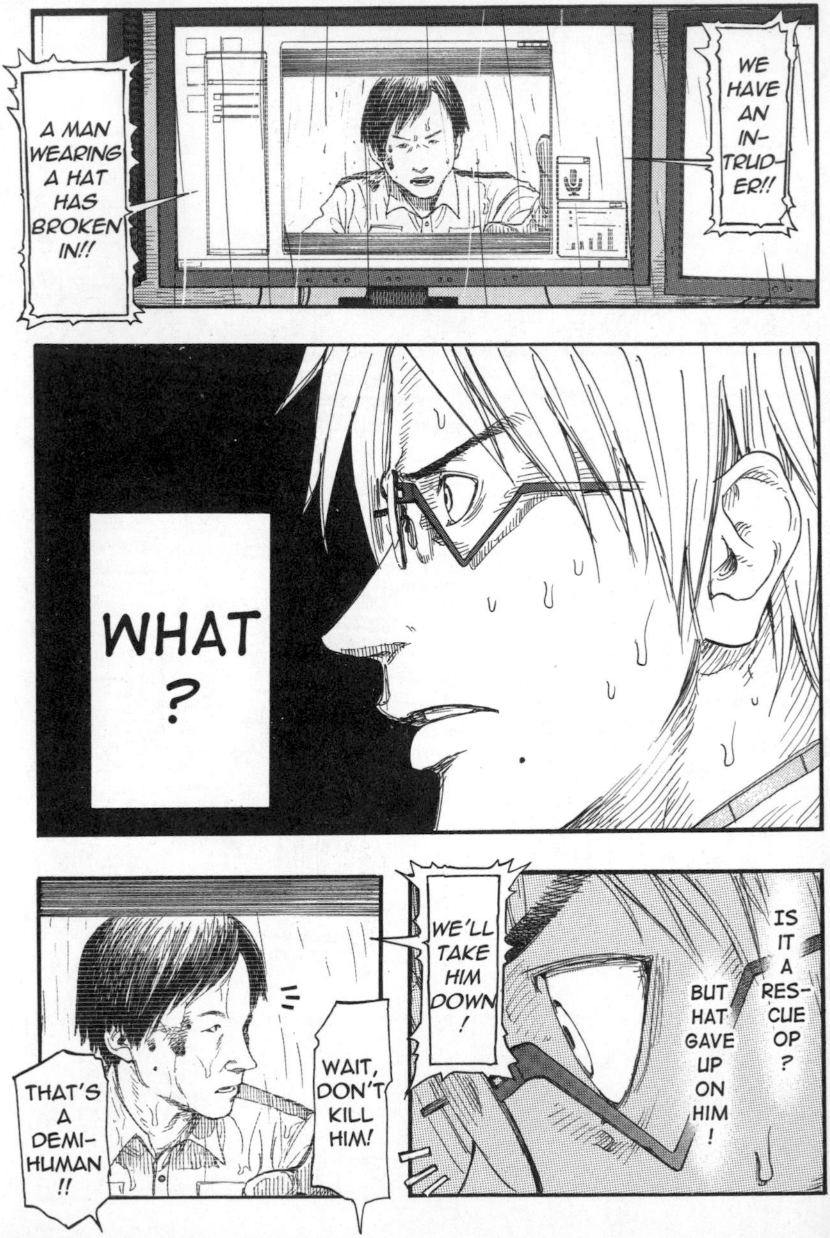
WE HAVE AN INTRUDER!!
A MAN WEARING A HAT HAS BROKEN IN!!
WHAT?
IS IT A RESCUE OP?
BUT HAT GAVE UP ON HIM!
WE'LL TAKE HIM DOWN!
WAIT, DON'T KILL HIM!
THAT'S A DEMI-HUMAN!!

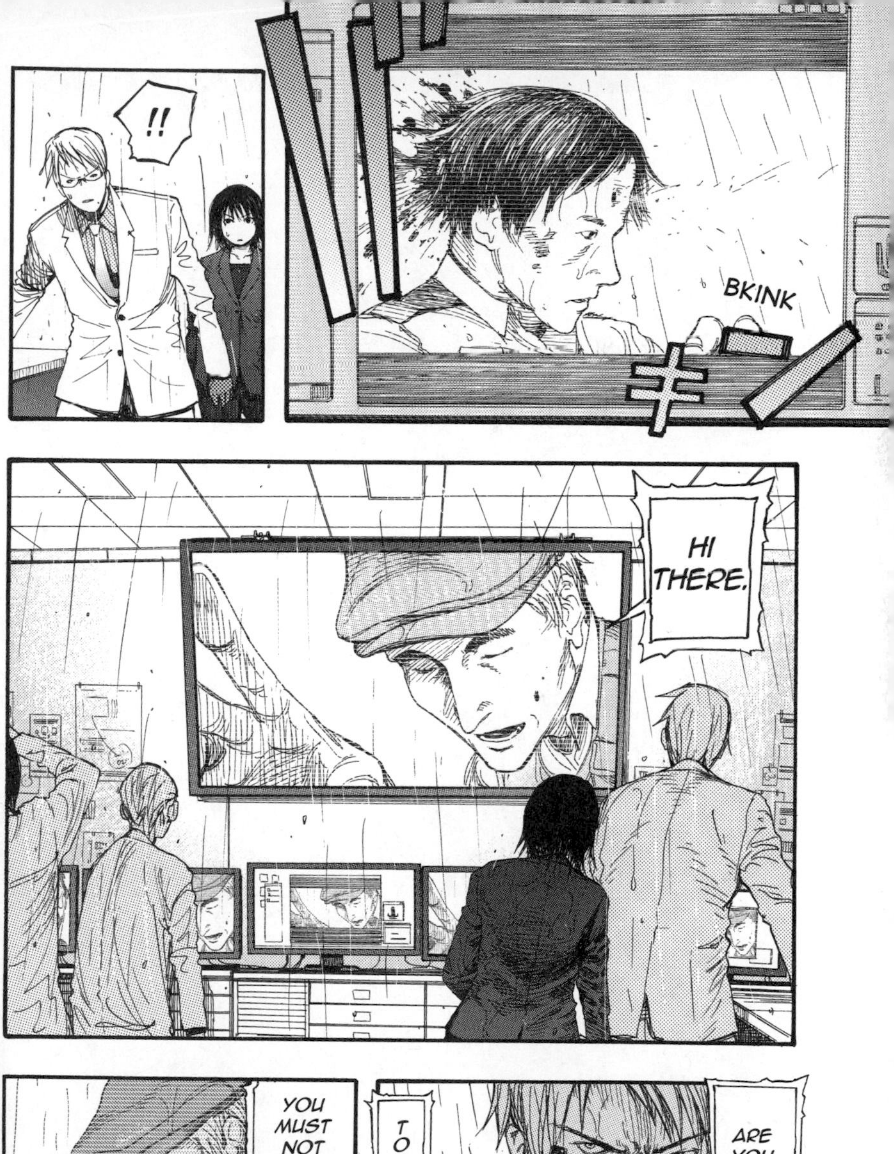
BKINK
!!
HI THERE.
ARE YOU HOME,
TOZAKI?
YOU MUST NOT KNOW WHY I'M HERE YET.
BUT ...

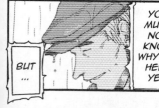

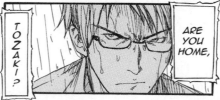

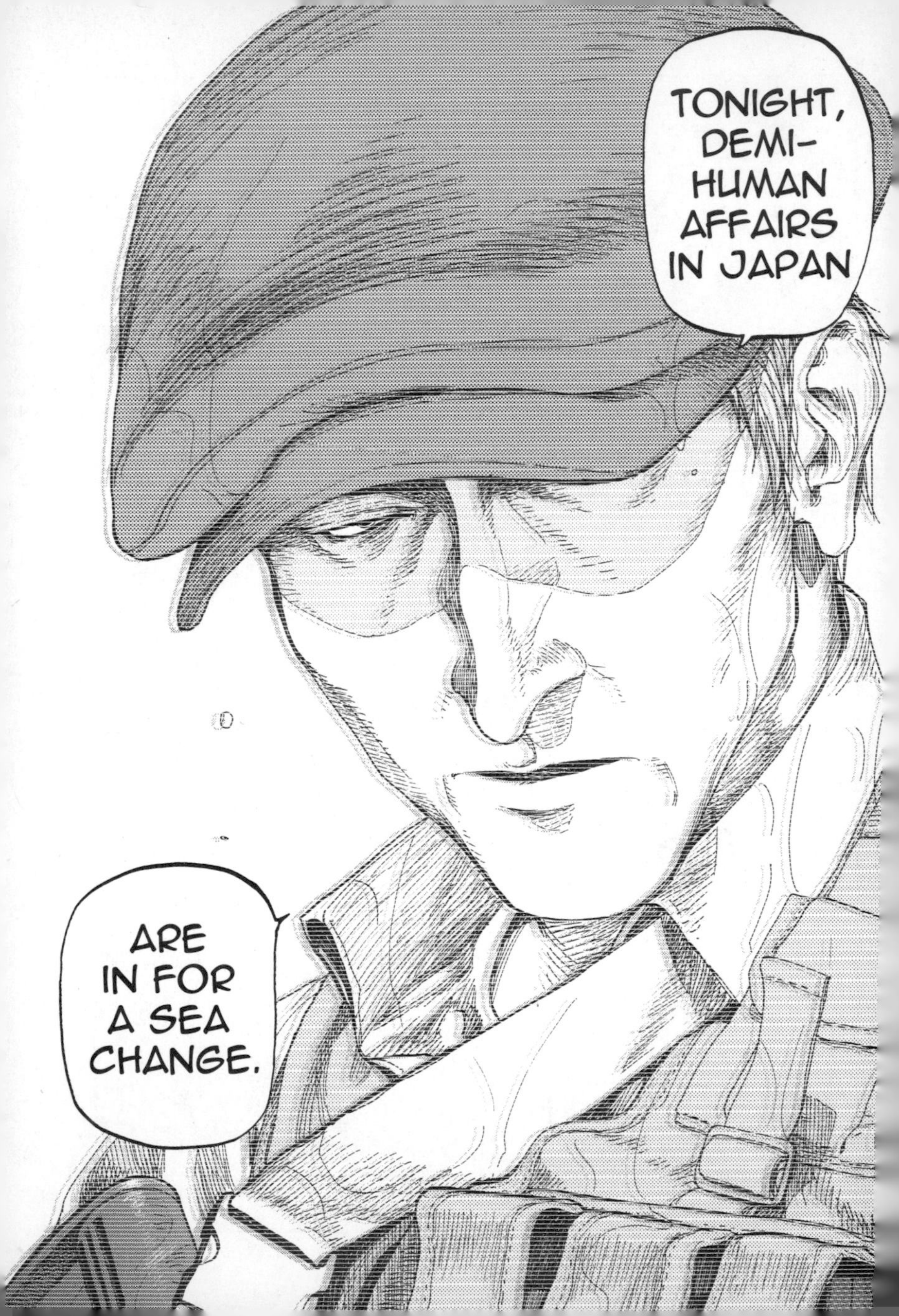
TONIGHT, DEMI-HUMAN AFFAIRS IN JAPAN
ARE IN FOR A SEA CHANGE.

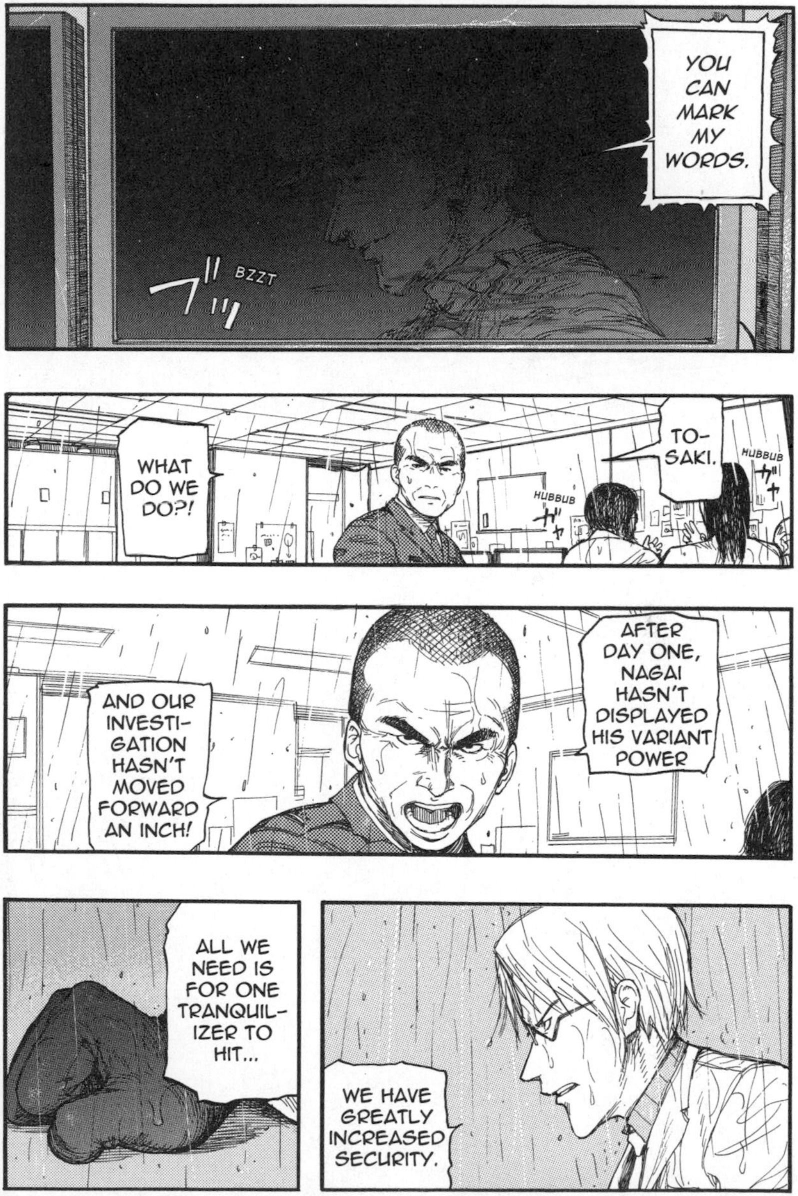
YOU CAN MARK MY WORDS.
BZZT
TO-SAKI.
HUBBUB
HUBBUB
WHAT DO WE DO?!
AFTER DAY ONE, NAGAI HASN'T DISPLAYED HIS VARIANT POWER
AND OUR INVESTIGATION HASN'T MOVED FORWARD AN INCH!
WE HAVE GREATLY INCREASED SECURITY.
ALL WE NEED IS FOR ONE TRANQUILIZER TO HIT...

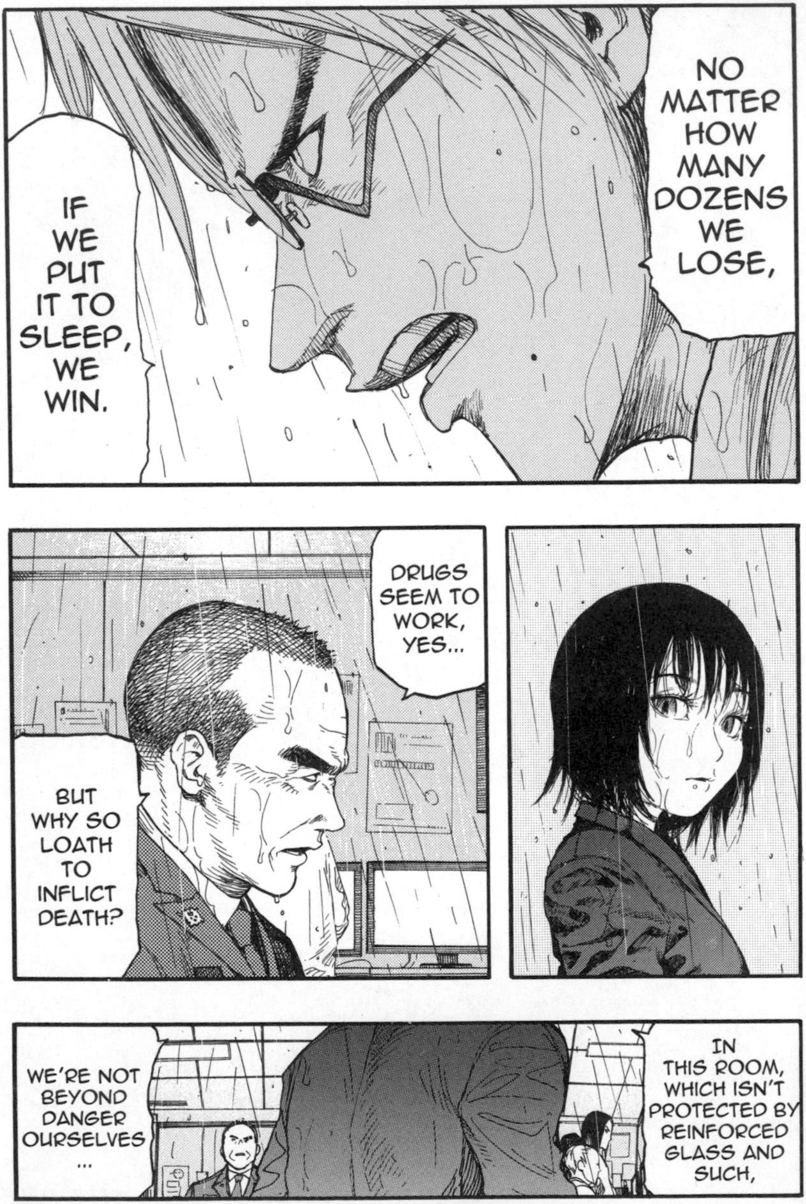
NO MATTER HOW MANY DOZENS WE LOSE,
IF WE PUT IT TO SLEEP, WE WIN.
DRUGS SEEM TO WORK, YES...
BUT WHY SO LOATH TO INFLICT DEATH?
IN THIS ROOM, WHICH ISN'T PROTECTED BY REINFORCED GLASS AND SUCH,
WE'RE NOT BEYOND DANGER OURSELVES ...

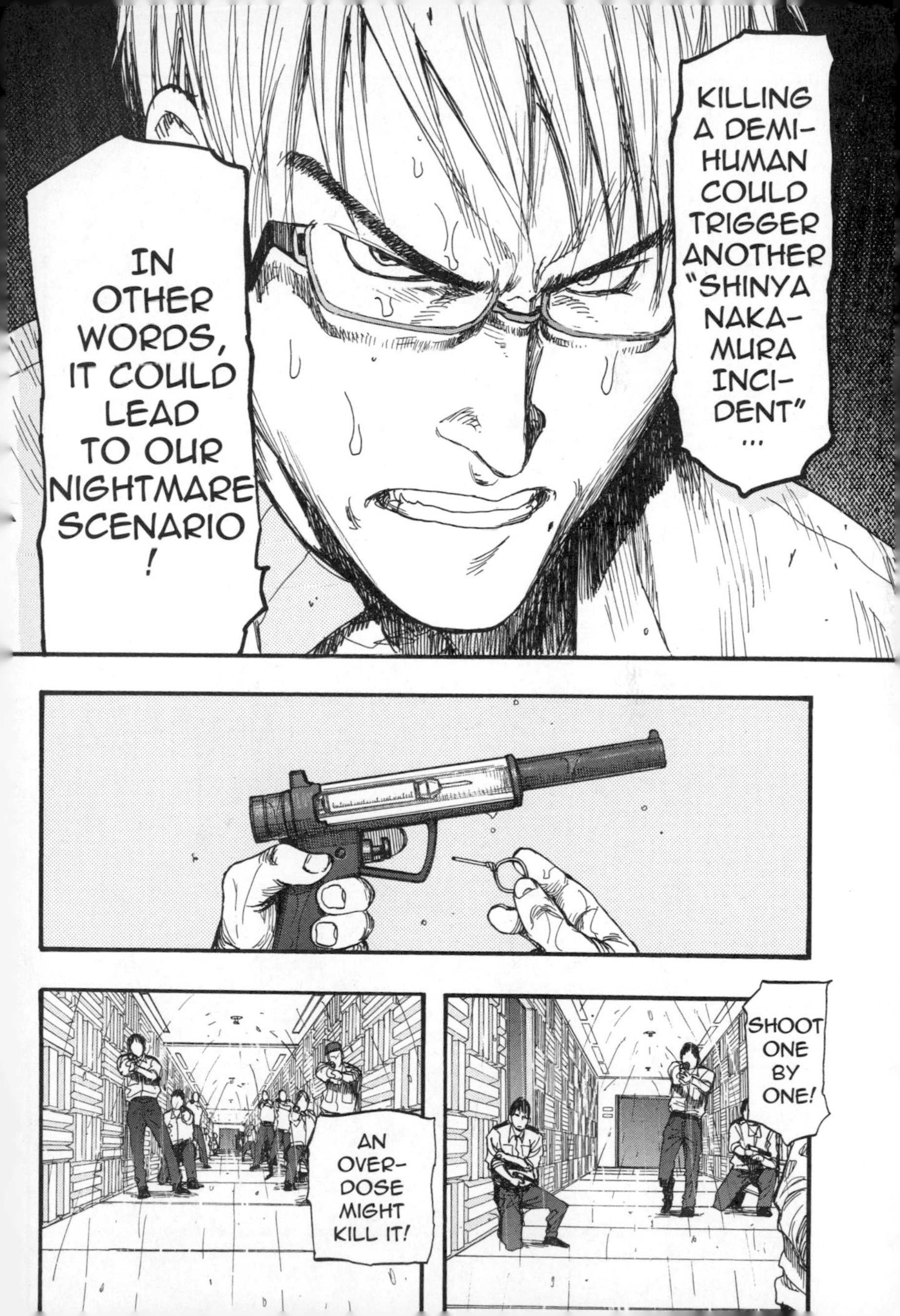
KILLING A DEMI-HUMAN COULD TRIGGER ANOTHER "SHINYA NAKAMURA INCIDENT"...
IN OTHER WORDS, IT COULD LEAD TO OUR NIGHTMARE SCENARIO!
SHOOT ONE BY ONE!
AN OVER-DOSE MIGHT KILL IT!

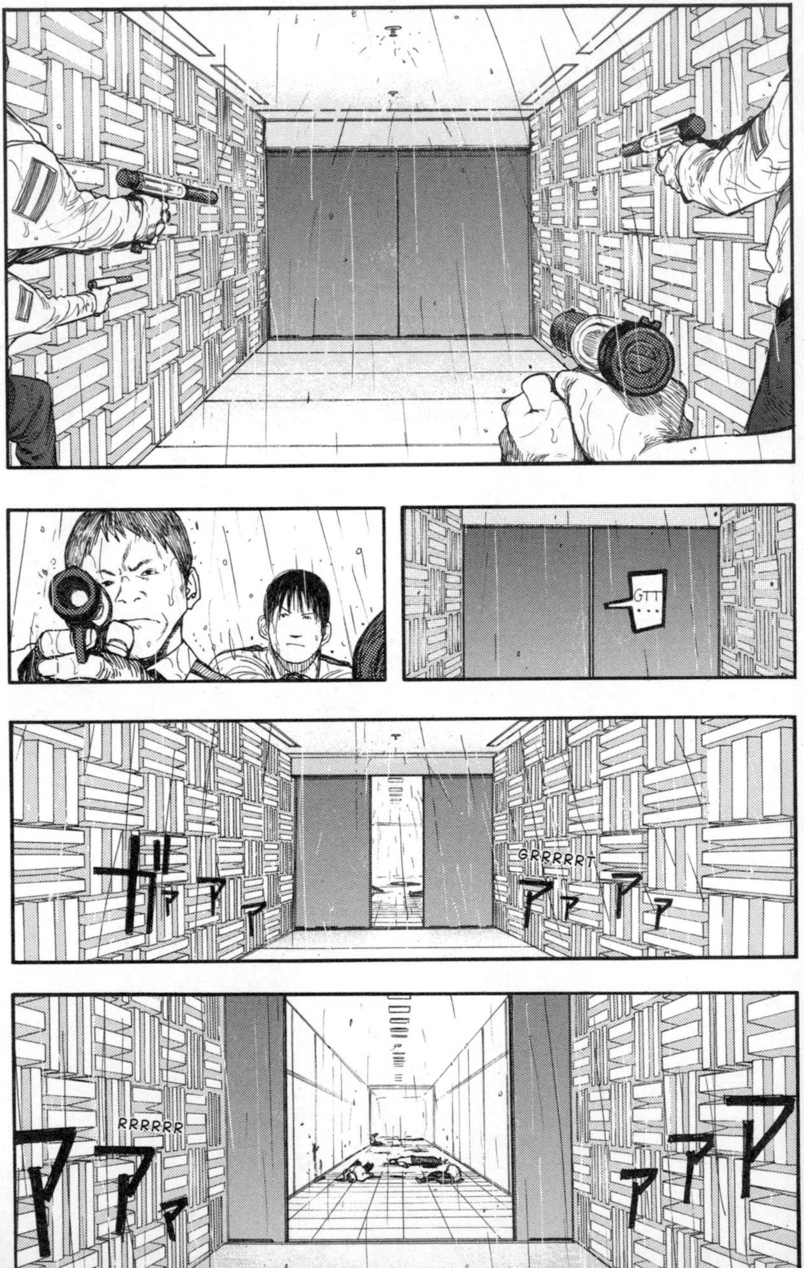
GTT
...
GRRRRRT
RRRRRR

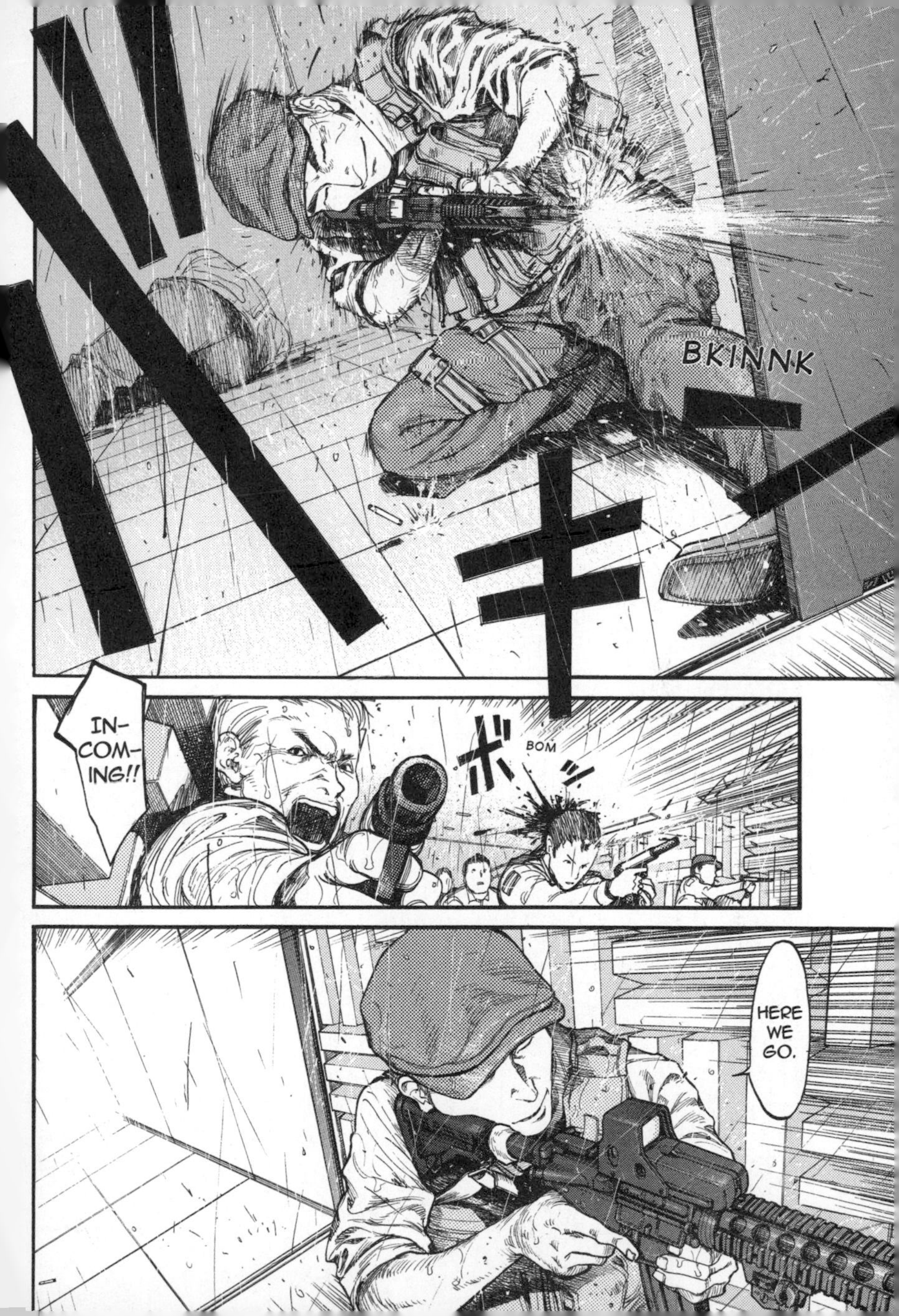
BKINNK
IN-COM-ING!!
ボッ
BOM
HERE WE GO.

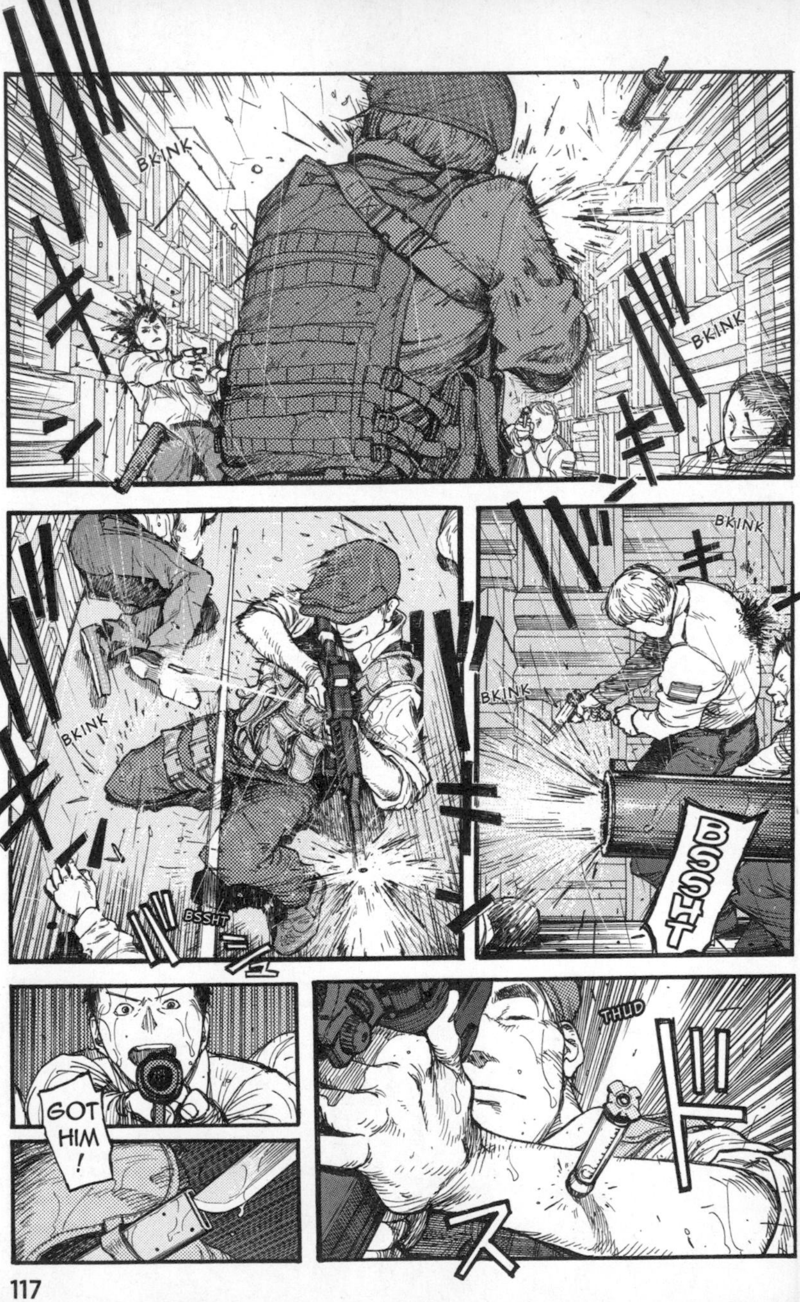
BKINK
BKINK
BKINK
BKINK
BSSSHT
BKINK
BSSHT
THUD
GOT HIM !

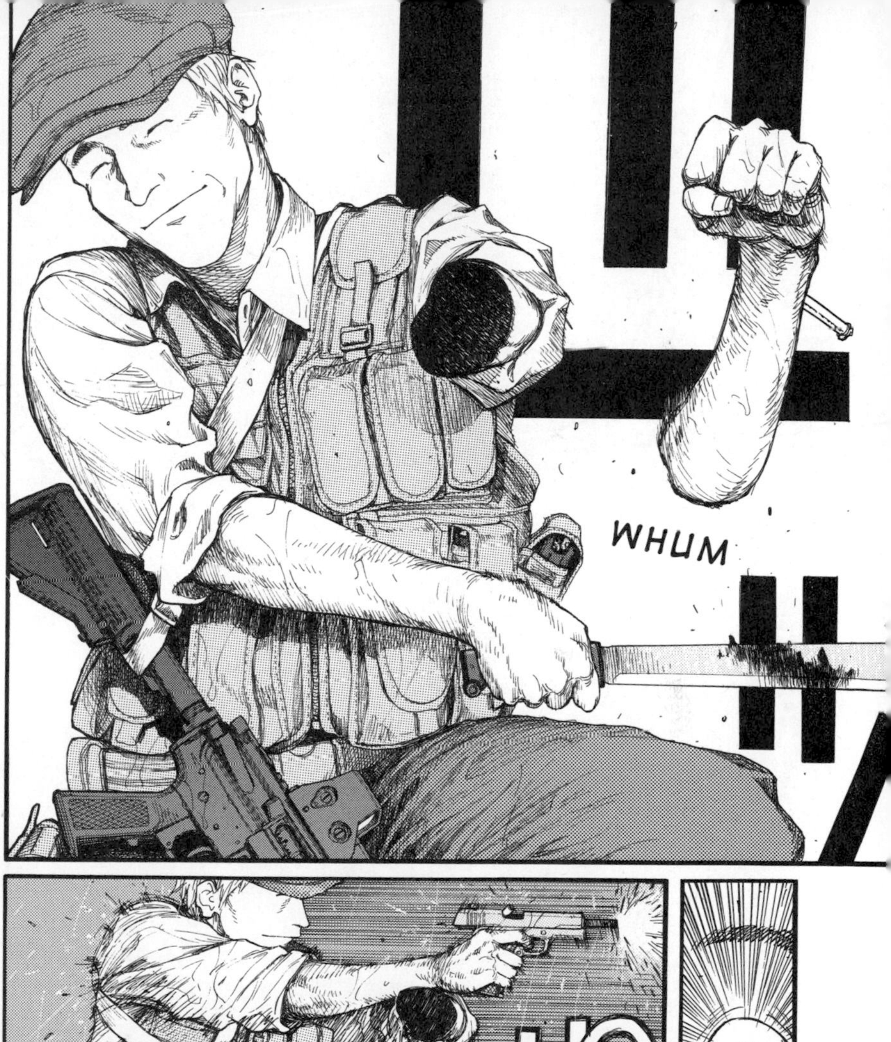
WHUM

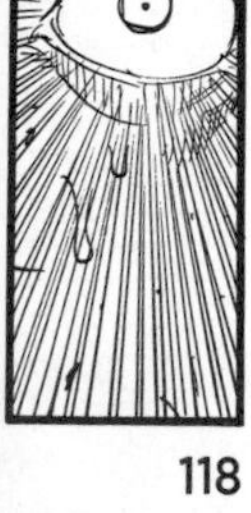

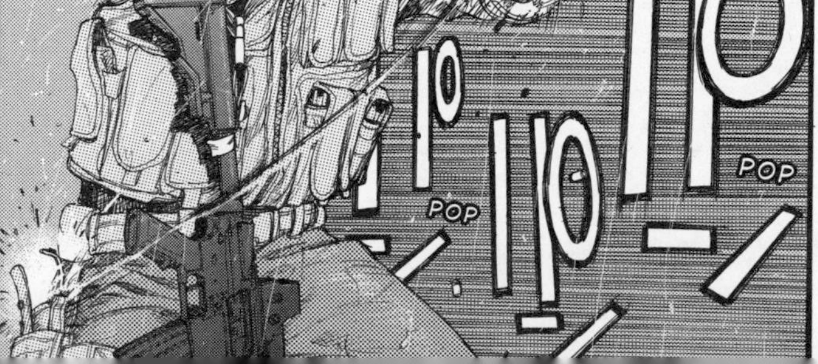
POP
POP

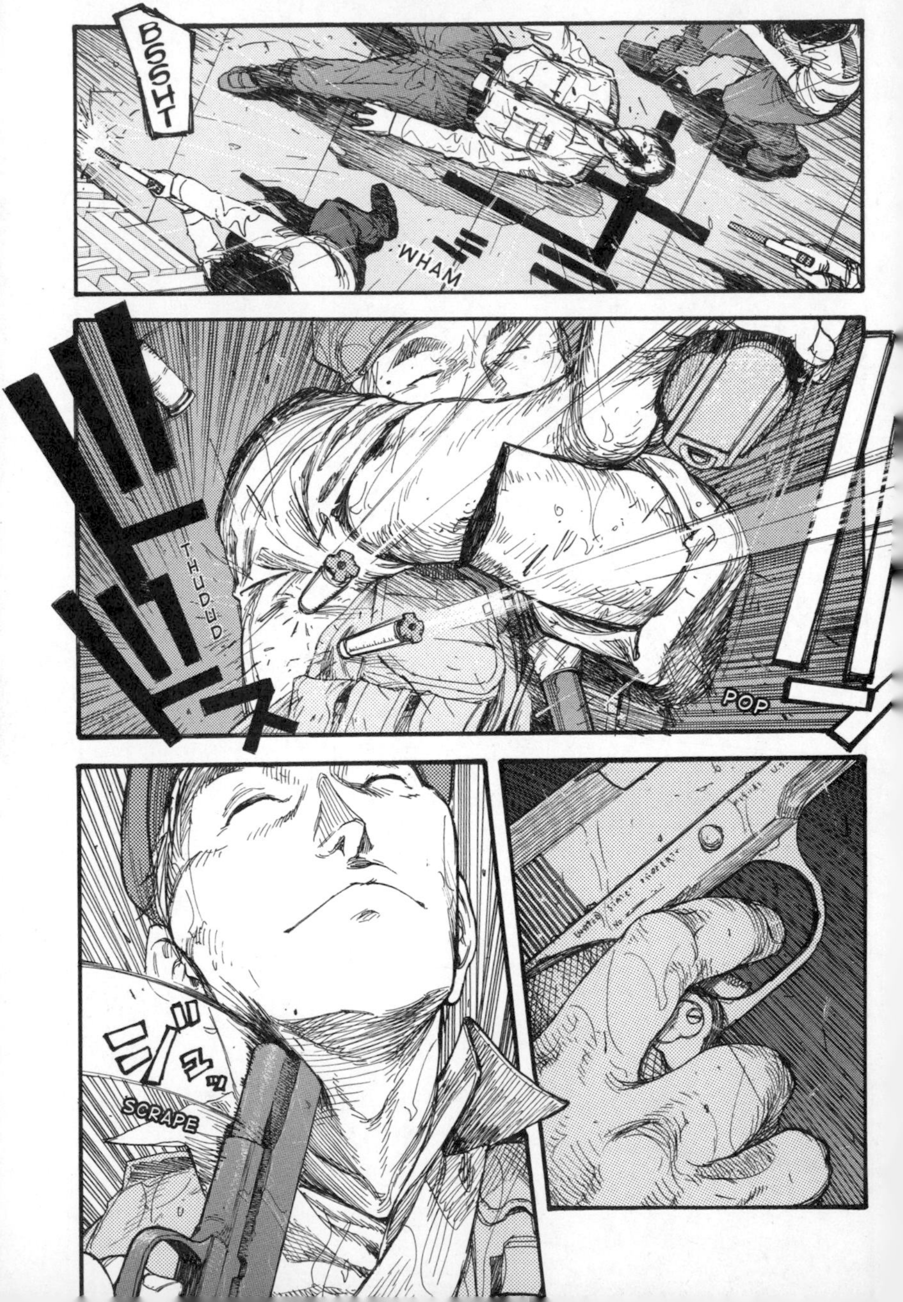
BSSHT
WHAM
THUDUD
POP
SCRAPE

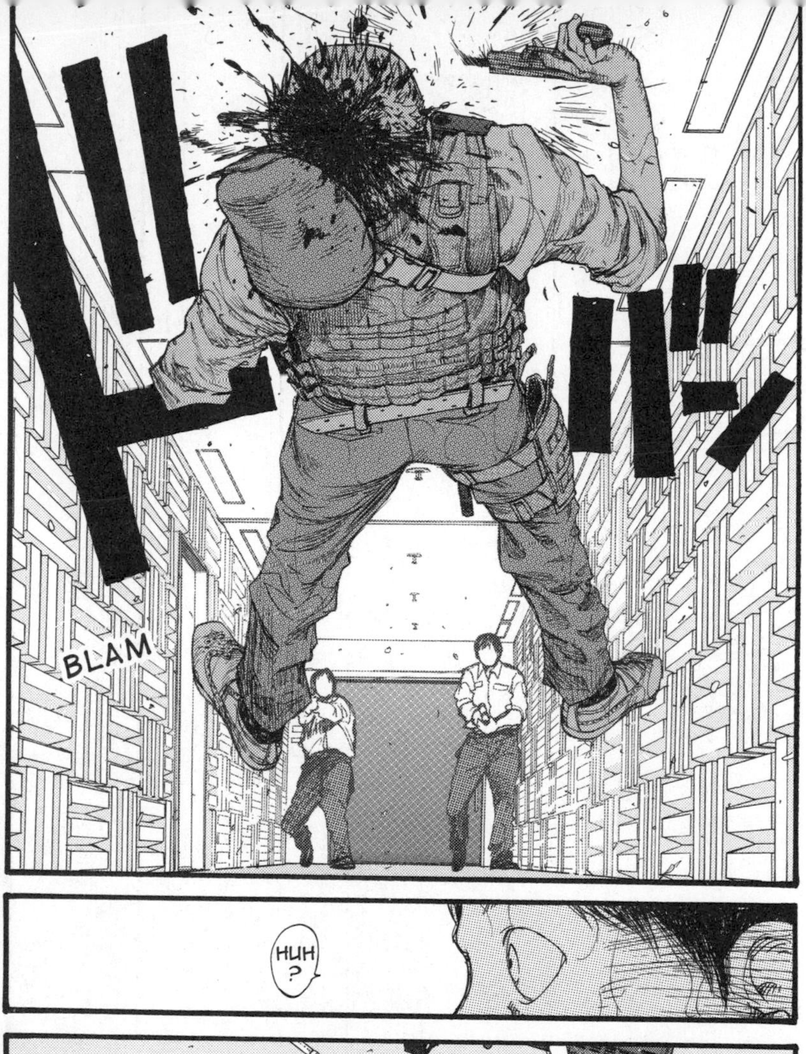
BLAM

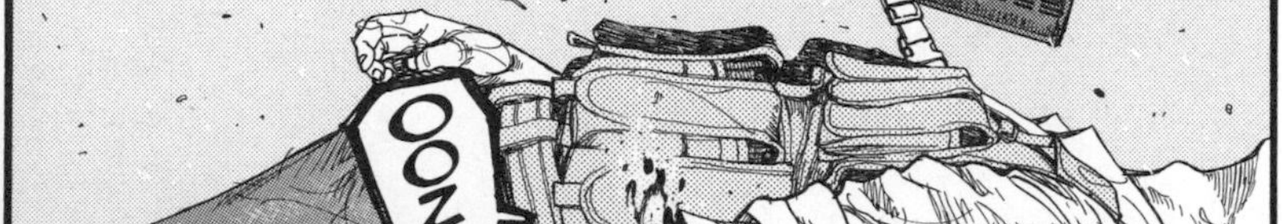
HUH?

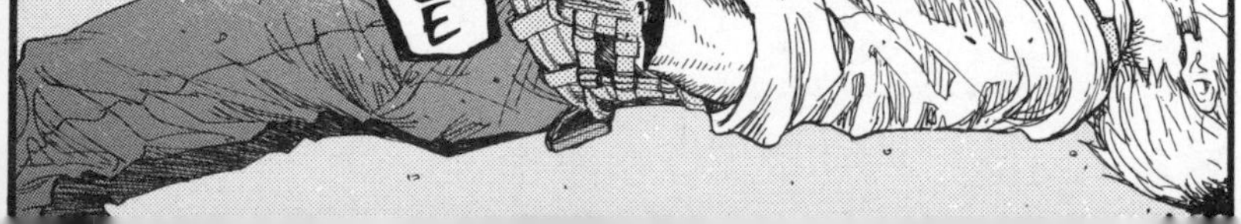
OOZE

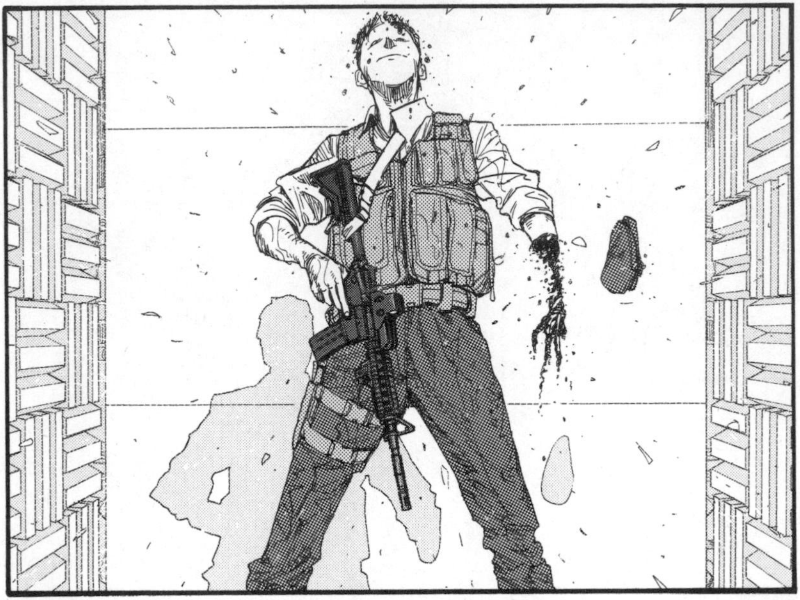
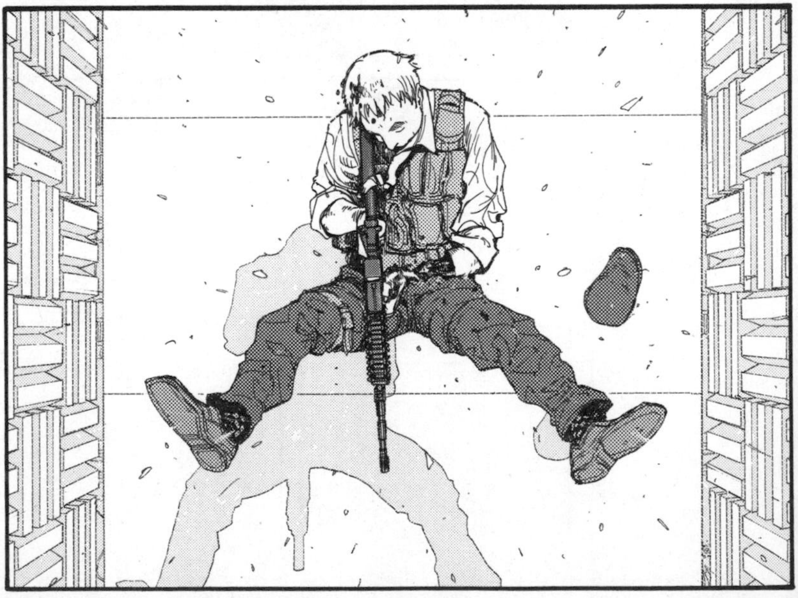

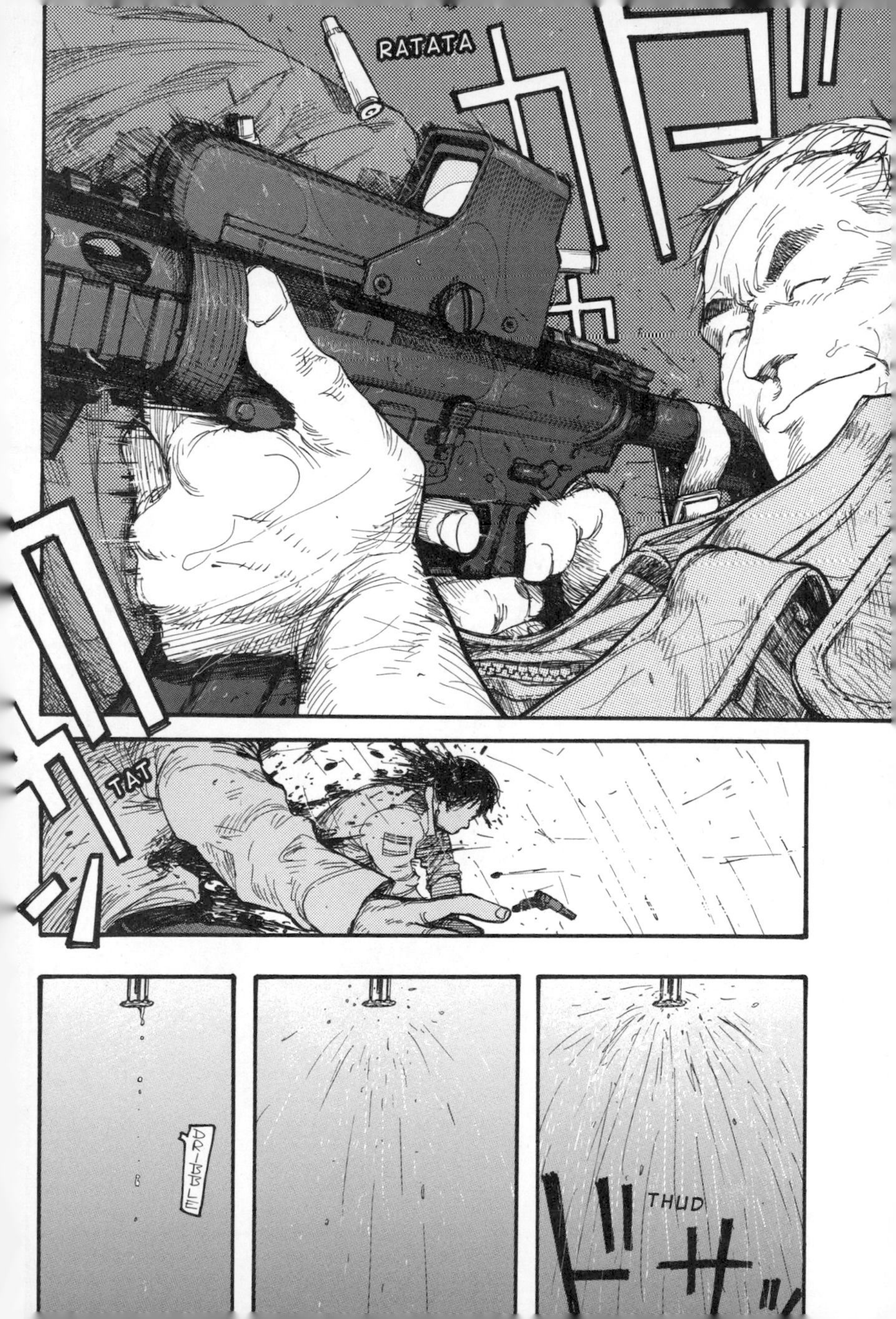
RATATA
TAT
THUD
DRIBBLE

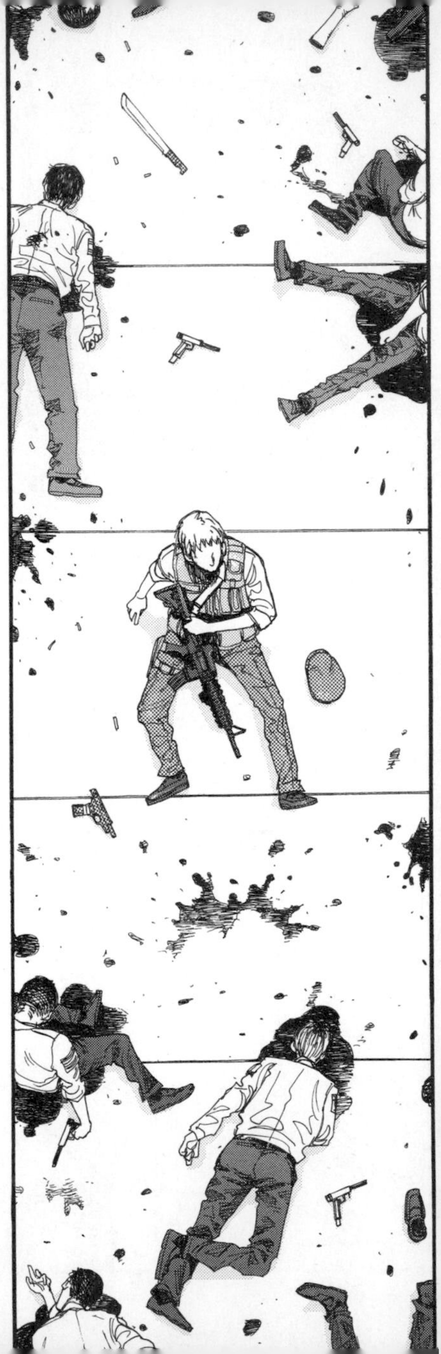
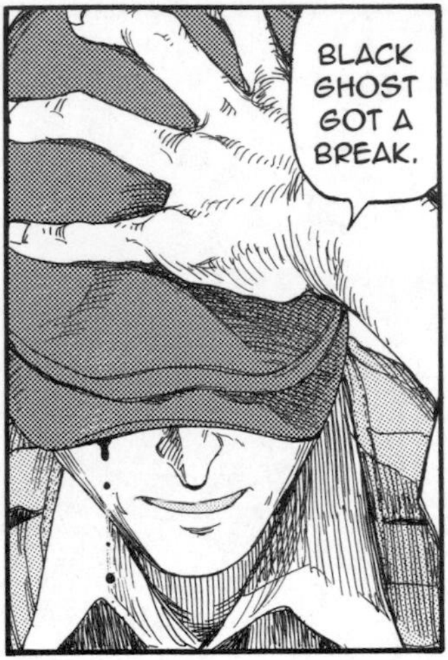
BLACK GHOST GOT A BREAK.
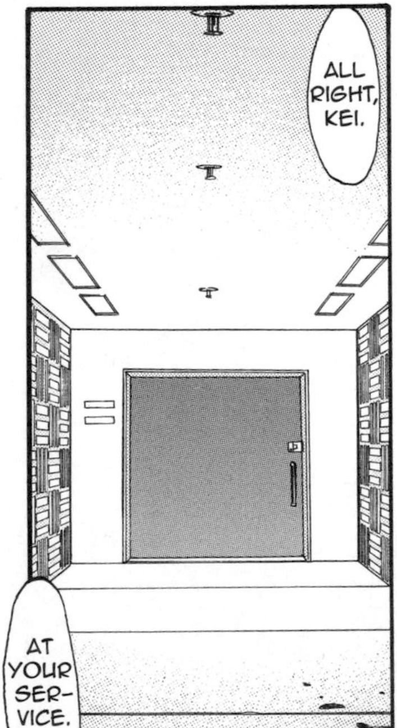
ALL RIGHT, KEI.
AT YOUR SER-VICE.

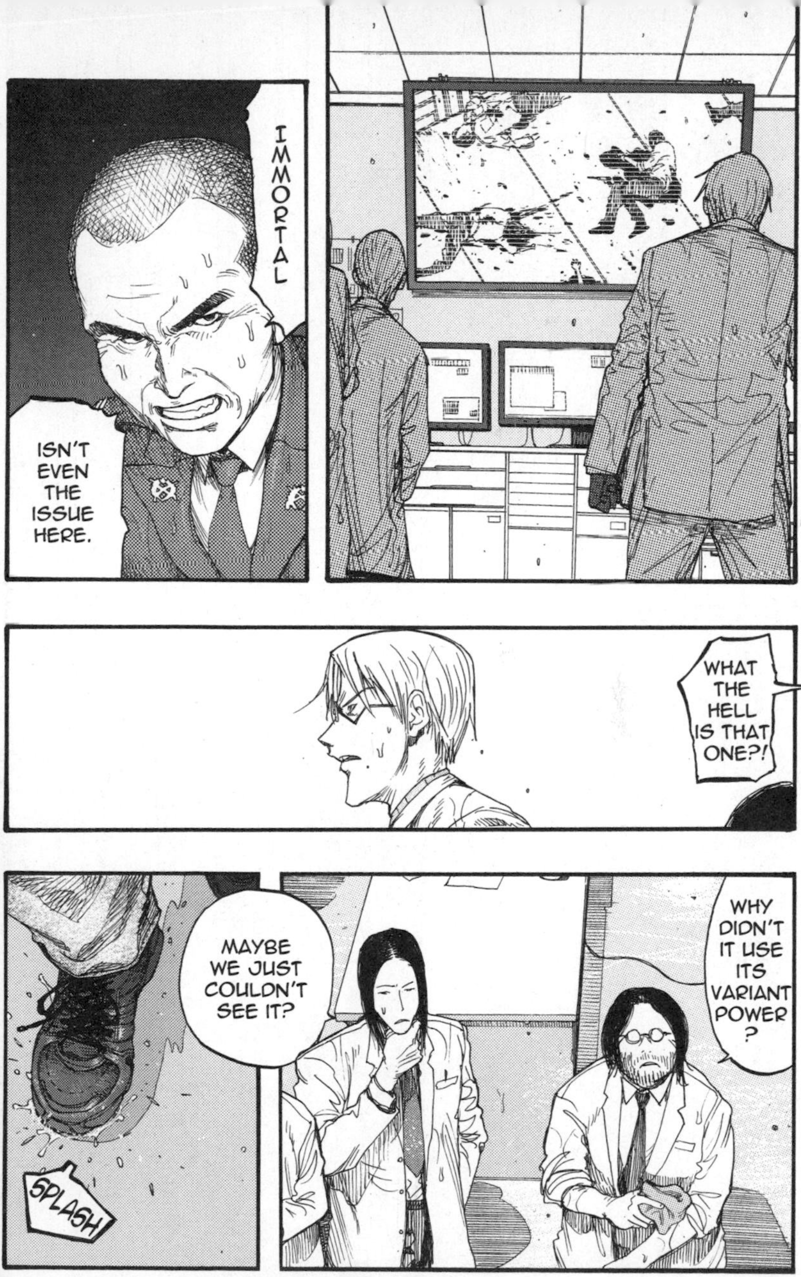
IMMORTAL
ISN'T EVEN THE ISSUE HERE.
WHAT THE HELL IS THAT ONE?!
WHY DIDN'T IT USE ITS VARIANT POWER?
MAYBE WE JUST COULDN'T SEE IT?
SPLASH

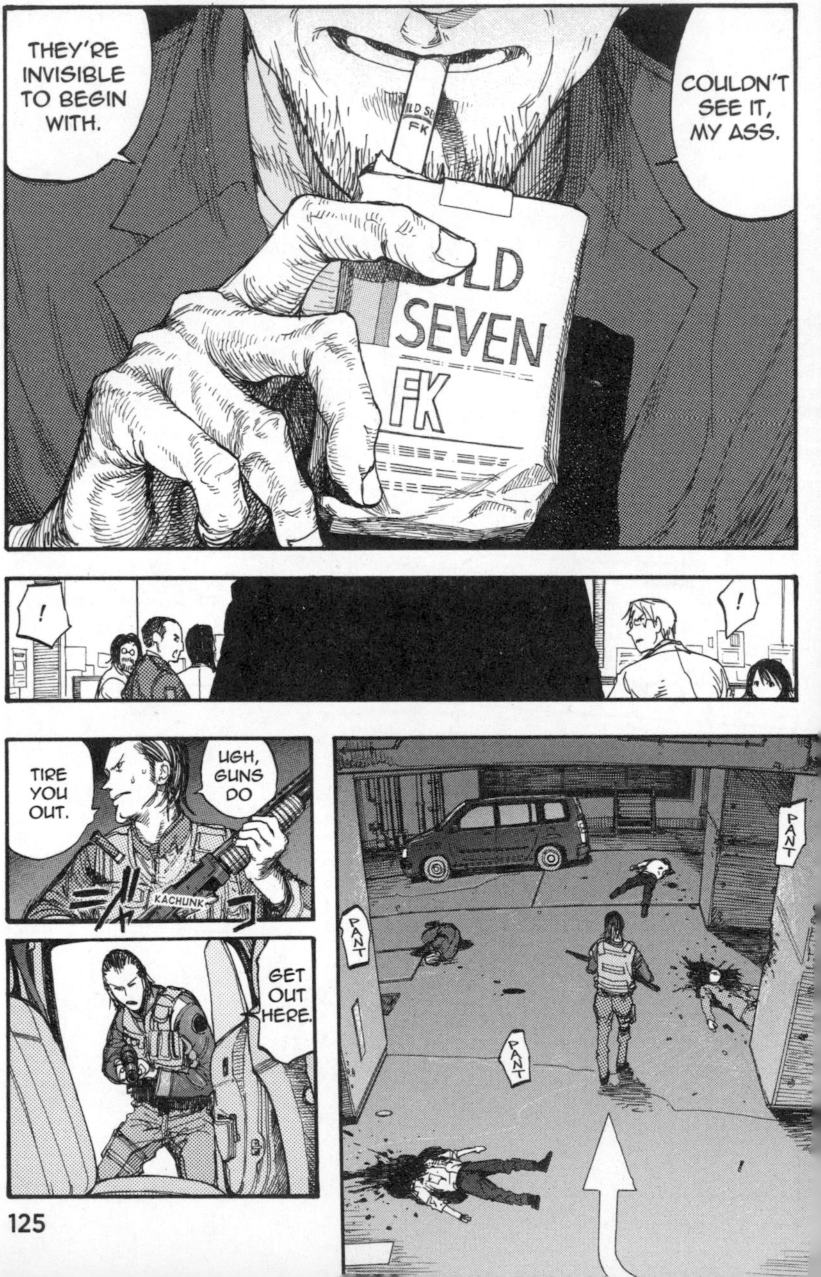
COULDN'T SEE IT, MY ASS.
THEY'RE INVISIBLE TO BEGIN WITH.
SEVEN
FK
!
!
PANT
PANT
PANT
UGH, GUNS DO
TIRE YOU OUT.
KACHUNK
GET OUT HERE.

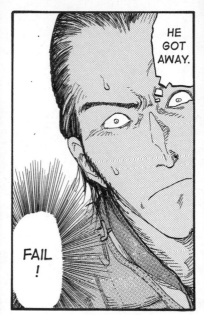

HE GOT AWAY.

FAIL!

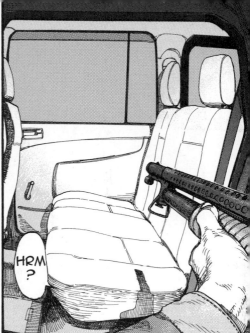

HRM?

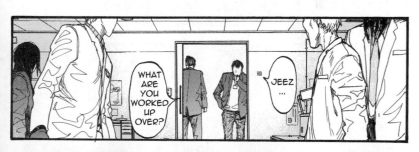

WHAT ARE YOU WORKED UP OVER?

JEEZ...

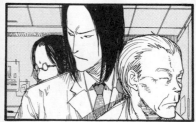

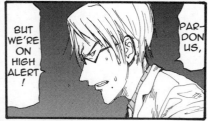

BUT WE'RE ON HIGH ALERT!

PARDON US,

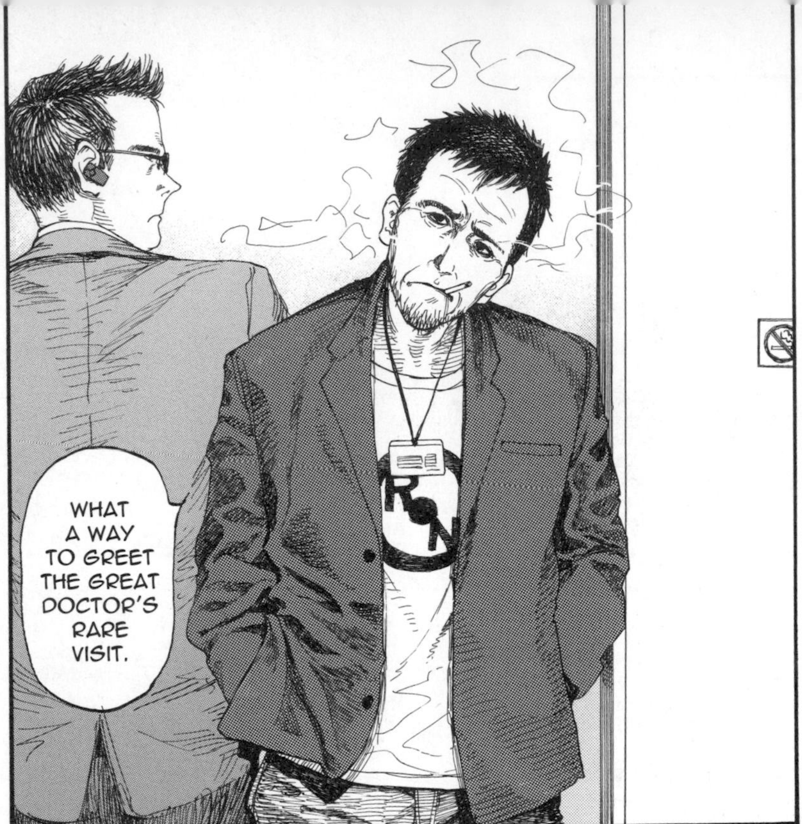
WHAT A WAY TO GREET THE GREAT DOCTOR'S RARE VISIT.

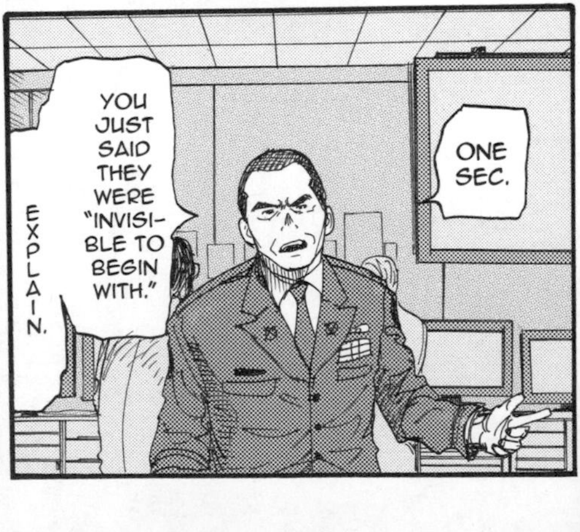
ONE SEC.
YOU JUST SAID THEY WERE "INVISIBLE TO BEGIN WITH."
EXPLAIN.

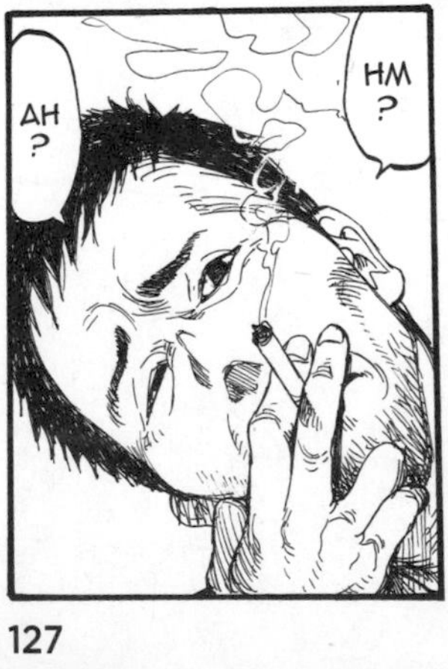
HM?
AH?

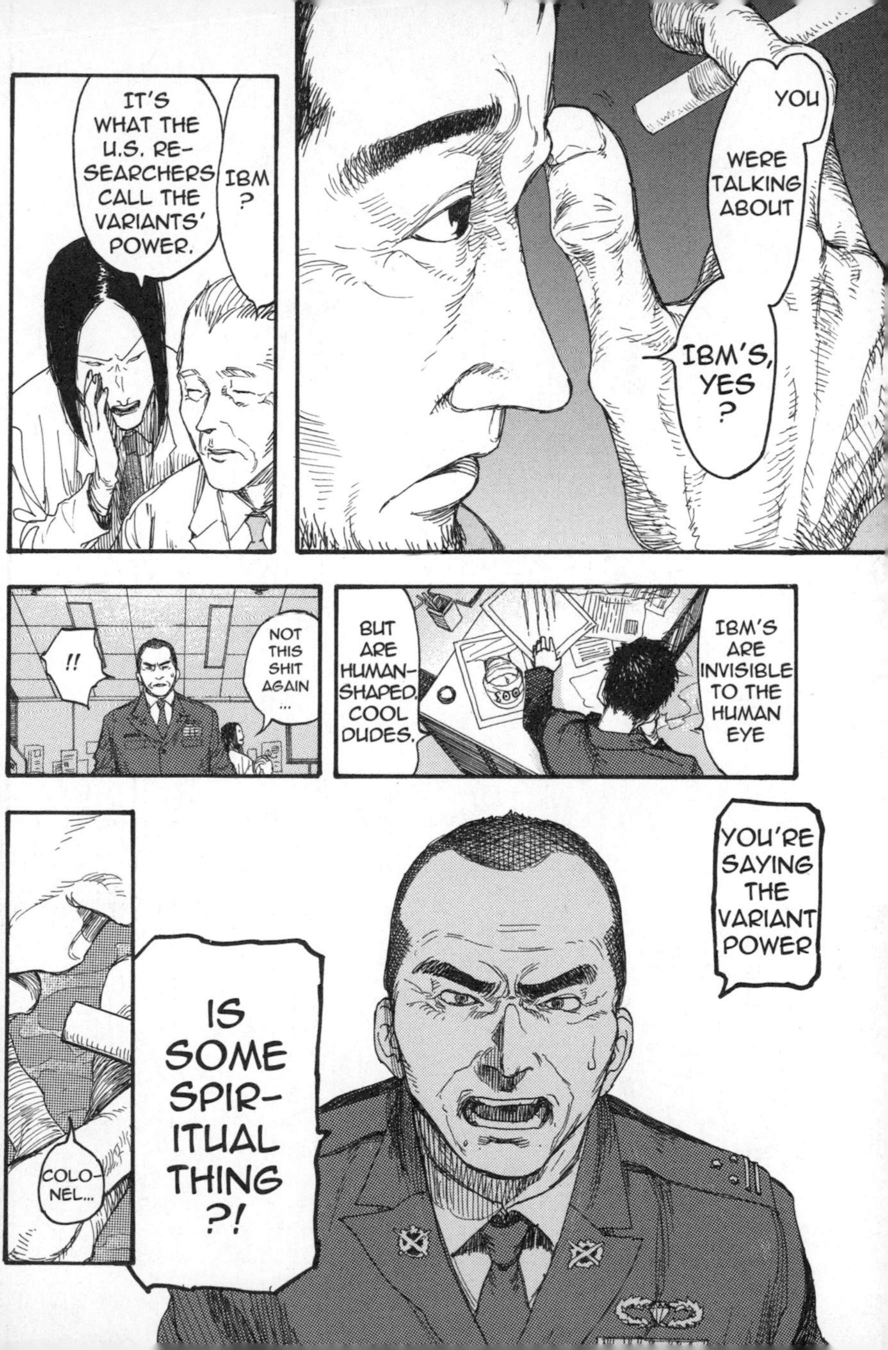
YOU WERE TALKING ABOUT IBM'S, YES?
IBM?
IT'S WHAT THE U.S. RESEARCHERS CALL THE VARIANTS' POWER.
IBM'S ARE INVISIBLE TO THE HUMAN EYE
BUT ARE HUMAN-SHAPED, COOL DUDES.
NOT THIS SHIT AGAIN ...
!!
YOU'RE SAYING THE VARIANT POWER
IS SOME SPIRITUAL THING?!
COLONEL...

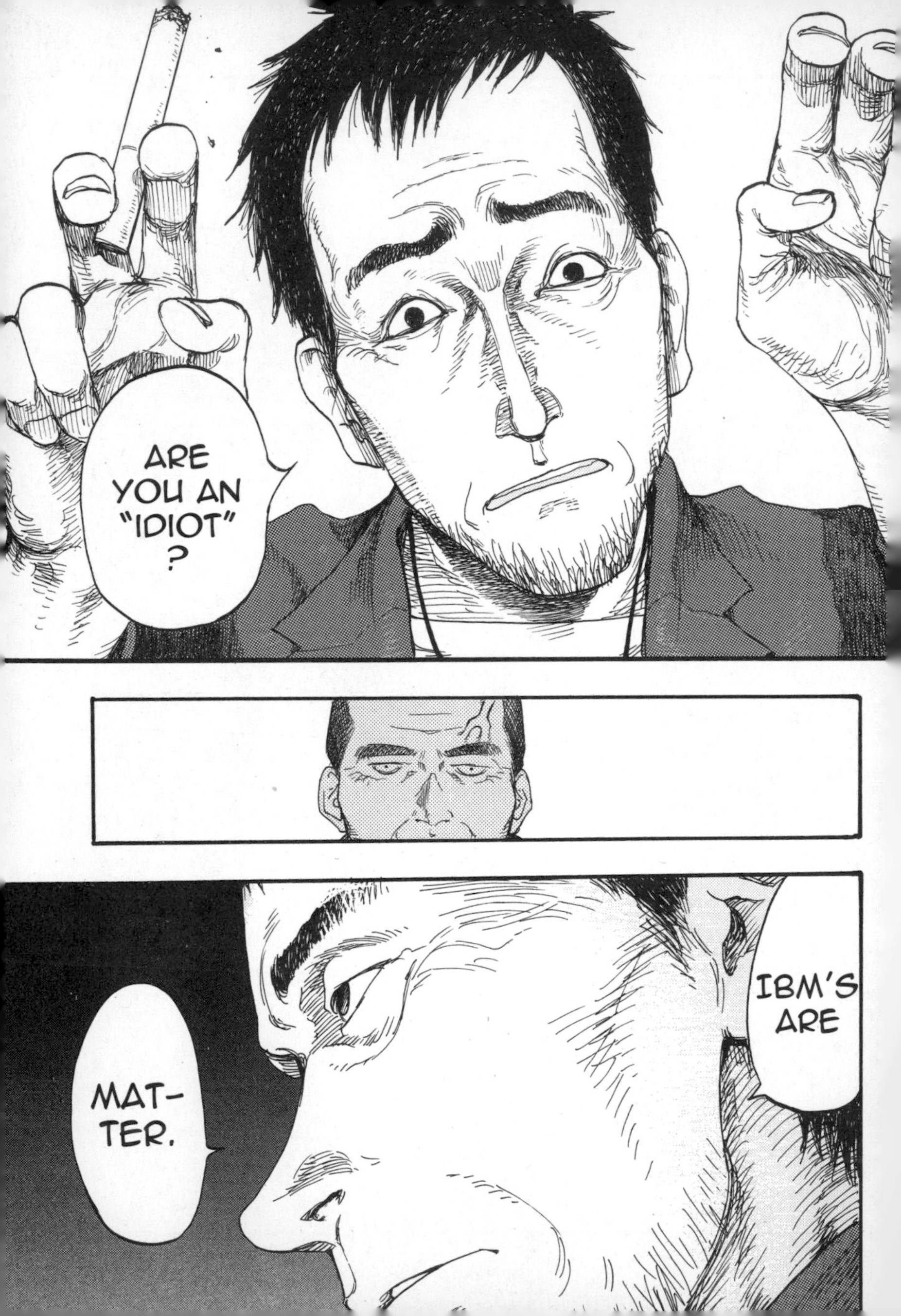
ARE YOU AN "IDIOT" ?
IBM'S ARE
MAT-TER.

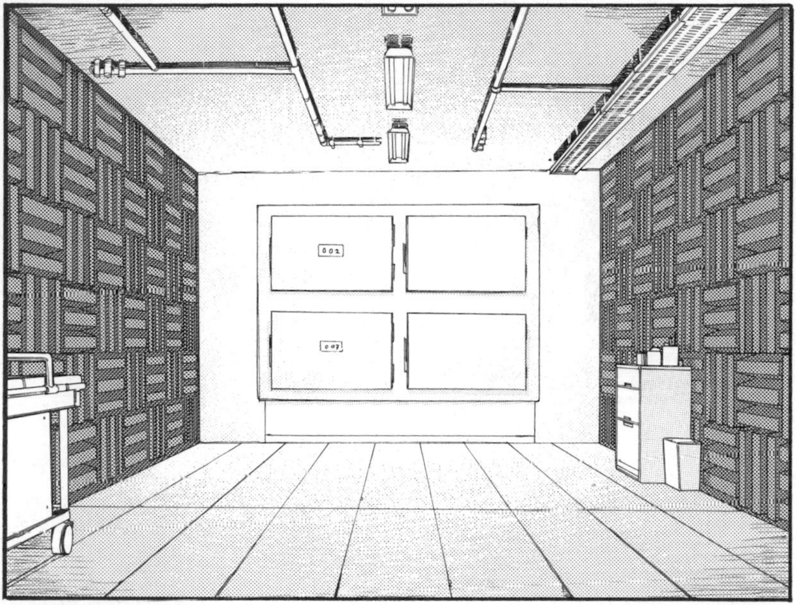
002
003

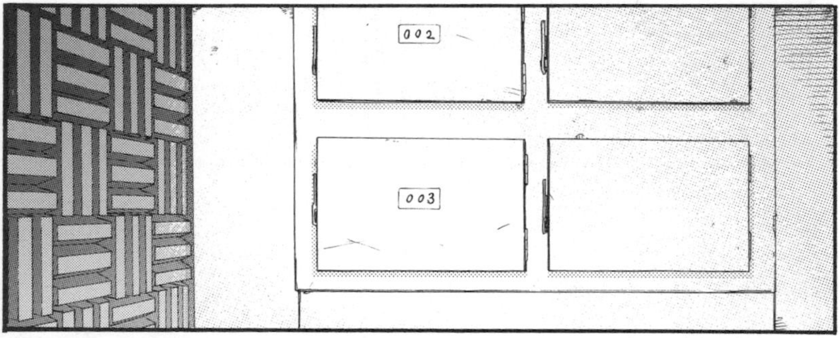
002
003

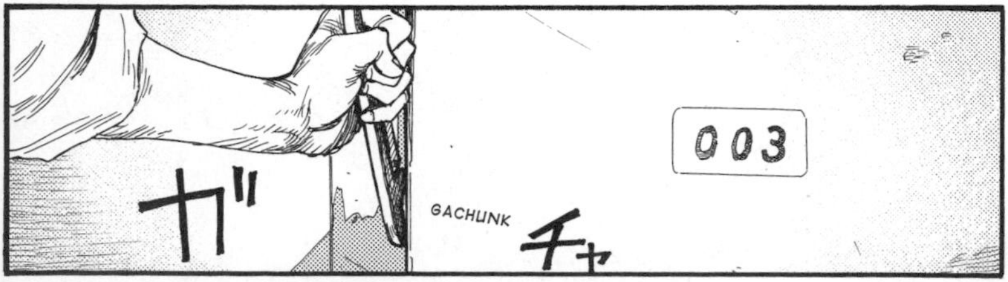
003
ガ
チャ
GACHUNK

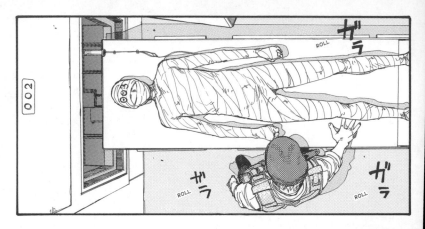

ROLL ガラ

ROLL ガラ

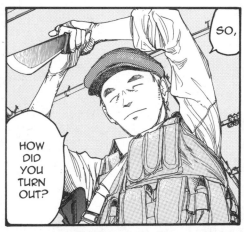

SO,

HOW DID YOU TURN OUT?

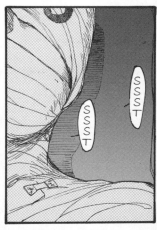

SSST

SSST

SSST

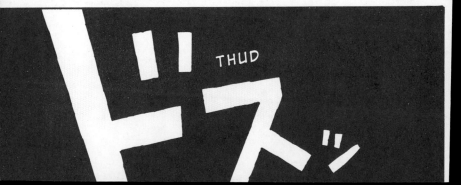

THUD

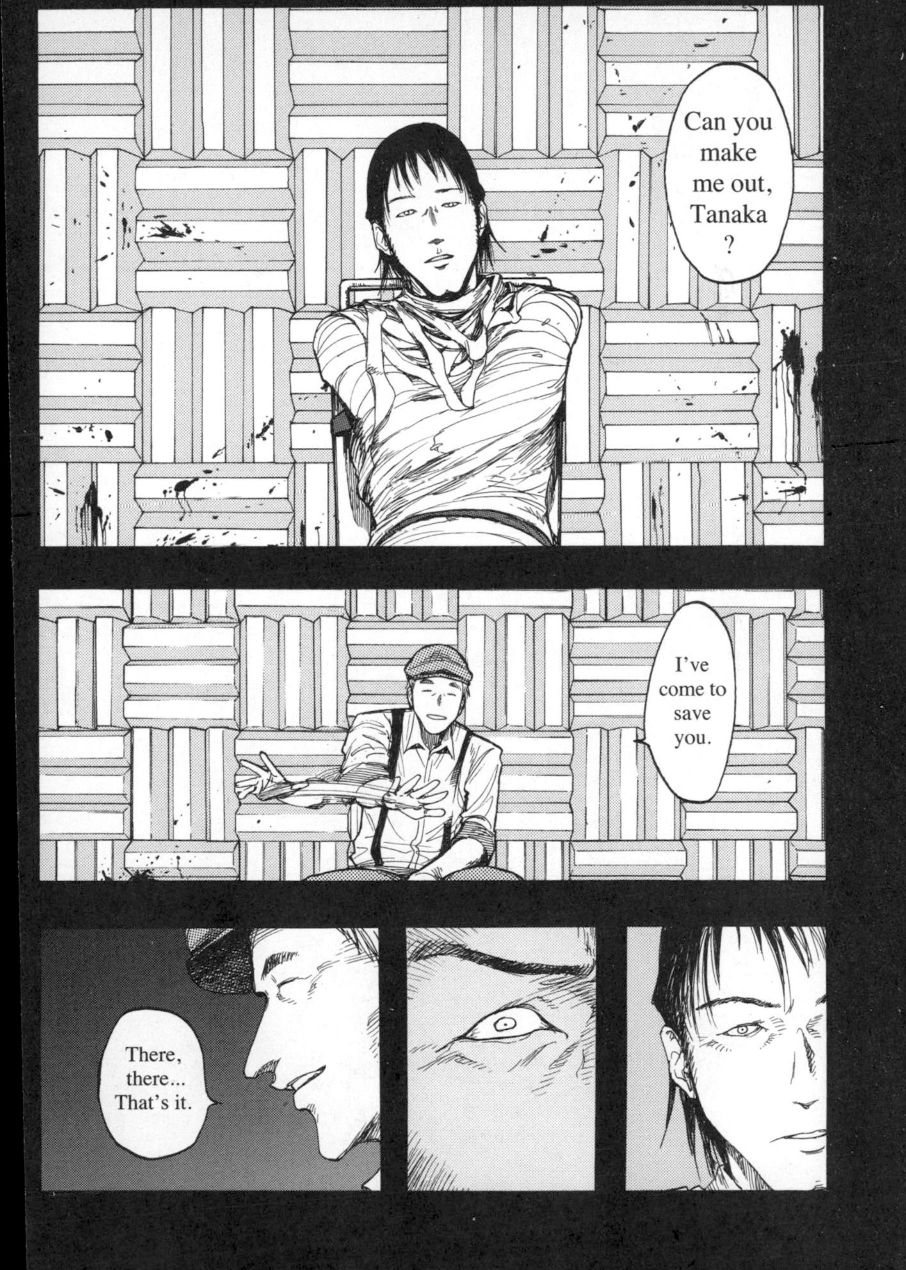
Can you make me out, Tanaka ?
I've come to save you.
There, there... That's it.

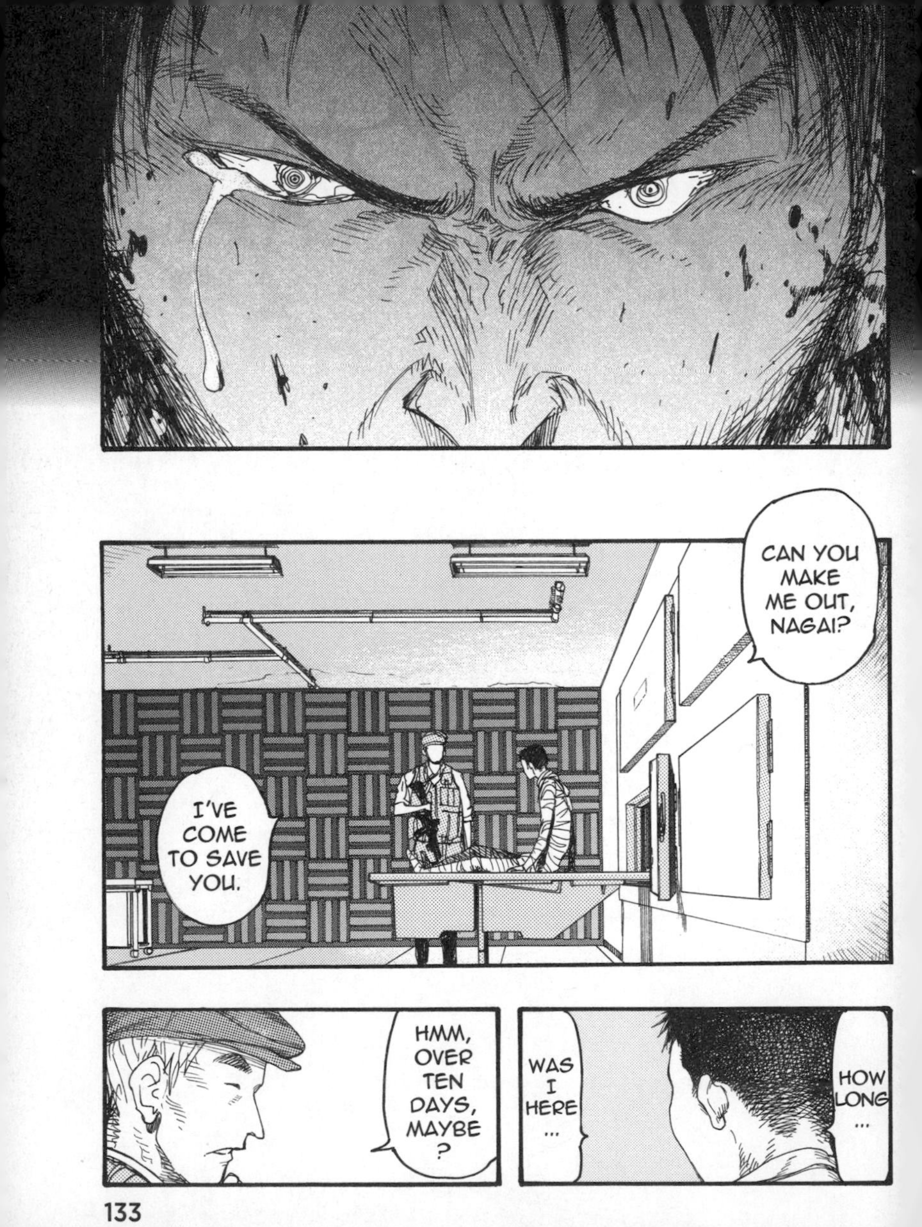
CAN YOU MAKE ME OUT, NAGAI?
I'VE COME TO SAVE YOU.
HOW LONG ...
WAS I HERE ...
HMM, OVER TEN DAYS, MAYBE?

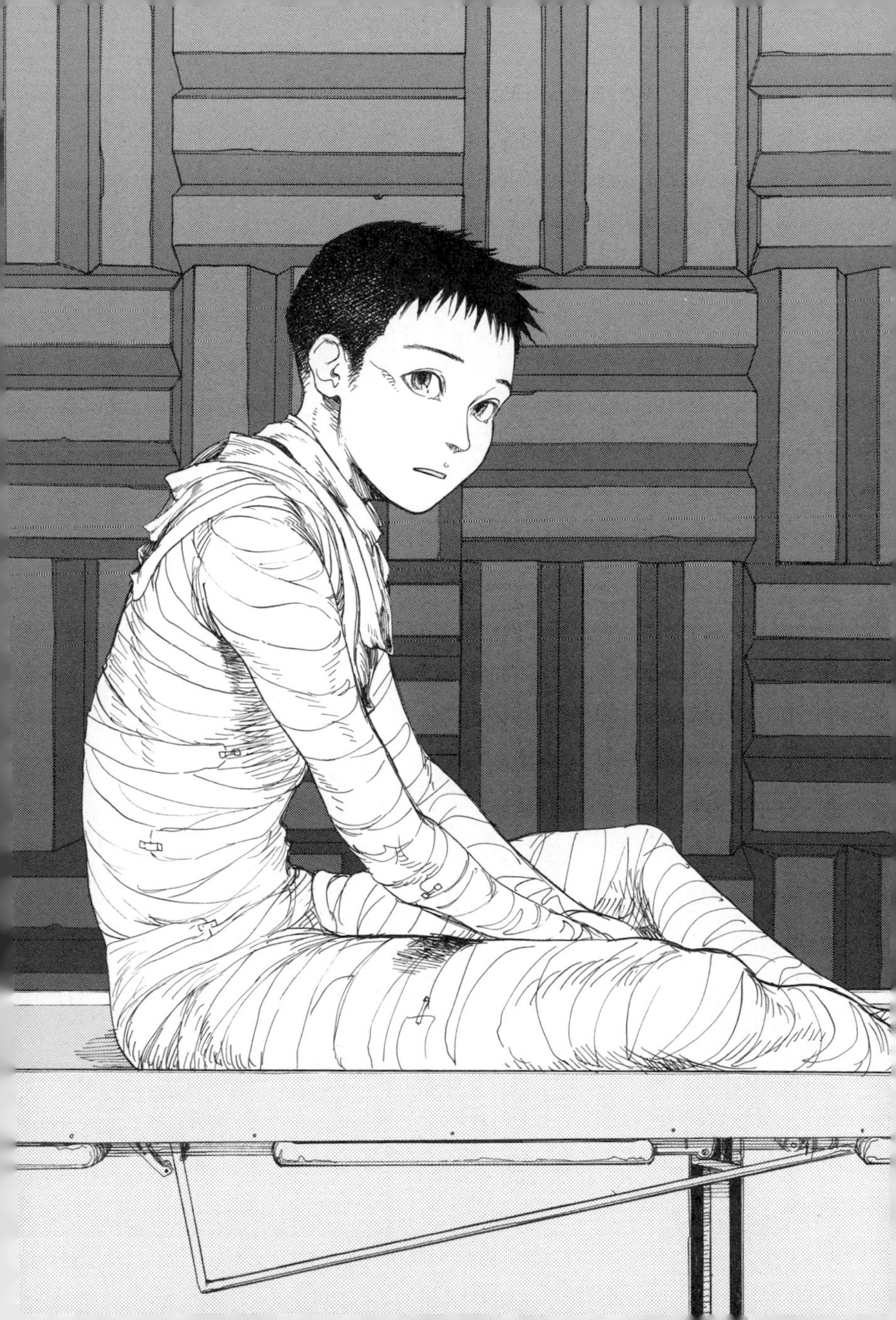

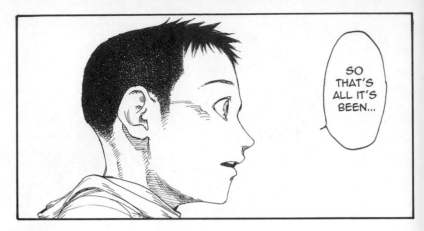

SO
THAT'S
ALL IT'S
BEEN...

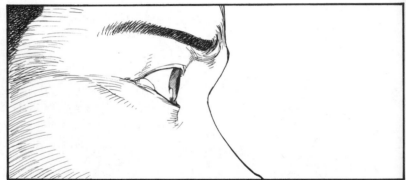

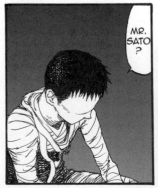

MR.
SATO
?

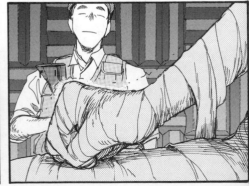

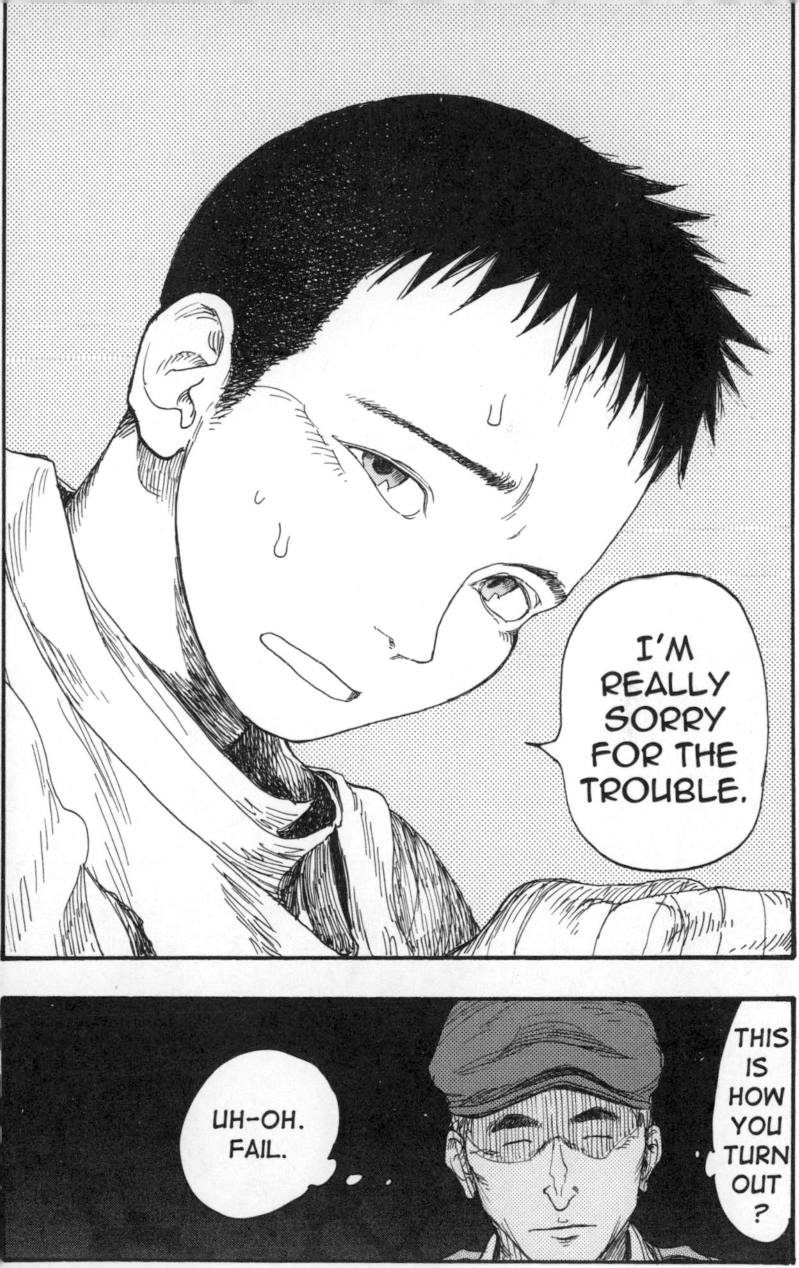
I'M REALLY SORRY FOR THE TROUBLE.
THIS IS HOW YOU TURN OUT?
UH-OH. FAIL.

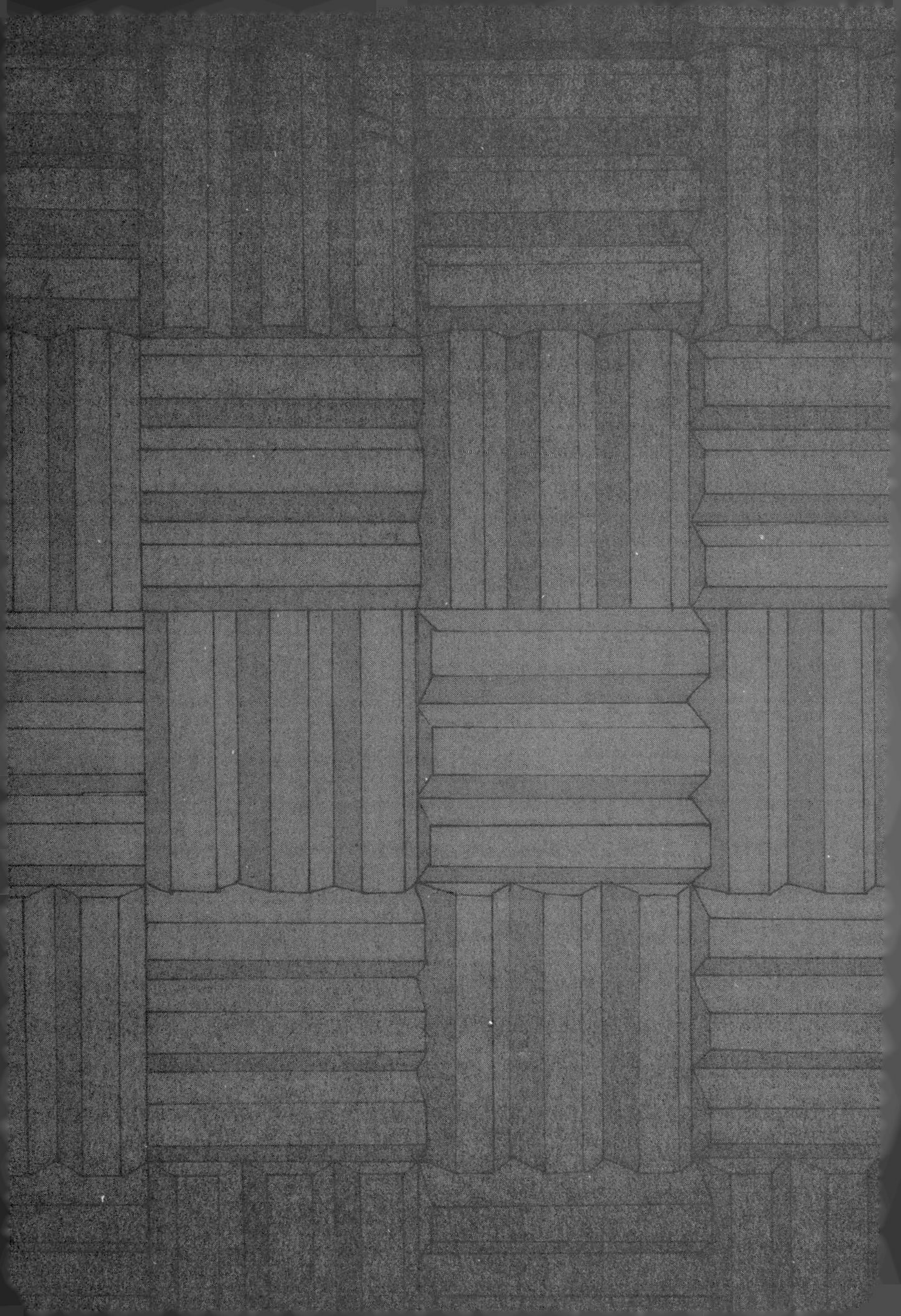

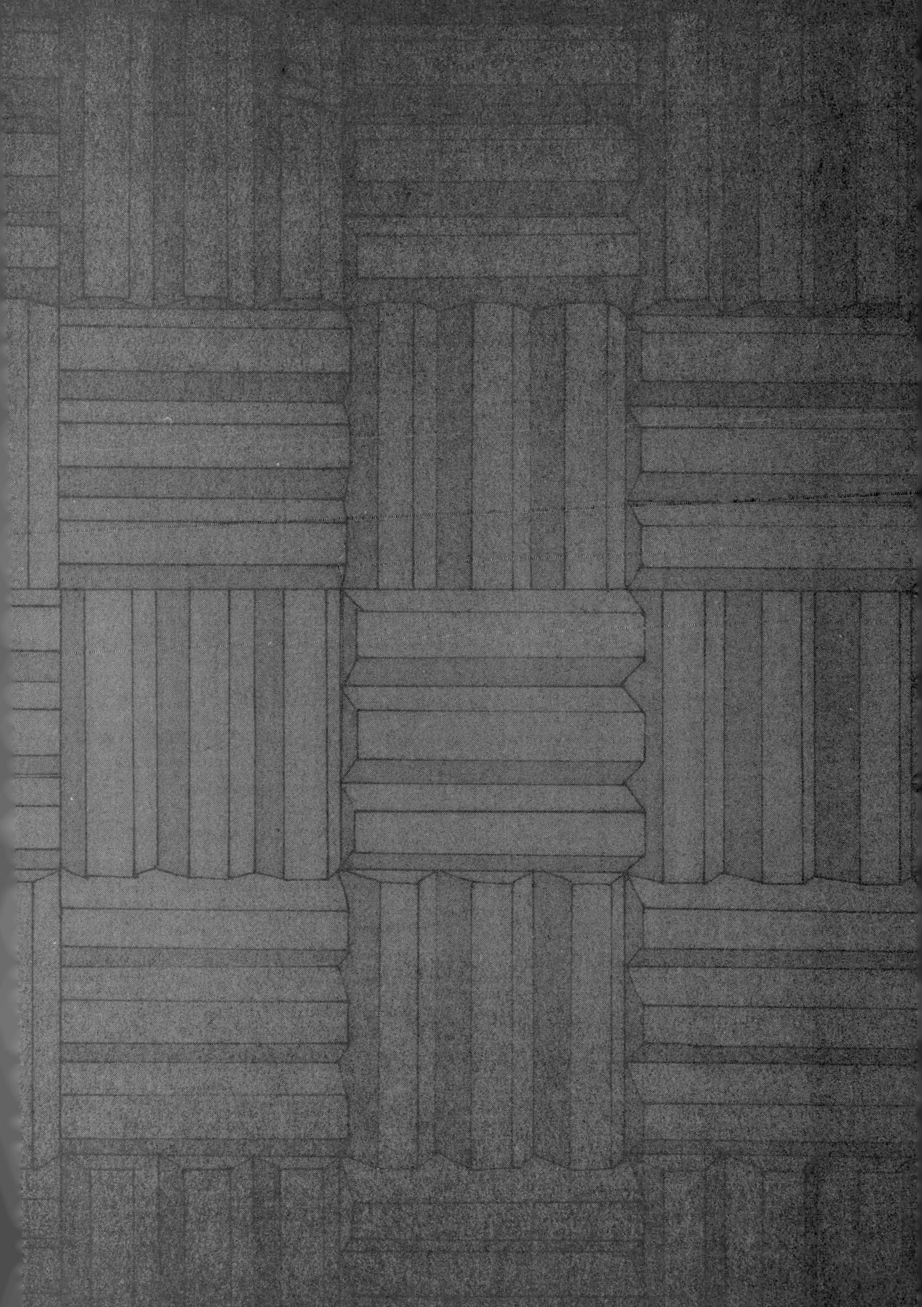

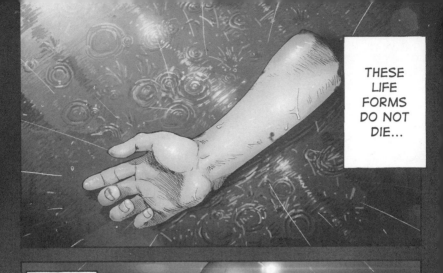

THESE
LIFE
FORMS
DO NOT
DIE...

THEY ARE
KNOWN
AS DEMI-
HUMANS.

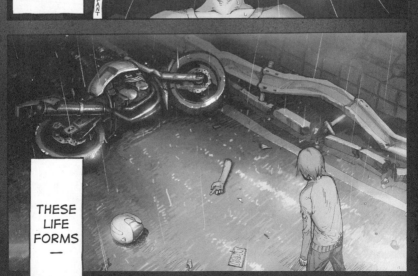

THESE
LIFE
FORMS —

File:00

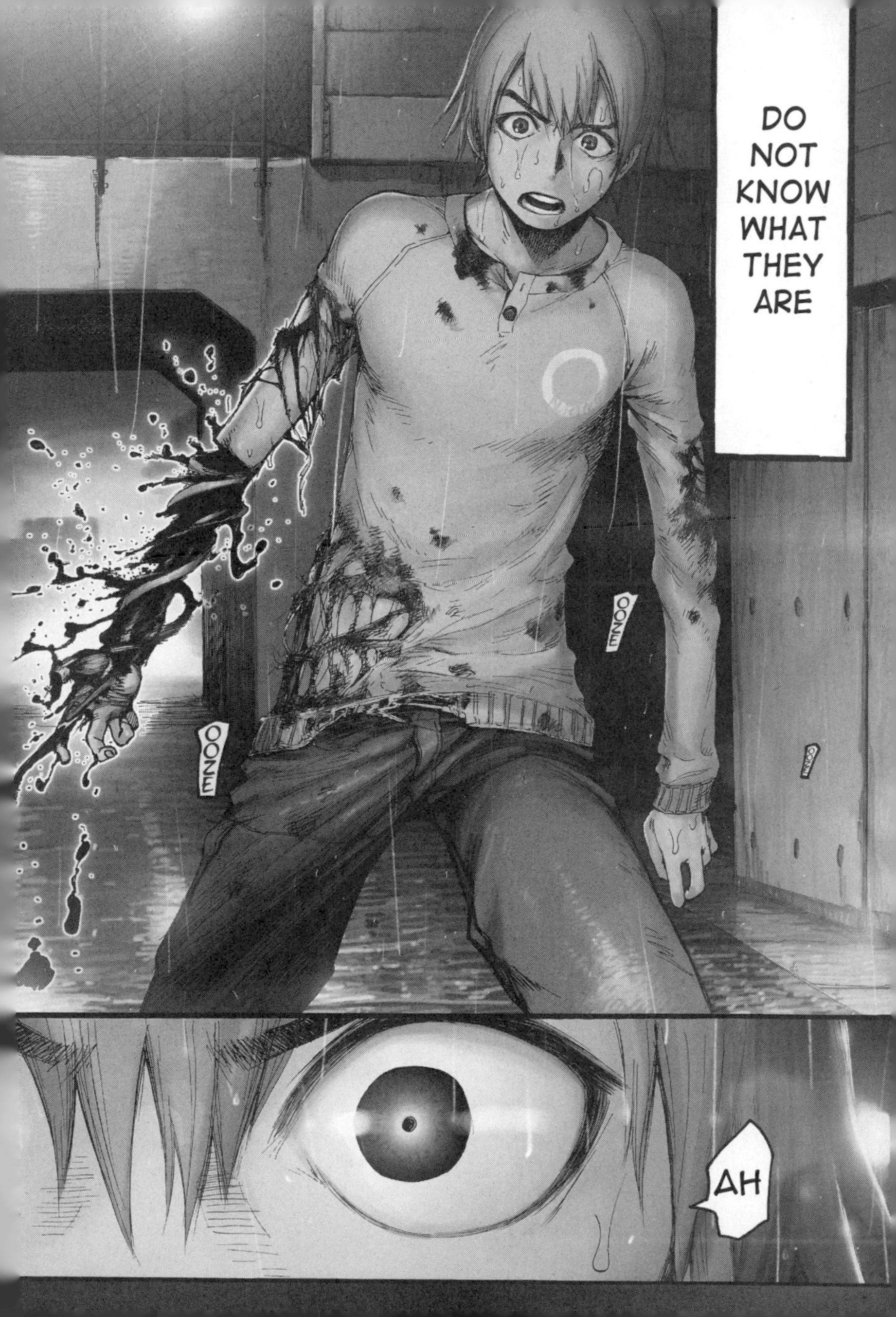
DO NOT KNOW WHAT THEY ARE
OOZE
OOZE
AH

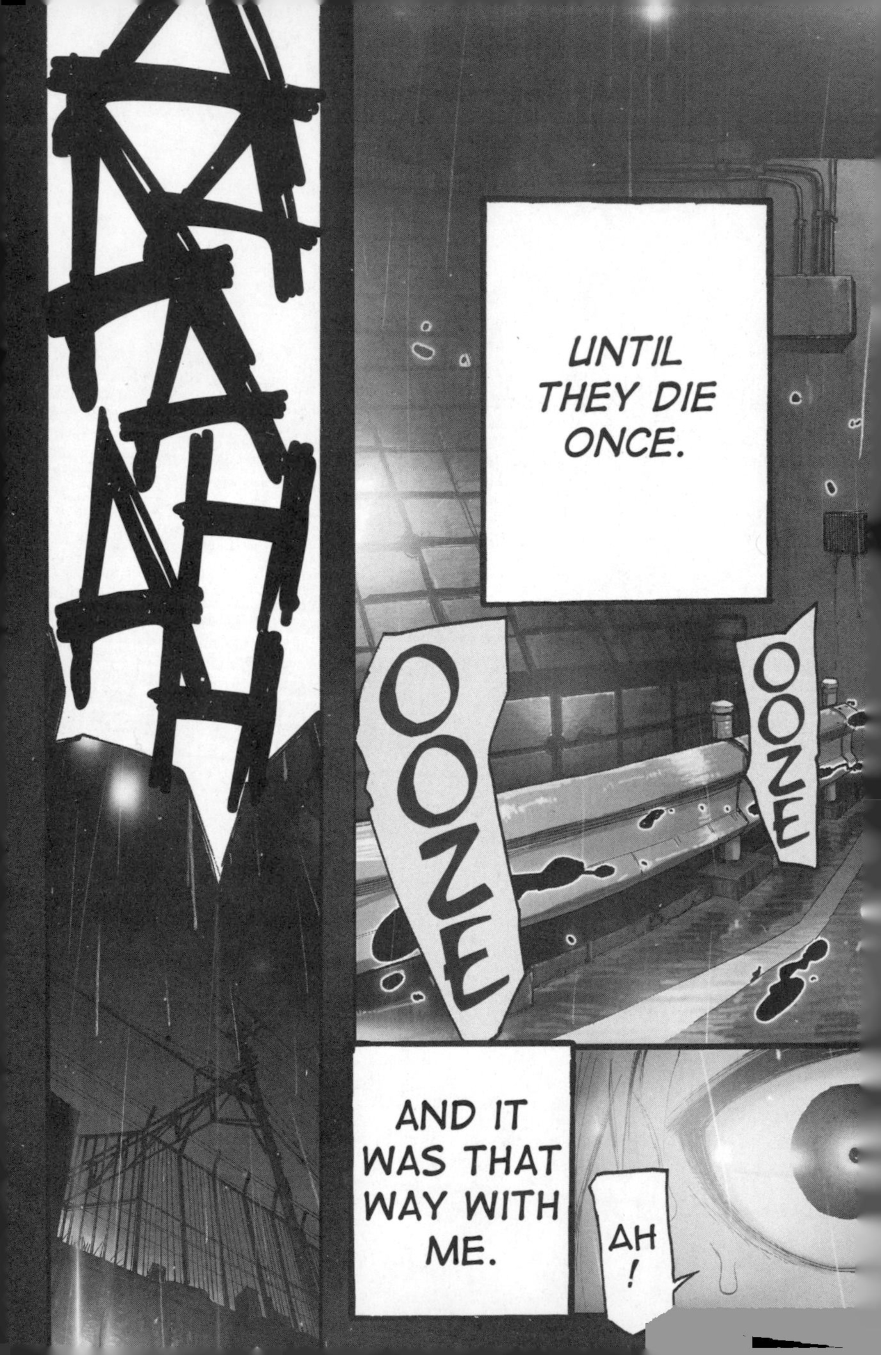
UNTIL THEY DIE ONCE.
OOZE
OOZE
AH!
AND IT WAS THAT WAY WITH ME.
AAAAHH

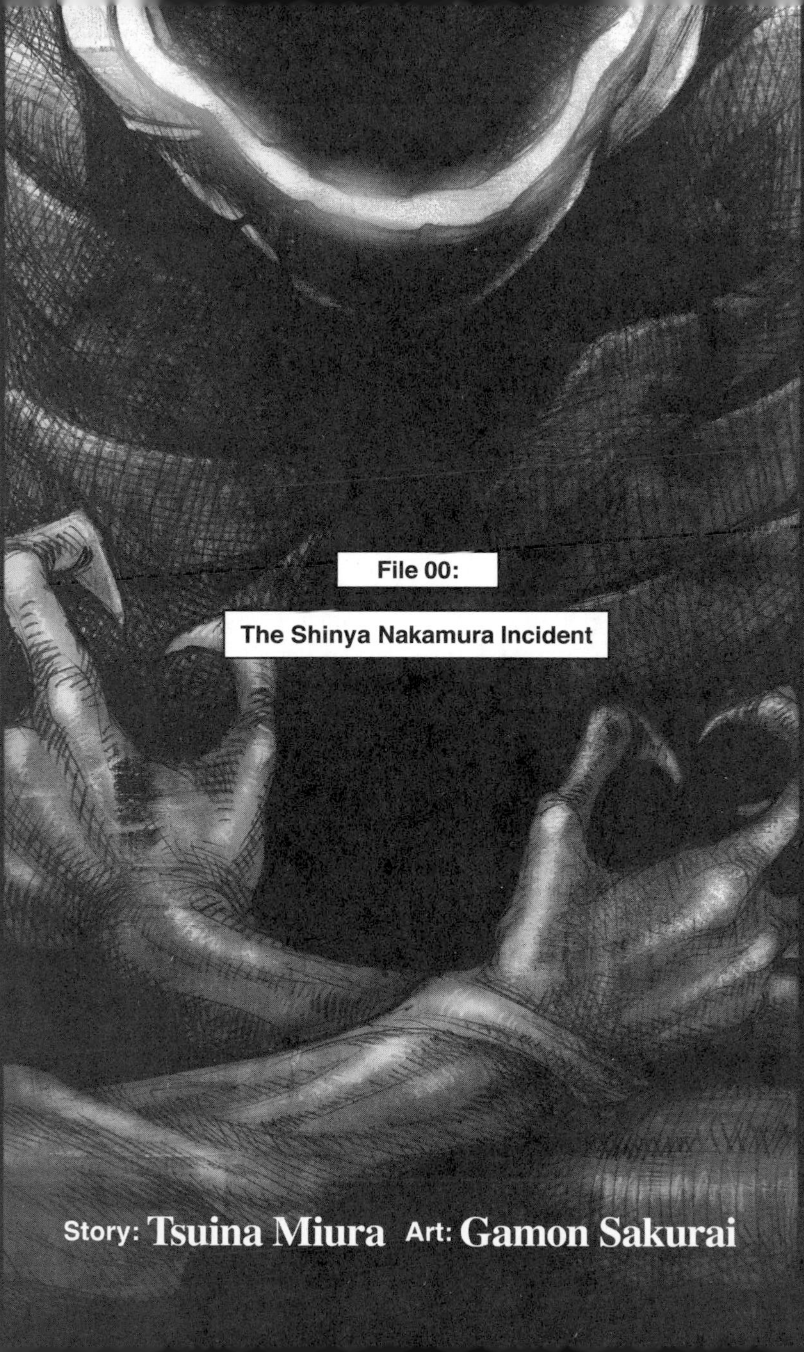
File 00:
The Shinya Nakamura Incident
Story: Tsuina Miura Art: Gamon Sakurai

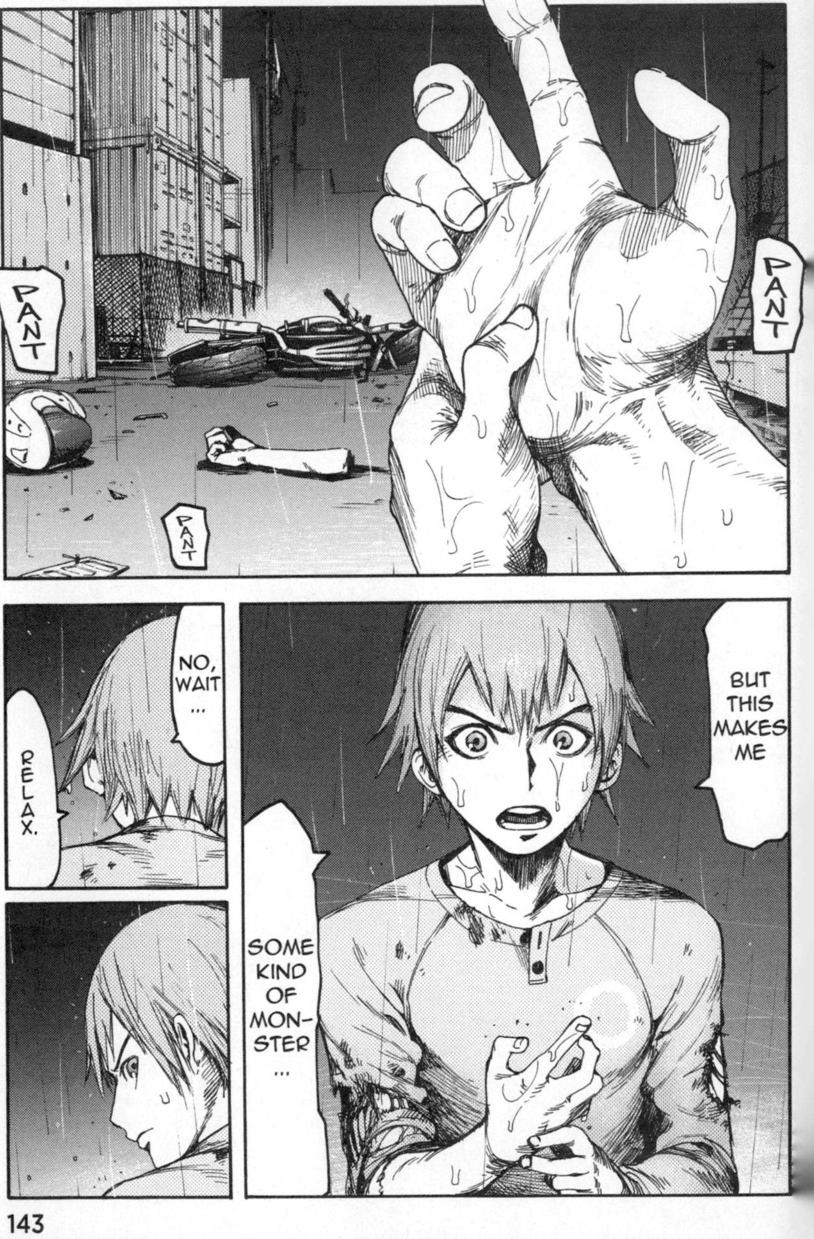
PANT
PANT
PANT
BUT THIS MAKES ME
SOME KIND OF MON-STER ...
NO, WAIT ...
RELAX.

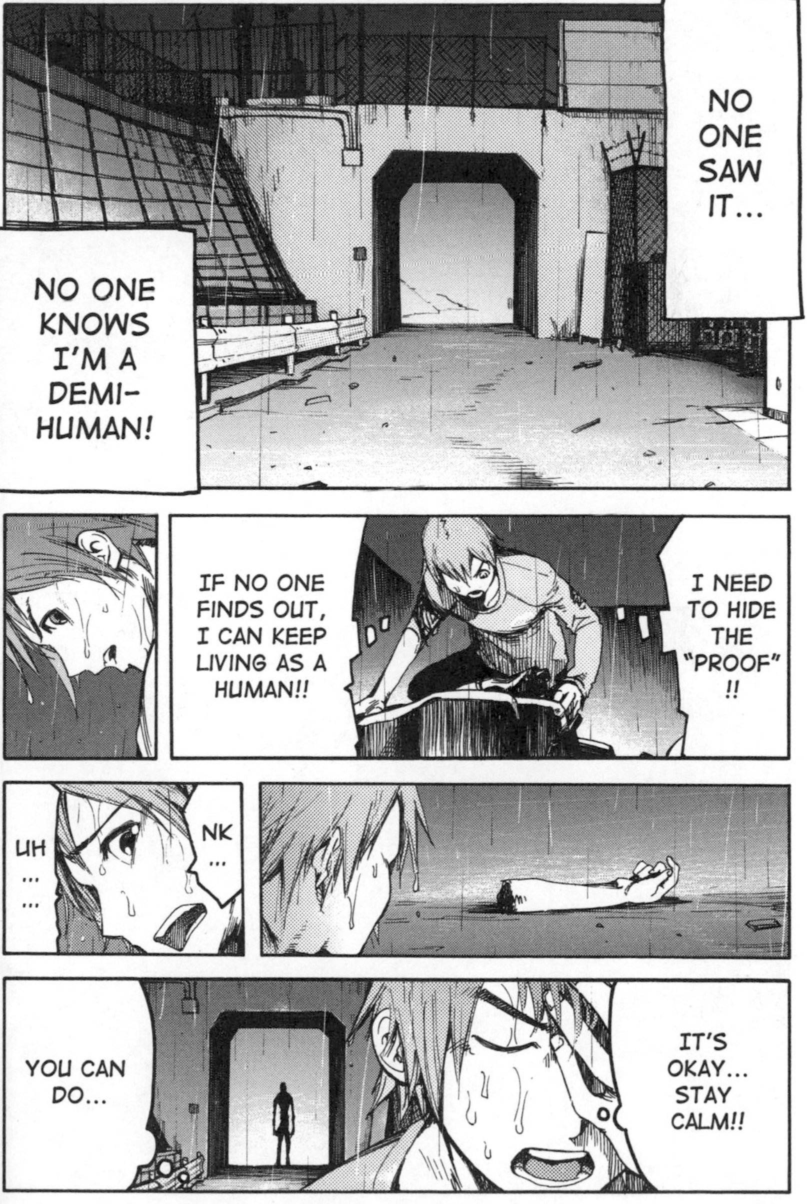
NO ONE SAW IT...
NO ONE KNOWS I'M A DEMI-HUMAN!
I NEED TO HIDE THE "PROOF" !!
IF NO ONE FINDS OUT, I CAN KEEP LIVING AS A HUMAN!!
NK ...
UH ... ...
IT'S OKAY... STAY CALM!!
YOU CAN DO...

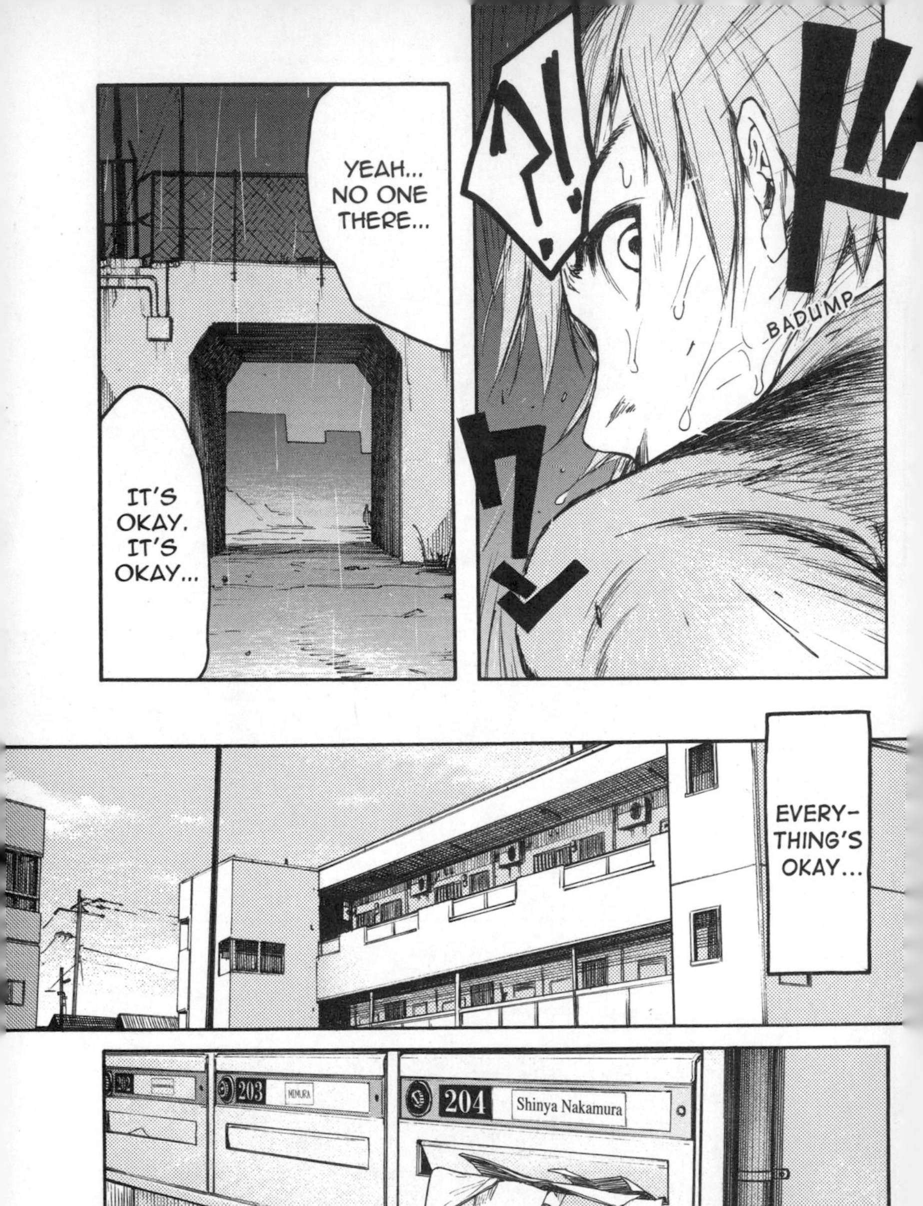
?!!
BADUMP
YEAH... NO ONE THERE...
IT'S OKAY. IT'S OKAY...
EVERY-THING'S OKAY...
203
MIMURA
204
Shinya Nakamura

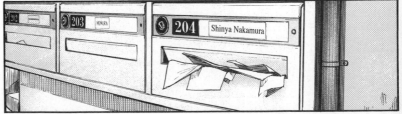

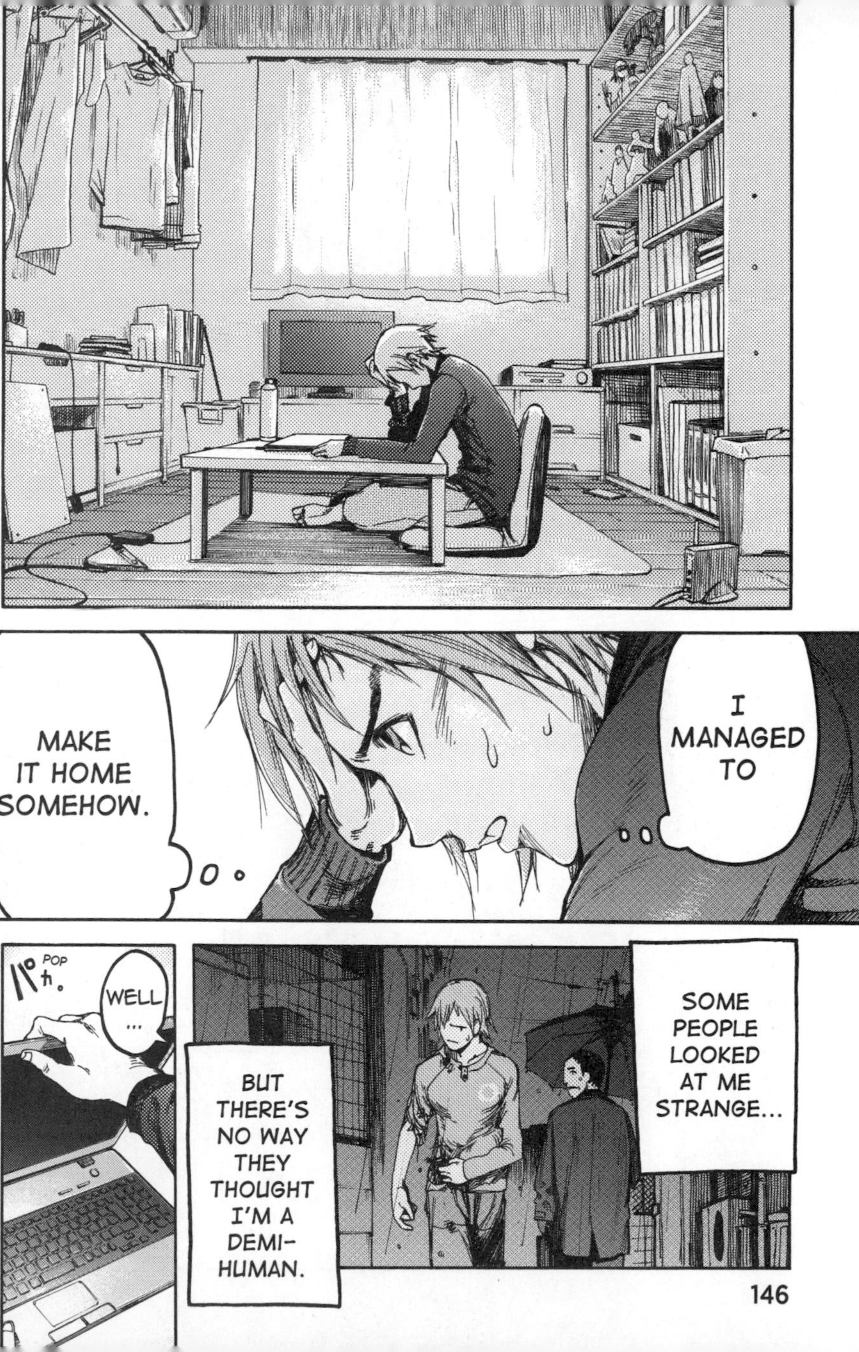
I MANAGED TO
MAKE IT HOME SOMEHOW.
SOME PEOPLE LOOKED AT ME STRANGE...
BUT THERE'S NO WAY THEY THOUGHT I'M A DEMI-HUMAN.
パカ。
POP
WELL ...

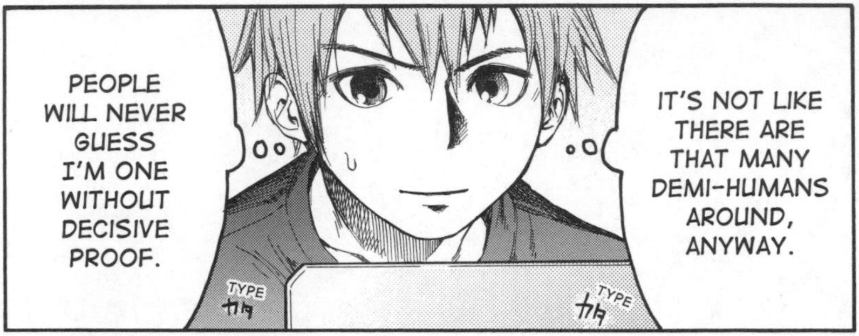
IT'S NOT LIKE THERE ARE THAT MANY DEMI-HUMANS AROUND, ANYWAY.
PEOPLE WILL NEVER GUESS I'M ONE WITHOUT DECISIVE PROOF.
TYPE カタ
TYPE カタ

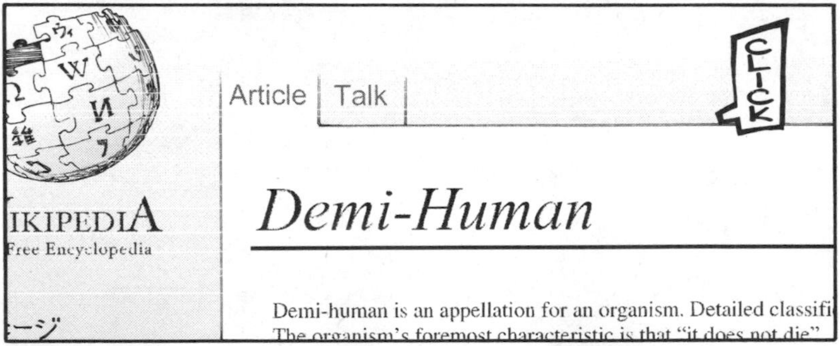
CLICK
IKIPEDIA
ree Encyclopedia
ージ
Article
Talk
Demi-Human
Demi-human is an appellation for an organism. Detailed classifi
The organism's foremost characteristic is that "it does not die"

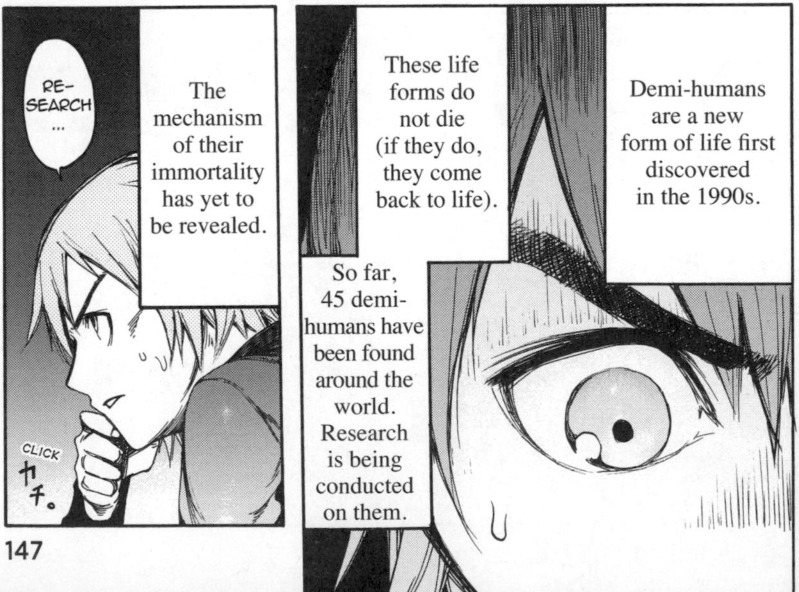
Demi-humans are a new form of life first discovered in the 1990s.
These life forms do not die (if they do, they come back to life).
So far, 45 demi-humans have been found around the world. Research is being conducted on them.
The mechanism of their immortality has yet to be revealed.
RE-SEARCH ...
CLICK カチ。

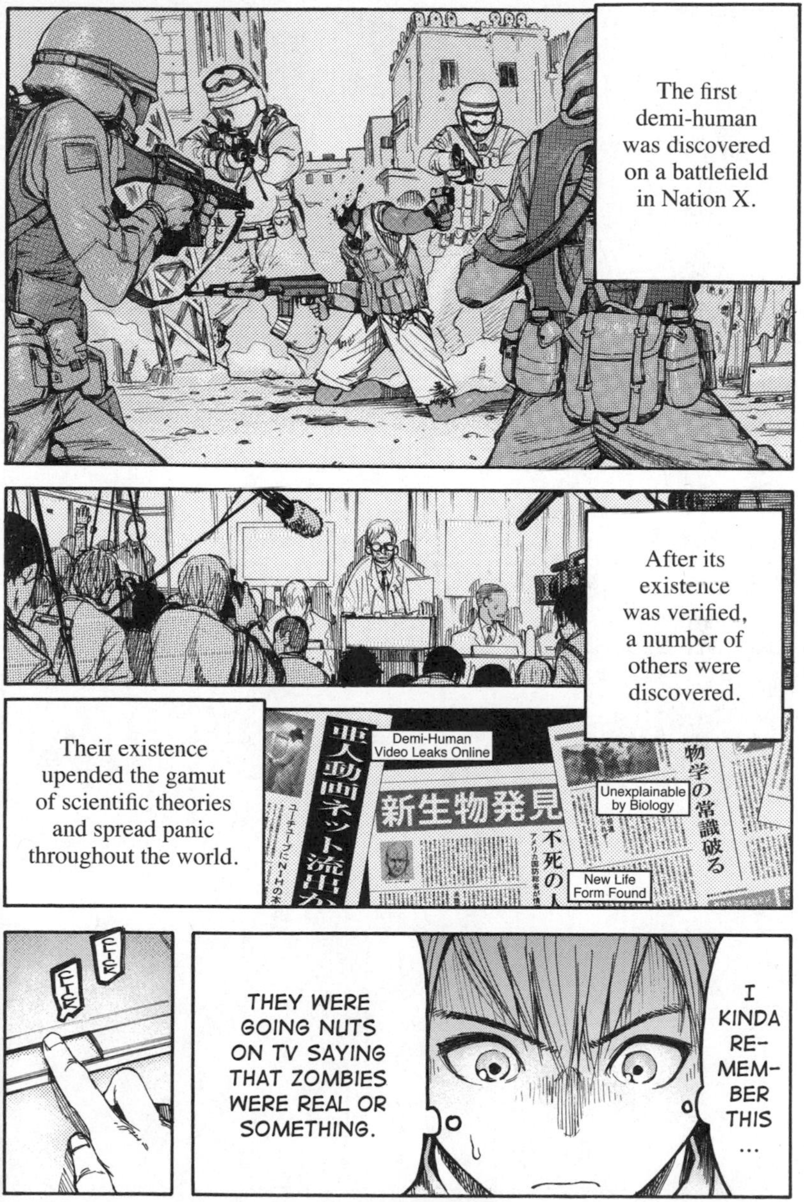
The first demi-human was discovered on a battlefield in Nation X.
After its existence was verified, a number of others were discovered.
Their existence upended the gamut of scientific theories and spread panic throughout the world.
Demi-Human Video Leaks Online
新生物発見
New Life Form Found
物学の常識破る
Unexplainable by Biology
I KINDA RE-MEMBER THIS ...
THEY WERE GOING NUTS ON TV SAYING THAT ZOMBIES WERE REAL OR SOMETHING.
CLICK
CLICK

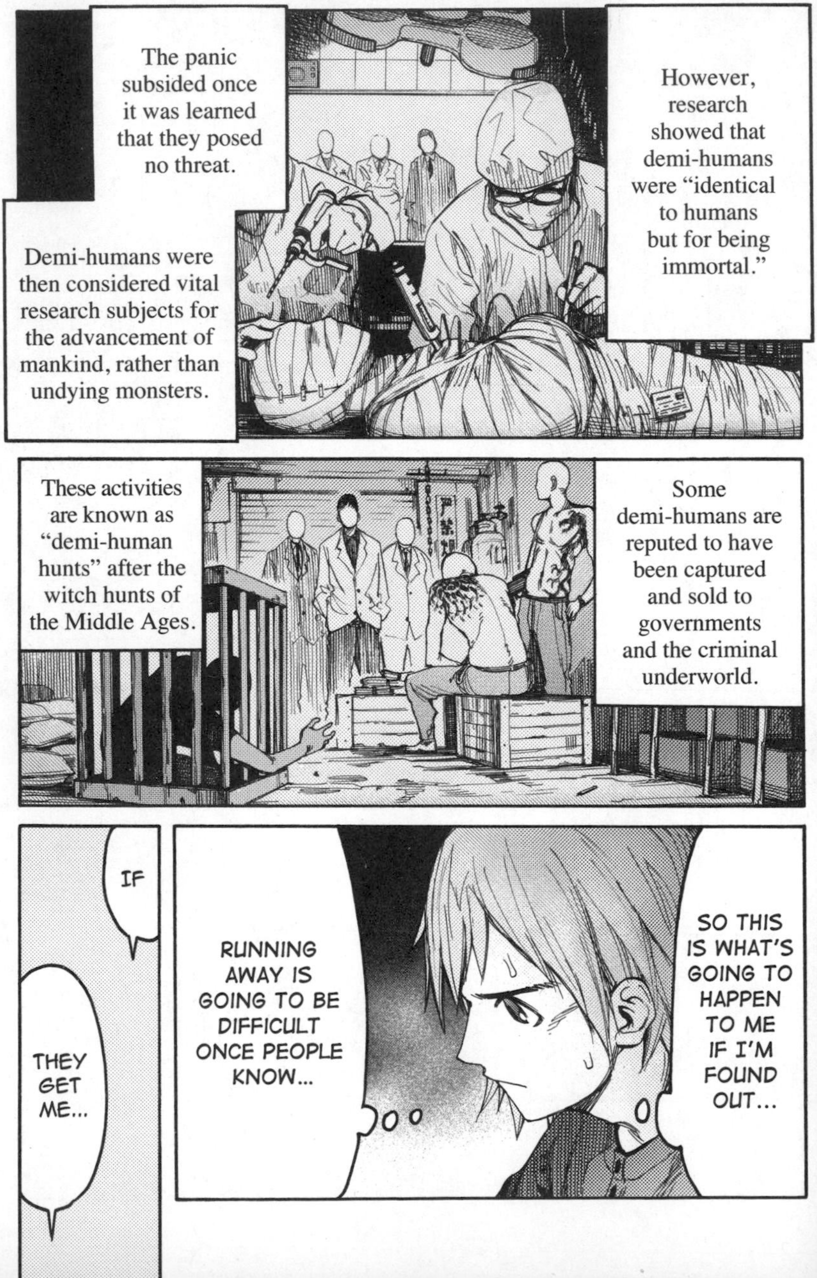
However, research showed that demi-humans were "identical to humans but for being immortal."
The panic subsided once it was learned that they posed no threat.
Demi-humans were then considered vital research subjects for the advancement of mankind, rather than undying monsters.
Some demi-humans are reputed to have been captured and sold to governments and the criminal underworld.
These activities are known as "demi-human hunts" after the witch hunts of the Middle Ages.
SO THIS IS WHAT'S GOING TO HAPPEN TO ME IF I'M FOUND OUT...
RUNNING AWAY IS GOING TO BE DIFFICULT ONCE PEOPLE KNOW...
IF
THEY GET ME...

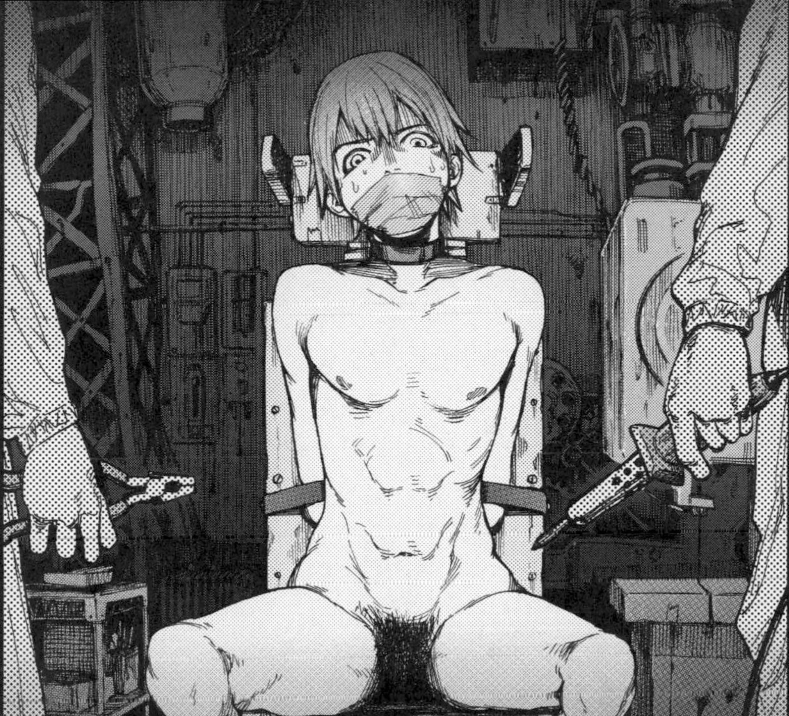

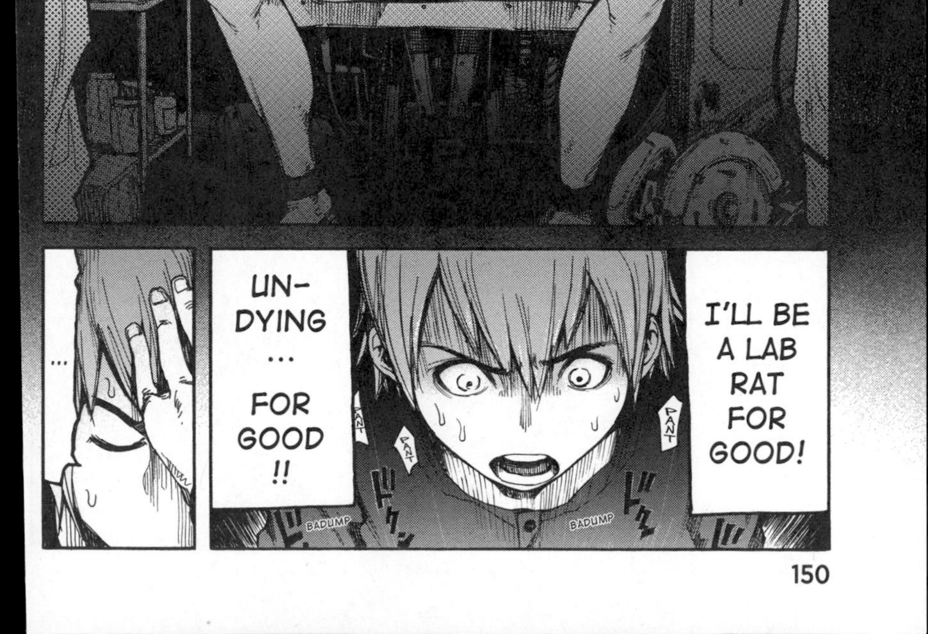
I'LL BE A LAB RAT FOR GOOD!
PANT
PANT
PANT
BADUMP
BADUMP
UN-DYING... FOR GOOD!!
...

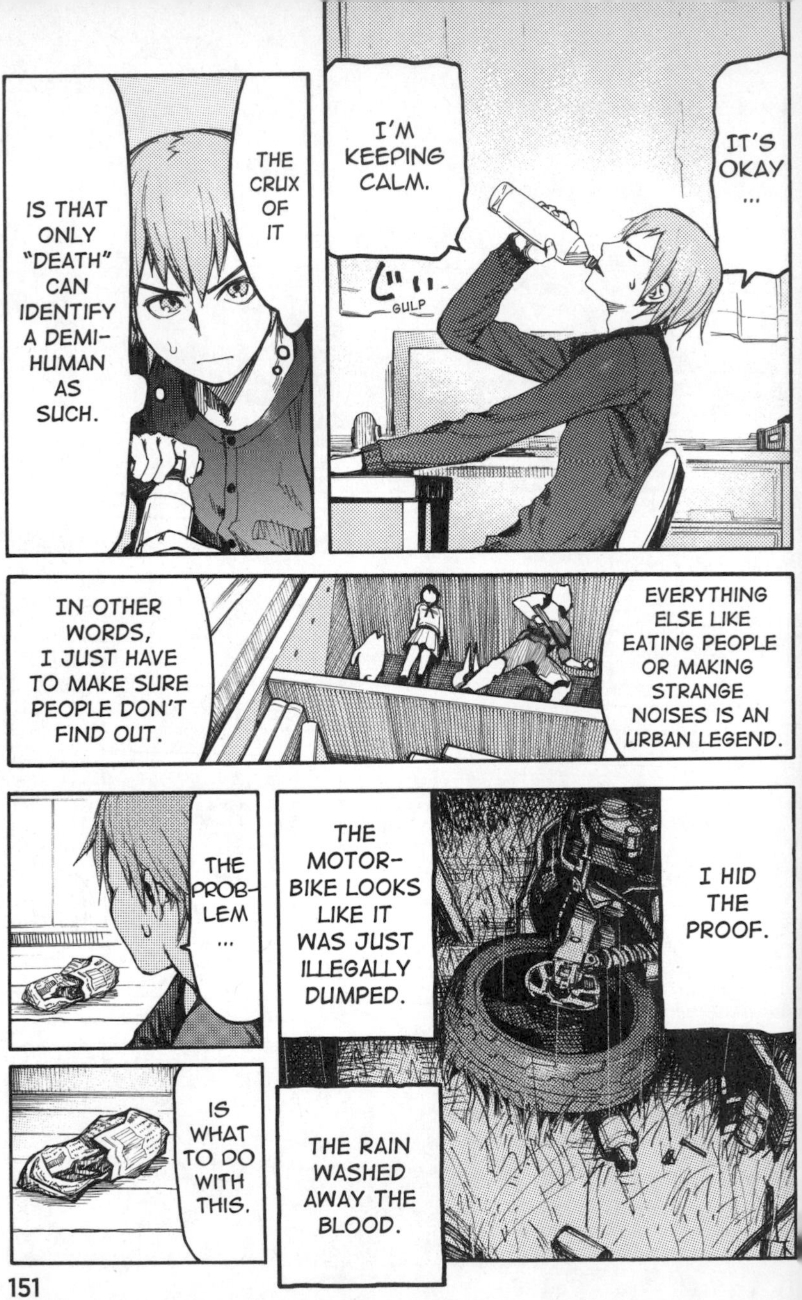
IT'S OKAY ...
I'M KEEPING CALM.
GULP
THE CRUX OF IT
IS THAT ONLY "DEATH" CAN IDENTIFY A DEMI-HUMAN AS SUCH.
EVERYTHING ELSE LIKE EATING PEOPLE OR MAKING STRANGE NOISES IS AN URBAN LEGEND.
IN OTHER WORDS, I JUST HAVE TO MAKE SURE PEOPLE DON'T FIND OUT.
I HID THE PROOF.
THE MOTOR-BIKE LOOKS LIKE IT WAS JUST ILLEGALLY DUMPED.
THE RAIN WASHED AWAY THE BLOOD.
THE PROB-LEM ...
IS WHAT TO DO WITH THIS.

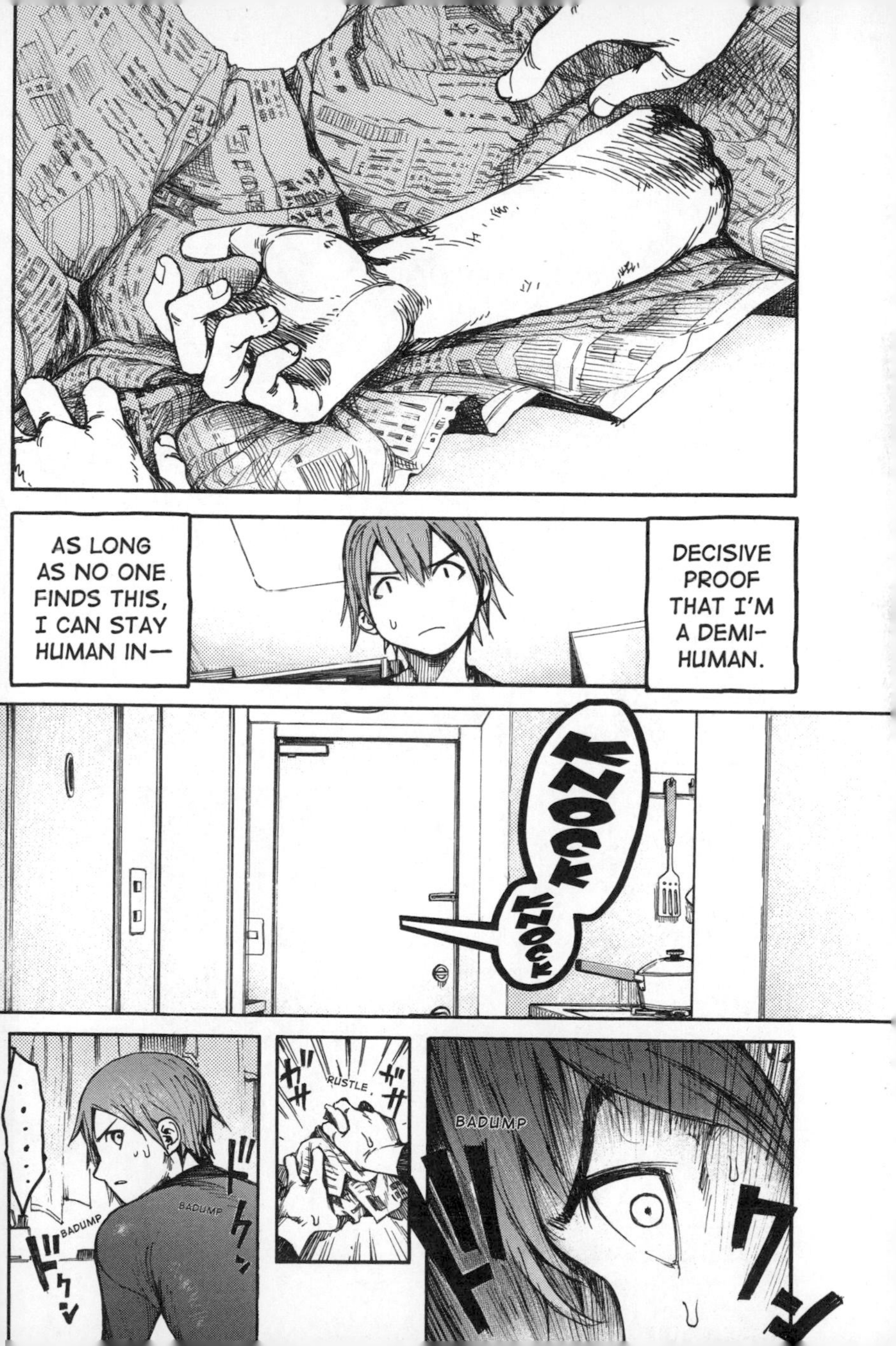
DECISIVE PROOF THAT I'M A DEMI-HUMAN.
AS LONG AS NO ONE FINDS THIS, I CAN STAY HUMAN IN—
KNOCK
KNOCK
BADUMP
RUSTLE
......
BADUMP
BADUMP

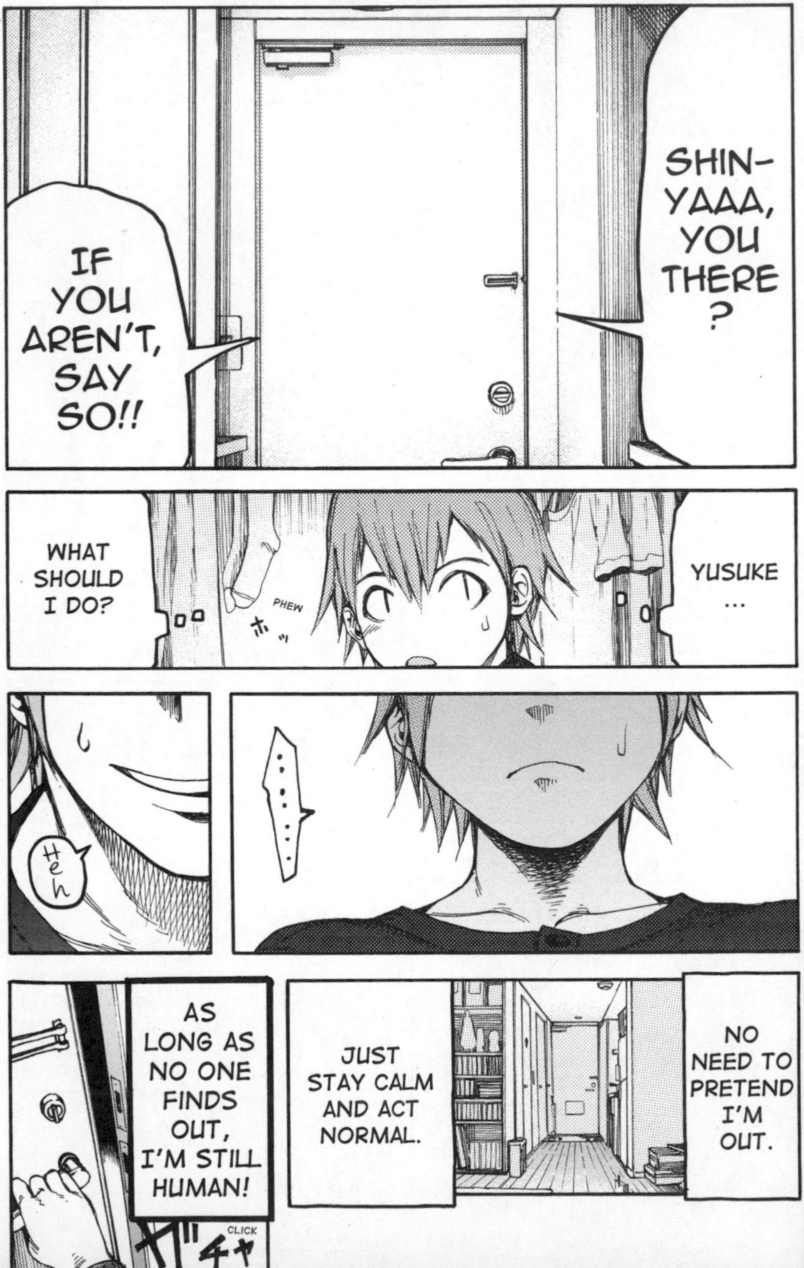
SHIN-YAAA, YOU THERE?
IF YOU AREN'T, SAY SO!!
YUSUKE...
PHEW
WHAT SHOULD I DO?
......
Heh
NO NEED TO PRETEND I'M OUT.
JUST STAY CALM AND ACT NORMAL.
AS LONG AS NO ONE FINDS OUT, I'M STILL HUMAN!
CLICK

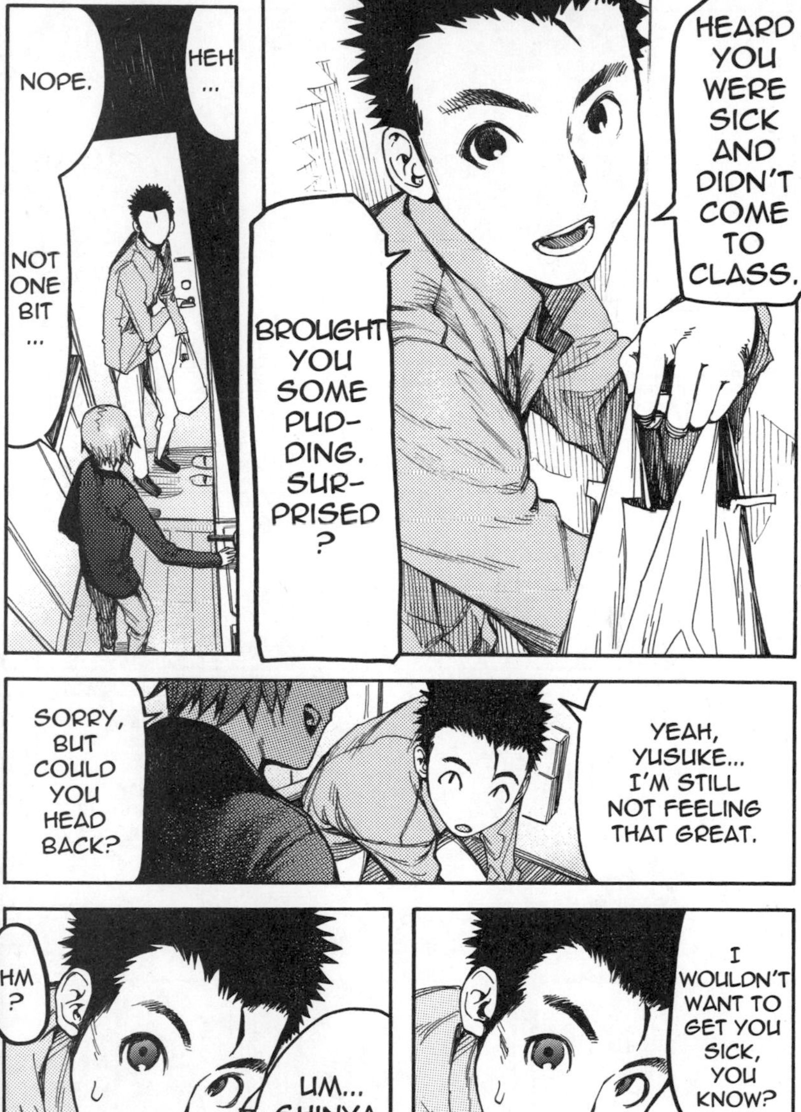
HEARD YOU WERE SICK AND DIDN'T COME TO CLASS.
BROUGHT YOU SOME PUD-DING. SURPRISED?
HEH...
NOPE.
NOT ONE BIT...
YEAH, YUSUKE... I'M STILL NOT FEELING THAT GREAT.
SORRY, BUT COULD YOU HEAD BACK?
I WOULDN'T WANT TO GET YOU SICK, YOU KNOW?
HM?
UM... SHINYA?

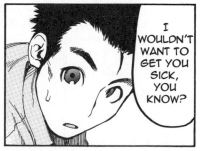

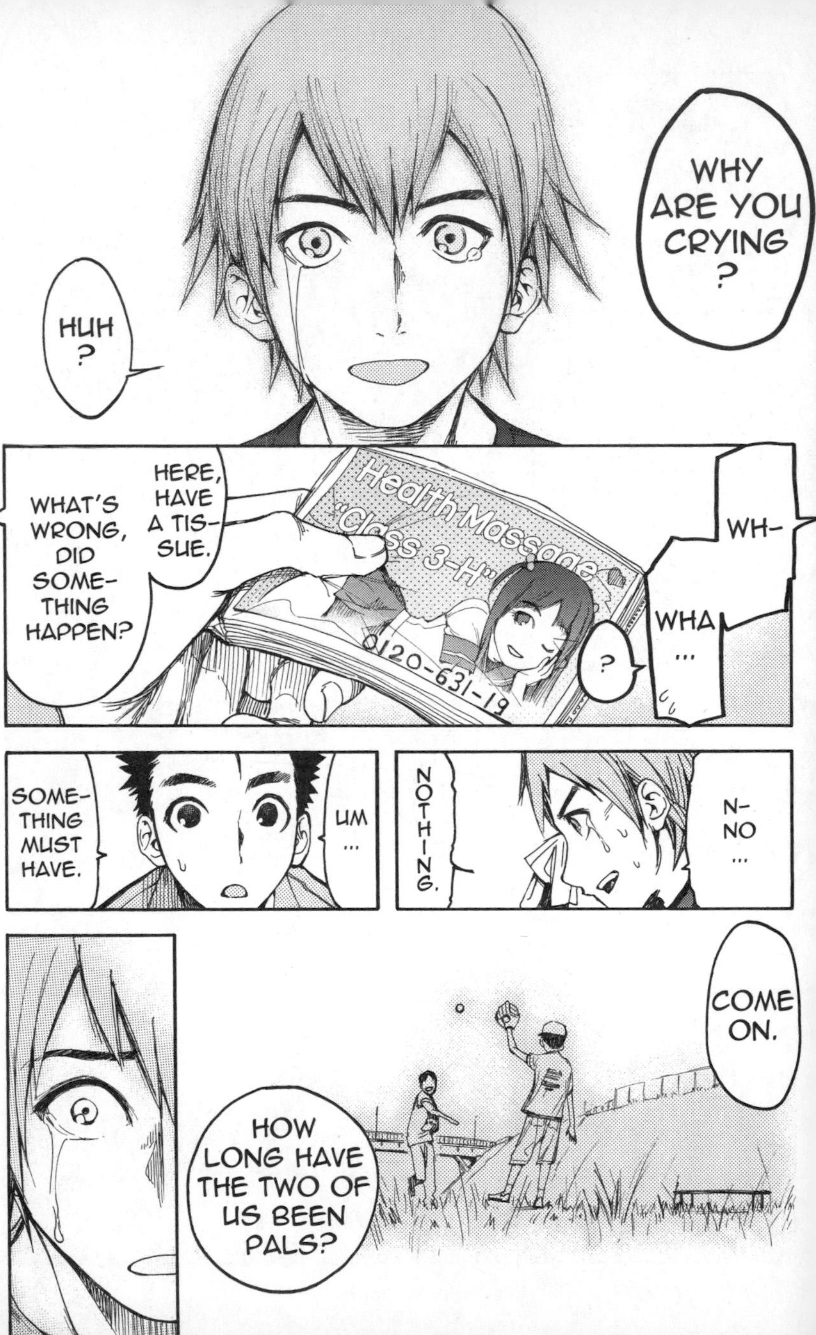
WHY ARE YOU CRYING ?
HUH ?
WH-
WHA ...
?
Health Massage
"Class 3-H"
0120-631-19
HERE, HAVE A TIS-SUE.
WHAT'S WRONG, DID SOME-THING HAPPEN?
N-NO ...
NOTHING.
UM ...
SOME-THING MUST HAVE.
COME ON.
HOW LONG HAVE THE TWO OF US BEEN PALS?

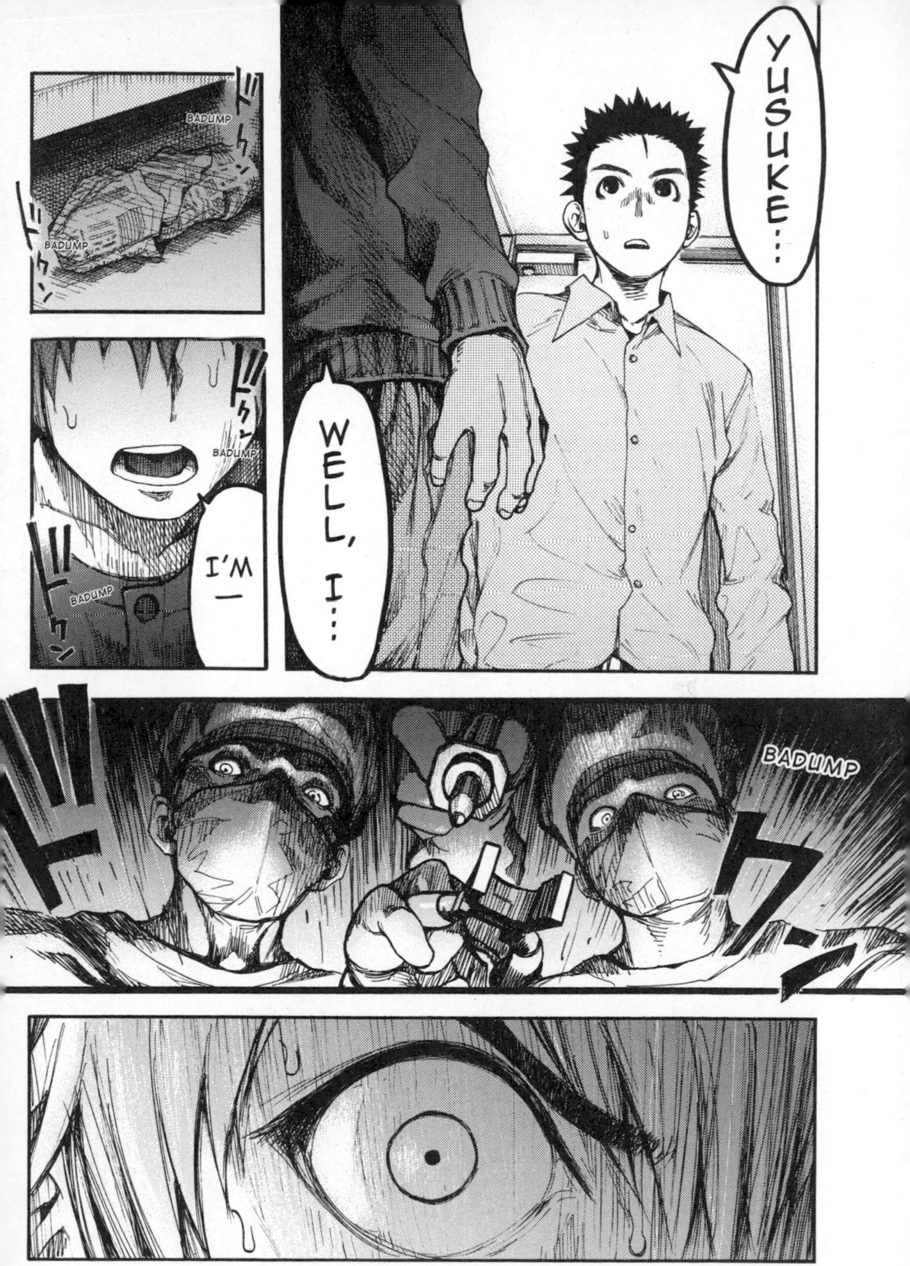
YUSUKE...
WELL, I...
BADUMP
BADUMP
BADUMP
I'M —
BADUMP
BADUMP

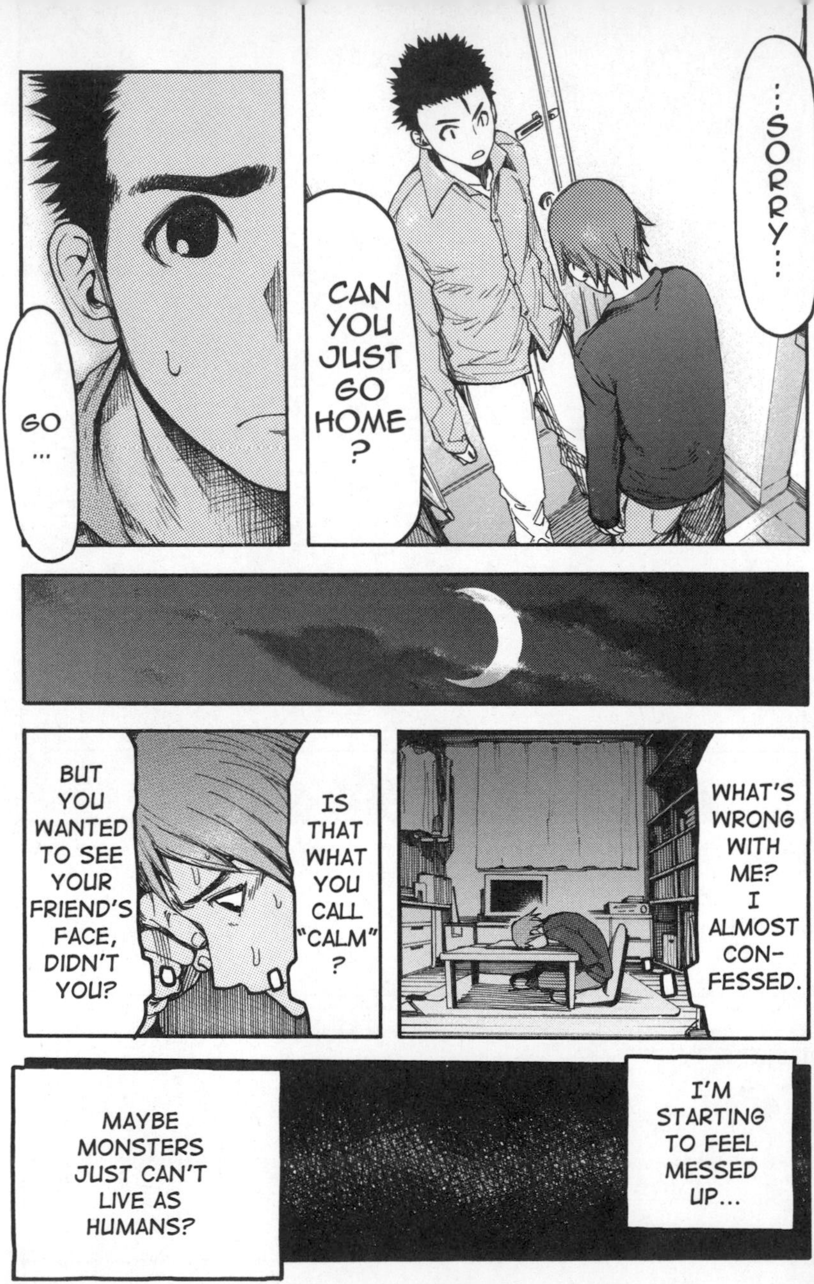
...SORRY...
CAN YOU JUST GO HOME?
GO...
WHAT'S WRONG WITH ME? I ALMOST CON-FESSED.
IS THAT WHAT YOU CALL "CALM"?
BUT YOU WANTED TO SEE YOUR FRIEND'S FACE, DIDN'T YOU?
I'M STARTING TO FEEL MESSED UP...
MAYBE MONSTERS JUST CAN'T LIVE AS HUMANS?

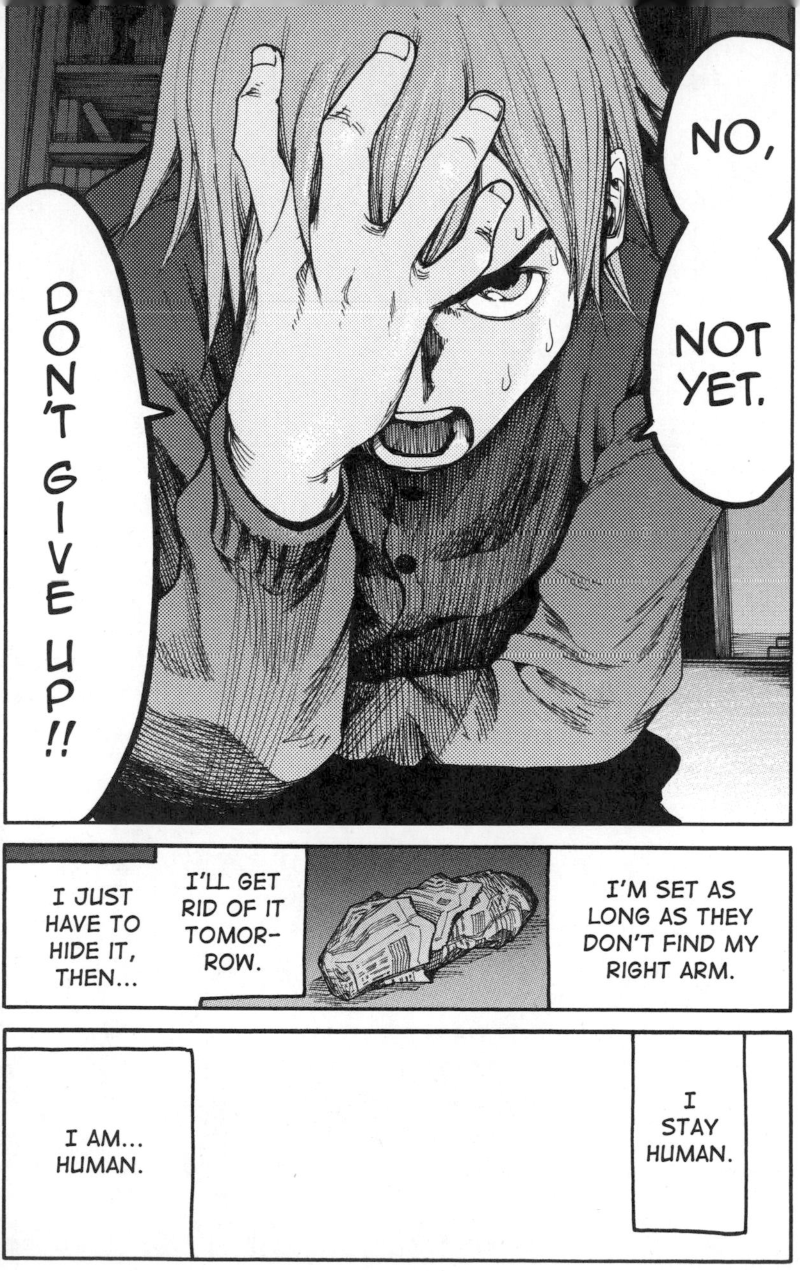
NO, NOT YET.
DON'T GIVE UP!!
I'M SET AS LONG AS THEY DON'T FIND MY RIGHT ARM.
I'LL GET RID OF IT TOMOR- ROW.
I JUST HAVE TO HIDE IT, THEN...
I STAY HUMAN.
I AM... HUMAN.

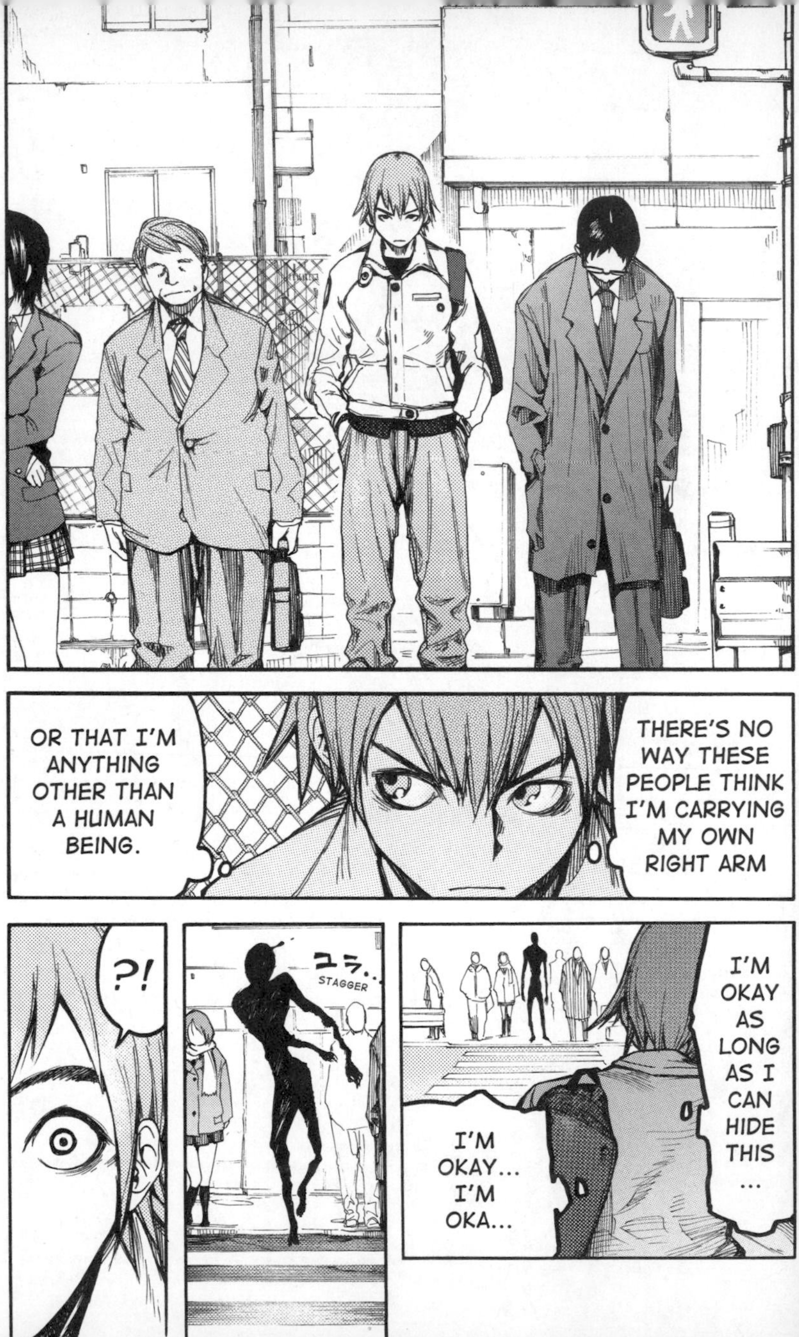
THERE'S NO WAY THESE PEOPLE THINK I'M CARRYING MY OWN RIGHT ARM
OR THAT I'M ANYTHING OTHER THAN A HUMAN BEING.
I'M OKAY AS LONG AS I CAN HIDE THIS ...
I'M OKAY... I'M OKA...
ユラ…
STAGGER
?!

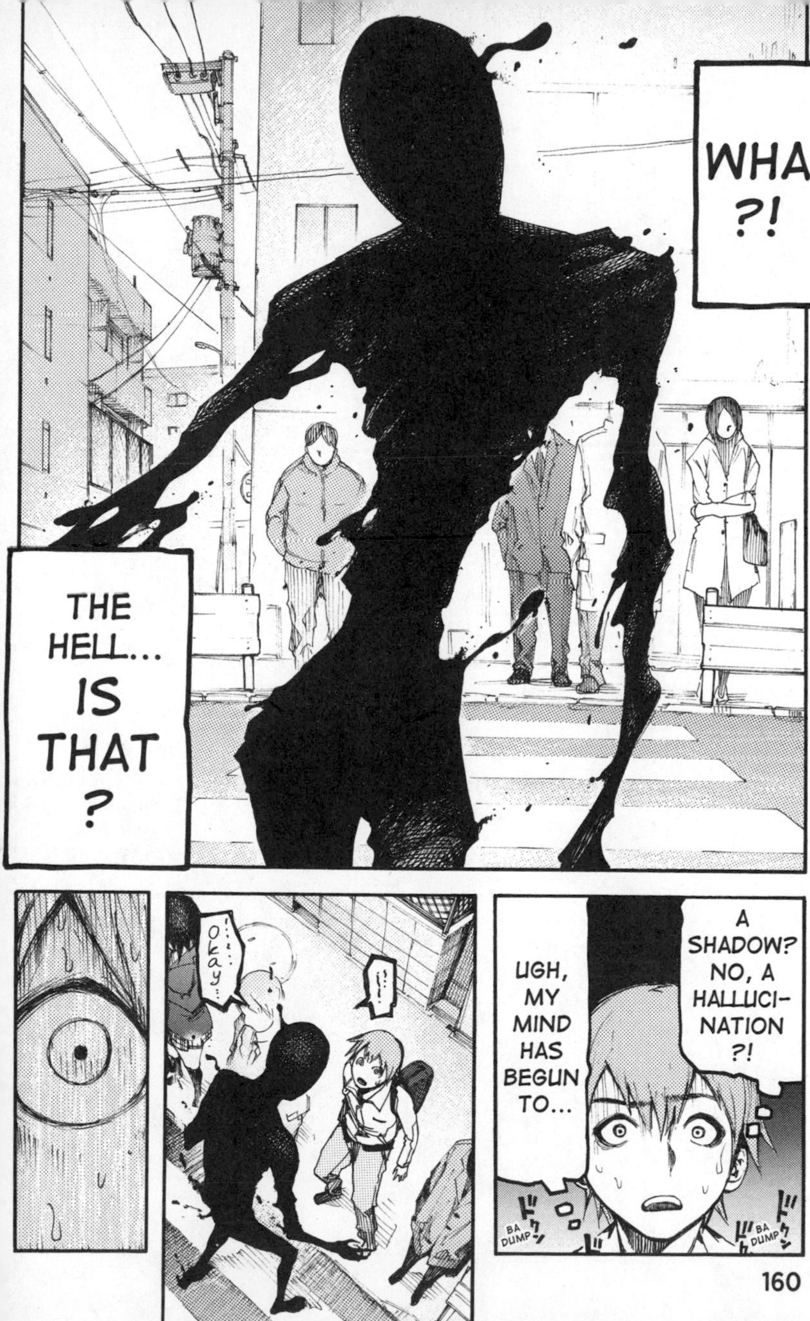
WHA ?!
THE HELL... IS THAT ?
A SHADOW? NO, A HALLUCI-NATION ?!
UGH, MY MIND HAS BEGUN TO...
BA DUMP
BA DUMP
!!
Okay...

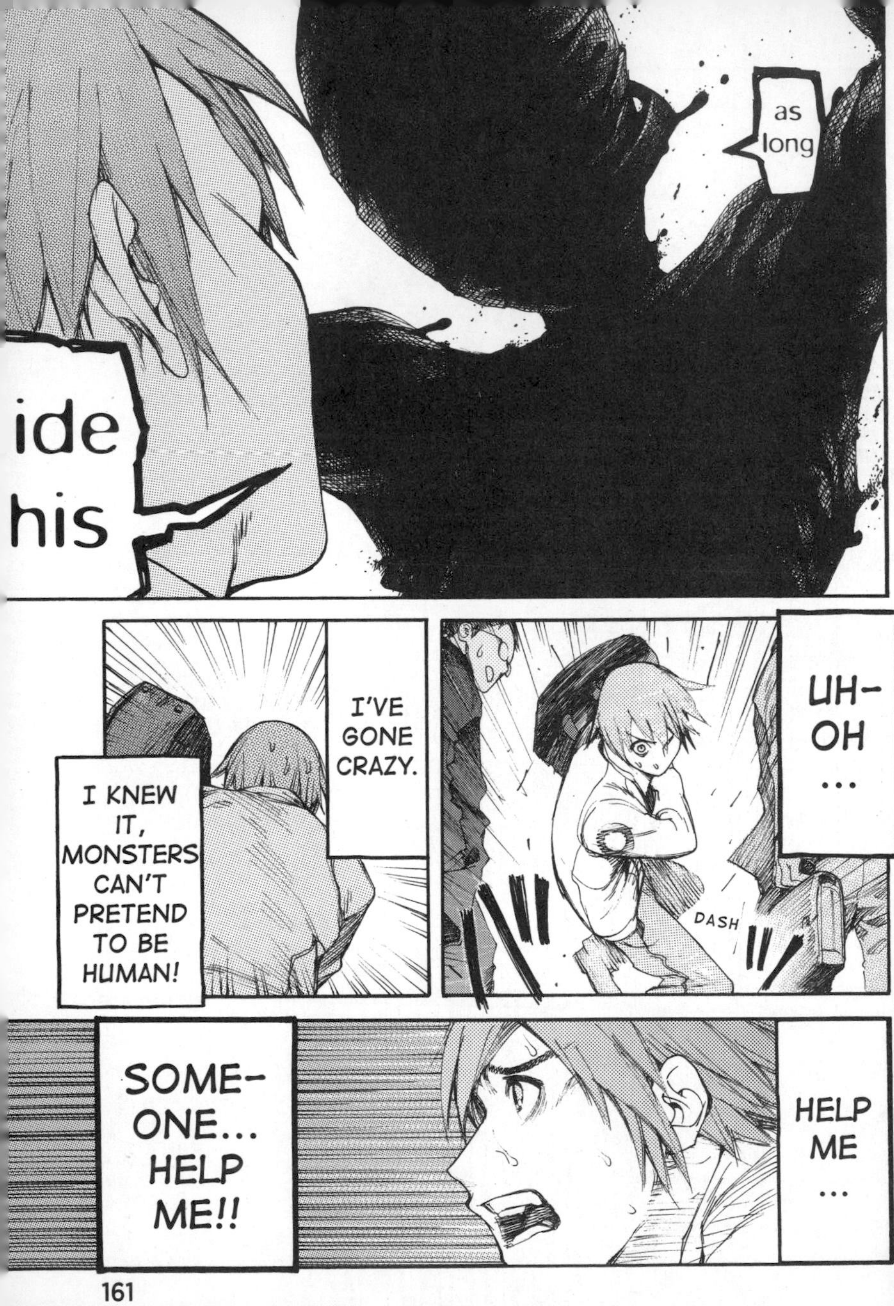
as long
ide his
UH-OH ...
DASH
I'VE GONE CRAZY.
I KNEW IT, MONSTERS CAN'T PRETEND TO BE HUMAN!
HELP ME ...
SOME-ONE... HELP ME!!

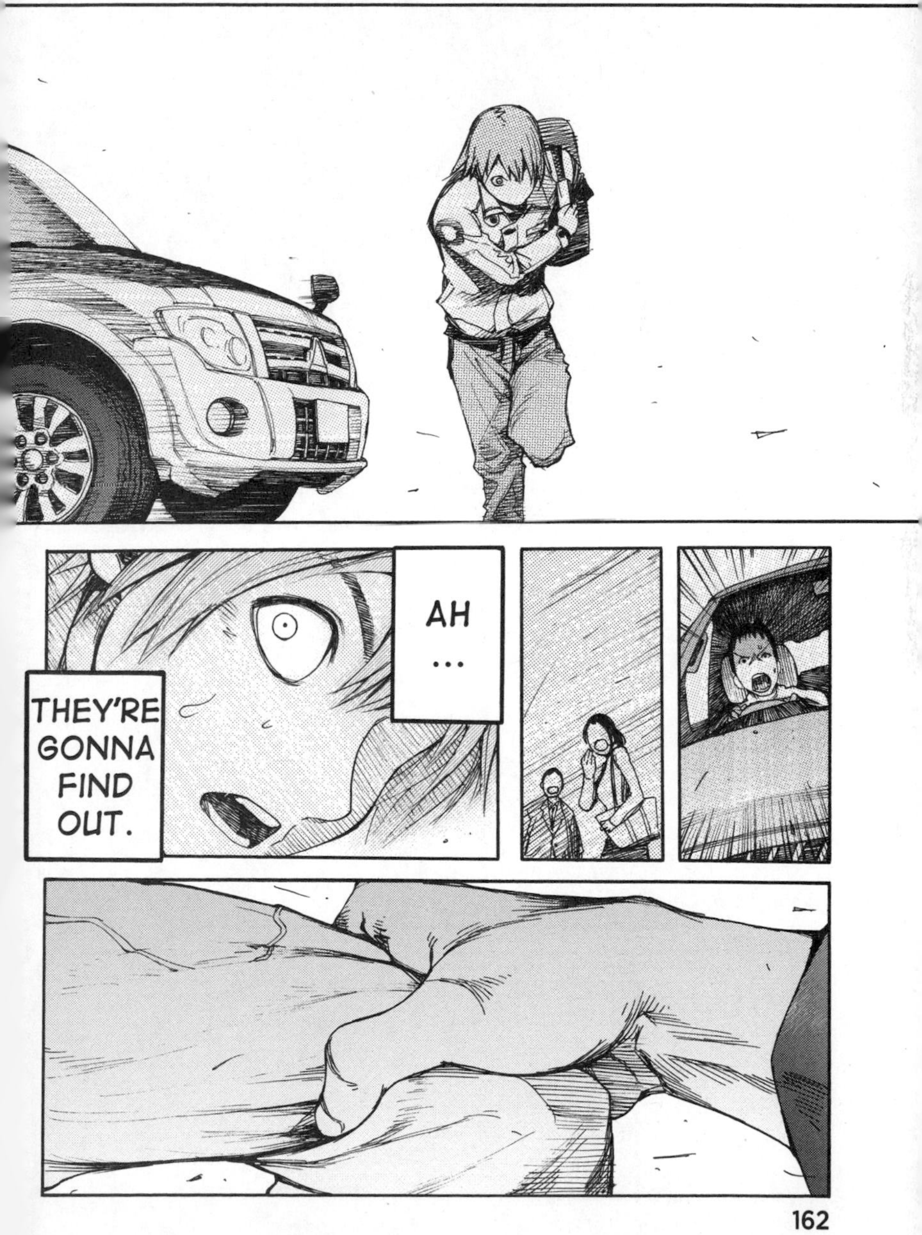
AH ...
THEY'RE GONNA FIND OUT.

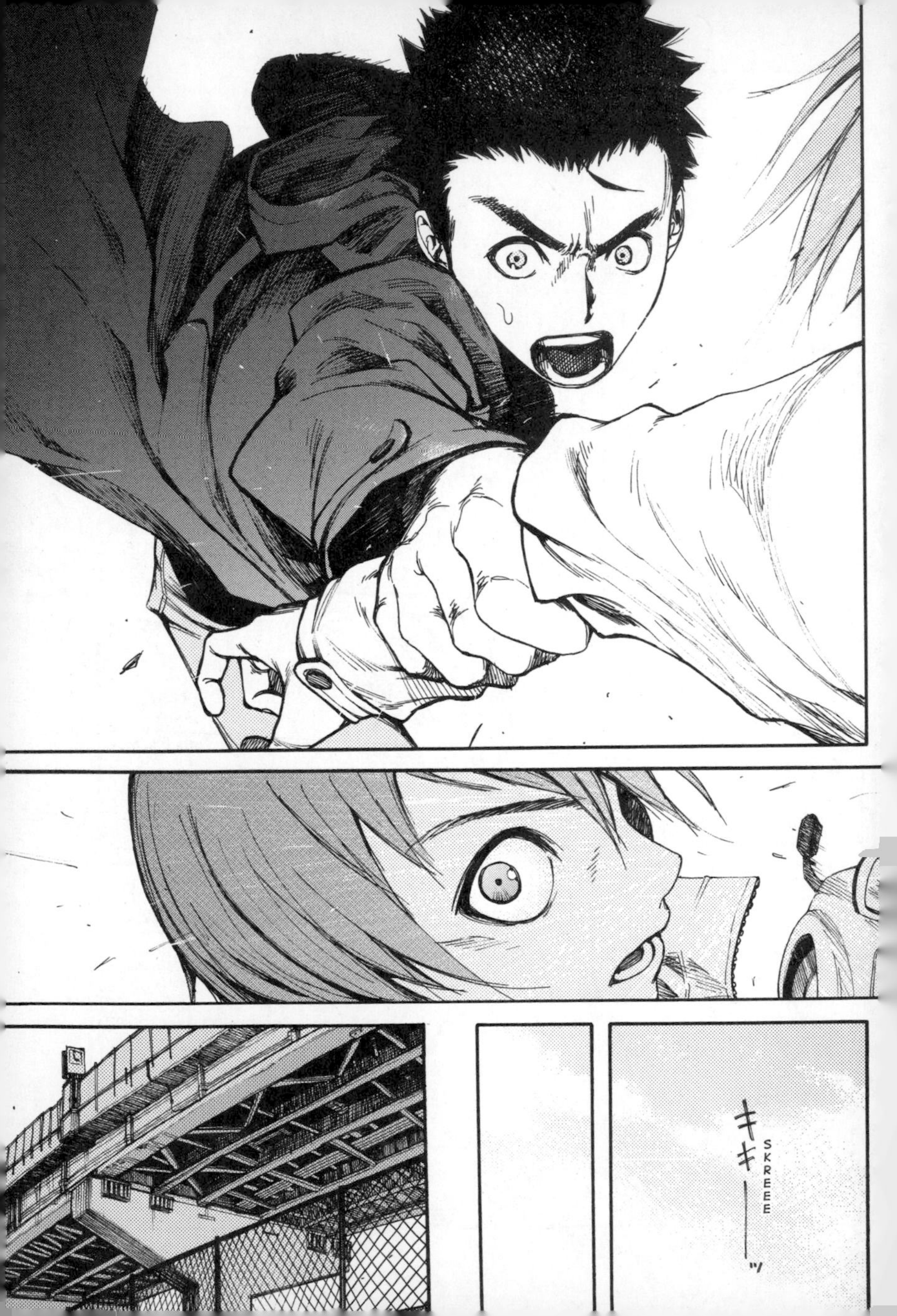
キキ———ッ
SKREEE

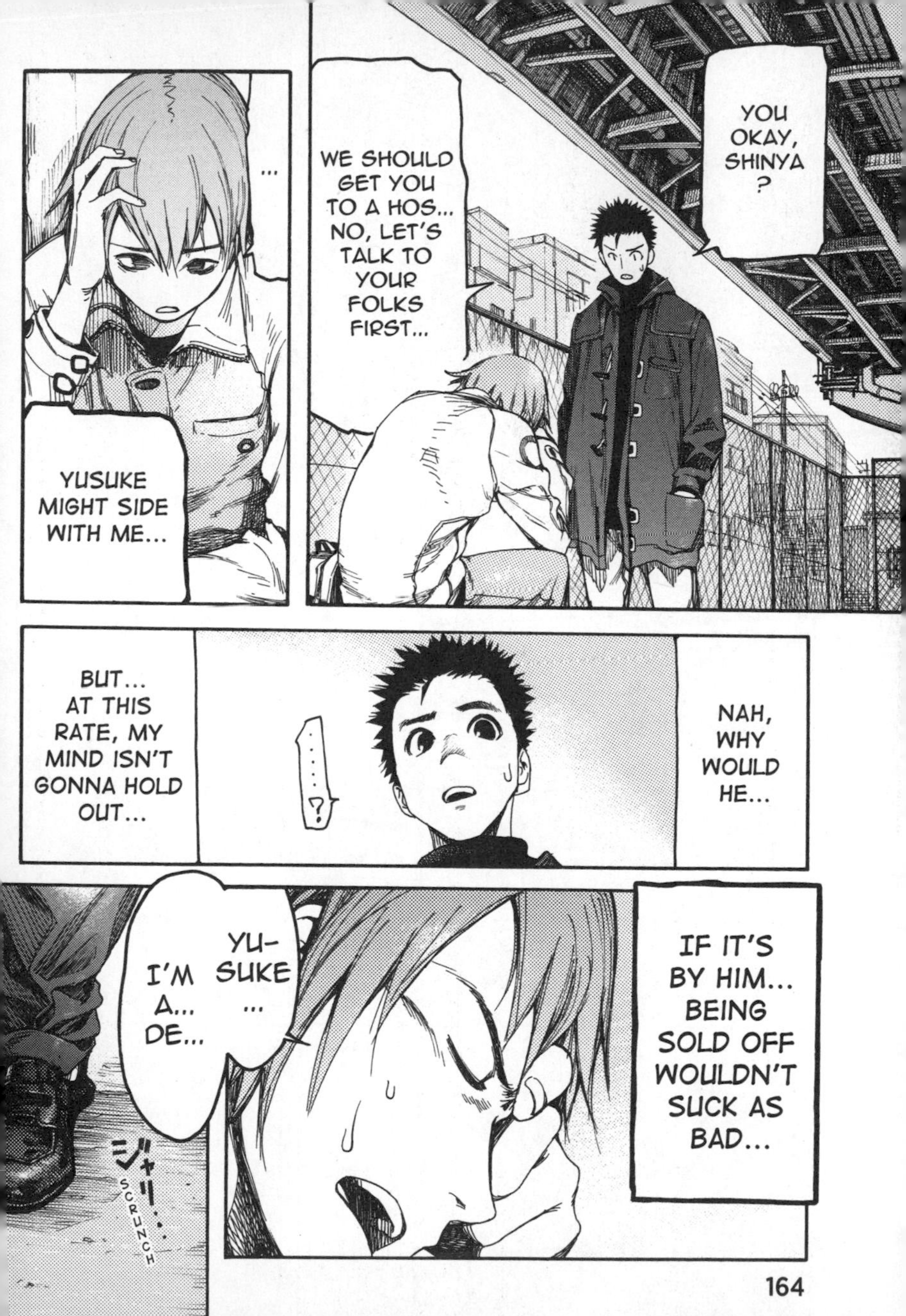
YOU OKAY, SHINYA?
WE SHOULD GET YOU TO A HOS... NO, LET'S TALK TO YOUR FOLKS FIRST...
...
YUSUKE MIGHT SIDE WITH ME...
NAH, WHY WOULD HE...
.....?
BUT... AT THIS RATE, MY MIND ISN'T GONNA HOLD OUT...
IF IT'S BY HIM... BEING SOLD OFF WOULDN'T SUCK AS BAD...
YU-SUKE...
I'M A... DE...
ジャリ...
SCRUNCH

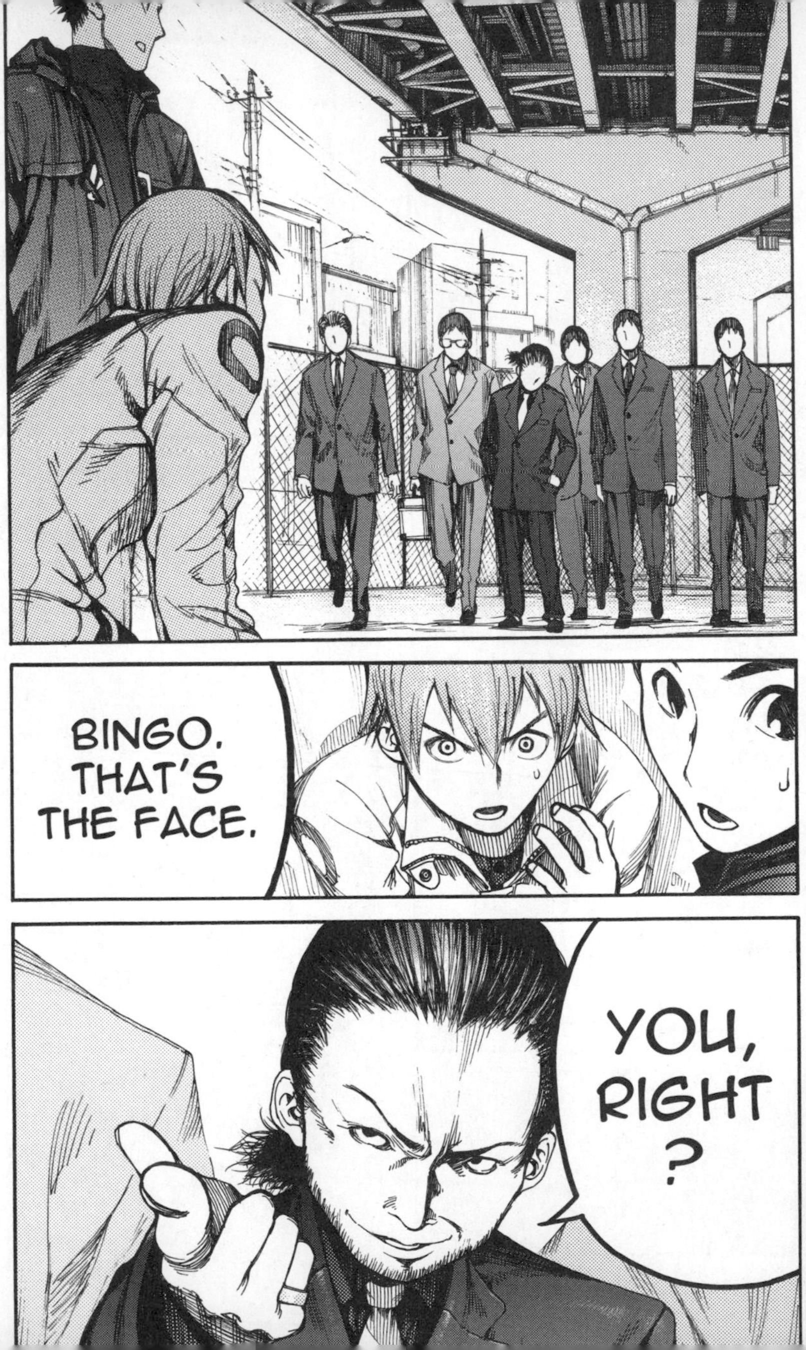
BINGO. THAT'S THE FACE.
YOU, RIGHT ?

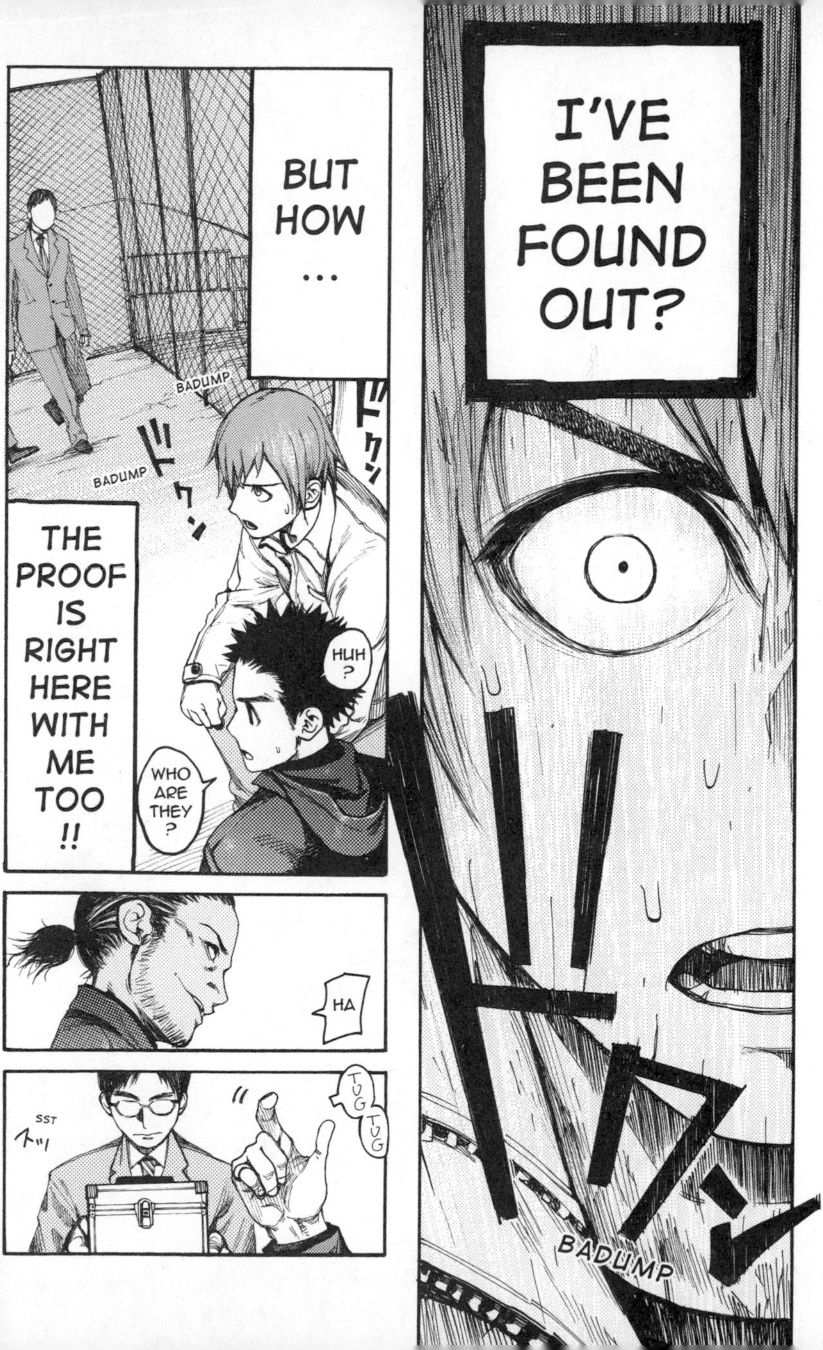
I'VE BEEN FOUND OUT?
ドクン
BADUMP
BUT HOW ...
BADUMP
ドクン
BADUMP
ドクン
THE PROOF IS RIGHT HERE WITH ME TOO !!
HUH ?
WHO ARE THEY ?
HA
SST
スッ
TUG TUG

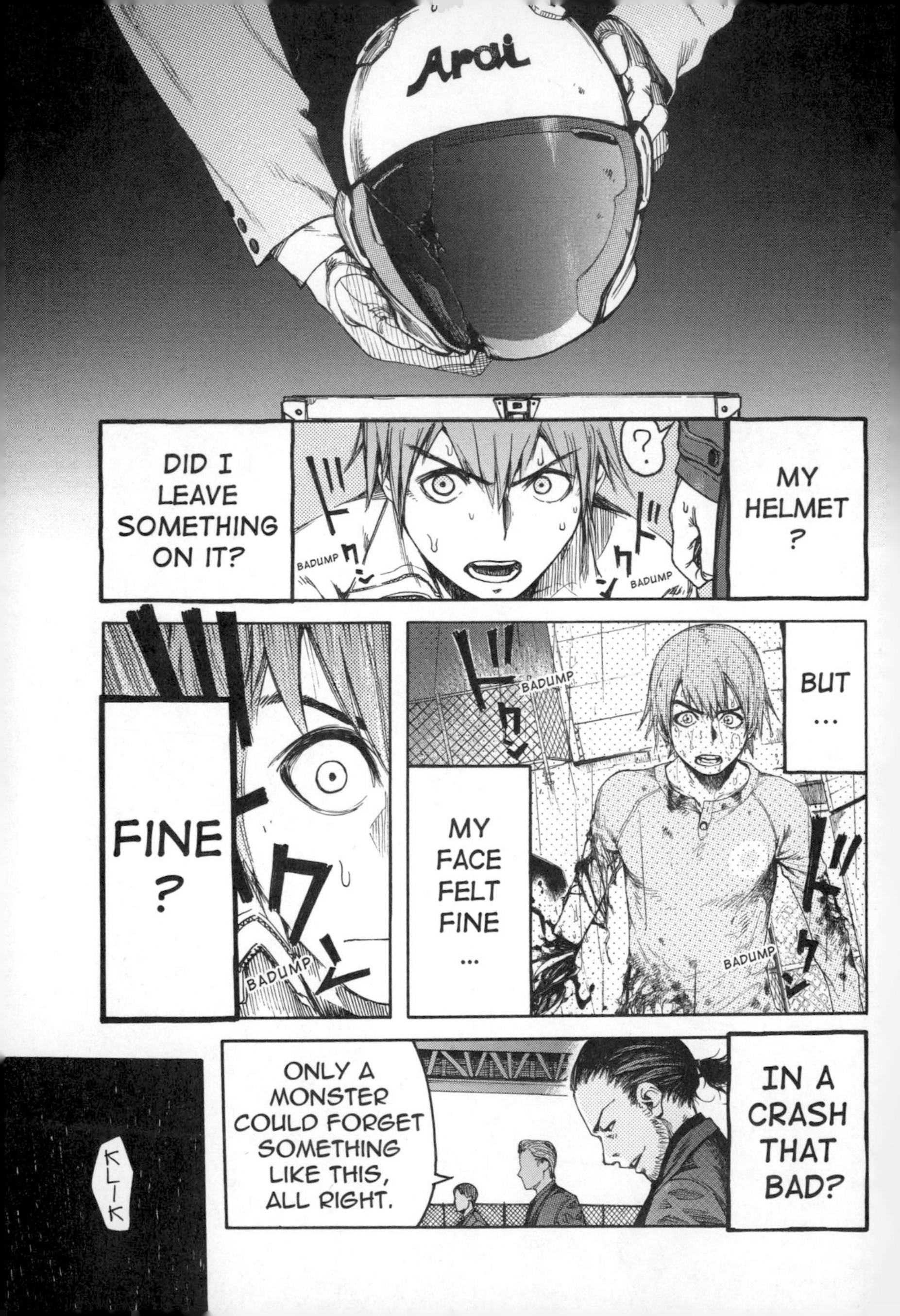
MY HELMET ?
?
BADUMP
BADUMP
DID I LEAVE SOMETHING ON IT?
BUT ...
BADUMP
MY FACE FELT FINE ...
BADUMP
FINE ?
BADUMP
IN A CRASH THAT BAD?
ONLY A MONSTER COULD FORGET SOMETHING LIKE THIS, ALL RIGHT.
KLIK

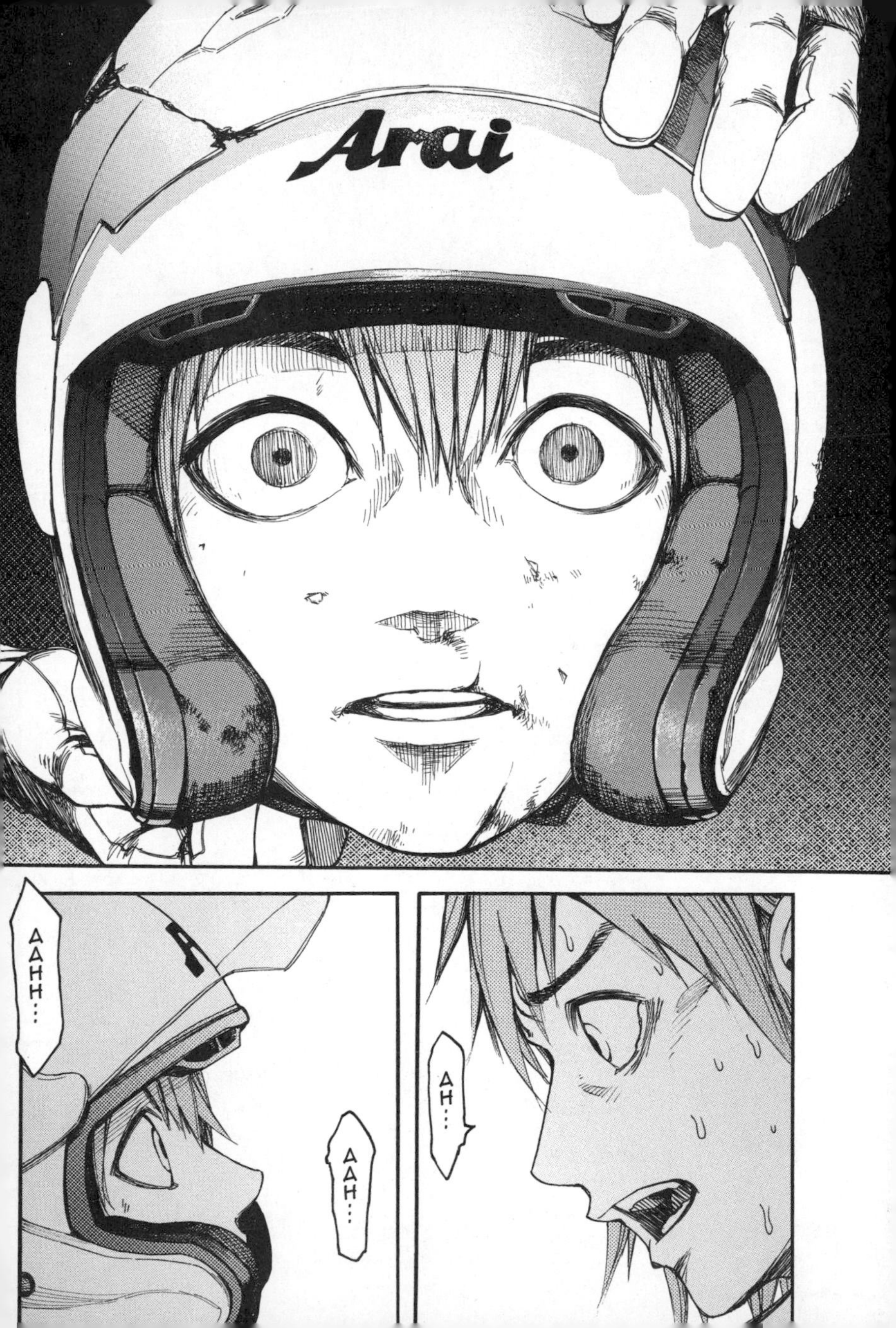
Arai
AH...
AAH...
AAHH...

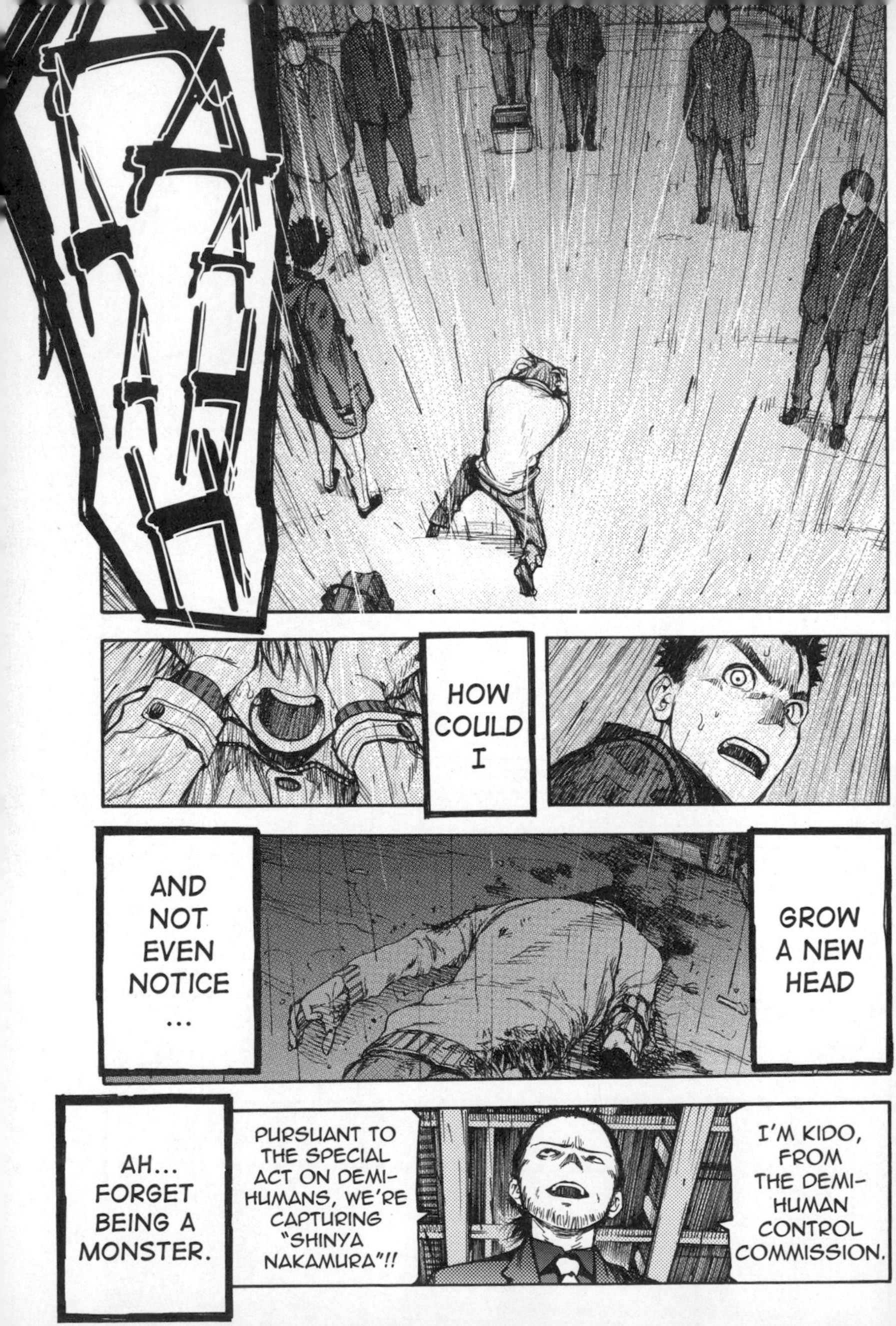
HOW COULD I
GROW A NEW HEAD
AND NOT EVEN NOTICE ...
I'M KIDO, FROM THE DEMI-HUMAN CONTROL COMMISSION.
PURSUANT TO THE SPECIAL ACT ON DEMI-HUMANS, WE'RE CAPTURING "SHINYA NAKAMURA"!!
AH... FORGET BEING A MONSTER.

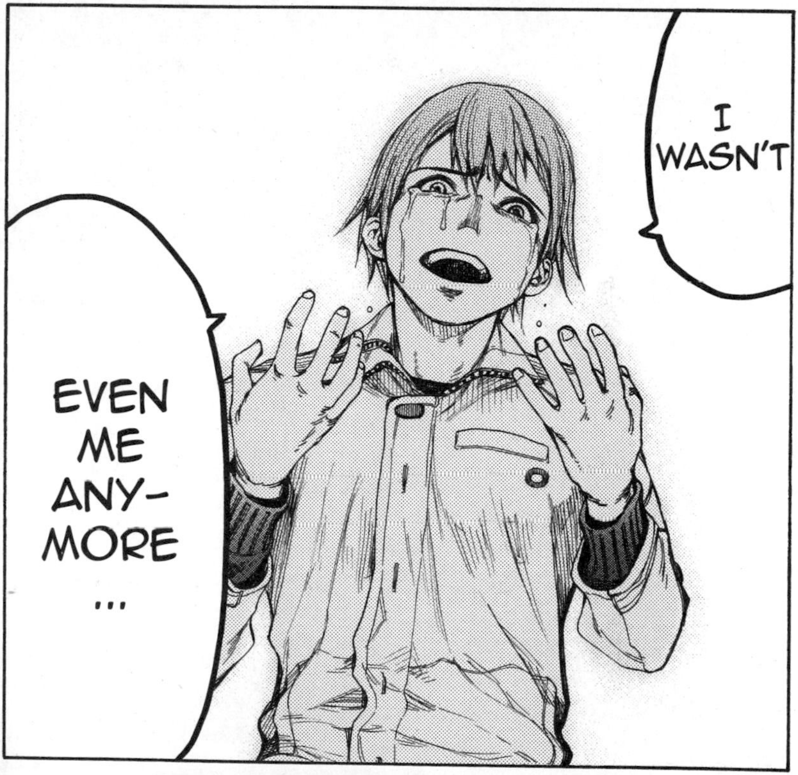
I WASN'T
EVEN ME ANYMORE ...
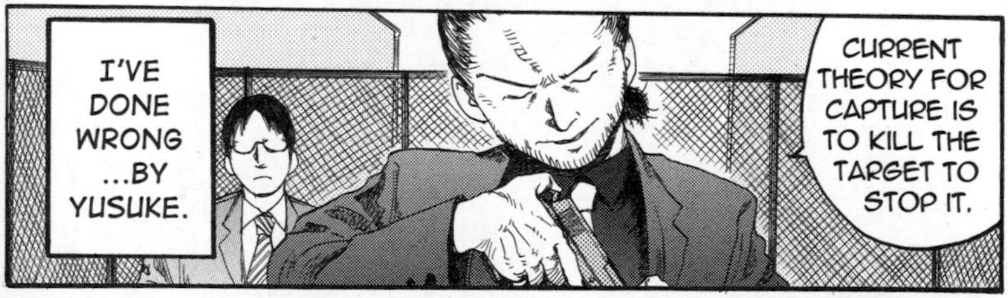
CURRENT THEORY FOR CAPTURE IS TO KILL THE TARGET TO STOP IT.
I'VE DONE WRONG ...BY YUSUKE.
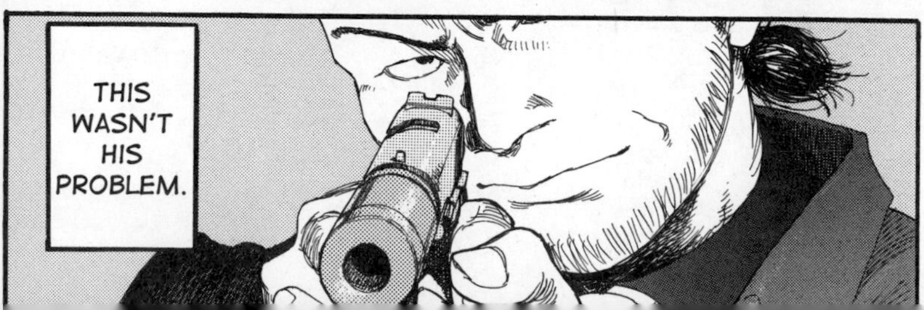
THIS WASN'T HIS PROBLEM.

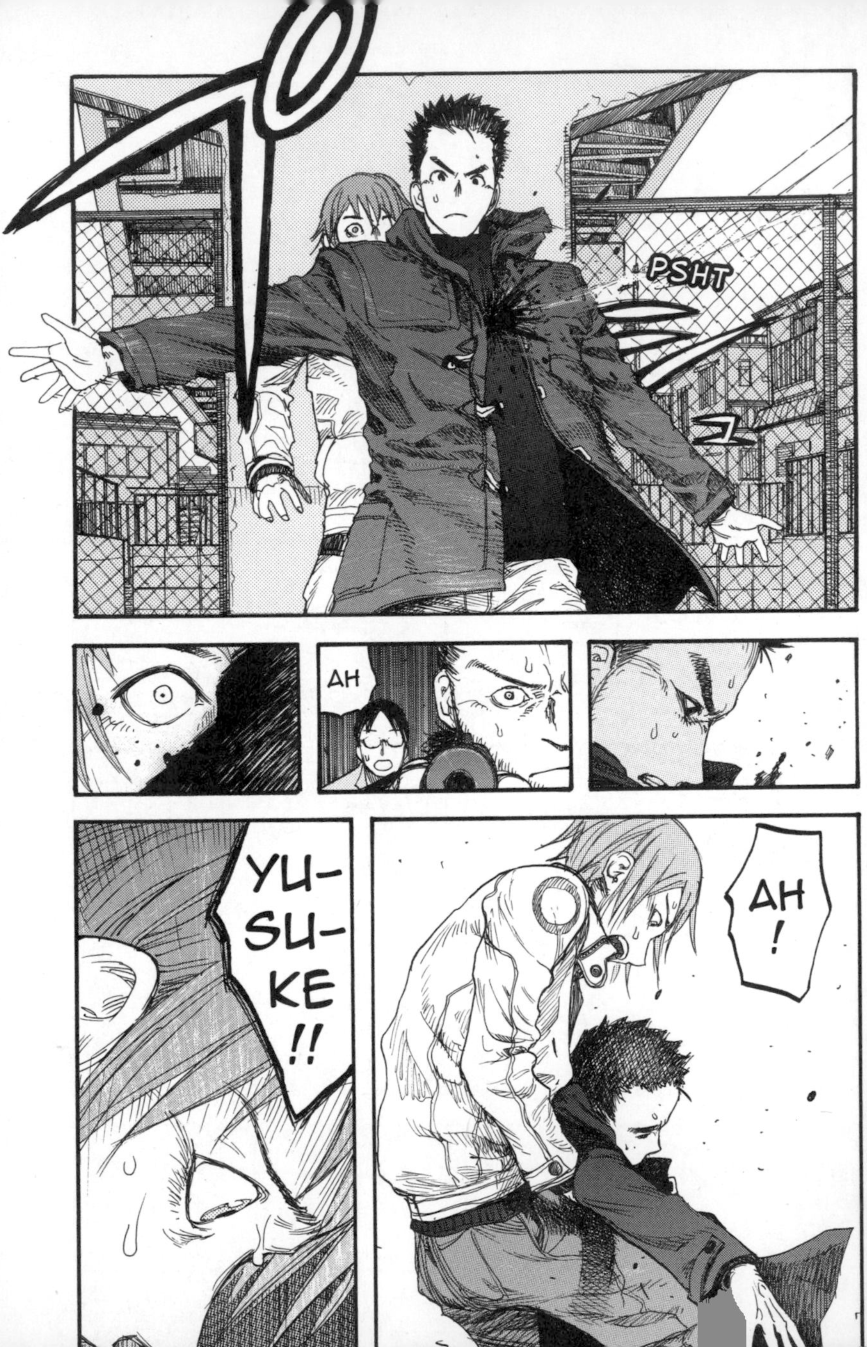
PSHT
AH
AH!
YU-SU-KE!!

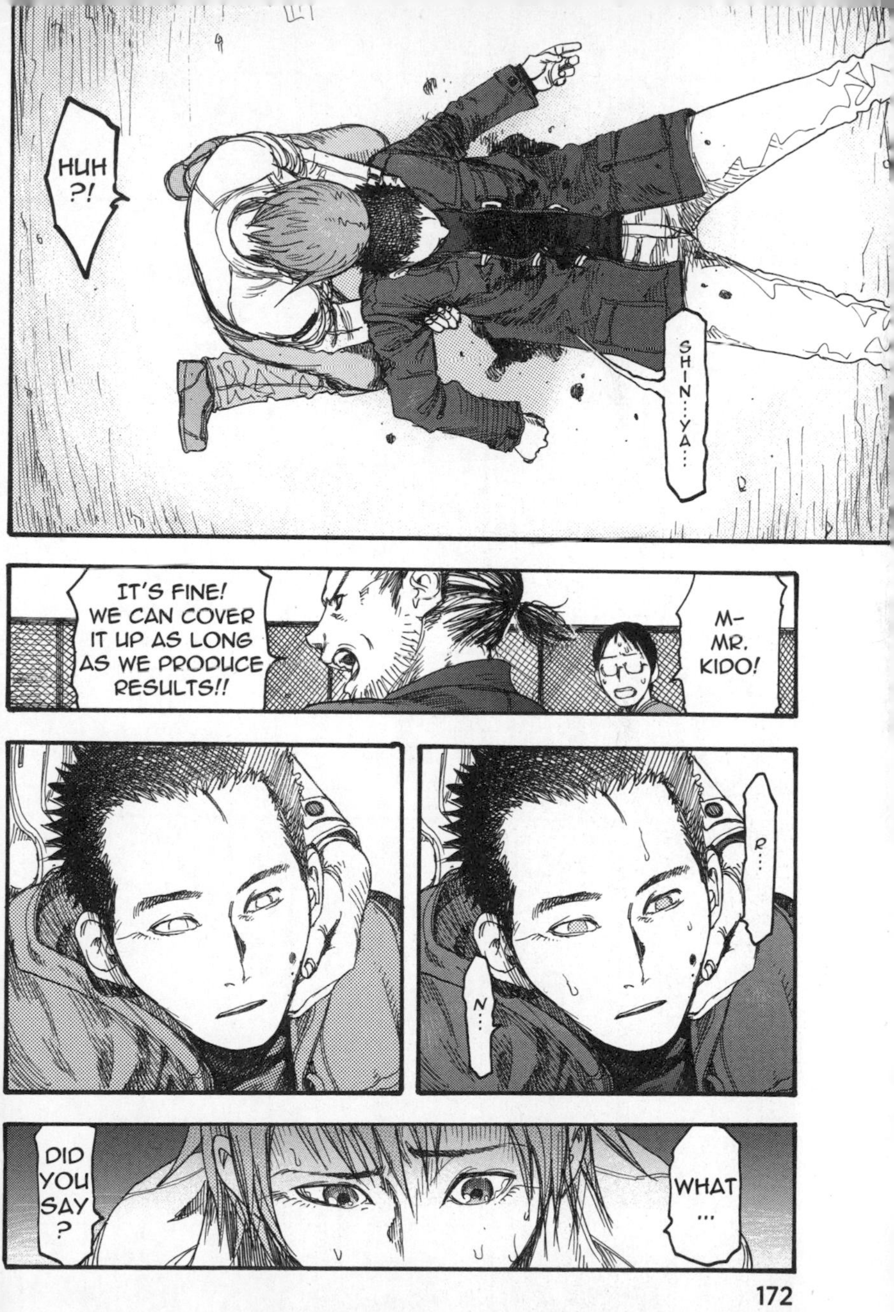
SHIN...YA...
HUH ?!
M- MR. KIDO!
IT'S FINE! WE CAN COVER IT UP AS LONG AS WE PRODUCE RESULTS!!
R...
N...
WHAT ...
DID YOU SAY ?

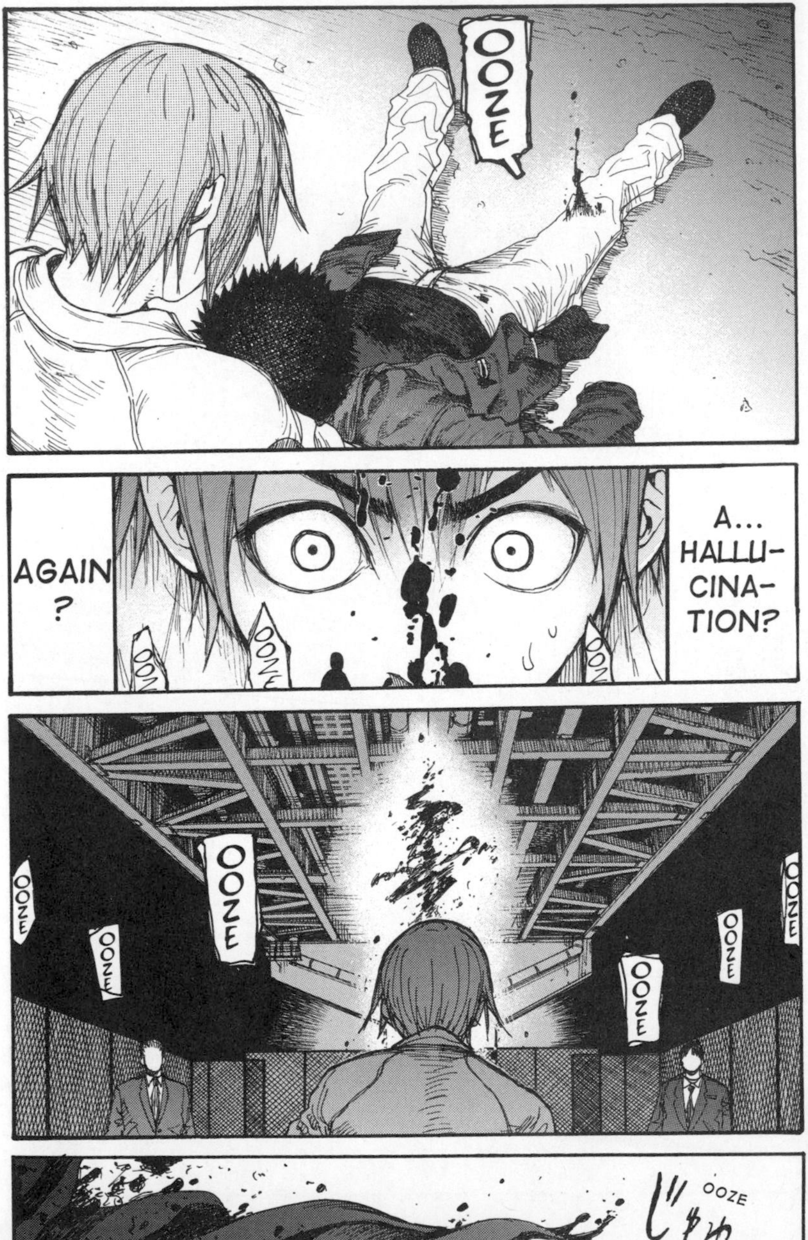
OOZE
A... HALLUCINATION?
AGAIN?
OOZE
OOZE
OOZE
OOZE
OOZE
OOZE
OOZE
OOZE
OOZE
OOZE
じゅわ...

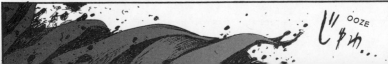

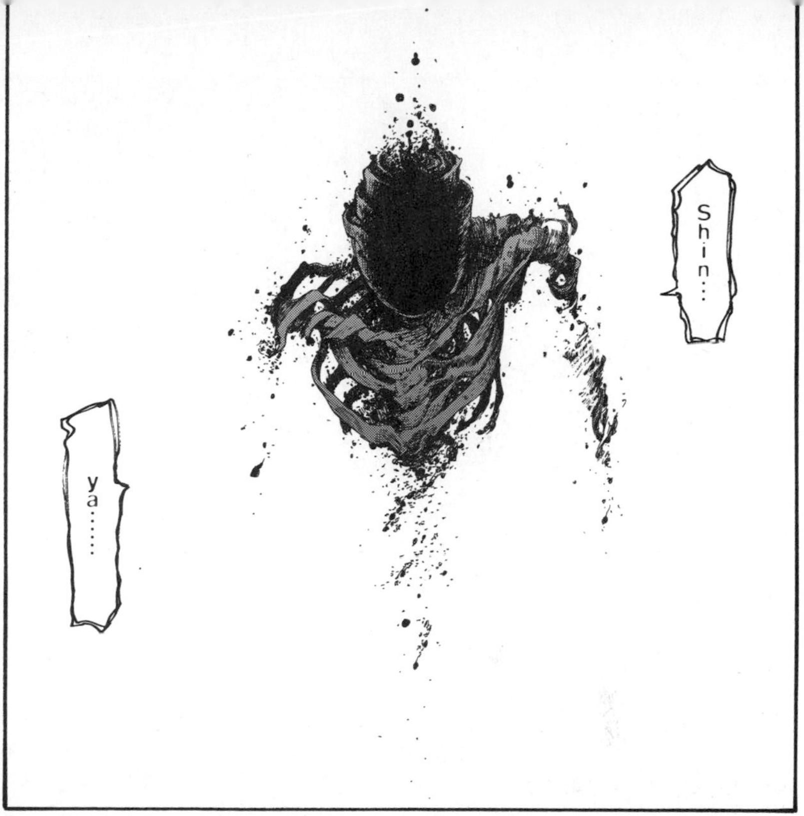
Shin...
ya......

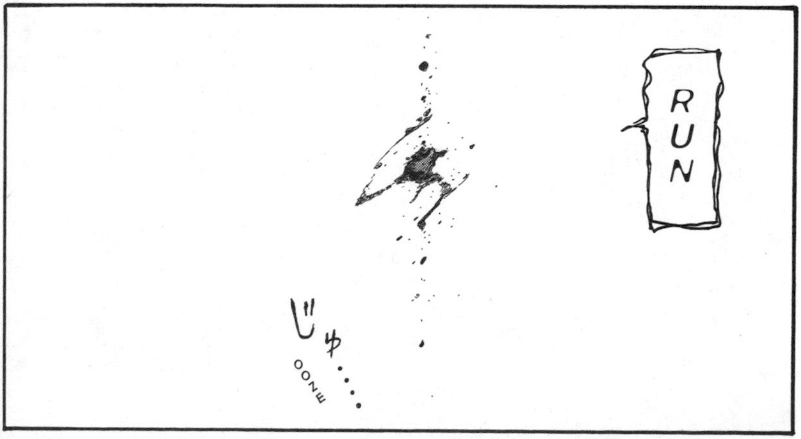
RUN
じゅ....
OOZE

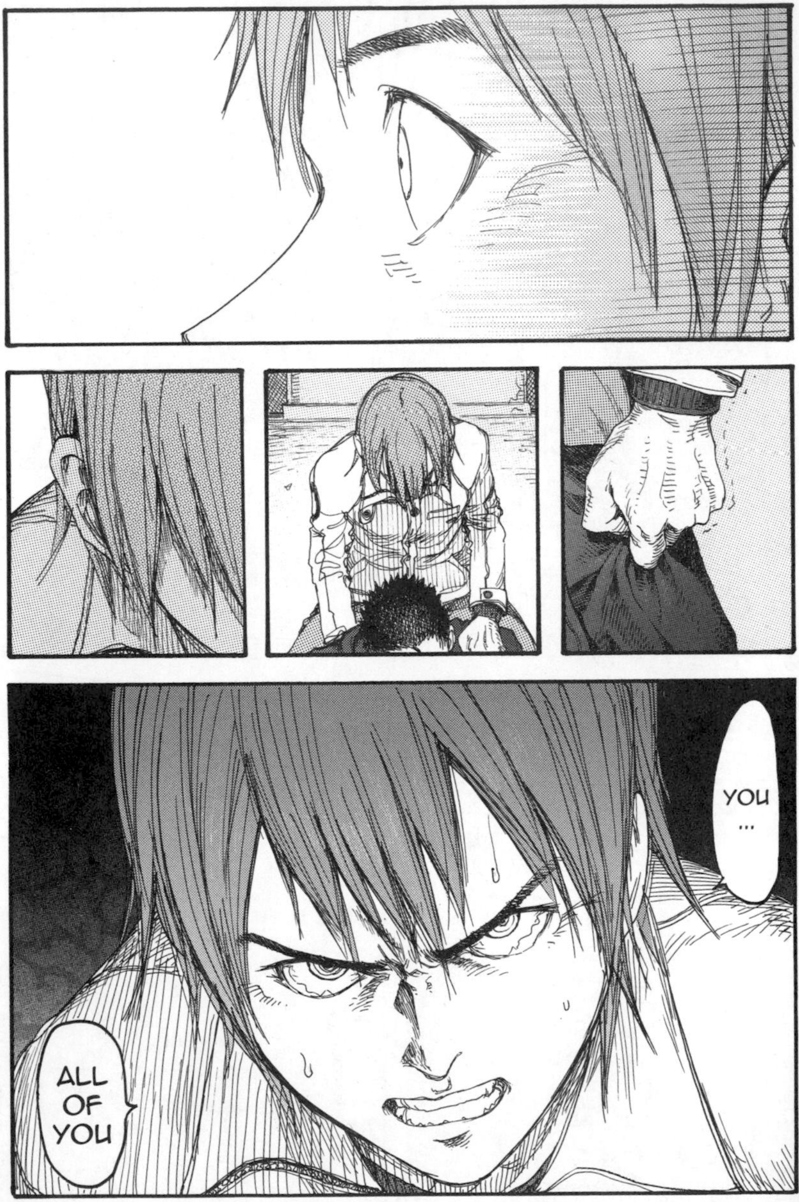
YOU ...
ALL OF YOU

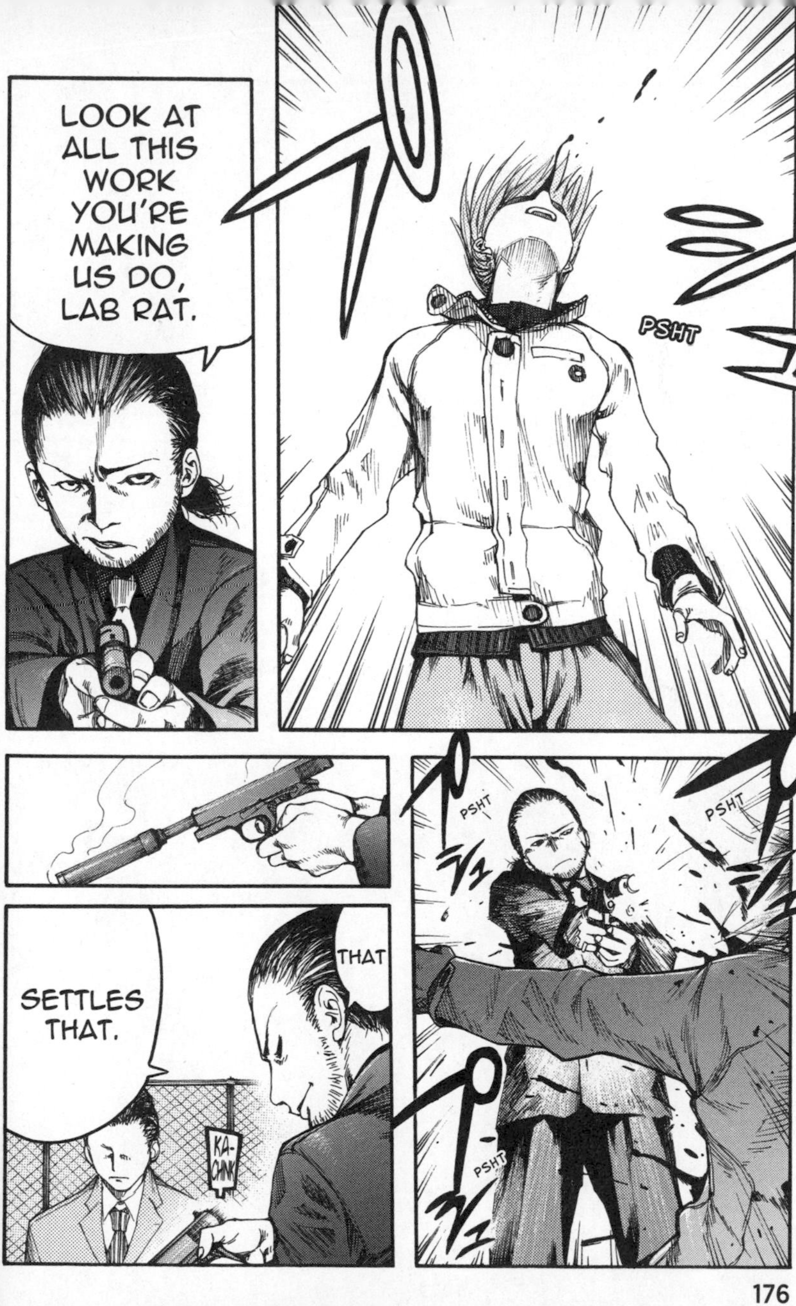
PSHT
LOOK AT ALL THIS WORK YOU'RE MAKING US DO, LAB RAT.
PSHT
PSHT
PSHT
THAT
SETTLES THAT.
KA-CHINK

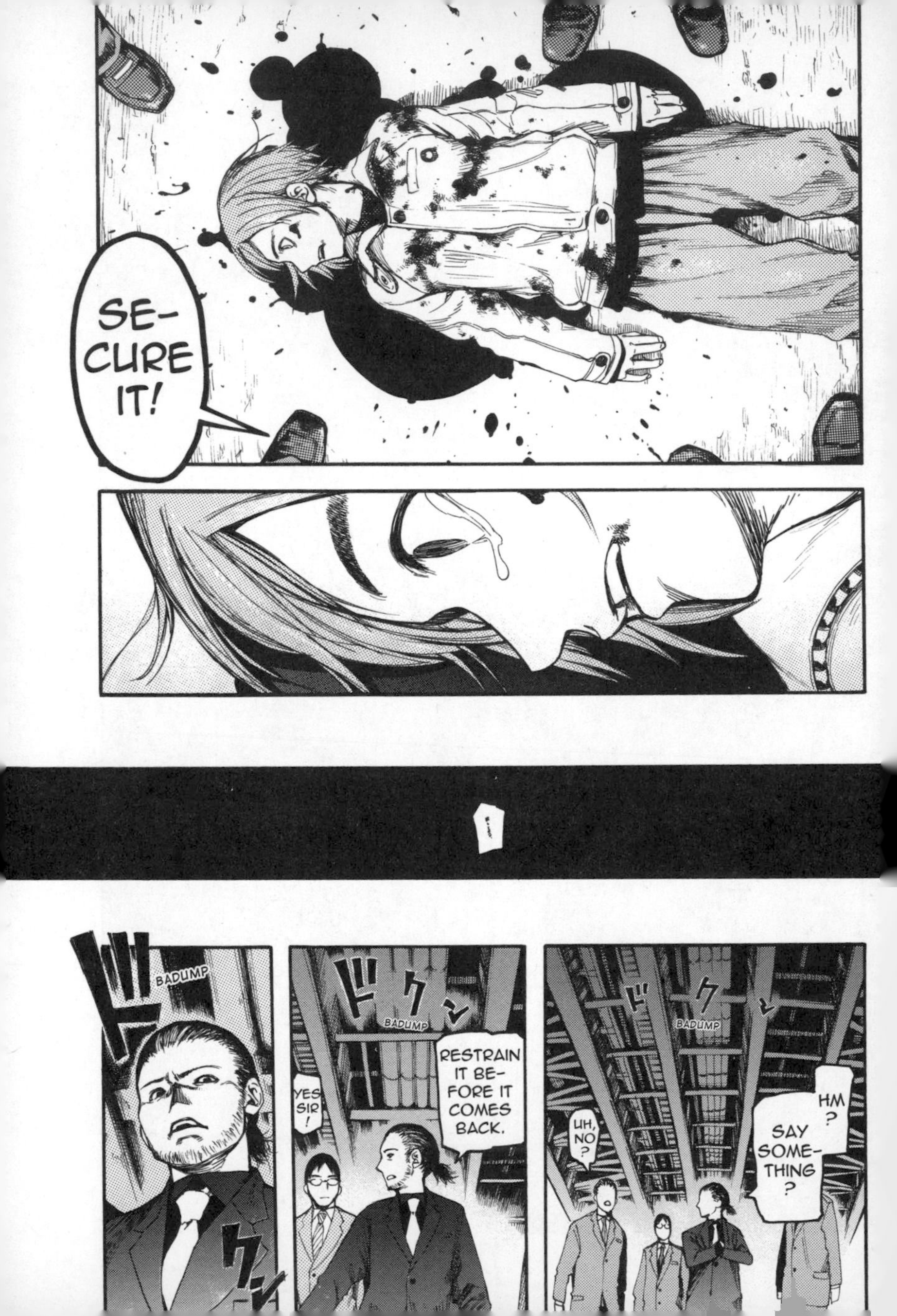
SE-CURE IT!
BADUMP
HM? SAY SOME-THING?
UH, NO?
BADUMP
RESTRAIN IT BE-FORE IT COMES BACK.
YES SIR!
BADUMP

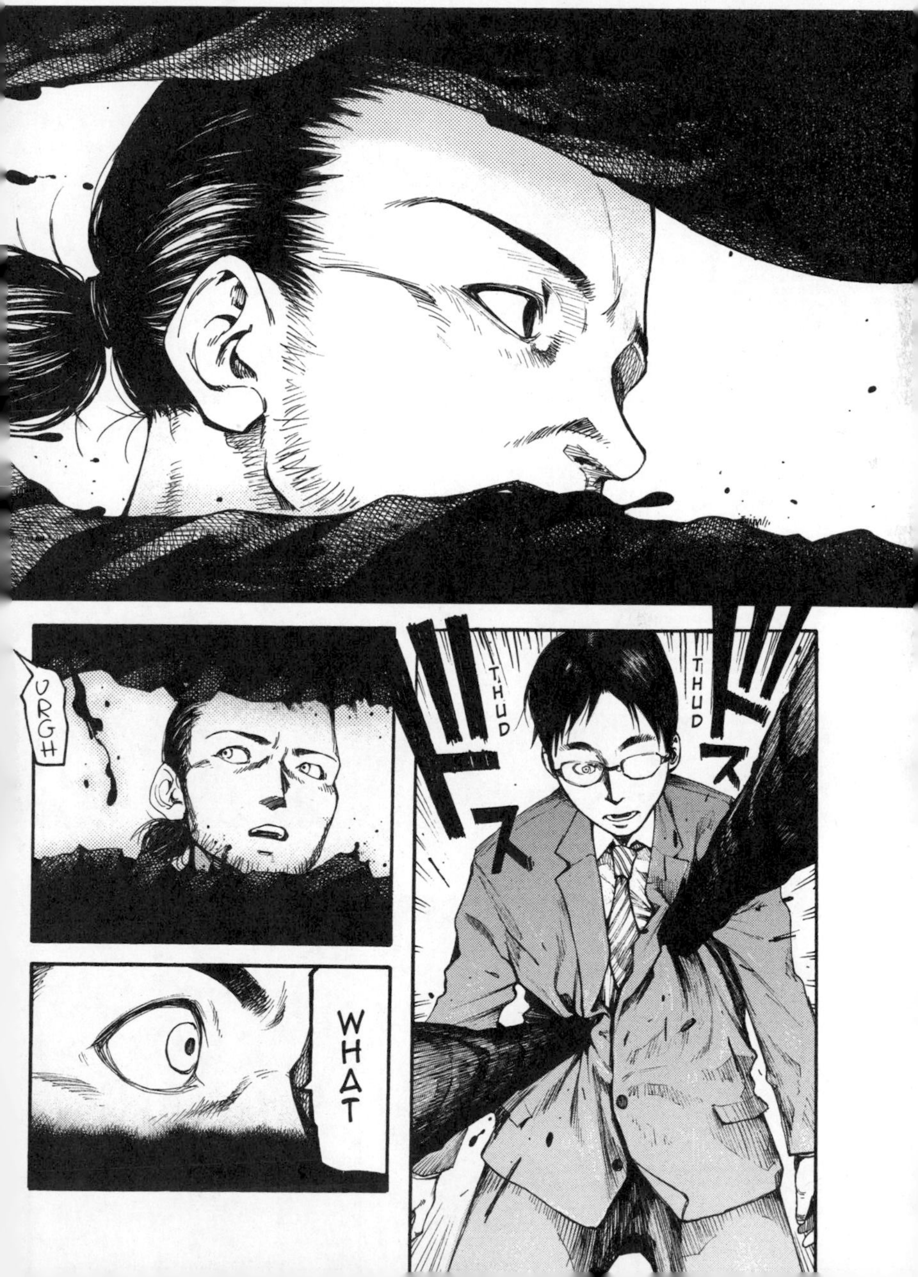
ドス
THUD
ドス
THUD
URGH
WHAT

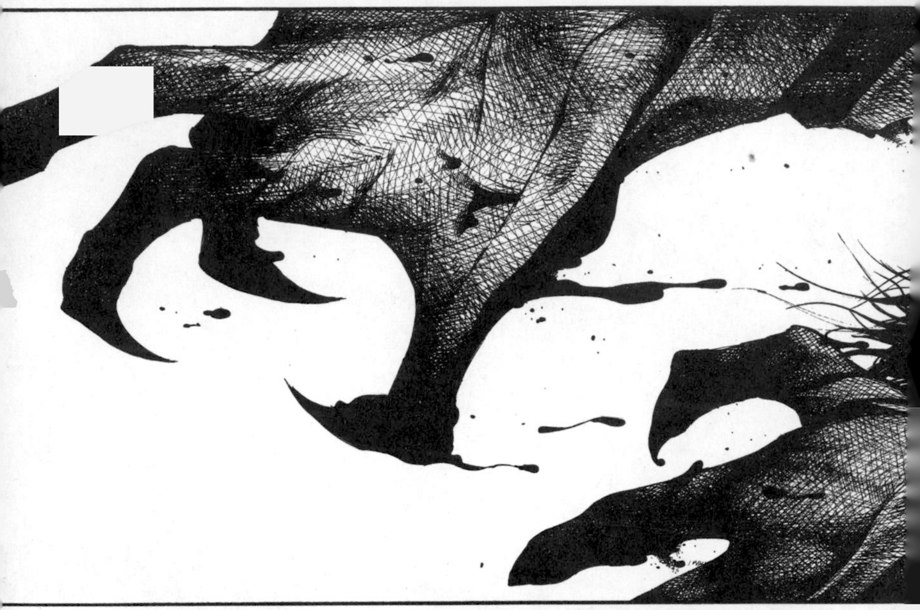

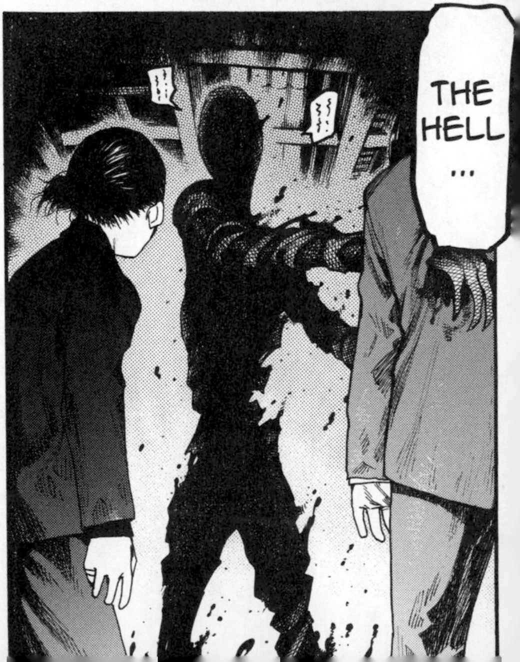
THE HELL ...

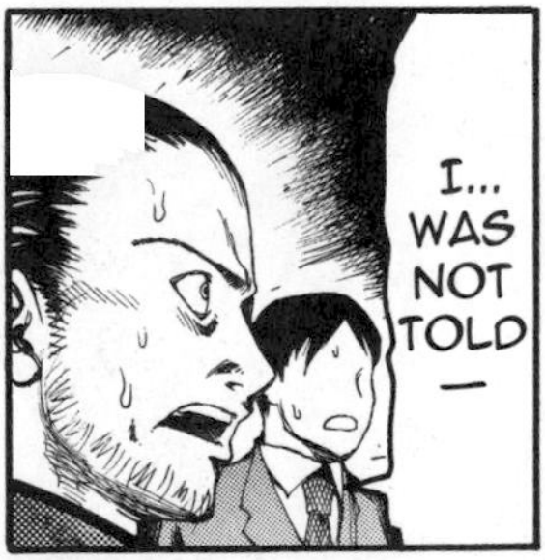
I... WAS NOT TOLD —

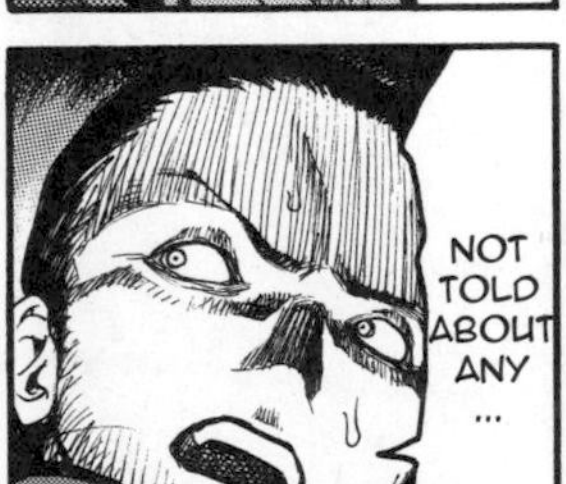
NOT TOLD ABOUT ANY ...

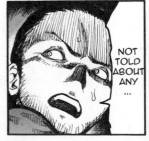

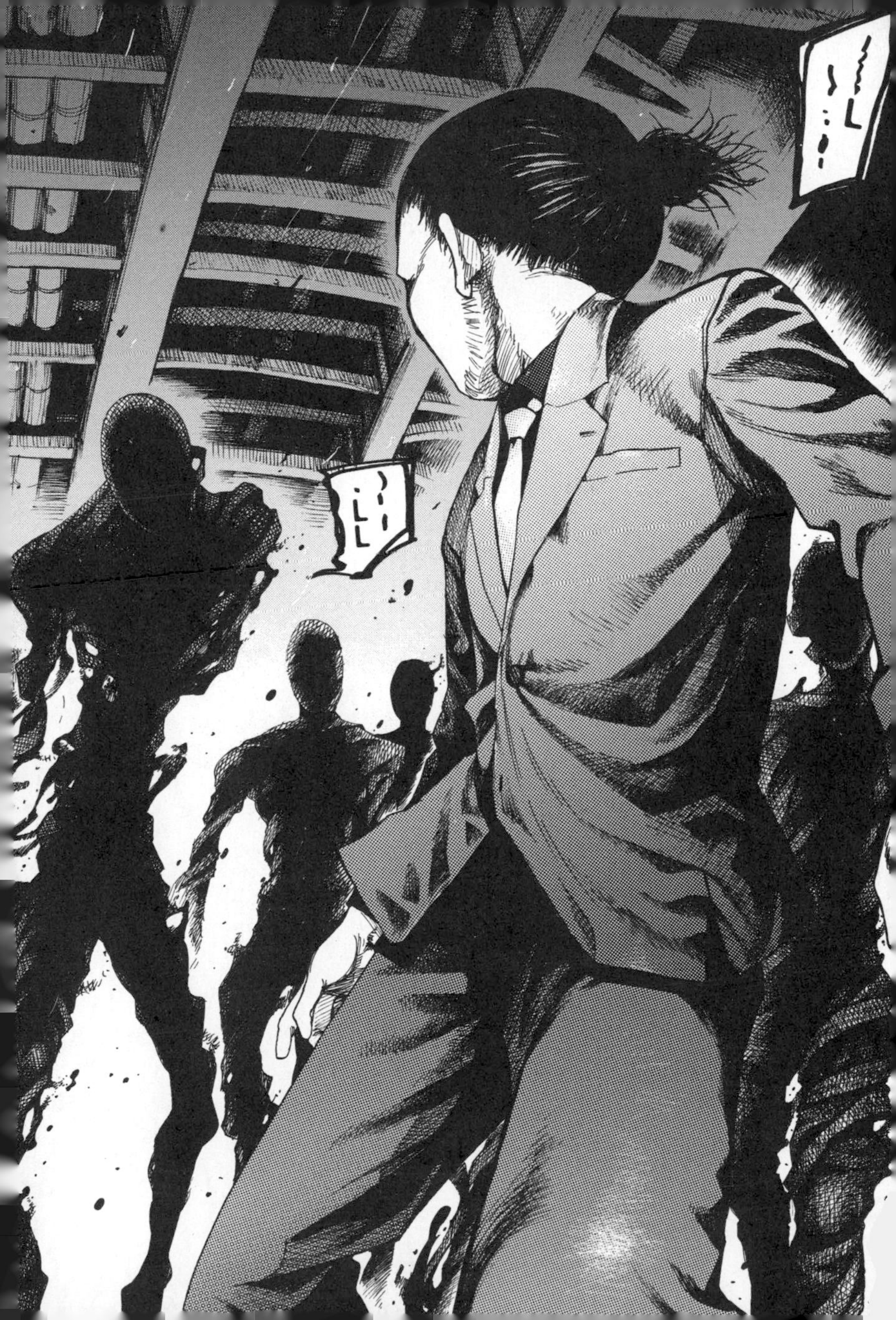

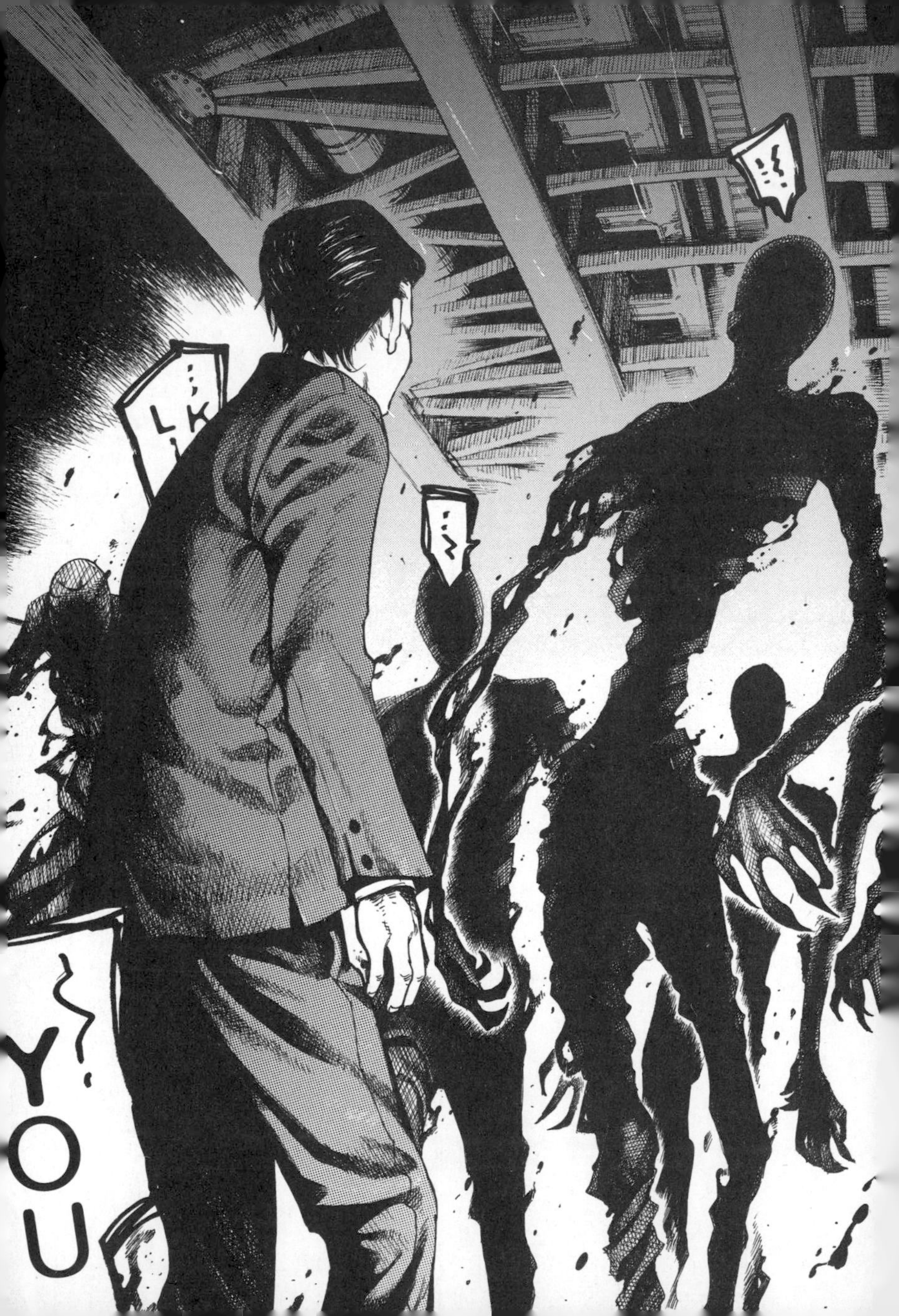
YOU

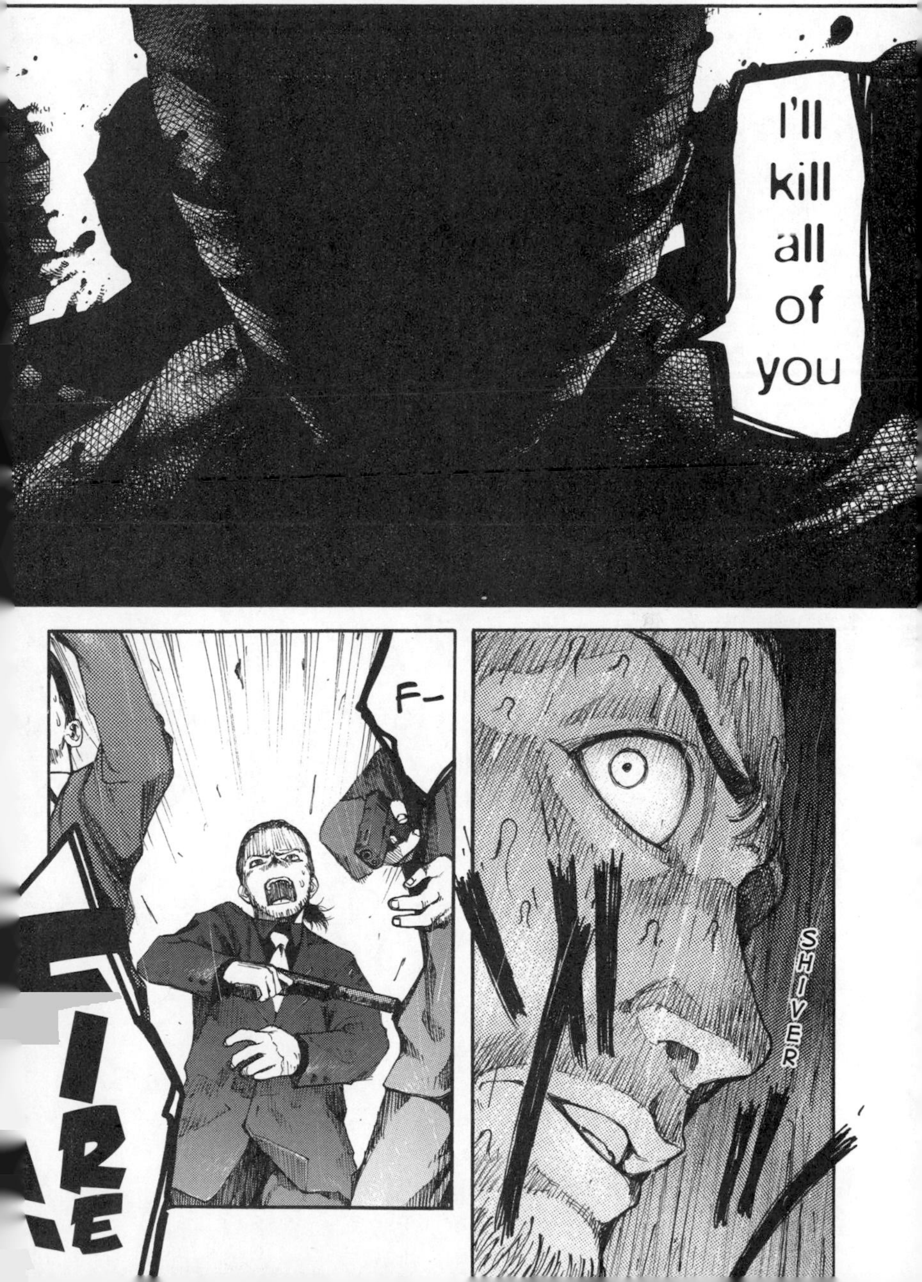
I'll kill all of you
SHIVER
F-

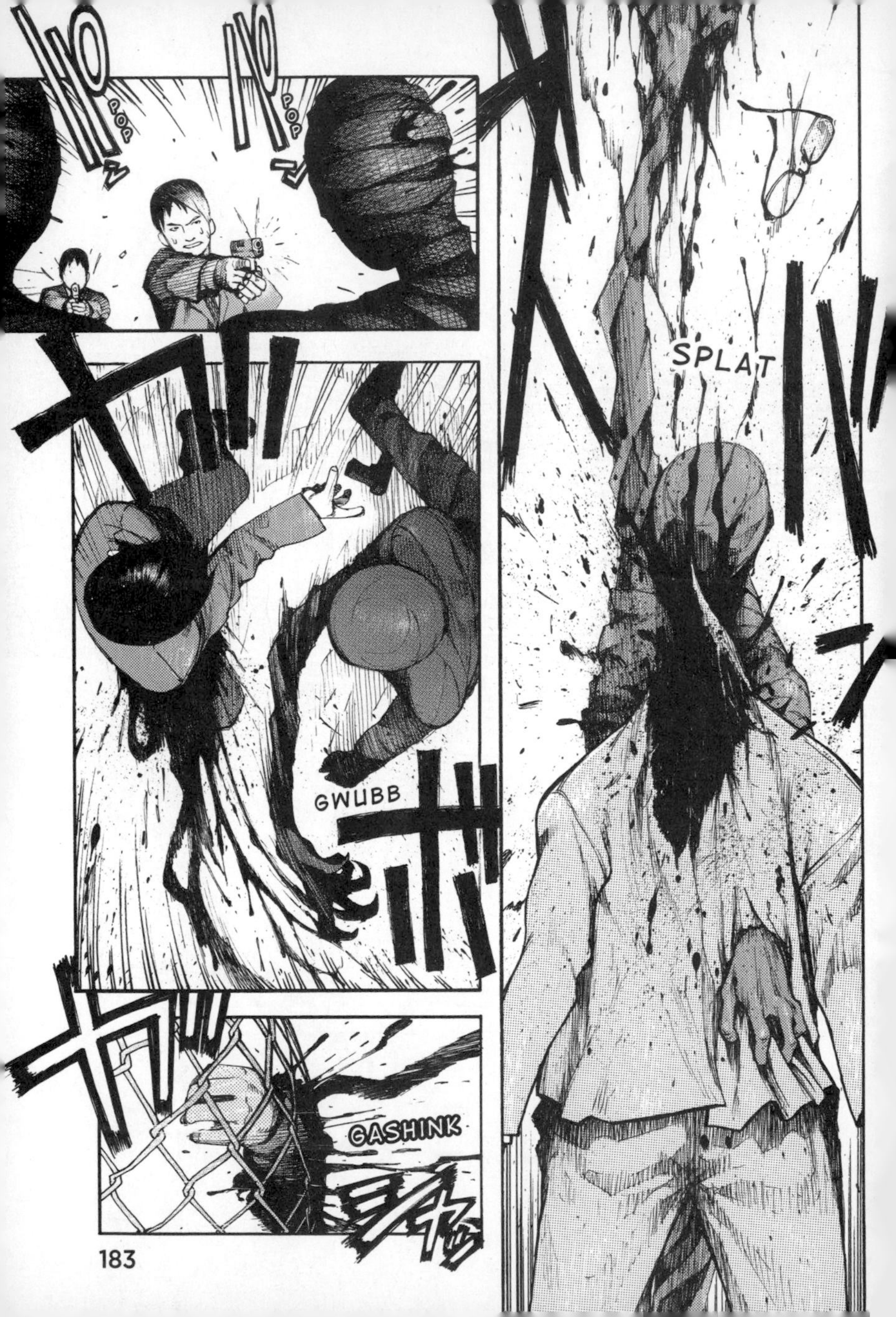
SPLAT
POP
POP
GWUBB
GASHINK

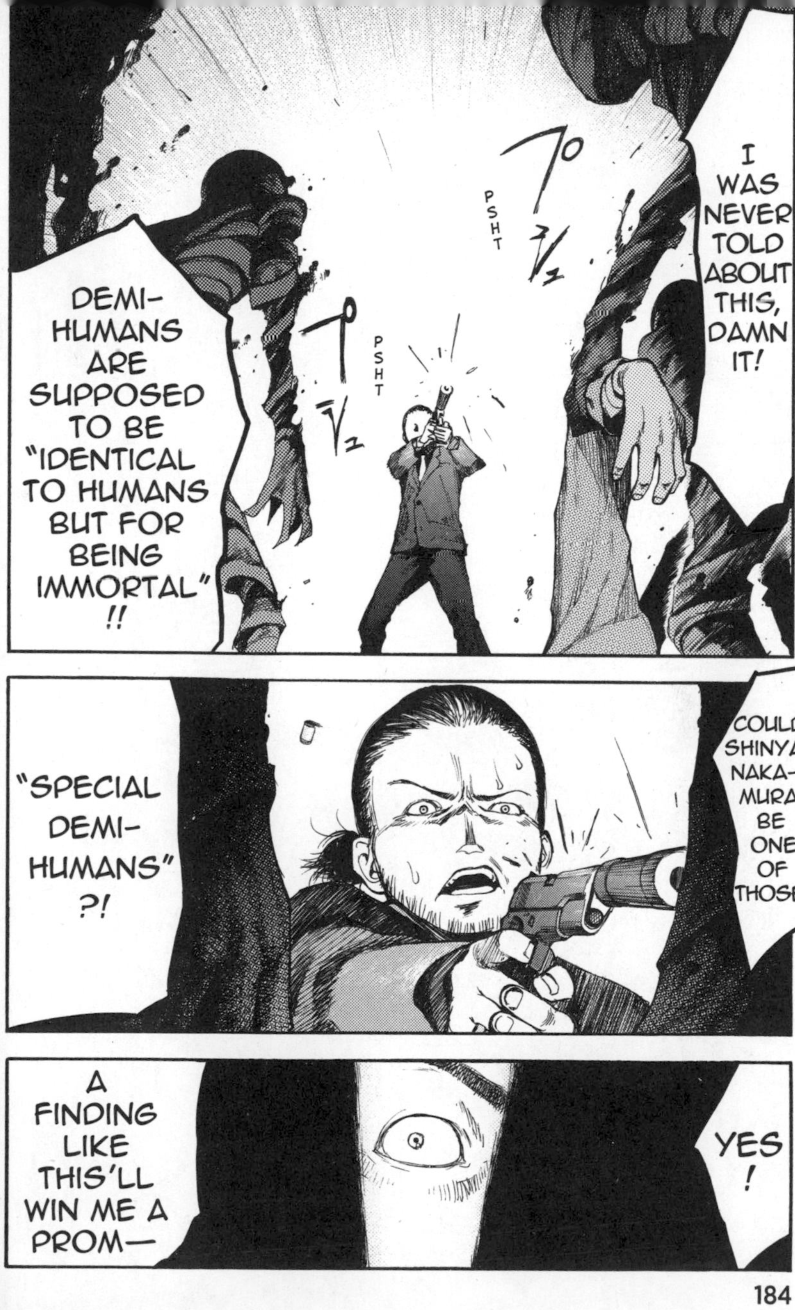
I WAS NEVER TOLD ABOUT THIS, DAMN IT!
PSHT
PSHT
DEMI-HUMANS ARE SUPPOSED TO BE "IDENTICAL TO HUMANS BUT FOR BEING IMMORTAL"!!
COULD SHINYA NAKAMURA BE ONE OF THOSE
"SPECIAL DEMI-HUMANS"?!
YES!
A FINDING LIKE THIS'LL WIN ME A PROM—

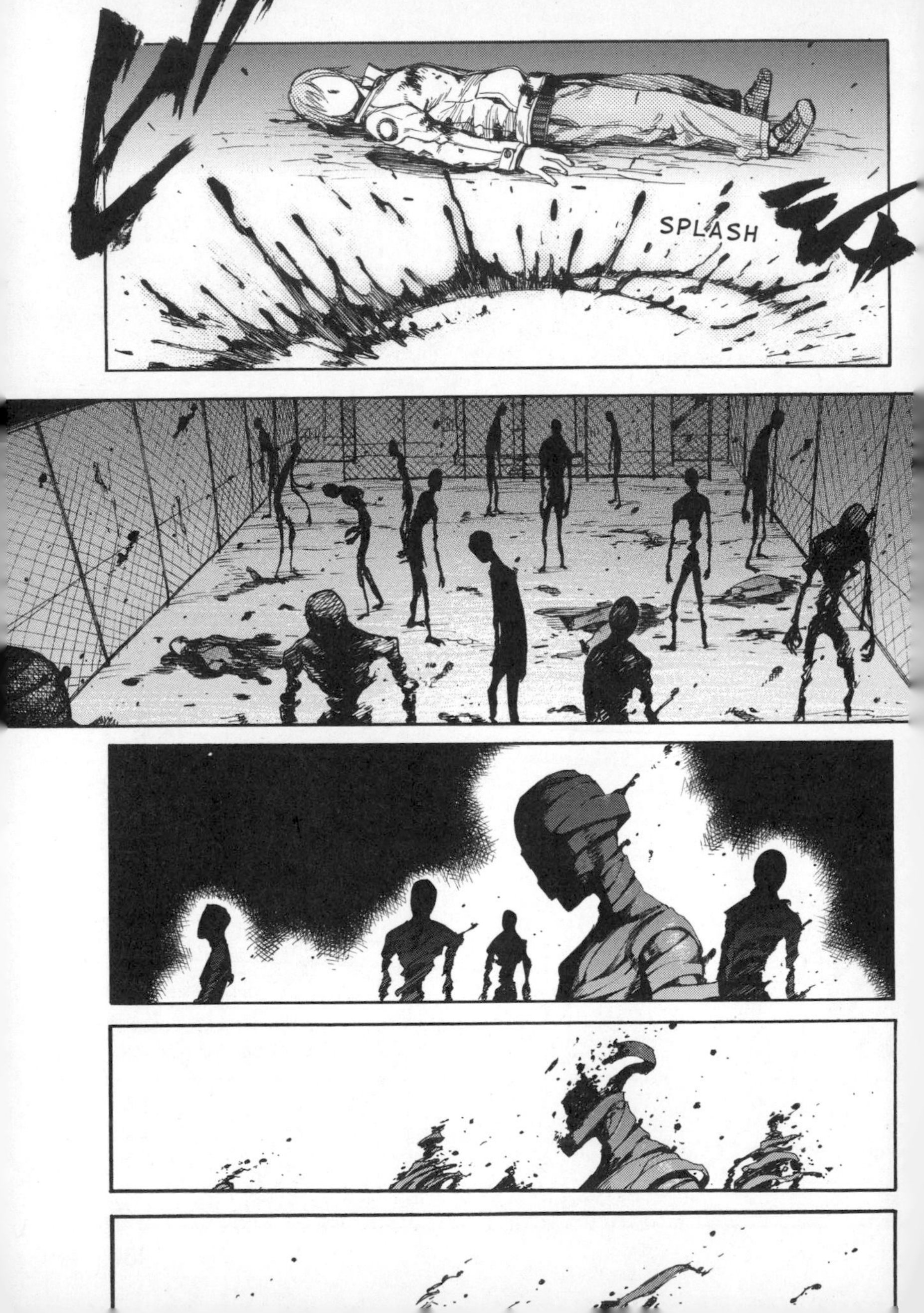
SPLASH

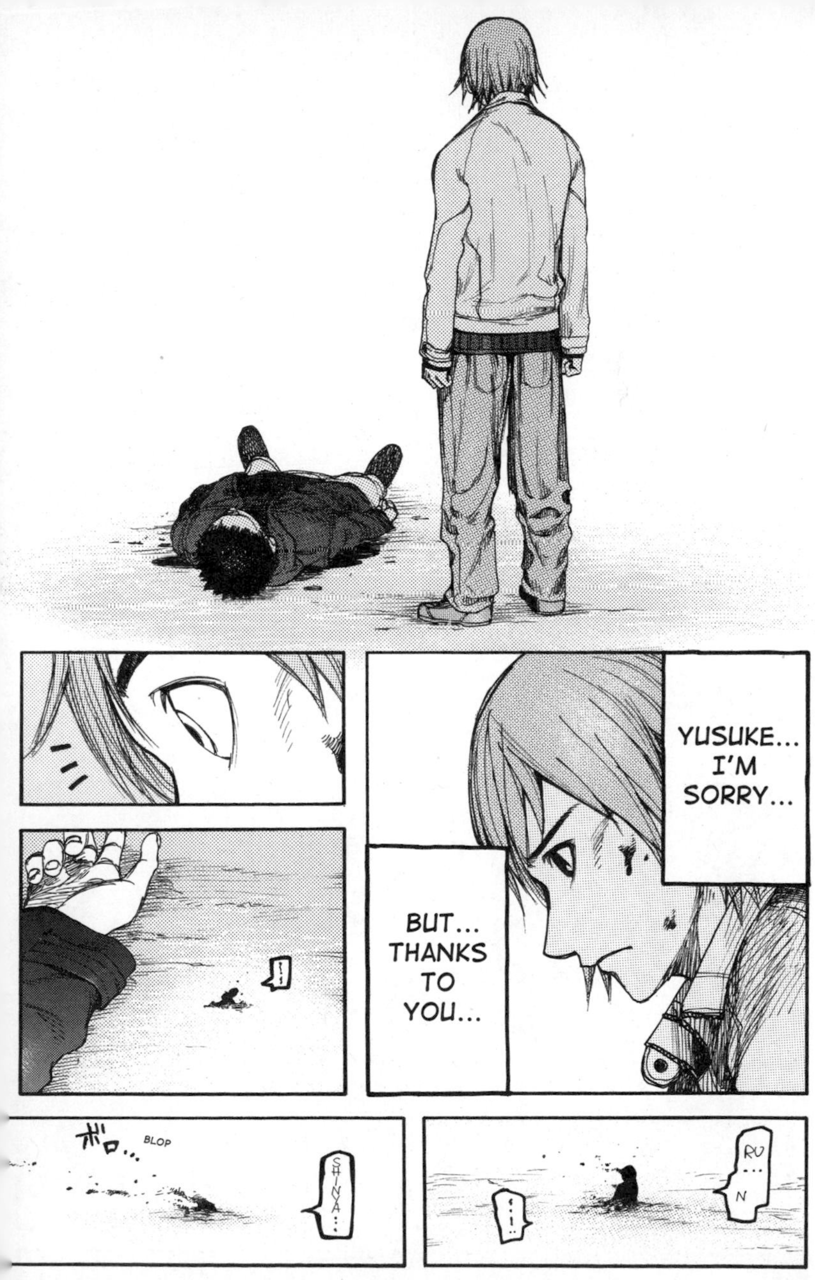
YUSUKE... I'M SORRY...
BUT... THANKS TO YOU...
RU... N
SHINYA...
ボロ...
BLOP

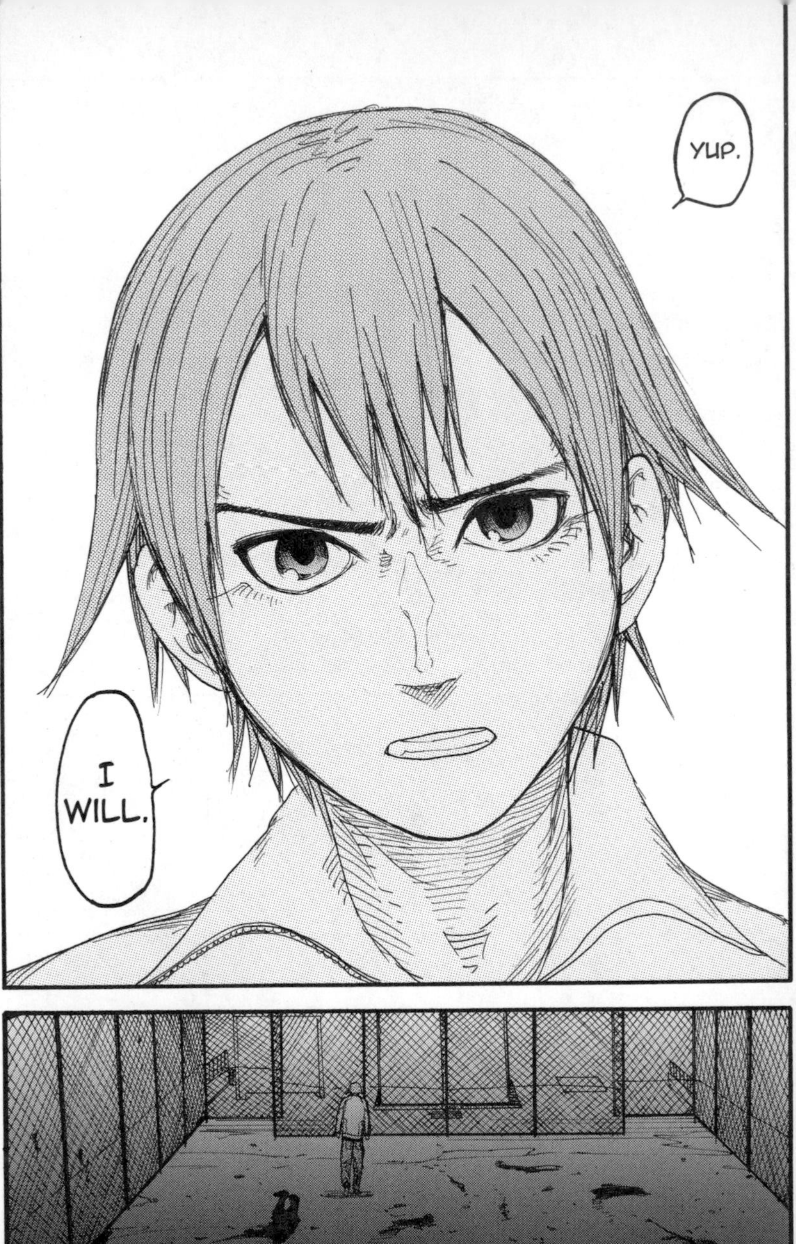
YUP.
I WILL.

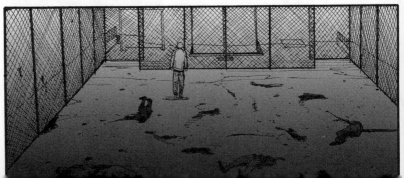

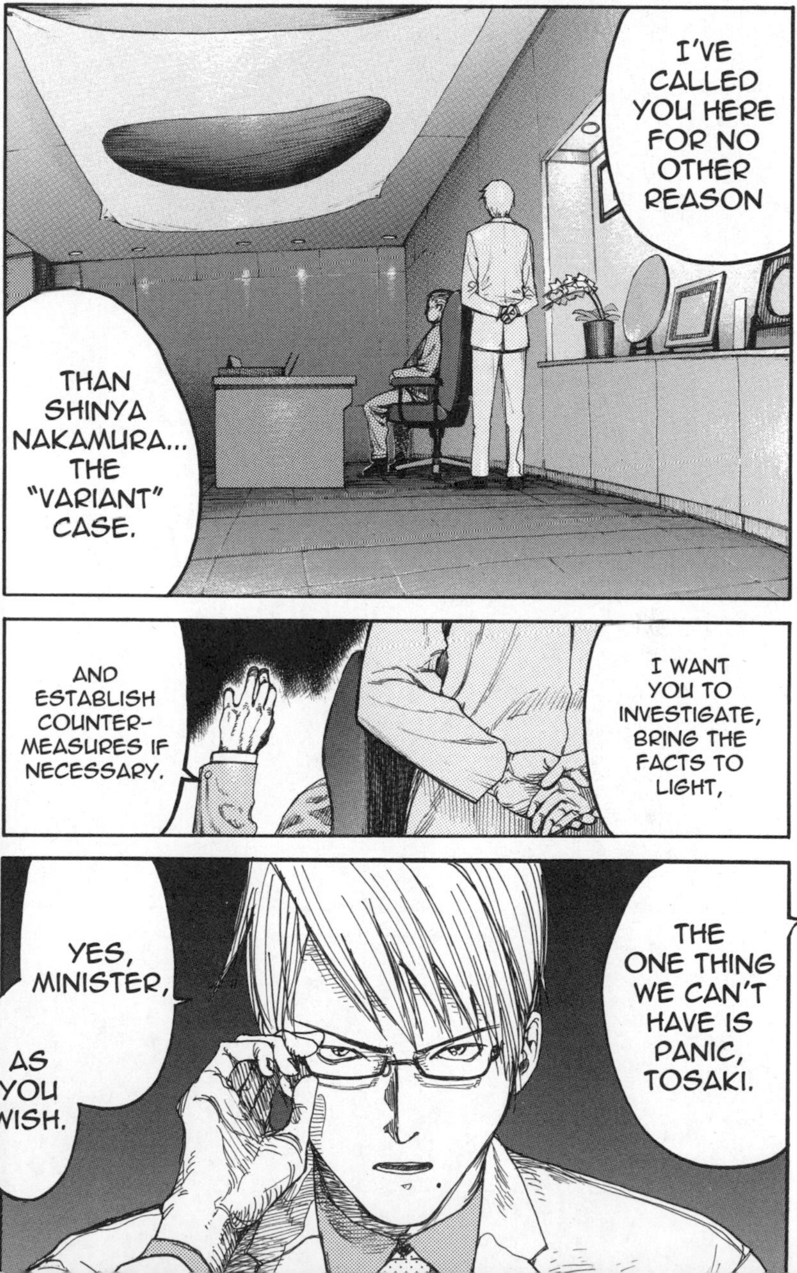
I'VE CALLED YOU HERE FOR NO OTHER REASON
THAN SHINYA NAKAMURA... THE "VARIANT" CASE.
I WANT YOU TO INVESTIGATE, BRING THE FACTS TO LIGHT,
AND ESTABLISH COUNTER-MEASURES IF NECESSARY.
THE ONE THING WE CAN'T HAVE IS PANIC, TOSAKI.
YES, MINISTER,
AS YOU WISH.

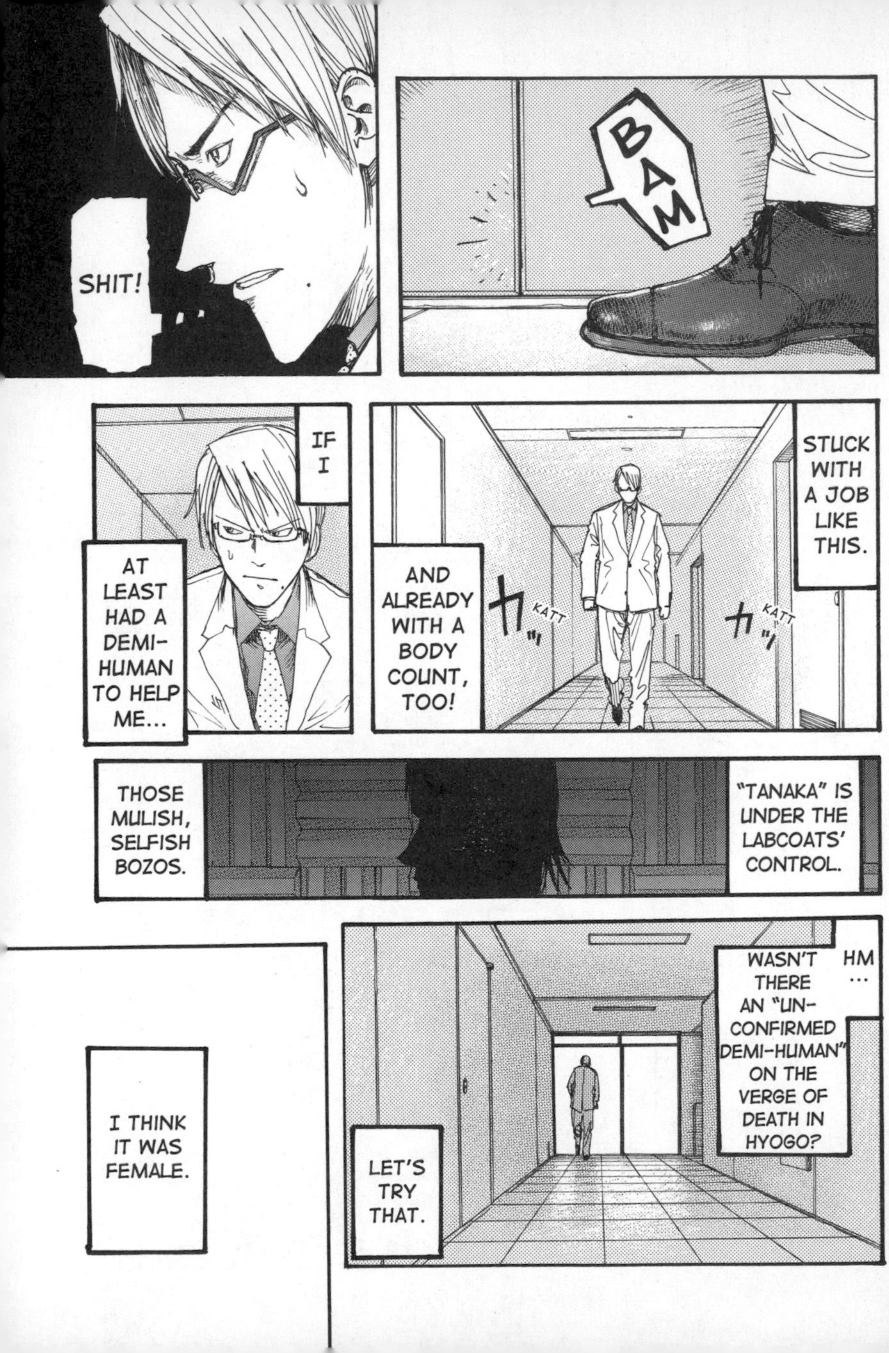
BAM
SHIT!
STUCK WITH A JOB LIKE THIS.
AND ALREADY WITH A BODY COUNT, TOO!
KATT
KATT
IF I
AT LEAST HAD A DEMI-HUMAN TO HELP ME...
"TANAKA" IS UNDER THE LABCOATS' CONTROL.
THOSE MULISH, SELFISH BOZOS.
HM...
WASN'T THERE AN "UN-CONFIRMED DEMI-HUMAN" ON THE VERGE OF DEATH IN HYOGO?
LET'S TRY THAT.
I THINK IT WAS FEMALE.

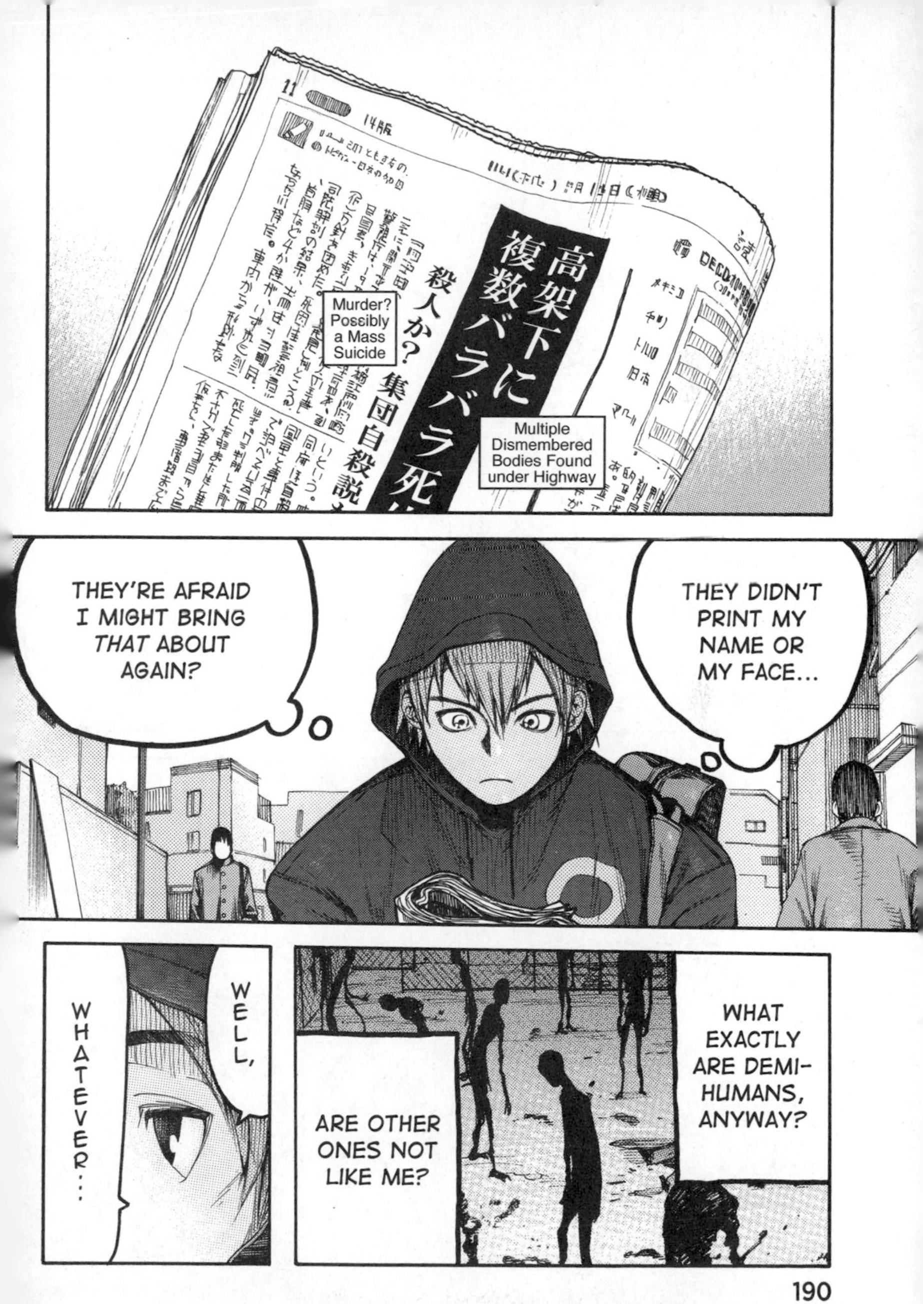
Multiple Dismembered Bodies Found under Highway
Murder? Possibly a Mass Suicide
THEY DIDN'T PRINT MY NAME OR MY FACE...
THEY'RE AFRAID I MIGHT BRING *THAT* ABOUT AGAIN?
WHAT EXACTLY ARE DEMI-HUMANS, ANYWAY?
ARE OTHER ONES NOT LIKE ME?
WELL,
WHATEVER...

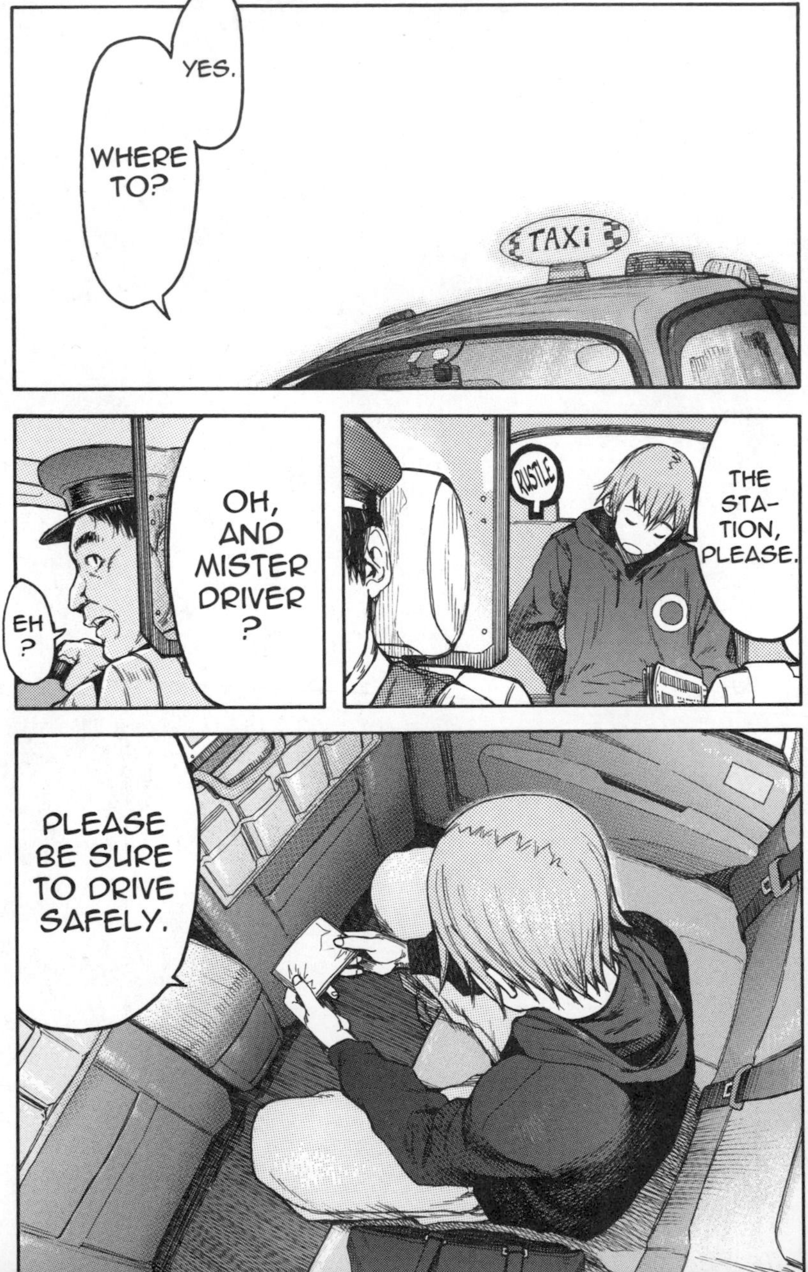
YES.
WHERE TO?
TAXi
THE STA-TION, PLEASE.
RUSTLE
OH, AND MISTER DRIVER?
EH?
PLEASE BE SURE TO DRIVE SAFELY.

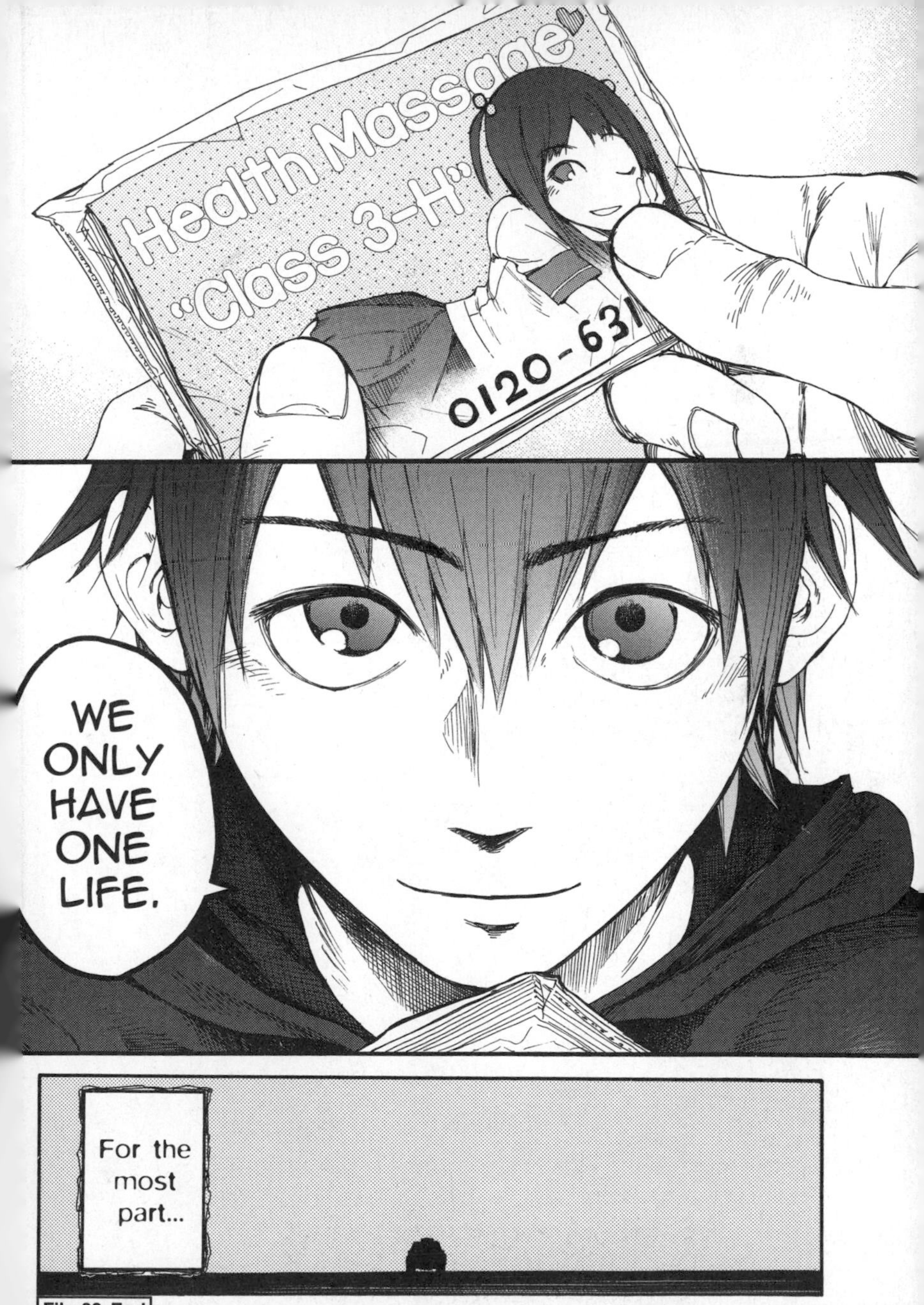
Health Massage
"Class 3-H"
0120-631
WE ONLY HAVE ONE LIFE.
For the most part...

File:00 End

COMIC: GAMON SAKURAI

ASSISTANT: CROUTON SANCHI (masking tones -for "File:00" only, blacking out and panel frames)

AJIN 2 End
DEMI-HUMAN

Ajin: Demi-Human, volume 2

Translation: Ko Ransom
Production: Risa Cho
Hiroko Mizuno

First published in Japan in 2013 by Kodansha, Ltd., Tokyo
Publication for this English edition arranged through Kodansha, Ltd., Tokyo

Published by Vertical, Inc., New York

Originally published in Japanese as *Ajin 2* by Kodansha, Ltd.
Ajin first serialized in *good! Afternoon*, Kodansha, Ltd., 2012-

This is a work of fiction.

ISBN: 978-1-939130-85-3

Manufactured in the United States of America

First Edition

Third Printing

Vertical, Inc.
451 Park Avenue South
7th Floor
New York, NY 10016
www.vertical-inc.com